The Making of the Africa-Nation

Pan-Africanism and the African Renaissance

Published by
Adonis & Abbey Publishers Ltd
P.O. Box 43418
London
SE11 4XZ
http://www.adonis-abbey.com

First Edition, November 2003

British Library Cataloguing-in-Publication Data
A catalogue record for this book is available from the British Library

ISBN 0-9545037-2-4

Cover Design   Ifeanyi Adibe

Printed and bound in Great Britain by Lightning Source UK Ltd.

The Making of the Africa-Nation

Pan-Africanism and the African Renaissance

Edited by
Mammo Muchie

Adonis & Abbey
Publishers ltd

Other Books by Adonis & Abbey include:

Broken Dreams (Fiction/Town Crier Series 1)
By Jideofor Adibe

Wooden Gongs and Drumbeats: African Folktales, Proverbs and Idioms (Fiction/Town Crier Series 2)
By Dahi Chris Onuchukwu

Nigeria and the Politics of Unreason (politics/political economy/history)
By Victor E. Dike

The Challenge of Authenticity: African Culture and Faith Commitment (religion/philosophy/theology)
By Jacob Hevi

Table of Contents

Messay Kebede

Part III
Africa-Nation, Pan-Africanism and the African Renaissance: Issues, Challenges and Prospects

Dedication

To Mikael, for his kindness, Adey for her wisdom and Negash Admasu for total integrity. I am proud to be the father of the first two, and the uncle of the third. Though I'm away from you physically, you have permanent residences in my soul and heart. Not a second passes without my thinking of you wherever I am.

To my dear father Muchie Getahun and my sister Yimgenushal Muchie and their families. Respect and deep sorrow for not having seen you since my long exile from the Ethiopia-Africa I deeply cherish and love.

By dedicating this book to kith and kin, I hope it will help convince Mikeal, Adey and Negash to choose to live in, and work for Africa.

Foreword

The idea to edit this book came when I had the opportunity to run an international workshop on: Pan-Africanism: An Idea Whose Time Has Come in Denmark in December 2000. Prior to this time, I have been trying to re-involve myself with the continent in practical ways since 1997 after a research visit to Kenya.

With the support of some of the leading scholars in South Africa, I was fortunate to have been invited by the University of Natal's School of Development Studies and the Centre for Civil Society to pursue work on 'Civil Society and African Integration.' The programme is funded and supported by the Ford Foundation. We express our deep appreciation for this generosity.

My remit as the director of the research programme on Civil Society in, and for African Integration, is to carry out a conceptualisation of civil society, and how the participation of ordinary people and communities could help in shaping African integration. Some of the crucial questions we hope to find answers to include: How can African integration be anchored on a pedigree of civil society and the millions of ordinary African people? How can multiple stakeholders be brought to undertake the task of African integration? How best can civil society engage with the official integration driven by the post-colonial state entities?

The research programme hopes to design a workable and practical strategy on how knowledge-producing institutions could function effectively in Africa. The programme will also offer research and post graduate education (M.SC and PhD) degrees in Civil Society and African Integration. The successes and lessons learnt from this venture will be used to build a model of knowledge integration, staff and student mobility and best practice that could be encouraged across the continent.

The programme will organise a series of workshops in every region of the continent, culminating in a final conference where the course plan and the research strategy will be articulated, endorsed and stamped with a pan-African perspective and scope. Regional advisory and coordinating groups will be formed. Concept papers covering each region will provide the input and guide for the workshops and the conference.

The Publisher has agreed to my request to use this book to publicise the programme on Civil Society and African Integration. The programme has also a website (see: www.nu.ac.za/ccs) If one clicks on research and integration, updates of the activities of the programme will follow.

The publisher of Adonis & Abbey, Dr. Jideofor Adibe, has been exceptionally helpful, and took much interest in getting this volume edited and published. I am grateful to Adonis & Abbey Publishers for the professional editorial work on the various contributions. Papers were solicited from different scholars to broaden the perspectives offered. Some who attended the Conference in Denmark in 2000 were asked to update their papers to make them more relevant for this volume. I sincerely thank all who responded to this clarion call, even at a short notice. By responding, they have contributed their Widow's Mite to The Making of the Africa-Nation.

My special thanks also go to Metassebia Tadesse, Kelvin Harewood, Amsallu Meheretu and Paul Opoku Mensah. To colleagues at Aalborg University - Berhanu, Beza, Li Xing, Jacques, Ellen, Susan, Zewdu Teklu and Andy, I say thanks for all the support and friendship. Also to my colleagues at Middlesex University, especially Prof. Abby Ghobadian, the Dean of the Business School and Prof. Denis Parker for allowing me to take up a secondment. Equally thanks to Dr. Anga Baskaran and Dr. Yi Zhu for their support and friendship. I also thank Alan Gully, Kirit Patel and Jonathan Liu for a different type of support. I am equally grateful to all my students at Middlesex University, UK, and all my post-graduate students at the University of Aalborg, Denmark, who helped directly or indirectly in organising the conference on: *Pan-Africanism: An Idea Whose Time Has Come?* in Denmark in December 2000. This book, as stated earlier, was inspired by that conference.

I am also grateful to my colleagues in the Civil Society and African Integration project, especially Adam Habib and Vishnu Padayachee for all their support. I also thank the University of Middlesex's Business School for seconding me to the programme.

———

Mammo Muchie, Director:
 Research Programme on Civil Society in, and for African Integration
School of Development Studies & Centre for Civil Society,
 University of Natal, Durban, South Africa; 28 August 2003.

Preface

Reflections on Pan-Africanism and the African Renaissance

Andrew Jamison

For many of us who took part in the movements of the 1960s and 1970s, the last decade has been filled with many disappointments. In Europe for instance, social democrats have tried to take back the initiative that they lost in the 1980s, but the one big union that was created in the neo-liberal epoch continues to cause problems for them. Is the European Union, an avowed capitalist project, able to be transformed so that its well-endowed institutions can show any real concern for the poor, the disenfranchised and, for that matter, the survival of the sustaining capacity of the planet itself? I have my doubts. In Africa, with the exception of South Africa – and what a wonderful exception its liberation was! - the decade has also been discouraging. Wars and conflicts have represented the main "news" that has emanated from the dark continent, as tyrants and villains of various kinds seem to have taken power almost wherever one cares to look. At the same time, Africa has continued to seep into the cultural lifeblood, providing globalisation with a beat and a number of colourful rhythms that almost serve to justify the rest. If you can dance and get into the music, it sometimes feels that the rapacious exploitation might just be worth it. After all, without CDs and the Internet, without globalisation itself, there would not be so much music to listen to, at least not that good and global.

It was in this kind of dispirited mood, as the decade was drawing to a close on a dark Danish December in 2000 that I met up with the African renaissance, and its wonderful sense of "post-pessimism". I had known that Mammo Muchie, who had been visiting our university in

Aalborg for the past couple of years, was involved in various interesting activities, but I never imagined that they were that interesting. As I listened, over an evening and a day, to speakers from several African countries, most of who live and work in Europe, I began to realise that a movement was afoot. From different fields and different points of departure, a number of African intellectuals seemed to be reinventing their past. In the name of some kind of continental unity – which Mammo and some of the others referred to as pan-Africanism – a search for roots, but also for new beginnings, were taking place. It reminded me of what we, in the environmental movement, had done so many years ago. We had also ransacked our historical legacy, looking for inspiration in the long lost works and deeds of our precursors and predecessors. We also had tried to construct a "usable past" for our emerging consciousness, as movement intellectuals have always done. And we had also tried to articulate a new set of "knowledge interests" – with a worldview, and specific projects connected to it. But, in this case, the movement was not confined to a single sector, or issue complex. It was much broader, but also perhaps much less coherent. It covered everything.

What I found most intriguing from Mammo's conference was the mixing of academic or intellectual sophistication with the passionate engagement that we associate with activism. And that too reminded me of the early days of the environmental movement. The speakers, who were mostly journalists and academics, shared what I have previously called a core cognitive praxis. For one thing, they had a common or collective cosmology: a worldview that places Africa in the centre of world history, but more importantly and even more ambitiously, seeks to reconnect the history of Africa to the history of the world. It was not all glory and heroism said Adotey Bing, Director of the Africa Centre in London. He told us of migrations from Egypt down to South Africa, which put in place a kind of productive system that simply was not able to counter the more mechanical and single-minded approach of the European imperialists. We were, however, also told of the ways in which that productive system had functioned: its ecology and patterns of culture. I was especially taken by the suggestion that African culture is, in some sense, more in tune with its natural environment than the European (and American) culture has been. That nature - so bounteous, so magnificent, so diverse had not required such ingenious forms of technology in order to be utilised effectively. It had encouraged a more benign technical development process, as well as a more rural or pastoral form of settlement. But, of course, that had been historically more of a weakness than strength.

There were also discussions of the effects of imperialism on Africa, a kind of reassessment of historical experiences that have tended to be previously seen in black and white terms. Here again, what struck me was the ambivalence, the dialectical reflection that so many of the speakers expressed. Colonialism had been evil in many ways, and we were told many gruesome stories that need to be remembered. But it had also brought to Africa new skills, new knowledge, new ambitions, and new opportunities for human creativity. The challenge was to appropriate that scientific, technical, and organisational competence, to make it African, to make it fit into and not replace the particular patterns of cultural and environmental adaptation that had been cultivated during the centuries. I was intrigued by the ongoing projects that were presented by the speakers: the effort to make a commercial business out of a folk instrument and transform musical education in the schools in the process, the attempt to examine the linguistic similarities of the ancient and contemporary African languages as a way to help develop new forms of communication and dialogue, the project on social capital which sought to identify the cultural basis for successful business in different African countries, and the monthly magazine, New African, which seeks to contribute to the fostering of a public sphere, a context of communication, across Africa.

Can all this really make a difference? Can there be an African renaissance? What more is needed for something to happen, for the rivers of time to change direction? And more specifically, what, if anything, can an aging 60s radical, a middle-class white boy from New Jersey, offer by way of advice?

As I look back on the event after a couple of months have passed, what is perhaps most striking is how transient it all seems. That one exciting day in the December darkness has been overwhelmed by all the other impressions that a university professor continually accumulates – from student papers (now I must really do something about biotechnology), completed manuscripts (will it find an audience? will it have an impact?), networks and projects (who should we contact? where should we apply for funds?). It is so easy for the African renaissance to slip off the agenda, drift away from one's consciousness: it needs to be more visible! It seems to me that one thing that is crucial for the African renaissance is to organise yourselves better. The movement's members need to create a more visible and operational public space for their activity. We need to know, and be constantly reminded, that you are out there. This could be done by establishing local branches and formal organisations in different countries - this is how most social movements develop. But it could also be in the form of creating new contexts of communication – between business and politics, between the universities and the media. You need to follow the example of New African magazine, by going further with internet publications and other, more specialised journals and outlets, making use of other media: film, TV, video, and, of course, music.

And then there is the question of strategy. What I heard on that December day were lots of different ideas about how to proceed, about how an African renaissance or a pan-African movement could develop further. But where is the strategic debate taking place? Where are you weighing the different options, formulating the different tactical and organisational choices, reaching out for commitment and involvement from those who have not yet heard about your movement? A social movement needs more than good ideas and a common cognitive core to pass what might be called the threshold of significance. Alain Touraine, in his many writings on social movements, has pointed to the importance of "historicity", the linking of one set of issues or one movement project to all the others, and, in particular, to the dominant social agenda. The movement for an African renaissance needs to meet the challenges of globalisation, on the one hand, and, on the other; it needs to distance itself from the stranglehold of traditionalism. At the same time, it needs to seek out and find common grounds with other "progressive" actors vying for historicity: feminists, environmentalists, concerned biotechnologists and local activists.

If the dreams of pan-Africanism or African unity are to come closer to being realised, they need to become both more exciting and more visible. There is a need for more meetings like the one organised by Mammo in December 2000, but try to make them more fun. Next time, do not forget to bring the music…

PART I

Introduction

I

Has the Pan-African Hour Come?

Mammo Muchie

My mind and my knowledge of myself are formed by the victories that are the jewels in our African crown, the victories we earned from Isandhlwana to Khartoum, as Ethiopians and as the Ashanti of Ghana, as the Berbers of the Desert. I am the grandchild who lays fresh flowers on the Boer graves at St Helena and the Bahamas, who sees in the mind's eyes and suffers the suffering of a simple peasant folk: death, concentration camps, destroyed homesteads, and dreams in ruins. I am the grandchild of Nongqause... I come of those who were transported from India and China, whose being resided in the fact, solely, that they were able to provide physical labour, who taught me that we could both be at home and be foreign, who taught me that human existence itself demanded that freedom was a necessary condition for that human existence. Being part of all these people, and in the knowledge that none dare contest that assertion I shall claim that I am an African.

(Thabo Mbeki, Africa: The Time Has Come (Cape Town & Johannesburg, Taelberg Publishers & Mafube Publishing, 1998, pp31-2)

Thabo Mbeki has woven historical experience, African resistance, African culture and African consciousness to anchor his own existential identity as an African. He did not use biology, the colour of his skin or the spatial location he hails from to define his existential co-ordinates. Naturally the colour of the people and the resources and geography of Africa have been the primary data ostensibly used as reasons to trigger the actions that finally brought the degradation and historical humiliation experienced/suffered by African people. Thus colour and place have mattered in the unfolding of world history. For Thabo Mbeki, historical experience and consciousness as *outcomes/outputs* mattered more to define the African than the *inputs* and ingredients of history. Others think the inputs of colour and geography matter more than the outcomes of historical experience and consciousness to identify or specify a global African soul and personality.

Beyond the playout of biological realities, a shared historical experience and shared consciousness can facilitate the constitution of a minimum common denominator for constructing Africa's unified and de-colonised futures. Biological and geographical varieties do not easily lend themselves to any algorithmic compression to provide a least common denominator. And the project to unite and free Africa requires perforce a shared minimum common base. Without such a shared bottom line, it is virtually impossible to sustain a free Africa unity project.

Mbeki has touched upon an important point of principle: the making of Africa requires a prior making of the African. We have Africa as a geographical reality, but the African as a social reality has yet to evolve. Over the last forty years, Pan-Africanism has been associated with trying to make the Organisation of African Unity (OAU) work. However, the yoking together of an assorted constellation of Africans and non-Africans to forge a union with discrete interests, aspirations and differences can and will hardly make a stable union. It is people that wish to deal with common problems and challenges by building a shared purpose that can unite. It is by recognising themselves as free Africans that Africans can forge a free Africa. It is free Africans as Africans that have to make unity. That presupposes an irreducible minimum of shared value and the existence of a shared African identity or purpose.

Neither a shared conception nor a shared reality can be taken for granted when it comes to describing or explaining the current unity projects in Africa. There is no shared idea of the African yet. Nor is the idea of Africa something that is settled. To date, this lack of shared understanding has made all well-intentioned attempts to unite and make Africa speak with a recognisable and distinct voice unstable. The conversion of the Organisation of African Unity into the African Union has not resolved this dilemma. It has, in fact, brought it forcefully on the agenda. Who is uniting? What is the unity for? How should the unity proceed? These are questions that have not been answered yet.

After forty years of the OAU, the basic concept for bringing 53 states in Africa and the historic and contemporary Diaspora to form the AU remains subordinate to the overriding need of the heads of states to maintain their largely hollow sovereignties. The key challenge remains to this day the creation of Africa as a sovereign entity. That can only happen if all sovereignties are pulled together and emerge with the synergistic effect of an African distinct voice. That requires that all those joining together evolve common positions not so much about the fluctuating issues of the day, but also on the enduring ideas about who they are, why do they need to come together and the shared basis for making common cause and evolving a common purpose.

Perhaps what has been missing most in all the efforts to unite Africa has been the lack of a concept or the idea of the African as a universality going beyond the specific identity. Others recognise the African, but Africans shun self-definition and self-recognition as first and foremost Africans. Only those scattered by slavery in the Diaspora add their African connection as a hybrid to their current settlement in Brazil, Cuba, America, the Caribbean and so on. In the continent, Africans seem to hold their other identities derived from blood or affiliation, location, clan and attachment to the post-colonial state more important than the existential fact of being Africans. A living people build for the future, but living people must know themselves first to forge ahead and forestall being a hazard to themselves and others.

There is a contradiction between the claims and assertions of specific identities and attachments and the lack of appeal to universal-African expression of identities and attachments. The concept of the African conveys the meaning, logo and significance of the coming of Africans, by sharing a universal identity. It comes up against a number of specific identities that African people can and should express in their lives. Whilst specific identities accentuate difference, the universal identity gives licence to a shared citizenship by promoting the construction of a shared purpose to deal with or respond to the environment. Some see universality as diluting their specific identity. Others see inurnment to specificity as an unsettling and an un-housing experience in any journey to unite Africa. There is a need to question the African national unity project based on the affirmation of specific and discrete interests and the desire to bring them together. Any partial get-together is by its very nature limited. Coming into regional blocs may be a step but it is not sufficient. Describing geographically based connections that a number of states or other entities make is to dilute the concept of Pan-Africanism. For the latter to come into being, there must be a shared principle anchoring the connection, and that principle must be a shared African national identity. It is better that those that share such principles associate than 53 odd states that can be tempted easily to break ranks for the sake of acquiring external aid. We have

seen such unity efforts from the OAU to the Arab League to
be largely a formula to continue ineffective and episodic get-together.

The right to carry out specific connections and interests is not
constrained by the affirmation of differing specific identities. Any
national unity project requires the affirmation of a universal common
bottom line that can legitimise the aspirations to forge common
connections and purposes. The idea of the African is universal. It is the
least common denominator - the atom or nucleus of the African
national project. The right to come together rather than remain different
is built from the fact that there is the African as a being and conscious
self. All that are potentially African are not yet there, but the work to
instantiate an African consciousness bearing the content of African
humanity and liberty through resistance and defiance against old and
current forms of oppression must be relentless and urgent.

An objection can be anticipated: how can the concept of the African
as a universal attribute exist given that Africans speak different
languages, practise different religions, come from different races,
express different interests, inhabit different ecosystems and are ruled
by different political arrangements and so on. If one wishes the
shopping list gaze on Africa, the differences that exist in Africa can be
seen as unwieldy and bewildering. But the shopping list framing of
Africa is a relic of 19th century anthropological type classification that
reduces people and their essence to the phenomenal attributes that they
share. It does not describe their essence, their heart, their existential
being and soul. To start with, no matter how many items one records or
buys from the shop, it does not prevent one from putting them in one
shelf or cooking them to add value, meaning or significance to the
purchase. The fact that Africans appear in a variety of ways, speak
different languages and practise different religions should not in
principle be an argument for making them suffer under the regime of
specificity by rejecting to construct a consciousness of universality. The
right to the universal or the African does not have to challenge the right
to remain different, speak different languages and worship different
deities. It can complement it and in fact it can enrich it, provided that
the dialectic between specificity and universality is resolved in favour
of producing the national nucleus for creating a sustainable unification
of Africa.

Indians speak many different languages and practise different
religions, but these have not prevented them from overcoming their
specific attributes and proclaiming an Indian national identity. The

success of the national liberation movement in India is to create the idea and reality of the Indian nation in spite of communal and other disaffections. Like India, there is no reason why Africans cannot transform into a nation by overcoming the tyranny of specificity and constructing a universal future. In Africa, Tanzania has achieved the ideal of a national universal African–Tanzanian by beating and overcoming ethnic self-assertions.

Thabo Mbeki has come up with a remarkable suggestion on how to escape from being trapped in the shopping list condemnation of Africans into 'unite-able' items. He suggests that we acquire universality as Africans through our history of resistance, consciousness, challenges and the problems we face, including our desire to become renascent. It is an important idea for finding the missing national common denominator to unite Africa.

Unless Africans inside and outside Africa see themselves, like Thabo Mbeki, as an African first (see opening quote of this chapter), making plans for unity and freedom may not deliver a united and free Africa. Africa cannot be made or transformed without the making of the African. The making of the African, in turn, is inseparably bound up with the making of the Africa-nation.

This questions the existing ways of uniting and proposes an alternative strategy to nation building in Africa. The fragmented pattern of nation building bequeathed from the post-colonial condition has proved a monumental disaster. It has turned Africa into a region of protracted conflicts and violence. The integrated pattern of nation building has not been tried. It remains the alternative vision Africa was never allowed to forge. It is time the vision was converted into reality. It is high time that we imagined an Africa- nation and made it. This enjoins that philosophies, principles and rationale for bringing together Africans in Africa and the rest of the world have to be revisited. There is a need to debate Africa's unity project fearlessly to inject new hope and ambition to the construction of Africa's voice. Fragmented and confronted with a one-way street go-go globalisation, Africa will lose out to others unless it strives to recompose and reconstitute itself as a one-nation society.

There is a need to start this debate now. Hopefully, the collections that we have put together in this book will spark a debate.

Pan-Africanism arose as a protest against the degradation of the African. On the one hand, it is a protest and rejection of the historical experience of slavery, colonialism and racial discrimination, and on the

other, it is an ideal to overcome the past and build a living
future based on a free and united Africa. Some people see Pan-
Africanism merely as a resistance, forgetting that this is only one
dimension to it. The more important dimension is the projection of an
ideal for uniting and freeing Africans and Africa. Whilst rooted in the
African historical experience, pan-Africanism goes beyond it and
escapes that degrading, negative and humiliating experience by
projecting a vision of a resurgent and renascent Africa. African
renaissance therefore becomes Pan-Africanism's future. In the words of
Thabo Mbeki the 'African Renaissance is upon us' (April 1997). He
enjoins all of us to be 'rebels' in the cause of renascent Africa. Some
commentators in the West tried to pour cold water by responding to
Mbeki's optimism with a hostile and negative claim that Africa is 'no-
nascent', not renascent! Africa should not be deterred by such negative
noises.

What Pan-African thinkers have not dared advance is that the pan-
African ideal cannot be achieved without the concept and reality of the
Africa-nation.

This concept of the Africa-nation requires a prior ontology of an
African citizen. The Africa-nation does not mean any of the current 53
odd post-colonial states. Nor can it come into being by using definitions
derived from genealogy, biology, region, language, religion or any
other discrete attribute. The Africa-nation is defined by an African
consciousness based on Africa's prolonged history and culture of
resistance against dehumanising beliefs, prejudices and practices. The
nation represents the logo of that consciousness and living resistance.
That is why in the title we have hyphenated Africa-nation to convey
powerfully the notion that the nation is Africa and Africa is the nation.
Geographical boundary should not limit the Africa- unification project.

The African continent is the territorial base for the Africa-nation,
but the Diaspora is also part of the same nation. The concept of the
Africa-nation is not exhausted by the territorial principle. It is a civic
concept that is anchored on history, culture, experience and
consciousness. It is above all consciousness and the knowledge,
aspiration and courage to make Africa free, humane, prosperous,
peaceful, stable, happy and united that the logo of the Africa-nation
concept embodies and spreads at the same time.

The notion of Africa-nation complements and deepens the theories
of pan-Africanism and African renaissance. This collection begins the
problematisation of the issue. It invites thinkers and researchers to

engage in the debate of making systematic conceptual links between Pan-Africanism, African Renaissance and the Africa-nation.

Like Pan-Africanism, the African Renaissance is not new. The striving for a new beginning has always accompanied major historical breakthroughs affecting the destiny of Africans. Renascent Africa, reborn Africa, renewed Africa, revolutionary Africa - these desires have been expressed from time immemorial. When apartheid - the last oppressive system that held Africans back - collapsed, it was inevitable that a resurgent South Africa and a governing party like the African National Congress (ANC) with a hundred years experience and its outstanding leadership, should come up with the idea of African Renaissance. It brings home forcefully the willingness to enlist South Africa's resources to renew the African world. It was appropriate and timely and strongly underlines the country's desire to further the cause of African unity.

African Renaissance complements rather than substitutes Pan-Africanism. It is not a new idea, but an old idea, which is renewed by the current challenges it faces in the global conjuncture. Like Pan-Africanism, the African Renaissance is not explicitly tied with the making of the Africa-nation.

We propose the thesis that efforts to free and unite Africa should integrate the idea of the African with the idea of making the Africa-nation, and both with pan-Africanism and African Renaissance. Only then can the problem of comprehensive structural transformation of the continent be seriously undertaken.

The African ←→ *Africa-Nation* ←→ *Pan-Africanism* ←→ *Africa Renaissance* ←→ *African Transformation*

Unity, freedom, development and structural transformation result from a re-conceptualisation of the African in relation to the building bloc of the Africa-nation. The collections here are bound by the theme, not ideology, and not even departure or destination. The views and narrative styles are as diverse as the authors that have contributed to the volume. We think there is strength in a plural expression of diverse voices. Each author has brought a fresh perspective on the issue they have selected to reflect upon.

The book is divided into five parts. Jamison and Muchie introduce the book (Part 1). Jamison observes that 'it is so easy for the African renaissance to slip off the agenda, drift away from one's consciousness: it needs to be more visible!' He calls on the movement's members to 'create a more visible and operational public space for their activity. We need to know, and be constantly reminded, that you are out there.' Mammo on his own (this chapter) wonders if the Pan-African hour is upon us now – given all that is happening.

Some of the contributors have explored the conceptual and theoretical issues involved in discussions of Africa-Nation, Nation-building, Pan-Africanism and African Renaissance (Part 2). Kwesi Prah, for instance, traces the history of Pan-Africanism and argues that 'early African nationalism was generically Pan-African'. He contends that the current jealous protection of fragmented sovereignties in Africa is a post-colonial phenomenon and challenges the view that nationalism should have little or no place in the affairs of Africans. Mammo Muchie suggests the reframing of Pan-Africanism to anchor it on a shared conception of African identity and interest based on shared history, culture and consciousness of resistance to oppression. Silvia Bercu on her part argues for a new humanist perspective, which will both promote a Pan-African regional integration and resist globalisation and the forces that dehumanise Africans through the promotion of violence and wars. In another contribution, Muchie argues that civil society in, and for Pan-Africanism, has to be conceptualised away from the global constitution of 'state failure and NGO success' and suggests co-operative relations between the triad of state, civil society and markets. For Chen Chimutengwende, what is urgently needed in Africa is a second liberation struggle anchored on Pan-Africanism and economic egalitarianism. This second liberation, he argues, 'has already started' and is the 'only process, which can defeat the forces of neo-colonialism and the re-colonisation of Africa'. Kebede is however sceptical, arguing that the project of Pan-Africanism is an endorsement of the colonial discourse in so far as it has been appropriated by the elites. He also argues that a Pan-African state (or Africa-nation) could put a 'severe strain on existing African states by taking away their legitimacy', and wonders what Africans could gain from a larger unit that they could not possibly gain from the present smaller units.

Part 3 of the book examines the key issues, challenges and prospects of the triadic projects of Africa-Nation, Pan-Africanism and African Renaissance. David Abdullai, for instance, challenges the *naysayers*, who see only despair and hopelessness in Africa and argues that the 'Africa of yesterday is different from the Africa of today'. He argues that in Africa 'political systems are more open than they were years ago, the press is freer than it was ten years ago and countries in the region are ridding themselves of outdated solutions, whilst drawing on the wealth of their cultural traditions.' Li Xing relates the history of the Chinese revolution to Pan-Africanism, and argues that the latter could borrow much from the logocentrism of the Chinese revolution. He contends that the effectiveness of the Chinese revolution was largely because of its 'devotion to inventing a nationwide logo in the form of common concepts, metaphors, ideologies, narratives and myths'. Baffour Ankomah, in his own contribution, challenges the notion of free press (as taught to African journalist students) and argues that in the West, the national interest defines the boundary of this 'free press'. He chastises African journalists for taking this 'press freedom' too literally, thereby unwittingly reporting stories that not only undermine Africa's national security but also contribute in reinforcing the negative stereotypes of the continent in the western media. Kimani Nehusi argues that since thoughts are framed in a language, a true decolonisation of Africa requires that the grip of the colonial languages, currently the official languages in most of Africa, must be loosened. Friedman focuses on the failure of the western-inspired democratisation project to create sustainable democratic institutions in Africa. He argues that the current wave of democratisation in Africa has not 'protected the ruled from the predations' of its rulers. Anna Leander examines the phenomenon of private military companies (PMCs) in Africa, and argues that the presence of the PMCs is widely accepted and will most likely remain so in the foreseeable future. She, however, contends that the PMCs undermine the state's authority to regulate violence. In his contribution, Desmond Davis discusses the weaknesses of African leadership, and argues that Africans must learn to take their destiny in their own hands by solving their own problems without waiting for outsiders to do so for them.

Part 4 of the book surveys Afro-Arab relations, historically and in modern times. Hawas raises the thorny question of the two failed nationalisms – Arab nationalism and its African variant. He describes Arab perceptions of Africans and the historical roots for those perceptions. He examines efforts by the late Nasser and Ghaddafi to promote Afro-Arab relations, and contends that Ghaddafi's current romance with Pan-Africanism is in part informed by his frustrations with Arab nationalism and its ineffableness. While Bankie does not rule out long-term co-operation between Arab and Africa, he contends that the conditions for such a co-operation will exist only after the Arab world has shown contrition for its role in the Trans-Saharan slave trade, and its present role in the ongoing slavery practices in Mauritania and Sudan. Muchie examines Afro-Arab relations in the post September-11 world order, and argues that the Afro-Arab perspective on terrorism includes the deeper causes of injustice – not just with dealing with the manifestations of terror acts. He calls for the revival of the anti-colonial project, which will this time include Arab, Afro-Asia and Latin America, in order to fight against a resurgent imperialism.

Part 5 surveys alternative guideposts to the Africa-Nation, Pan-Africanism and African Renaissance. Jacques Hersh, for instance, sees Pan-Africanism as being trapped between Afro-pessimism and Afro-optimism. The Afro-pessimists, he argues, have given up on Africa and would even welcome re-colonisation while the optimists are still full of hope. Hersh proposes Pan-Africanism as an alternative social project for surmounting the tension between the 'pessimism of the intellect' and the 'optimism of the will'. In separate articles, Arnold and Muchie examine the potentials of NEPAD (the New Economic Partnership for Africa's Development) and arrive at similar conclusions. They argue that NEPAD, under the current regime of aid and loan dependency, coupled with the strangulating effects of the high level of indebtedness of most African countries, is unlikely to work. Arnold, in fact, argues that Africa's paramount challenge is how to rid itself of the weight of external pressures, pointing out that the 'question of how Africa can shake off dependence upon the outside world is quite separate from engagement with the world'.

In the General Conclusions (Part 6), Muchie argues that by linking dialectically the projects of Africa-Nation, Pan-Africanism and African Renaissance, the contributors to the volume have driven home the fact that 'Africa needs to evolve its own power of definition, discourse, ideology, narrative, myth and metaphysics to deal with, and overcome the imperialist-colonial domination that militates against its chances of becoming free, empowered and attaining a comprehensive agency'. He contends that 'Pan-Africanism, African Renaissance and Africa-Nation are Africa's counter-hegemonic projects for instantiating and inscribing Africans' will not to remain isolated leaves but to become part of a dense network that the tropical forest symbolises'

PART II

Conceptual and Theoretical Issues

2

The Wish to Unite: The Historical and Political Context of the Pan-African Movement

Kwesi Kwaa Prah

Introduction

"The wish to unite" is a persistent and universal sentiment in nationalist thought. Few voices have made this point more lucidly than Ernest Renan (1823-1892), who in his 1882 Sorbonne lecture, *Qu'est-ce qu'une nation?* (What is a nation?), identified this wish as a key ingredient in nationalism. Nearer our times, it found great resonance in the formulation of Sukarno's philosophy of Indonesian nationalism. The Pan-Slavic and Slavophile movements were articulated in the language of unity. The unification of country and people was the supreme dream of the father of the Chinese nation, Sun Yat-sen. Pan-Arabism and the Ba'athist movement were ideologically constructed on the idea of the unity of the Arab nation. The European movement of the post-2nd World War period has carried this view as a central tenet. It is therefore no surprise that among African nationalists, unity is a central and undying theme.

Of all the ideas, which have shaped the African freedom movement over the past hundred years, African nationalism and its wider frame of reference, Pan-Africanism, have been the most potent and historically consequential. What do I mean, when I say that Pan-Africanism is the wider frame of reference for African nationalism? African nationalism as a manifestation of African assertiveness and political awakening in the era of colonialism tended to be organisationally captured within the specific colonial territories and borders as determined by the colonial powers. Thus, when we make reference to Congolese nationalism, Nigerian nationalism, Kenyan nationalism or Zambian nationalism we are historically referring to the specific exposition of this self-assertiveness for political independence within the context of a given colonial state.

What we know is that much of this history has played out as parallel processes on the continent, with the 1960s as its high-watermark. In 1960, 17 African countries, including the Belgian Congo achieved colonial freedom. Indeed, the 1960s are frequently described in the literature as "the decade of African independence". Obviously, the processes inter-relate and inter-penetrate. This becomes clear each time we examine these processes within some of the larger colonial regions, which preceded most of the final colonial states just before independence. It is not accidental that *Nkosi Sikelele Afrika*, for most of its history, as an anthem of African freedom, was used regionally; in South Africa, Lesotho, Zambia, Swaziland and Zimbabwe, it was the acknowledged anthem of African nationalism, and remains, till today, the national anthem in Zimbabwe, South Africa, Tanzania (with Swahili lyrics) and Zambia (with English lyrics). It is, indeed, arguably the greatest candidate for anthem for a united Africa.

Most of the political leadership of the independence movement in English-speaking Southern Africa won their spurs under the inspiration of the Congress movement of South Africa. In West Africa, the *Rassemblement Démocratique Africain*, founded in Bamako in 1946, and which was largely a brainchild of Felix Houphouet-Boigny, was a regional political organization covering the whole of French West Africa. The National Congress of British West Africa founded in 1919 was the prime source of nationalist thought and activity, for English-speaking West Africa, throughout the period between the 1st and the 2nd World Wars. Nnamdi Azikiwe, the father figure of modern Nigerian politics, started out as a politician and journalist in the Gold Coast. Milton Obote of Uganda, came first into politics in Kenya between 1950 and 1955, and was a founder member of the Kenya African Union. In 1952, when Amilcar Cabral and Agostinho Neto helped establish the *Centre of African Studies* in Lisbon, the objective was to provide an intellectual forum for the discussion and development of a nationalist agenda for all the Portuguese colonies in Africa. While Jomo Kenyatta is best known as the first president of Kenya, it is less known that in his earlier, politically formative years in Europe, the focus of his nationalism was Pan-African. Kenyatta was for sometime caretaker of the *West African Student's Union* (WASU) hostel in London during the inter-war years.

Indeed, Kenyatta took an active part in black liberation politics in London in the 1930s, and wrote a historic article "Hands off Abyssinia", as a member of the *International African Friends of Abyssinia* group in London, in the wake of Mussolini's fascist invasion of Abyssinia. This group which fielded a variety of nationalist thinking Africans from all corners of Africa and its Diaspora, included Jomo Kenyatta, Peter Milliard, Kwame Nkrumah, Makonnen, Wallace Johnson, George Padmore, C.L.R. James and Amy Ashwood Garvey (the ex-wife of Marcus Garvey). Amy Garvey was a founder member of the *Nigerian Progress Union* (1924), one of the first British based Pan-African organisations.[1]

In the history of the past 100 years, as far as Pan-African activism is concerned, few events lent themselves as easily and as expressively to Pan-Africanist sentiments as the Italian invasion of Abyssinia. Record has it that African reaction on the continent was intense, emotive and diligent. A correspondent of the *Gambia Outlook and Senegambian Reporter* in the issue of 13 February 1936 in an article entitled *Abyssinia and We* argued that:

> Many do not seem to realise their obligation to Abyssinia in this her hour of crisis; they are not proving themselves worthy of the example of leading in all parts of the civilised world. Excitement to support the Abyssinian forces financially and otherwise is rife in the three West African Colonies, and almost everywhere that African races are to be found. Pan-Africanism, or African race-consciousness, is remarkably pronounced, even in South Africa, where Africans boycott Italian trade …. It seems to be the idea of some that the Abyssinia crisis does not concern us. I even understand that collectors of the fund have been confronted with the suggestion that the money being collected for Abyssinia could be given to the poor. I wonder if those who think so really care for the poor. They subscribe liberally to Earl Haig's Fund and they do well. But should not their charity begin at home?[2]

The point is that early African nationalism, was generically Pan-African, and accepted implicitly or explicitly sociological terms of reference, which defied and transcended the later borders of African states. Thus, for example, before the existence of the Ivory Coast, Mali or Burkina, the nationalism expressed in these areas, which later became these countries, was projected on a larger geographical or ethnic canvass.

The fragmentation of the nationalist argument and the tailoring of its language to suit the realities of the late colonial state, were a direct response to the balkanisation of Africa on the eve of the independence era. Africa in 1970 was more chopped up into bits and pieces than it was in the late 19th century, in the wake of "the scramble for Africa". It is remarkable to note that French West Africa in 1958 was a monolithic colonial territory of 45 million people. Cameron described it as a:

> …huge and once apparently immutable stretch of territory that enshrined the French mystique of overseas rule from the Sahara to the Atlantic. Nowhere except perhaps the Belgian Congo had seemed so permanently established in independence, so thoroughly sewn into the elastic straitjacket of French colonial policy. … It was eight times bigger than France herself; within a year this vast area had fragmented and balkanised itself into twelve separate republics, autonomous, yet all, with one spectacular exception, *Guinea*, owing allegiance to the Gaullist abstraction created for the new age: the "French Community", Commonwealth of the Fifth Republic.[3]

This latter new entity was the French answer to the British Commonwealth. Both the French Community and the British Commonwealth were, in important senses, attempts to salvage what could be rescued, with the co-operation of the newly ascendant elites, from the remains of the old colonial empires, and maintain spheres of influence in neo-colonial contexts. Nationalist concerns had by the 1960s and 1970s been reduced to parochial interests and limited *étatiste* preoccupations. The larger and wider, earlier African frames of reference were geographically and politically scaled down. The core issues have however remained, till today, the same. Africans wanted freedom, greater emancipation, a better quality of life, and just and democratic governance. The authorities in all the post-colonial states, openly or quietly, swore allegiance to these ideals. The practice, as we have known it over the past 50 years, has been on the whole, a dismal failure.

Africa was effectively not only, or simply, geographically chopped up. Even more importantly, the further balkanisation of Africa on the eve of independence created more inhibiting conditions for the development of an African national consciousness rooted in Africa's deep history, cultural affinities, common modern experience and a chance to build on this heritage. The gross artificiality and conceptual arbitrariness of the post-colonial state created new Africans without histories, truncated cultures, and pure creatures of the imagination and interests of the western powers. The retreating colonial powers left these historically bereft entities in the hands of a carefully groomed elite, faithful to "his master's voice", beliefs and tastes. These entities were politically announced and baptised as "nation-states" or "nations in the making", ostensibly *en route* to nation building.

Nkrumah exhorted Africans that "Africa Must Unite", and Gabriel d'Arboussier prophesied that: "We see French Africa surmounting both colonialism and its own petty loyalties of tribalism … Within ten years we may have come together to form a great new federal state, bilingual in French and English; not a unitary state, but a federation of Federations – a loosely organised but progressive association of fifty or sixty million African people."[4] Cameron rightly identified such expression as visionary language and imagery. He added that it was however a vision which was shared by many Africans who felt that "in a continent dedicated wholly to unrestrained nationalism the multitude of smaller nation-states stood small chance of independent progress."[5] It was a sentiment which was clearly rampant during that period and was shared by others like Sekou Toure, Modibo Keita, Azikiwe, Kenyatta, Nkrumah and Sobukwe amongst others. Note Sobukwe's words of 21st March 1960 at Orlando Police Station (Johannesburg, South Africa): "Sons and Daughters of Africa, we are standing on the threshold of an historic era. We are blazing a new trail and we invite you to be, with us, creators of history. Join us in the march to freedom. March with us to independence. To independence now. Tomorrow, the United States of Africa. IZWE LETHU!" [6]

However, it was not an exclusively African perceived vision. Fenner Brockway, the long time British member of parliament for Eton and Slough, who was dubbed (tongue in cheek) in the British parliament, "the MP for Africa", wrote that: "The United States of Africa will be a United Socialist States of Africa. It may be the end of this century before it is achieved, but no survey of the continent can lead to any other conclusion than that the creative forces of Africa are now fashioning both unity and socialism."[7]

The idea of socialism in Africa has for most of the post-colonial period been a populist formulation. Different leaders like Kenyatta, Nkrumah, Toure, Nyerere, Kaunda and Keita have all variously articulated positions, which they described as socialist. In some cases, like Tanzania, Ethiopia, Guinea and Ghana, the claim to socialism and a socialist programme of development was openly acknowledged. Much has not been achieved, in terms of prosperity and successful implementation of this ideal, but by and large the ideal has remained strong and resilient in the hearts of many, especially the youth.

In non-Arab Africa, three countries have a relatively long history of the institutionalisation of a Marxian socialist grouping or party. These are Senegal, Cameroon and South Africa. Of these three, it is in South Africa that Marxian socialist claims have been, societally most openly articulated as a political platform by adherents. Much of this, in fact, can be said to be theoretically close to the 4th International. Trotskyism has the strongest base on the African continent in South Africa, especially in the Western Cape. Trotskyism in South Africa has been largely expressed as a *workerist* tendency. There is, however, little evidence that it was treated with serious caution and fear by the erstwhile apartheid regime. The South African Communist Party's (SACP) case is remarkable, in that for a great part of its history, it has been in alliance with the African National Congress (ANC). Founded in 1921, it rapidly moved into active politics in the country. Dubow writes that:

> the Communist Party began actively to recruit African support and by 1928 the great majority of its 1,750 members were blacks. Links were also forged with the ICU, which reached the peak of its influence in the late 1920s but thereafter went into rapid decline. In 1927 James la Guma travelled to Moscow as a representative of the CPSA, together with Josiah Gumede, the new president of the ANC. Gumede had been strongly influenced by Garveyite ideas and pronounced himself highly impressed by what he saw of the Bolshevik Revolution. The Gumede-La Guma trip inaugurated a relationship between the ANC and the CPSA which has endured in one form or another ever since. This association was cemented when the CPSA, in 1928, defined its principal objective as the fight

for an "independent native republic". The "native republic" declaration acknowledged that South Africa was not yet ripe for revolution and that, as a "British dominion of a colonial type", it was necessary to secure a bourgeois nationalist revolution before socialism could be achieved. In subsequent years this position was revised, elaborated and redefined, but the presumption of a two-stage revolution remained an article of faith for the Communist Party. Although this formulation drew to some extent on local experience of peasant insurrection and reflected the Party's growing Africanisation, it was in fact decreed by the Comintern. The "native republic" policy offered considerable potential to create an alliance between nationalist and socialist forces, but it was deeply resented by those who felt that communism's class-based objectives had been diluted.[8]

Other groups like the Pan Africanist Congress of South Africa, (PAC South Africa) and the Azanian People's Organization (AZAPO) have also had some Marxian cadres. But, in these latter instances, their Marxism has been largely subsumed within the dominant Africanist ideological frame.

Cheikh Anta Diop and Nkrumah set themselves the task of demonstrating how Africa's enormous resources could be collectively harnessed to benefit its people. In the aftermath of the assassination of Lumumba and the turbulence that followed in the Congo (which has not come to an end), and in the wake of the Unilateral Declaration of Independence (UDI) in Rhodesia/Zimbabwe, Nkrumah suggested the setting up of an *African High Command* (AHC) as a military capacity, based in Africa and controlled by Africans, to deal with problems and neo-colonialists impositions and confrontations with African interests.[9] The idea did not fly.

Thus, if what is usually described as African nationalism defined its terrain within the framework of the post-colonial state, pan-Africanism has consisted of the same ideas pegged within the parameters of Africa and its Diaspora. I would largely agree with Hodgkin's view that:

African "nationalism" operates, or tries to operate, at a variety of levels: at the level of a particular language-group, or greater tribe – Yoruba, Ewe, Baganda, Banyarwanda, Kikuyu; of a particular colonial territory – Ubangui-Shari, the Gold Coast, Uganda; or

Federation – Nigeria; or former colonial territory – Togoland and the Cameroons, of a wider "trans-territorial" region – *Afrique Noire,* West Africa; and, finally, of "Pan-Africa". Effective political organisations have been built up at each of the first three levels, e.g. the Yoruba Action Group, the Gold Coast Convention People's Party and the Pan-French-African *Rassemblement Démocratique Africain*. The last level belongs so far mainly to the world of ideas and projects – those conceived for example, by Kwame Nkrumah in the Gold Coast and Harry Nkumbula in Northern Rhodesia – rather than of practical politics. But it is not a peculiarly African phenomenon that, during a period of struggle for independence from foreign rule, the shape of the nations-to-be should remain somewhat cloudy and undefined or that various competing or coexisting nationalisms, appealing to wider or narrower loyalties, should be thrown up in the process.[10]

Because African nationalism was so tied to the movement for colonial freedom, it has in its classical form, lost the ear of African intelligentsia. The myth that is current today suggests that African nationalism should have little or no place in the affairs of Africans. This view frequently carries with it the argument that nationalism, in all its forms, is negative and atavistic. This is in fact, on closer examination, a lame argument. Nationalism appears both in progressive and reactionary forms; it appears in both right and left wing varieties. In Africa, nationalism still has a long way to go for societies in which the national and democratic character of the social and economic majorities have for centuries been oppressed. Under such circumstances, the national question in economic, political and cultural senses represents part of the process for democracy and the emancipation of mass society.

The national question remains a dominant issue in contemporary Africa. The question is how can Africa carry the democratic masses to greater and fuller emancipation beyond the politics of anti-colonial/anti-settler colonial liberation movements and processes. Once independence or settler colonial regimes have been overcome, the challenge is then, the empowerment and emancipation of mass society so that democracy and social justice have meaning. The national question needs to be pursued in its multifarious dimensions. It includes issues of economic empowerment of deprived constituencies, the development of social welfare policies, the education and acknowledgement of the masses, based on their cultures and languages and the liberation of the identities of the masses suppressed under the culture of Eurocentric African elites and the cultural hegemony of the west in the era of globalisation.

The Evolution of African National Consciousness

There is a saying that "you never see Africa whole until you are out of it". In this respect, it is not surprising that it was in bondage and enslavement of the African, in the "new world", that the early stirrings and formulations of a pan-Africanist agenda emerged. It was in the African Diaspora, in the western hemisphere, that the modern articulation of the history and destiny of Africans, as a people, first took tentative conceptual representation. From early beginnings in the 18th century, the Diaspora linkage has been a permanent feature of the evolution of African nationalism. In the history of this evolution, understandably, concerns of Africans on the continent have broadly differed from those of the Diaspora. This is primarily because the historical and sociological contexts of the two constituencies have consistently varied. Until the very late 19th century convergence between Diaspora Black nationalist concerns and continent-based views was weak and thin. However, the linkages have, both theoretically and practically, been abiding features of this history. Cummings makes the point well that, "we cannot understand the history and substance of the Pan-African Movement without drawing heavily upon sources now classified as Afro-American Studies on the one hand, and Caribbean and African Studies on the other" .[11]

It is possible to sketch out the evolution of pan-Africanism into four broad historical stages. The first period roughly runs from the end of the 18th century to the closing decades of the 19th century. The second stage continues from the *fin de siecle* period to 1945. The third stage runs into the 1990s, and the fourth period continues into the present. The periodisation scheme is hardly precise and has thematically considerable overlap.

During the first period, much of the proto-nationalist ideas were based in the New World in general and North America in particular. Across the Diaspora, under slavery, rebellions were frequent and persistent occurrences. On the African continent, the 18th and 19th centuries were a period of primary anti-colonial resistance. Apart from inter-African wars, Africans were locked in wars against western expansion and attempts by westerners to gain controlling influence in different parts of the continent. There were also in the Sahel, West and East Africa (all the way down to 20 degrees, south latitude), the much older institution of Arab-led slavery, which fed into West Asia and beyond. There were in all areas where African slaves were taken, sporadic and spasmodic outbreaks of revolt, however, none of these expressions of resistance evolved into any sustained movement of a nationalist kind. Across the world of the Diaspora proto-nationalism and nativism often found religious expression. The better known examples of these include the *Jeje, Voodun* in Haiti, *Candomble-Nago* in Brazil, *Lucumi* in Cuba, *Obeyie* (sometimes spelt *Obeah*) in some parts of the West Indies, *Orisha* worship, *Palo Mayombe, Macumba, Abakwa* and others. In some instances, such institutions developed organised and routinised systems of priesthood, for example the *Santeros* and *Babalaos*, which are names of different types of *Lucumi* priests.

Nationalism in a modern sense first made an appearance on the African continent in the 1860s. The position in the Diaspora was different. We are informed that as far back as the 1770s, Africans in North America were training as missionaries for Africa. Sierra Leone was founded in 1787 and rapidly over years, saw the arrival of immigrants from the West Indies, Nova Scotia and other parts of the British colonial world. Lynch has drawn attention to the fact that almost all Black organisations in the United States, up to about the third decade of the 19th century, made reference to Africa or African in their titles. Some examples were "Prince Hall's African Lodge No.1, the Free African Societies of Philadelphia and Newport, the African Baptist Churches, and the African Methodist Church. From about the third decade on, when American Negroes became convinced that the American Colonisation Society (founded in 1817) wished forcibly to deport them to Africa, the title "African" became less popular among them and was replaced by "Coloured."[12] The American War of Independence and its aftermath saw the dispersal of thousands of Blacks to different British possessions, some of them ending up back in Africa.[13] Bell writes that in the period following the American War of Independence, from time to time, certain Negro Americans thought of Africa as a land of opportunity, as a world to which they owed a debt of loyalty for having been the land of their forebears, as land for missionary effort, or as an area of economic opportunity for which blacks were qualified physically, mentally, and emotionally in greater degree than whites. A number of Negroes from Boston expressed an interest in emigration to Africa in 1787, and before the end of the century a Rhode Island group had asked permission to enter the British colony of Sierra Leone. But the first American Negro to make an individual attempt to tie Africa and North America together commercially by cords of black was Paul Cuffee, a Quaker of Negro-Indian ancestry, a self-made fisherman, whaler, merchant. Cuffee sought with some degree of success to persuade American blacks to take an interest in his joint scheme for emigration and commercial exploitation, but it was brought to a halt by the War in 1812. After the war he did transport a group of emigrants, but died soon afterwards.[14]

The earliest epoch-making representation of black nationalism in the Diaspora is rooted in the ideas of emancipation from slavery, which undergirded the Haitian revolution of 1791- 1804. It sought freedom from slavery for African slaves in France's most important slave colony in the West Indies. The effects of the Haitian revolution, under Toussaint L'Ouverture, spread far beyond Haiti. Its success was a catalyst for the arrest of French colonial aspirations in the western hemisphere. It was instrumental in inducing France to sell its substantial territory in North America to the United States through the Louisiana Purchase in 1803. The emergence of a free Haiti was the initial vindication of the strand of African nationalism in the Diaspora, which sought a destiny in the New World and not as returnees; "back to Africa". With respect to North America, Cummings summarised the experience of these two tendencies thus: "Long before the end of slavery in America, many blacks had raised the issue: what are we? Are we Americans or Africans? Frederick Douglass, the prominent abolitionist, sought to resolve the issue once and for all. In a now famous statement, Douglass told Americans, black and white, that Afro-Americans are Americans, although descendants of Africa. While Douglass raised the standard for Americanism, other contemporaries of his such as Martin R. Delany and Bishop Henry McNeal Turner championed their own back-to-Africa movements. With the benefit of hindsight, we now can assert that Douglass won the debate and the Civil Rights Movement led by Martin Luther King, Jr. in the 1960s reaffirmed his position."[15]

Cuffee's friends and disciples, particularly Daniel Coker and Lott Cary, became eloquent voices for the returnee idea. Coker was active and influential in the Africanist break from the Methodist Episcopal Church to form the African Methodist Episcopal Church. The beginnings of Liberia emerged largely as an inspiration of Coker. Until its independence in 1847, control over Liberia was vested in the hands of the American Colonisation Society. John B. Russwurm was another figure of significance in the establishment of early Liberia. Through various colonisation societies and associations, which proliferated in the United States and the West Indies at that time, the back to Africa movement in the 19th century, established a foothold for returnees in West Africa. It is within this milieu that some of the more articulate ideologues of pan-Negro nationalism like Edward W. Blyden, Robert Campell and Alexander Crummell took centre-stage. Ayodele Langley has pointed out that:

> Crummell like Blyden originally had great faith in the ability of the Afro-American colonists and in the Americo-Liberian class in general to build a Liberian nation through the integration of the indigenous Africans of Liberia and like Blyden, he was gradually disillusioned and constantly warned the Americo-Liberians of their shortcomings and of the dangers of black colonialism and oligarchy. Like Blyden he believed in the modernising role of imperialism, and gave high priority to Christianity and free trade, though unlike Blyden he was not a cultural nationalist or a believer in the integrative virtues of Islam.[16]

We know that following the Bahia slave rebellion of 1835, returnees from Brazil to various parts of Africa, especially West Africa, increased. The Aguda or Brazilian returnees to principally Dahomey/Benin, are noteworthy for being (as compared to the returnees from the West Indies and North America – Sierra Leone and Liberia) Diaspora Africans who assimilated western cultural values in Brazil, but managed to resiliently maintain African habits and customs to the extent that, on return, they were able to culturally readapt to a greater degree of effectiveness.[17] Over the years, these Afro-Brazilian elements have successively dispersed throughout West African littoral and largely "re-tribalised". Some have emerged even in South Africa as the Ribeiros and the Peregrinos.

The return of sizeable numbers of returnees ended with the 19th century. However, the intellectual tradition of the "back-to-Africa" kind has persisted in various forms to the present time. During the twentieth century, its most powerful expression appeared in the work of Marcus Garvey and his Universal Negro Improvement Association (UNIA). Socio-psychologically, Garvey's movement of the 1920s was a tremendous boost for the flagging self-respect and pride of people of African descent, particularly in the Diaspora. For some Garvey's ideas appeared fanciful and drew derisory commentary. Cronon writes that:

> Most American Negro editors scoffed at the Back to Africa talk and loudly proclaimed the desire of Negroes to remain in the United States. The *Chicago Defender*, which generally avoided use of the word Negro in its columns, announced proudly: "The Race considers itself African no more than white Americans consider themselves European." The *Defender* went on to suggest pointedly that "in the United states lunacy commissions still have legal standing". An anti-Garvey cartoon showed a strong manly Negro holding a small nondescript "Back to Africa fanatic" and advising: "The best thing you can do is stay right *here* and fight out your salvation." Even the white press, when it deigned to notice Garvey, was hostile to the idea of redemption of Africa. Negro intellectuals generally opposed Garvey's methods if not his interest in Africa. Booker T. Washington had preached against any idea of a return to Africa and doubtless his philosophy still carried great weight with many American Negroes.[18]

Today, the back-to-Africa tradition has become an even more marginal tendency with a shrinking and limited constituency. Its strongest substratum in the West Indies is currently the Rastafarian movement.

The second period saw the cross-fertilisation of the ideas of Blyden, Hilary Teage and Crummell and Africanus Horton with those of a slightly younger generation of continentally based nationalist thinkers like Sarbah and Casely Hayford. I have elsewhere pointed out that the earlier figures tended to favour extensive cultural, linguistic and religious westernisation.[19] Crummell's idea that African languages are "characterised by lowness of ideas. As the speech of rude barbarians marked by brutal and vindictive sentiments....", or Ajayi Crowther's judgement that "if we have any regard for the elevation of Africa ... our wisdom would be to cry to those Christian nations which have been so long labouring for our conversion, to redouble their Christian efforts for the evangelisation of this continent ..." were classic cases.[20] Such views were conceptually partially negated by figures like Attoh Ahuma, Casely Hayford, Sarbah and particularly Kobina Sekyi. Sarbah's nativism, which bears a strong Afro-centric strain, is exemplified by the following passage from his preface to his *Fanti National Constitution (1906)*. "The American slave trade, in the opinion of many intelligent Africans, was Africa's greatest curse. The phrase 'gone Fantee', originated, however, at a time when Gold Coast natives, being dissatisfied with the demoralising effects of certain European influences, determined to stop further encroachments into their nationality. Fully convinced that it is better to be called by one's own name than be known by a foreign one, that it is possible to acquire Western learning and be expert in scientific attainments without neglecting one's mother tongue".[21] The sentiment was echoed with equal conviction by the Nigerian pastor Mojola Agbebi that "the introduction of the usages and institutions of European life into the African social system has resulted in a disordering and a dislocation of the latter which threatens to overthrow the system altogether and produce a social state of anarchy".[22] We hear also here, nearer our times, Chinua Achebe's views from his novel, *No Longer at Ease*.

In a letter written by Joseph Dawson, the secretary of the Fanti Confederacy to the editor of the *African Times* dated August 21, 1870, which appeared in the 24 October issue of the newspaper, Dawson in this letter about the objects of the Fanti Confederacy explained that: "The love of my country and a desire to see it rise, if it be the will of God, to the class of civilised nations, have emboldened me to set aside all fear of the consequences in stepping out openly to do my share of the business, and leave the result to God and the sons of Fanti".[23] In his *West African Countries and Peoples (1868)*, James Africanus Horton argued that ".... we have seen European nations who in years long passed were themselves as barbarous and unenlightened as the Negro Africans are at present, and who have exhibited wonderful improvements within the last century.

This should urge the Africans to increased exertions, so that their race may, in course of time, take its proper stand in the world's history".[24] Elsewhere in the same text, basing himself on a cyclical theory of civilisation, he wrote that "nations rise and fall; the once flourishing and civilised degenerates into a semi-barbarous state; and those who lived in utter barbarism, after a lapse of time become the standing nation ... the nations of Western Africa must live in the hope, that in process of time their turn will come ..."[25] By the end of the 19th century, western trained Africans were beginning to see and sing to the promised land, however far it was from immediate view. In 1892, John L. Dube, later first President of the ANC, in a pamphlet entitled *A Talk Upon My Native Land* had this to say:

Hail, O Africa, thy ransom!
Raise to heaven, thy grateful song!
Last in rang among the nations,
Thou shalt lead the choral throng, -
Land of promise!
Thy Redeemer's praise prolong! [26]

During the 20th century such minds included Pixley Isaka Seme, a founder member of the African National Congress in 1912, and later president of the organisation. In 1905, he spoke of a *Regeneration of Africa*. In that presentation, he remarked: "I have chosen to speak to you on this occasion upon *The Regeneration of Africa*. I am an African, and set my pride in my race over against a hostile public opinion.... The African recognises his anomalous position and desires a change. The brighter day is rising upon Africa. Already I seem to see her chains dissolved, her desert plains red with harvest, her Abyssinia and her Zululand the seats of science and of religion, reflecting the glory of the rising sun from the spires of their churches and universities. Her Congo and her Gambia whitened with commerce ..."[27] The conviction that Africa is on the rebound, that we are in the darkness before dawn, has been a steadily resonating theme throughout the 20th century.

The idea of Pan-Africanism much as it is associated with the work of W.E.B. Du Bois, is actually a creation of the mind of Henry Sylvester Williams. Williams, a Trinidadian from Arouca, had been profoundly affected by his experiences in North America and Britain. His biographer, J.R. Hooker, informs us that from 1897 onwards, he was increasingly occupied with African conditions both in the Diaspora and the continent. He had been particularly influenced by the experiences of an African woman married to a Scotsman, a mining engineer who had worked in South Africa in the Rand. Her addresses in Britain on the conditions in the mining compounds had triggered an idea in Williams about the need to fight for the improvement of African conditions. Apparently Williams was appalled by the testimony of Mrs

Kinloch. Hooker writes that this resulted in the "formation of the world's first Pan-African Association (PAA), sometime after June 1897. Its Constitution charged the PAA with securing "to Africans and their descendants throughout the world their true civil and political rights, to ameliorate the condition of our oppressed brethren in the continents of Africa, America, and other parts of the world, by promoting efforts to secure effective legislation, to encourage our people in education, industrial and commercial enterprises, to foster friendly relations between the Caucasian and African races, to organise a bureau, a depository for the collection of authorised writings and statistics relating to our people everywhere, and to raise a fund to be used solely for forwarding these purposes".[28] This period saw Williams develop a strong interest in African affairs, and led directly to the emergence of the Pan-African Congress Movement. Williams' views were much like the other African nationalists of the period, Casely Hayford, Sarbah, Dube, Molema, who were all basically accommodationists interested in finding sympathy for African causes amongst the western powers.

Williams moved into Cape Town, South Africa in 1903 and was in South Africa until 1904. He was, according to Hooker, the only black barrister in Cape Town at that point in time. He was admitted as an advocate of the Supreme Court in the Colony of the Cape of Good Hope on the 29th October 1903. In a letter dated 17th November, 1903 he wrote to his wife in London that: "The whole of South Africa is looking upon me and I must see to it that my debut in the criminal arena will be memorable." [29] He was active in the cause of the Basuto and became the first non-white on the municipal council of Cape Town.[30] Hooker presents evidence to show that he was in touch with D.D.T. Jabavu and A. Abdul Rahman.[31]

It needs to be remembered that this was during the period of the frantic scramble for colonies in Africa by the imperial powers. There was no talk of independence or outright rejection of colonialism. The idea was that Africans would and should accept benign colonial rule, which was kind and sympathetic to the colonial wards of the western powers. Marc Kojo Tovalou Houenou, the Dahomeyan/Beninois founder of the *Ligue Universelle pour la Defense de la Race Negre* (1924) wrote in the journal of the *Ligue* at the opening stages of the First World War (1914) that all pro-French patriotic colonial subjects should support France in the war, and that after the war all they desired was that "the colonies should have possibilities of making their voices heard in the

affairs of the Government …"[32] Attoh Ahuma was equally agreeable to
the imperial power. Writing in 1911 his views were that:

> … there has been established within our territories an *imperium in
> imperio* - the highest organised form of government in creation,
> which binds us as an integral part of an empire over which the sun
> never sets. We are being welded together under one umbrageous
> Flag – a Flag that is the symbol of justice, freedom, and fair play:
> and we have ruling over us, as king of our kings and in the bond of
> peace, one paramount emperor – His Majesty King George V. The
> Gold Coast under the aegis of the Union Jack is the unanswerable
> argument to all who may incontinently withhold from us the
> common rights, privileges, and status of nationality.[33]

Hooker suggests that the first notice that the PAA was planning a
conference appeared in the form of a letter written by B. T. Washington
in 1899 to African-American newspapers, in which he stated that:

> In connection with the assembling of so many Negroes in
> London from different parts of the world, a very important
> movement has just been put upon foot. It is known as the Pan-
> African Conference. Representatives from Africa, the West
> Indian Islands and other parts of the world, asked me to meet
> them a few days ago with a view to making a preliminary
> programme for this conference, and we had a most interesting
> meeting. It is surprising to see the strong intellectual mould,
> which many of these Africans and West Indians possess. The
> object and character of the Pan-African Conference is best told
> in the words of the resolution, which was adopted at the
> meeting referred to, viz: "In view of the widespread ignorance
> which is prevalent in England about the treatment of native
> races under European and American rule, the African
> Association, which consists of members of the race resident in
> England, and which has been in existence now for nearly two
> years, has resolved during the Paris Exposition of 1900 (which
> many representatives of the race may be visiting) to hold a
> conference in London in the month of May of the said year, in
> order to take steps to influence public opinion on existing
> proceedings and conditions affecting the welfare of the natives

in various parts of the world, viz. South Africa, West Africa, the West Indies and the United States. The resolution is signed by Mr. H. Mason Joseph, President, and Mr. H. Sylvester Williams, as Honourable Secretary. The Honourable Secretary will be pleased to hear from representative natives who are desirous of attending, at an early date. He may be addressed, Common Room, Grey's [sic] Inn, London, W.C.[34]

This is how B.T. Washington registered for the African-American public the first Pan-African Conference. The Conference amongst other things established a committee to address the Nations of the World with W.E.B. Du Bois as Chairperson of this group. The address, which was provided by Du Bois, brought into historical record what has become his famous quote that the problem of the 20th century is the problem of the colour line. The well-known paragraph reads: "In the metropolis of the modern world, in this the closing year of the nineteenth century, there has been assembled a congress of men and women of African blood, to deliberate solemnly upon the present situation and outlook of the darker races of mankind. The problem of the twentieth century is the problem of the colour line, the question as to how far differences of race – which show themselves chiefly in the colour of the skin and the texture of the hair – will hereafter be made the basis of denying to over half the world the right of sharing to their utmost ability the opportunities and privileges of modern civilisation."[35]

If Williams inaugurated the idea of Pan-Africanism, it was Du Bois whose steadfast work, in focusing minds around successive congresses between 1900 and 1945, laid the foundations of the movement that has come to be known as the Pan-Africanist Movement (1919, 1921, 1923,1927 and 1945). The greatest significance of this movement was that it ultimately created the platform for what can be regarded as the launch of the African independence movement after the Second World War, in Manchester, England. Padmore and Makonnen by this time had become differently key role players in the evolution of this process.

The series of congresses represented by this movement by no means exclusively monopolised the spirit and direction of the African freedom movement during this period, but the 1945 Manchester congress virtually moved the idea of African freedom and independence from a theoretical level to the pursuit of practical solutions. The Manchester congress included many of the figures who later became famous in the independence movement such as Kwame Nkrumah, Jomo Kenyatta, Kamuzu Banda, Koinange and Joe Appiah. Distinctly, while in the period between 1900 and the beginning of the Second World War African nationalists had sought an accommodationist relationship with the colonial power, after 1945, starting with Nkrumah, the thrust of the struggle was for colonial freedom and independence. The driving impulses of Pan-Africanism became, more clearly, continentally-based Africans. From 1945 to the demise of apartheid in 1994, Pan-Africanism went through another evolutionary stage. Both colonialism and settler-colonialism were overthrown. The dream of a united Africa has lived in the hearts and minds of African nationalists, but has remained in substance a dream. The post-Manchester 1945 story is the story of a successful defeat of colonialism but also a failure to institutionalise a firm and concrete African unity.

Nkrumah led the way and soon created greater scope for other younger nationalists in Africa to follow suit. During the speech for independence, at the Old Polo Ground in Accra on 6 March, 1957 he announced that "the independence of Ghana is meaningless unless it is linked with the total liberation of Africa". This policy and pronouncement led quickly to the creation of facilities, of various sorts, for the prosecution of the anti-colonial struggle in both peaceful and violent ways. The Bureau of African Affairs in Accra became the focal point of activity in support of the struggles led by people like Joshua Nkomo (Rhodesia), Felix Moumie (Cameroon), Holden Roberto (Angola), Neto (Angola), Mondlane (Mozambique), Obote (Uganda), Toure (Guinea), Keita (Mali) and others.

The hope had been that the emerging independent states of Africa would rapidly move towards unity. This turned out to be an extravagant dream. The realities and forces of neo-colonialism were in fact grossly underestimated. The split between the Monrovia and Casablanca groups in 1961 underscored the entrenchment of divergent interests and different views as to the way forward. With the creation of the Organisation of African Unity (OAU) on 25 May, 1963 the rift between the Monrovia and Casablanca groups was healed. But the OAU was, in fact, practically a regional organisation. It was, in fact, more a continental (regional) association than a federation of states. In its charter, it simply expressed the wish "to promote unity"; it asserted the "sovereign equality of all Member States"; and upheld "the non-interference in the internal affairs of States". To Nkrumah's exhortations of unity now, Nyerere inveighed that "there is no god who will bring about African unity by merely saying 'let there be unity'." [36]

The contradiction between these two positions can be expressed in terms of those who wanted an immediate realisation of unity and others, who although they were equally in favour of unity, felt that the process needed to be undertaken piecemeal. An example of this is provided by Nkrumah and Azikiwe. In an address to the Ghana National Assembly on 8 August 1960, against the background of the crisis in the Congo created by the presence of Belgian troops and the secession of Katanga, Nkrumah argued that:

> … The African struggle for independence and unity must begin with political union. A loose confederation of economic cooperation is deceptively time delaying. It is only a political union that will ensure uniformity in our foreign policy projecting the African personality and presenting Africa as a force important to be reckoned with. I repeat, a loose economic co-operation means a screen behind which detractors, imperialist and colonialist protagonists and African puppet leaders hide to operate and weaken the concept of any effort to realise African unity and independence. A political union envisages a common foreign and defence policy, and rapid social, economic and industrial developments. The economic resources of Africa are immense and staggering. It is only by unity that these resources can be utilised for the progress of the Continent and for the happiness of mankind.[37]

Azikiwe's position contrasted sharply in the sense that he articulated clearly the gradualist argument to unity. In an address given in London on 31 July 1959, as Prime Minister of the eastern region of Nigeria and leader of the National Council of Nigeria and the Cameroons (NCNC), he articulated his position thus:

> I believe that economic and social integration will enable Nigeria and its neighbours to bring to pass the United States of Africa, which is the dream of African nationalists. It would be capital folly to assume that hard-bargaining politicians who

passed through the ordeal of victimisation and the crucible of persecution to win their political independence will easily surrender their newly won political power in the interest of a political leviathan which is populated by people who are alien to one another in their social and economic relations. It has not been possible in Europe or America.... I reiterate that I firmly believe in the attainment of an association or union of African states either on a regional or continental basis in the future. I would regard such a future as not within the life-time of the heroes and heroines who have spearheaded the struggle for freedom in Africa, these four decades... In other words, the prerequisite of political integration in Africa are the economic and social integration of African peoples.[38]

The OAU lumbered on until 2002, when largely through the self-interested zeal of Colonel Ghaddafi of Libya, a revamped version, revised as an improvement on the old body, was conceived and helped to birth by South Africa. There are many who regard the South African initiative of facilitating the birth of the African Union (AU) as fortuitous. Fresh from the legacy of apartheid, and empowered with a new democratic Constitution, with better resources than any other African country, South Africa was able to rescue the idea out of the hands of what could possibly be regarded as Ghaddafi's mercurial politics. With the birth of the African Union, African nationalism and Pan-Africanism have entered a new stage. Notions like "peer review" of the democratic performance of states, the nascent conceptualisation of an African parliament, the use of African languages in the affairs of the African Union and the back-paddling of the principle of non-interference in the affairs of member states, all go to indicate that the parameters for the pursuit of the ideal of African unity are changing.

An almost half-century of post-colonialism has revealed the hand of neo-colonialism. African states are ostensibly recognised and treated as sovereign states on the councils of the world. In fact, almost all are "banana republics" - free and sovereign in name but effectively and totally dependent on the designs, institutions and intentions of the Western powers. African countries have all started with great expectations for development, economic growth, and the eradication of poverty, but not one African state has been able to emerge economically and developmentally triumphant in the half century of post-colonial history. The truth is that it is unlikely that African states can move forward to development singly. It should be obvious to all that even in the present conditions of extreme difficulties facing Africa, a united Africa would be in a better position to negotiate with all-comers on a basis of equality and parity.

Pan-Africanism in our era is straining to break the leash of neo-colonialism. Political realities on the ground are dictating the pace of this process, in the sense that the emerging scenario of generalised war and conflict is challenging the original OAU protocol, which imposed the non-interference of African states on each other's affairs. Today two-thirds of sub-Saharan Africa is at war. In the Eastern part and Horn of Africa area, the Eritrean war of independence took a heavy toll on the human and economic resources of both the victor and the vanquished. Subsequently, the cruel border war has worsened conditions further. In Somalia, internecine conflict and clan rivalries have more or less shredded the state. Sudan continues to be the terrain of Africa's longest war, which started in August 1955. In Uganda, the Museveni government has continued for twelve years a war in the north of the country against atavistic millenarian and messianic movements. The Museveni regime has refused to countenance the sort of political solution, which could bring the war to an end. Across the border, in the Democratic Republic of the Congo, war continues in an extensive and calamitous bloodletting way. Genocide of unprecedented proportions is going on in the eastern Congo, in Kivu, while Ugandan and Rwandese troops loot the country. In Rwanda a decade ago, genocide was visited on the Tutsi minority by the Hutu majority, the tensions and sporadic blood-letting between the two groups have continued since the end of Belgian rule in the area. The Angolan war which was fought for almost three decades has recently come to an end and the country is saddled with untold hardship, suffering and unprecedented poverty. In the Central African Republic, sporadic war and fighting continues. The same is true for Chad where civil war has for decades divided north-south, east-west of the country. For now the Tuareg war in Mali, Niger and Chad appears to have abated, but recent signs continue to be ominous. In West Africa littoral, countries have been falling into civil war like dominoes. Senegal is at war with itself, Guinea Bissau, Guinea, Sierra Leone, Liberia and Côte d'Ivoire is on the threshold of full-blown war. Tension in northern Ghana threatens to plunge the country into war. Almost three decades of dictatorship in

Togo has created deep tensions in the country, which are contained only through ruthless repressions. Madagascar has been for two years now teetering on the edge of civil war. Afro-Arab tensions and conflicts in Mauritania, the Western Sahara and Sudan continue. All in all, the situation in Africa is most unpromising.

In a recent email sent to a number of recipients, Ekwe Ekwe makes the useful observation that "with 10 major ongoing armed conflicts, Africa has more wars raging on its territory than any other continent in the world. Since the end of the Second World War in 1945, more than 100 wars have been fought in Africa, the Middle East, Asia and Latin America/the Caribbean resulting in the death of 36 million people. This figure represents about 70 per cent of the total number of those killed during the Second World War. Of these 36 million fatalities, one-third or 12 million are Africans, killed in the so-called 'internal' wars that have been fought across Africa since the 1960s".[39] It is doubtful if banning arms *per se* will solve the problem of growing and expanding armed conflict across the continent. For one thing, it would be very difficult, under the present circumstances of porous borders to seal off entry and exit points for arms. What is more important is to remove the roots of the tensions and the structural problems, which make Africa conflict-prone. Africa's wars have become so interlocking and interrelated that it is no longer possible to treat them as issues, which face single countries. Indeed, it is impossible to solve these interlocking conflicts unless their Pan-African character is first acknowledged. We have collectively to go back to the drawing board and find ways of solving our problems as problems facing Africans as a whole and not as single countries.

In Conclusion: Continentalism and its Critique

Of all the limitations of the Pan-Africanist ideology as we have known it throughout the 20th century, particularly since the beginning of the independence era, is the question of continentalism. By continentalism, I mean the idea that the unity of Africa is to be based on firstly, the geographical unity of the whole continent and secondly, constructed with the post-colonial/neo-colonial states as the building blocks. This conception of African unity is fundamentally a geographical or regional understanding of African unity and not a unity of people with affiliation to commonalities of history and culture and subjective attachments to these. In other words, African unity based on historical and cultural factors cannot exclude the African Diaspora. In fact, it includes the Diaspora more than it includes the states, which belong to the Arab League. This latter seeks unity of the Arab world and the Arab nation, which is a legitimate and noble aspiration of the Arab people. Continentalism as a concept of African unity sees African unity in the same sense as other regional bodies like the Organisation of the American States (OAS) or the Association of South East Asian Nations (ASEAN) see themselves - not as historical and cultural unities in the first instance. I have elsewhere argued that "*continentalism* is the bane of Pan-Africanism. The geographical definition of Africans simply means that everybody in Africa is an African, even where some of such people insist they are not Africans. Everybody becomes an African, and therefore nobody is an African. The dialectic takes its course. *Continentalism* means those who are not on the continent are not Africans, therefore, the Diaspora is not African, (*quod erat demonstrandum*). This is the sort of bizarre direction *continentalism* logically takes us".

As we confront the realities of the decomposition of the post-colonial state, we have the opportunity to redesign our political futures afresh and collectively. We need to move away from the design of an Africa imposed on us by the old colonial powers. A united Africa, which acknowledges its Diaspora beckons. An Africa united is an Africa capable of solving the problems we currently face. A disunited Africa has no chance of advancement. A half-century of the latest African history is enough for us to know this truth.

References

[1] .S.K.B. Asante. *Pan-African Protest: West Africa and the Italo-Ethiopian Crisis 1934 – 194 1*(Longman, Britain. 1977). P. 48; writes that "the focal point of the protest of West Africans in Britain to the Italo-Ethiopian conflict was the West African Students' Union (WASU) founded in August 1925. Its chief architect was H.C. Bankole-Bright, a medical doctor and member of the Sierra Leone Legislative Council and of the National Congress of British West Africa. A meeting of about a dozen West Africans, most of them law students, held on 7 August 1925,

adopted a resolution to inaugurate a West African Students' Union. At that time, there existed three African students' organisations in England: the Union for Students of African Descent formed in 1917 primarily for literary and social activities; the Gold Coast Students' Association and the Nigerian Progress Union established in 1924."

2.*Gambia Outlook and Senegambia Reporter*. February 1936. In, S.K.B Asante. *Pan-African Protest: West Africa and the Italo-Ethiopian Crisis 1934 – 1941* (Longman. Britain 1977). P. 147.

3.James Cameron: *The African Revolution* (Thames and Hudson, London, 1961). P.102.

4.Ibid. Pp. 106 – 107.

5.Ibid. P. 107.

6.See, Elias L. Ntloedibe: *Here is a Tree: Political Biography of Robert Mangaliso Sobukwe* (Century-Turn Publishers, Mogoditshane/Botswana. 1995). P.74.

7.Fenner Brockway: *African Socialism* (The Bodley Head, London. 1963) P.124.

8.Saul Dubow: *The African National Congress*, (Johnathan Ball Publishers. Johannesburg. 2000). Pp.13-14.

9.At the time Nkrumah first launched this idea, he was fiercely criticised by many as wanting to create an instrument for his domination of Africa. Recently, the *Accra Mail* of 23 November 2001 reported that "the time for the formation of an African High Command (AHC) as envisaged by the late President of Ghana, Dr. Kwame Nkrumah has arrived. Such a command under the direction of the African Union could be deployed for peacekeeping operations in cases of armed conflict between two sister African countries." Nkrumah's idea was that the AHC would confront and thwart neo-colonialist intentions in Africa, halt the balkanisation process, and speed up the unity of Africa.

10. Thomas Hodgkin: *Nationalism in Colonial Africa*. Frederick Muller. London. 1956. P.21.

11.Robert J. Cummings. "Africa Between the Ages" in *African Studies Review*. Vol. 29. No. 3. September 1986. P.6.

12. Hollis R. Lynch. "Pan-Negro Nationalism in the New World Before 1862" in Jeffrey Butler (ed). *Boston University Papers on Africa. Vol. II.* (Boston University Press. Boston, 1966) P.151.

13. Howard H. Bell: "Introduction" in M.R. Delany and Robert Campbell: *Search for a Place: Black Separatism and Africa, 1860.* (Ann Arbor Paperbacck, University of Michigan Press. 1971 edition) pp.2-3.

14. Ibid. p.3.

15. Robert J. Cummings. *"Africa Between the Ages"* (Presidential Address Delivered at the 28th Annual Meeting of the African Studies Association, November 24, 1985, New Orleans in *The African Studies Review* (The African Studies Association, Los Angeles, Vol.29. No. 3. September 1986) P.8

16. J. Ayo Langley: "Ideologies of Liberation in Black Africa, 1856 – 1970." *Documents on Modern African Political Thought from Colonial Times to the Present* (Rex Collings, London, 1979). P.24.

17. See, Olabiyi Babalola Yai. "The Identity, Contributions and Ideology of the Aguda (Afro-Brazilians) of the Gulf of Benin: A Reinterpretation". in, Kristin Mann and Edna G. Bay (ed). *Slavery & Abolition* (Special Issue, Volume 22. 1. 2001) "Rethinking the African Diaspora: The Making of a Black Atlantic World in the Bight of Benin and Brazil." See also, Elisée Soumonni. "Some Reflections on the Brazilian Legacy in Dahomey" in *Slavery & Abolition,* Ibid

18. E. David Cronon: *Black Moses: The Story of Marcus Garvey and the Universal Negro Improvement Association* (The University of Wisconsin Press, Wisconsin. 1955). P.186.

19. K.K. Prah: "The Idea of an African Renaissance, the Language of the Renaissance and the Challenges of the 21st Century", in Eisei Kurimoto (ed), *Rewriting Africa: Towards Renaissance or Collapse* (The Japan Centre for Area Studies Series. No.14. Osaka. 2001) pp-178-179.

20. Alexander Crummell: *The English Language in Liberia 1861*. Quoted in J. Ayo Langley. Op cit. P.357. Bishop A. Crowther's charge at Lokoja, 13 September 1869: "Africa for the Africans Alone". Quoted in H.S. Wilson (ed) *Origins of West African Nationalism* (Macmillan, St. Martin's Press, London, 1969) p.150

21. J. M. Sarbah: "Preface" in *Fanti National Constitution*. Quoted from H.S. Wilson. Ibid. p.274.

22. Mojola Agbebi. "Pastor Mojola Agbebi on the West African Problem." Quoted from H.S. Wilson (ed). Ibid. p.304.

23. H.S. Wilson. Op cit. p.208.

24. Ibid. p.167.

25. Ibid. p.170

26. Quoted from Hans Kohn and Wallace Sokolsky: *"African Nationalism in the Twentieth Century"* (Van Nostrand Company, Inc. New York. 1965) P.60.

[27] Pixley Isaka Seme: "The Regeneration of Africa" in the *Journal of the Royal Africa Society*, Vol.5. 1905-1906. Quoted from J. Ayo Langley. Op cit. 1979. p.261.

[28] J.R. Hooker: *Henry Sylvester Williams: Imperial Pan-Africanist* (Rex Collins, London, 1975) p.23

[29] Ibid. p.65.

[30] Ibid. p.79.

[31] Ibid. p.70.

[32] Kojo Tovalou Houenou: *The Problem of Negroes in French Colonial Africa*. Quoted in J. Ayo Langley. Op cit. P.229.

[33] S.R.B. Attoh Ahuma: *The Gold Coast Nation and National Consciousness* (1911) Pp i-ii. Quoted from, H.S. Wilson. Op cit. P.267.

[34] Ibid. P.29.

[35] Philip S. Foner (ed). *W.E.B. Du Bois Speaks: Speeches and Addresses 1890 – 1919* (Pathfinder Press, New York, 1970) P.125.

[36] See, Hans Kohn and Wallace Sokolsky. Op cit. p.96.

[37] Ibid. P.179.

[38] Nnamdi Azikiwe: *Selected Speeches of Dr Nnamdi Azikiwe* (Cambridge University Press, Cambridge). 1961. P.72. Quoted here from, Hans Kohn and Wallace Sokolshy. Ibid. P.183.

[39] Herbert Ekwe Ekwe: *"Ban all Arms Exports to Africa. Exclusive Commentary for USAfricaonline.com"*,
http://www.usafricaonline.com/ekweekwe.africaarms.html

3

Re-framing Pan-Africanism

Mammo Muchie

I have often been accused of pursuing a "policy of the impossible". But I cannot believe in the impossibility of achieving African union any more than I could ever have thought of the impossibility of attaining African freedom... Africa must unite. We have before us not only an opportunity but a historic duty.
(Nkrumah 1963: 231)

Introduction

In this chapter the argument is made for re-launching the debate on Pan-African unity to recapture the lost ground and make good the opportunity cost incurred by Africa in choosing the minimalist aims of settling for fragile and weak states with an equally enfeebled Organisation of African Unity, and possibly the new African Union (AU). It reviews the clash between Afro-pessimism and Afro-optimism in relation to the possibility of a continental unity as a feasible alternative to the African malaise.

The construction of a Pan-African identity through the development of a shared goal and the common social and historical experiences of struggling to lift up Africa from its untenable status as a marginal, oppressed and largely written off continent, is a timely undertaking. While state actors have made many Pan-African declarations, actual movement towards Pan-Africanism seemed to be inversely proportional to the number of declarations by African leaders in their annual ritual meetings at the behest of the Organisation of African Unity, now re-baptised African Union (AU). Unity is not an act. It is a process, which comes through a sustained fostering of communication, conversation, deliberation, dialogue, coordination, cooperation and solidarity. For Africans, unity could only be based on a shared African identity, consciousness and interest irrespective of colour, creed, racial origin, nationality, region and so on. On the basis of the evolution of a shared conception of an African identity and interest, Pan-African movements, which can sustain and deepen a Pan-African project, need to be encouraged from every part of the continent.

Rescuing the Pan-African Idea from the Clashes between Afro-Optimism and Afro-Pessimism

A change will be possible when the feeling of defeat is defeated (Loppes 1995: 37). Afro-pessimists stress the enormity of the problems that divide Africa rather than those things that unite it, and start with a presumption of self-defeat, allowing the African crises to prey on their judgement and limit their imagination. After de-colonisation this Afro-pessimist temper oppressed the African imagination. Afro-optimists on the other hand seem to say that despite the many differences, Africans have enough in common to unite them. The optimists can be said to have at least defeated the feeling of being defeated by, seeing the possibility of renewal, despite the prevailing despair in large swathes of the African continent. Except for a brief period immediately after de-colonisation, the African continent has suffered as much from material crises as from pessimistic projections on the capacities and possibilities of Africans to shape their own future.

Many of the current heads of states are readily willing to espouse rhetoric on the need for African solidarity while being totally unwilling to invest practically to bring that unity about. They also fail to act in a manner that will foster that unity and solidarity. Their hypocritical stance is as much a problem to African unity as the forces whose interest appears to lie in the oppressive continuation of African fracturing and fragmentation. Stressing differences as unbridgeable, exaggerating problems and lacking in imagination and intellectual stamina, many African leaders are satisfied as long as they have a political real estate with a few million people to rule over.

Some commentators have dreamt up essentialist discourses for the failure of African solidarity and lack of organisational spirit and confidence. They often reduce the problem of the African crises to the essentialism of what they call African character and culture. But such reductions cannot answer why Africa's growth rate was higher in the

41

1960s than those of the present day newly industrialising countries (Barratt-Brown 1995: 47). Africa's crises have intellectual, political and economic reasons much of which has been a relic from the incomplete decolonisation of the continent. That this is the case can be attested from the unchanging vertical links between African states and former colonial powers arresting the development of any horizontal link between each other. About 85 per cent of Africa's total exports are marketed in the industrialised countries of the North compared to 75 per cent of Latin America and 68 per cent for South and East Asia (http://www.hartford-hwp.com/archives/30/033.html 1998: 13). Only a very small fraction of officially recorded exports, between 3 and 6 per cent, go to other African countries (ibid.). Even intra community trade in the economic region of West African States (ECOWAS) was a mere 4.9 per cent in 1988 (ibid.). When one reads such figures one is justified to doubt all the declarations, cooperation schemes and conversations to forge continental unity. Some 40 years after decolonisation, the pattern of vertical linkage and virtual absence of horizontal inter-African linkages is an indictment.

Paradoxically, it is precisely to decolonise economically and culturally that a unified strategy was thought to be a viable alternative in the 1960s by such leading theorists of Pan-Africanism as K. F. Nkrumah. Africa must unite or perish was Nkrumah's famous exhortations. He wrote: "Just as our strength lies in a unified policy and action for progress and development, so the strength of the imperialists lies in our disunity. We in Africa can only meet them effectively by presenting a unified front and a continental purpose." (K. Nkrumah 1963: xvi) He added: "Our freedom stands open to danger just as long as the independent states of Africa remain apart." (K. Nkrumah, 1963: xvii) These words were spoken in the 1960s at a time when the possibility of rejecting the casual tearing of the continent at the 1885 Berlin Conference (otherwise known as the European Scramble for Africa) was open, when something like 32 of the current states were gaining their flag independence. That historical moment offered opportunities, which are no longer available.

Nkrumah captured with extraordinary foresight the importance of the opportunity presented by political decolonisation: "Here is a challenge which destiny has thrown out to the leaders of Africa. It is for us to grasp what is a golden opportunity to prove that the genius of the African people can surmount the separatist tendencies in sovereign nationhood by coming together speedily, for the sake of Africa's greater glory and infinite well-being, into a Union of African States." (ibid:22-222). He kept insisting that Africans must make "superfluous and obsolete" the "territorial boundaries which are the relics of colonialism," because the "forces that unite (Africans) are greater than the difficulties that divide us at present" (ibid: 221). The price for speaking so well for Africa was to be paid by his own overthrow.[1] The pursuit of Pan-African goals in the face of opposition from powerful forces was fraught with difficulties. If Nkrumah exhibited some tendencies for personality cult and restrictions in civil liberties, it has to be seen in the context of his overall project. He wished to crystallise a Pan-African power during the cold war when the US rulers could not tolerate anyone who was not following their policy against the USSR. The tension of the time took its toll. The contradictions involved in leading a historic Pan-African movement while being saddled with the task of managing an economy and state of Ghana were crippling. The Government of Ghana was under constant sabotage by external powers who understood Nkrumah's project better than his African colleagues. That contradiction exposed Nkrumah to fatal vulnerabilities. When all is said and done his record on the whole was clean in the sense of not doing what most African leaders came to see as their right - stashing national wealth in private banks for their own use. That was not Nkrumah's vice. His lack of personal corruption largely vindicates his record despite criticisms of his handling of Ghana's domestic difficulties, which were more a result of external pressure than any weaknesses and mistakes on the part of Ghana's policy makers.

Whilst Nkrumah's record in handling Ghana's economic and political affairs may be contested and subject to debate, his Pan-African commitment was remarkably consistent and speaks to the generations past, present and future with an incisive and piercing clarity. Nkrumah saw clearly the historical importance of rejecting Africa's humiliation through the promotion of African unity. He saw the redeeming value of resistance, defiance and courage in an African burst into world history. He kept driving home with proselytising zeal that he was willing to sacrifice Ghana's sovereignty for the larger good of Africa's rebirth. The more he wrote, spoke and organised, the more he exposed himself to the forces that harboured ill-intentions and ill-thought on Africa. They won, he lost. Not long before he died, Nyerere recognised the errors of those who saw lurking behind Nkrumah's push for African union a simple ambition for personal aggrandisement. Nigeria and some of the states grouped around a meeting they held in Monrovia opposed Nkrumah's project to turn Africa's moment of political decolonisation into a real festival for the complete rejection of the divisive consequences of the European 1885 Berlin Treaty. As if letting slip such a "golden opportunity or moment" to reject emphatically the casual tearing up of the continent was not bad enough, the post-colonial elite seems content to make do with the apparatus of colonial oppression that enriches it while the vast majority of the people in Africa remain poor. According to the World Bank, the population in sub-Saharan Africa (SSA) living below $1.00 a day (PPP[2] 1985 prices) was 179.6 million (1987), 201.2 million (1990), 218.6 million (1993) (World Bank 1996). In per cent population terms, this was 38.5 per cent (1987), 39.3 (1990) and 39.1 (1993) (ibid.).

The alternative for African unity is the attempt to entrench within arbitrary borders non-viable states retaining much of the colonial baggage, albeit in an attenuated form. Africa turned into the hands of a transnational elite allied to a local elite. They created a political economy for mutual survival, with scant regard, if at all, to the vast majority of the population, which remain largely excluded from well-being development. If there is any failure of purpose, vision, imagination and actual progress, it is the failure of those who inherited the post-colonial mantle and not the failure of Africa.

Presently, what Nkrumah spoke of some four decades ago is beginning to resonate with increased vigour. The long experience of South Africa's ANC in political struggle produced some leaders of exceptionally high moral stature unequalled in the world. Mandela has become a world hero and his successor, Thabo Mbeki, has quickly put a wider African signature to their victory. Optimism for Africa's future seemed to have come with the birth of the new South Africa.

The African Renaissance from South Africa: Can It Revive African Unity?

The most significant positive development for Africa after the end of the cold war is the emergence of South Africa from its apartheid era exclusion and isolation. South Africa accounts for 44 per cent of the total GDP of all Sub-Saharan African countries, and 52 per cent of its industrial output" (Castells 1999: 122). In 1993 real GDP per capita in

SSA excluding South Africa was US$1,288 billion, while South Africa's GDP alone was $3,127 billion (ibid.). Its GDP is thus roughly three times that of the entire SSA combined.

South Africa needs the rest of Africa to avoid being pushed aside from the harsh competition in the new global economy. The South African connection will also help to insulate the weaker African economies by providing an alternative to the global economy. The relationship between South Africa and the rest of Africa can be mutually beneficial if both sides develop a Pan-African outlook, perspective and shared goals and interests. The problem is thus twofold. First, South Africa has to evolve a Pan-African perspective from the debris of its apartheid past involving all sections of its communities. Second, the rest of Africa cherishes the opportunity provided by South Africa to enter the world economy on terms, for a change, not dictated against Africa's best interests.

Thus, if South Africa evolves a clear Africa role, opportunities exist to add new energy and vitality to conversations regarding the revival and renewal of African unity. Something like a second edition of Pan African ideals, potentialities and projections under the changed circumstances of the time can be fostered. This will open up opportunities for South Africa and its leaders to utilise their hard-earned reputation to repair Africa's fractured identity, unity, future and destiny. Indeed, it would be a shame if this reputation is squandered unwisely and the effort of adding South Africa's influence, wealth and power to Africa is not aligned or coupled with fostering unity, cooperation, coordination and solidarity amongst the peoples, states, societies, communities and individuals of Africa. To their credit, South Africa's new leaders have lost no time in seizing the historical moment of the country's emergence from the apartheid era exclusion to talk up Africa's opportunities such as through the coining of the optimistic phrase, "African Renaissance." How far this contribution becomes a reality or dissipates into thin air like the earlier and equally attractive phrase of "the African wind of change" of the 1960s remains to be seen. At least, the rhetoric of renaissance by Mbeki has revealed a broad intention and willingness to create public awareness in South Africa to shoulder a wider African role.

Whether others in Africa will welcome this South African desire to play a leadership role is still early to say. Other African countries should try to see the positive value of a substantial commitment from

South Africa to serve the cause of Africa. It is when South Africa retreats from an African role by being seduced or allured to other trappings that criticism would be justified. At the moment Mbeki's idea of an "African Renaissance" should be promoted. If he pursues this idea with the seriousness and certainty of Nkrumah, there will be no doubt that those who do not wish Africa to rise would also target him as they did Nkrumah. If however the talk of an African Renaissance is simply a rhetorical flourish without any conviction, those who find Africa's unified potential a problem can live with him.

Africans can either fear, or see it as a bonus to have South Africa's power on the side of Africa's future. It is difficult to trust that some African heads of states who are jealous of their positions will allow South Africa to play the full role it should play in the continent. If feared, there will be a conspiracy to frustrate South Africa from playing a positive role. If accepted, opportunities to build Africa's future in new and imaginative ways will be broadly opened up. Which choice will be made remains an open question. If the forces of foresight and vision win, South Africa has the potential to recoup Africa's lost opportunities. If the forces of surrender and enclave-state egoism and mentality win, we are back to the drawing board. One hopes imagination and moral purpose will win over cynicism and selfishness.

Nigeria: No longer the giant without an African purpose?

Another significant development is the emergence of Nigeria as a budding democracy. The slow and ponderous move of Nigeria, an African giant, from military rule to democracy, at least electorally, is a plus not just for that country but also more widely for Africa. The emergence of Nigeria as a democratic power is no light matter with respect to reckoning possibilities in building Africa's future. Its emergence must be seen against the background of Africa, which has been largely written off by the media and other Afro-pessimistic commentators as a place where "practically nothing works". The late but seemingly certain emergence of Nigeria as a young democracy has given stimulus to the optimistic scenario of building Africa's future. Nigeria has not exploited its potential power, wealth and influence in building itself and the continent. If the current direction brings out the full potential of Nigeria, in terms of its role in Africa, this can only be a positive reinforcement of the hopeful signals coming from South Africa.

There are good reasons to believe that the current leadership is different from the old venal military sort in Nigeria. Obasanjo also lost no time in declaring a wider African role by his "New Dawn for Africa" speech. We can safely agree that there is a sort of democratic turn in Nigeria though it is also recognised that it is still early days in that experimentation.

And From Libya Comes A Clear Message: The Sahara Does Not Divide But Can Unite Africa

The recent addition of Muammar al-Gaddaffi to the Pan-African voice is another milestone to reverse the voices of disunity, fragmentation and African enfeeblement. The Libyan leader called an extraordinary session of the Organisation of African Unity to bring back on the agenda something like Kwame Nkrumah's 1963 Pan-Africanist vision of a "united, proud, strong, and commanding" Africa. Forty-three African states attended the summit in Sirte, Libya from September 8-9, 1999. Libya's initiative has been hailed for having rekindled the energies for a Pan-African alternative to the continent's current fragmentation. In a speech justifying why a special summit of the OAU was required, Gaddaffi made some important conceptual clarification regarding the relationship of Arab and African identity. He said: "We do not deny that racially or historically we are Arabs. But politically and geographically we are Africans for thousands of years until the last migration 944 years ago - the migration of Bani Hilal and Bani Salim. We are Africans. We are Africans since our forefathers emigrated over land (Bir...Bir) that is why they were called Berbers." (PAM News March 1999: 9)

He added emphatically that the "Libyan people as from today should know that they are an African people. You are in Africa. You are Africans. Anyone who is on African soil and does not accept his African nature should leave Africa. Anyone who does not like the black colour of the African should ask himself what his white colour has achieved for him. The colour - whatever you call it, and which is found in North Africa, from Egypt through to Mauritania. If the peoples who exist from Egypt to Mauritania do not wish to belong to Africa and the nationality of Africa and integrate into Africa and share her destiny they should leave. Africa is for Africans" (ibid). Following from the reappraisal that Libyans and generally Arabs within the African continent are Africans, Gaddaffi recommended that, "all borders should be erased to the nationals of Africa from Pretoria to Tripoli... in order to "unite one thousand tribes... into the United States of Africa" (ibid).

If, as Libya, all the other Northern African countries share an African identity along with, or combining with their Arab identity, it will make the effort to re-frame Pan-Africanism much easier. It is not clear whether Libya's leader's conversion to Pan-Africanism is as a result of his loss of complete hope in Arab nationalism or a genuine commitment to add Arabs as part and parcel of Africa's destiny. Regardless of the reasons that prompted this commentary from Gaddaffi, it contributes to a new dialogue between Arab Africa and the rest of Africa. And that dialogue should help to put firmly behind us the nasty roles Arab traders played in the slave trade, and look forward to a new partnership and new relationship as equal and different people.

Some New Sceptical Voices Have Lent Their Support

Though sceptical himself, Museveni has lent his voice to Pan-African ideals. He has spoken of a Bantuphone Africa to break up Francophone, Anglophone and Lusophone Africa. Though not sold to the idea of continental unity, his public pronouncements suggest a Pan-African orientation. In addition, in Uganda, there is a Global Pan African Movement with Yoweri Museveni as the patron.

OAU at Abuja in 1991 Declared Pan-African Measures

In 1963 Nkrumah saw with extraordinary foresight what the Europeans were unable to imagine, even for themselves. They were then tinkering with a union of coal and steel in the Treaty of Rome, trying to harmonise custom and tariff regulations. Nkrumah called for a united Africa, which the idea of the European Union seemed to have borrowed from without any acknowledgement. In his report on a "Continental Government for Africa," Nkrumah stated three objectives: a) a common market of a united Africa; a common currency, a monetary zone and a central bank of issue, b) a unified security with a combined military and defence strategy with an overall land, sea and air defence command for

Africa, and c) "If we in Africa set up a unified economic planning organisation and a unified military and defence strategy, it will be necessary for us to adopt a unified foreign policy and diplomacy to give political direction to our joint efforts for the protection and economic development of our continent" (ibid.: 219-220). Nkrumah fully appreciated the value of making Africa take her rightful place in world affairs: "The unity of Africa and the strength it would gather from continental integration of its economic and industrial development, supported by a united policy of non-alignment, could have a most powerful effect on World Peace" (Nkrumah 1963: 222).

After a quarter of century of Nkrumah's admonition, the Treaty at Abuja, Nigeria (3.6.91) was signed at the 27th Summit of the OAU establishing the African Economic Community (AEC). The Treaty contains 106 articles, and provides a time table for implementing "...the phased removal of barriers to intra-African trade, the strengthening of the existing regional economic groupings, and other steps towards African economic cooperation," and the formation of an "Africa-wide monetary union and economic community by the year 2025" (OAU 1991). The Abuja Treaty setting up the African Economic Community did not state any protocol of implementation but curiously Article 4 states six stages of implementation, which together will take a period of 34 years.

None of the leaders who signed the treaty at Abuja should be there in the year 2025 if both democracy and the biological clock were to have the final word on the matter. The Abuja declaration picks up Nkrumah's ideals very late. Perhaps it is better late than never. The question is whether those who signed it have a fraction of Nkrumah's political will, imagination, intellectual courage, foresight, commitment and discernment. Or is this a belated imitation of the Pan-European incremental project and approach of economic community building? The time frame for each segment appears precise but curiously there is no protocol of implementation, neither are the relevant bodies of implementation specified. Given the speed at which the world is moving, setting out a generation to form an economic community seems far too long, especially given the exigencies of the crises threatening to overwhelm the continent. Having said this, the fact that African leaders found it necessary to resuscitate Nkrumah's vision of a united Africa is in itself remarkable. If a movement from civil society complements this state level desire for closer integration, the momentum to abbreviate the plan of a generation to set an economic community probably will be accelerated.[3]

While there are enough indicators of a positive trend towards Pan-Africanism, the old problems, which frustrated the efforts in the 1960s are still around, posing formidable barriers to the realisation of a Pan-African ideal. Externally the major powers may not find the emergence of a strong and united Africa an attractive proposition. The best to expect from the external world is some hypocritical understanding. Internally the major difficulty is the seemingly unending economic, political, security and cultural crises in Africa.

Perhaps the most enduring difficulty is a lack of shared African national identity. This is an important issue. Africa must evolve a value, a vision and mission to articulate common approaches and responses in dealing with the external environment. This can happen if Africans share a Pan-African outlook, work to create the African renaissance and build the idea and reality of the African nation. If a unit or people is more pro-Arab than African, more pro-French than African, more pro-British than African, then the unity amongst the others will not be real. It can only be cosmetic. For the unity to be real, they all must be first Africans or subscribe to an African nation. That self-conception must come to give stability and reduce the falsity of any African unity project. Otherwise with a first serious problem, different groups and states will take positions that will harm Africa.

Some Formidable Barriers against a Pan-African Ideal

While the desire for Pan-African integration has been always strong, the actual moves to forge unity have been undermined by the continued and protracted security, economic and political crises afflicting every region of the continent. A theory of Pan-African unity must reckon with the formidable barriers, which can potentially disrupt any best-laid plan. History cannot be made as Africans choose. They have to contend with the existing security, political and economic circumstances which are largely a consequence of external and internal clashes of interest. There is no economic, political, social and cultural level-playing field to erect a Pan-African edifice, which will endure.

Unity, coordination and cooperation among states can be facilitated if the economic and political situation is broadly similar in the countries concerned. If the economic and political circumstances are so uneven and divergent, this makes it harder to design social arrangements, which will be seen as fair, just, ethical and equitable. If all states share the norms and standards of a democratic social arrangement, the barriers to fostering integration will be easier compared to a situation where there are authoritarian dictators, monarchists, military regimes and other species of government. It is therefore important to review the existing political, economic and security circumstances in Africa before suggesting a theory of Pan-African integration for the continent.

Another obstacle is one related to the quality of leadership in Africa. Knowledge and those who have it appear largely shunned. Those who come to power often tend to abhor knowledge and knowledge producers – even when they are appointed as state functionaries. The leaderships stand condemned in depriving society the benefits of a knowledge-guided development.

Politically there is the question of the shallowness of democratic roots even in those countries that have "successfully" conducted multi-party elections. Change of power from one set of elite to another almost invariably involves violence except in a few states. And that is a formidable barrier to sustainable institutional arrangements for Pan-African integration. Fragile democracy is not the best space to fashion an enduring Pan-African architecture.

Pan-Africanism should take on board these negative constraints and barriers into account. At least, they cannot be ignored. In addition, the African military has not fully retreated. While it may be forced to validate its intervention with a democratic facade, it has not exhausted its ambition for political power. This is partly reinforced by the continuing economic and political crises, which encourage the military to spoil for political office.

There are also some formidable economic barriers relating to historical peculiarities of Africa's insertion in the world economy and current export-orientated policies imposed by the external donor agencies. To start with, colonialism in Africa did not do a Hong Kong or Taiwan for Africa. It left in nearly every African country weak industrial structures and low level of industrial diversity and depth. Sub-Saharan Africa's share of global GDP to global population has, for instance, continued to decline. World imports, terms of trade and relative position of shares in trade, investment, production and consumption showed similar decline.

African agricultural and food production have declined. Population is growing at a higher rate than agricultural production. Some 76 per cent of the export earnings of SSA come from agriculture. The social consequence of this lack of industrialisation, agricultural decline and weak linkage with world economic trends is dereliction of a majority of African humanity. Standards of living are said to have fallen by nearly 25 per cent since 1960. Unemployment is rising. In 1985, at the height of the crises some 47 per cent of the population lived below the poverty level. The International Labour Organisation (ILO) estimated that real wages have declined between 50 per cent and 60 per cent since the early 1980s in most countries.

More worrying is the failure by most African states to deliver services, support industrial and agricultural production, and improve the well-being and livelihood of their citizens. The failure of most African states to engage in any meaningful radical social project for the benefit of the least advantaged is truly depressing. The state here therefore seems more of a burden than a support to the population.

Another barrier is the endemic conflict and violence, which has turned the continent into a security no-go area. Much of the security hazard is related to the prevailing economic ruin and poverty afflicting large sections of the population of Africa. As stated earlier, many of the countries in the continent suffer the open sore of conflict. The continent is thus sizzling in an active state conflict from civil war to interstate war. The most outrageous aspect to the conflict is that children as young as seven years of age have been armed as child soldiers (UNICEF 1999). UNICEF claims that of the 300,000 child soldiers, 120,000 are from Africa (ibid.). Mass recruitment of child soldiers has taken place in Angola, Burundi, the two Congos, Liberia, Rwanda, Sierra Leone, Sudan and Uganda (ibid.). Tens of thousands are reported to have been forcibly recruited. The worst offender is Sierra Leone where child soldiers of less than nine years old took part in a two-week reign of terror by the Revolutionary United Front (RUF) rebels in January, 1999, in which thousands of civilians were killed, maimed or raped. In Uganda children, including girls, have been abducted by the rebel Lord's Resistance Army (ibid.). Rehabilitation and reintegration of demobilised children is difficult. Perhaps there is nothing more repugnant and morally offensive than using children who should be in school to be soldiers.

While some non-mineral wealthy countries are in a conflict, some key mineral wealthy countries seem to attract conflict. For example, in Angola and also in Sierra Leone, it has been reported that companies helped to fuel the conflict because the prevailing instability is lucrative to them. For example, UNITA in Angola under Savimbi controlled the diamond rich part of Angola. Angola has some of the best diamond fields in the world - "80 per cent are of the highest gem quality." (TWR No.103: 37) From 1992-1997 UNITA is said to have run the biggest diamond-smuggling operation using the proceeds to buy arms. Despite the UN sanctions, many observers reported that diamond dealers continued to trade with the rebels. The Angolan Government on its part used the country's oil wealth to finance its own war effort. It appeared the end of the Cold War and its attendant superpower rivalry was replaced by corporate and conglomerate competition (for example, diamond magnets against oil magnets). The situation in the Congo, which attracted so many types of interference in the past and has continued to do so till the present, is largely due to the country's mineral wealth.

Thus, the overall picture that emerges is that military action and violence, both internal and inter-state, have been rife. The defunct Organisation of African Unity tried to mediate on most of the conflicts but its resolutions were either too ambiguous or not taken serious enough by the warring parties. The pervasive conflict conflagration seemed to support the argument of those who say that any talk of Pan-Africanism is more of a "pipe dream" than a feasible project. An OAU backed by a strong security system could have had a chance to contain most of the conflicts in the continent.

Each state is vulnerable to outside interference and does not have the security capacity to neutralise hostile activities against it. Nkrumah did recognise this fact and therefore insisted on a common defence and security arrangement as part of his drive for a continental unity. Unfortunately, when the OAU was formed African countries settled for the balkanisation of the African continent by confirming, rather than rejecting the same external design, which split one family from another. In doing so they showed a singular lack of imagination and intellectual, moral and political courage. They decided to do their own thing and set up a very weak forum and secretariat with neither a big idea nor a large budget. It is therefore no exaggeration to say that the OAU was from its inception an abortion of Pan-Africanism rather than its renewal and further development.

There is also another formidable barrier relating to the identity crisis in Africa. The continent is not only an ethnic mosaic; it has been usual to divide it in cultural terms. Those colonies constituted by France are called Francophone, those formed by Britain are called Anglophone, and those ruled by Portugal are called Lusophone while those north of the Sahara belong to the Levantine world. This continued cultural division makes it harder to develop a dynamic integrated African culture centred on the concept of an "Afro-philia". The latter simply means the rejection of Afrophobia and the emergence of an African-anchored cultural identity.

Classification and Hypotheses

- Those people of African origin scattered mainly in Europe, the Americas and the Caribbean may be said to constitute "Cultural Africa".
- Those who have settled in Africa from various parts of the world and made permanent homes there belong to "Continental Africa", irrespective of the origin of their initial migration to Africa.
- Africans need to integrate into the rest of the world as an emancipated people and not as oppressed people.
- One of the major challenges facing Cultural Africa is racism while Continental Africa suffers from domination, exploitation, violence, conflict, poverty and marginalisation.
- Building up Continental Africa will help to reduce the discriminatory threshold in Cultural Africa.
- Assistance by Cultural Africa to Continental Africa partly serves its own emancipation.
- In principle, other races can become part of Africa. The only condition is that they develop an African attitude. They must accept, endorse and promote the emancipation of Africa.
- There is a need to build a new African identity using both the positive experiences of Africa's ancient history of relative success, and the negative history of oppression since 1500.

- There is a need to develop a common industrial and communication programme for the continent on the basis of a shared African attitude and identity.

Re-framing Pan-Africanism along the above lines of thought should be a worthy engagement for scholars, politicians and academics and all those who are taking Pan-African orientated initiatives from within and outside the continent.

Africans are confidant and comfortable being Africans without disparaging others and their cultures. Political decolonisation, as discussed earlier, did not include the decolonisation of cultural domination. In fact, the suggestion by Nkrumah to replace colonial languages by at least the selection of one language from each region of the continent did not seem to have got a hearing. The official languages of the defunct OAU were English, French and Arabic. The choice of one of the local languages, for example, Zulu in the South, Ki-Swahili in the East, Arabic in the North and Hausa or one of the West African languages for the OAU was rejected.

Culture and identity formations in Africa should be part of the self-liberation of the African. Some Africans may harbour inner self-hate and phobia, making it easier for them to submit to forces that dominate them rather than working with other Africans as their equals. The idea of killing Afrophobia and creating an enduring Africa-philia should be central to any Pan-African project.

Some African states are now suffering from the unattractive hazard of ethnic involution and dispersion. After nearly forty years of "nation-building" the post-colonial state has not managed to forge a single nation called Somalia, Liberia, Sierra Leone, Rwanda, Kenya, Nigeria, Tanzania, and so forth, by a dissolution of the mosaic of criss-crossing ethnic loyalties. Pan-Africanism therefore appears to be a credible alternative to a failed nation-building project and ethnic corporatism.

The negative pictures painted above as "formidable barriers" would seem to argue against African unity. In reality they do not – on the contrary. They are more like signs and calls urging those who wish Africa well to hurry and unite the continent. Problems have compounded and multiplied precisely because of the failure to build solidarity amongst Africans. Pan-Africanism may therefore be the most potent weapon for dismantling the barriers to unity discussed above.

Towards a Theory for Re-framing Pan-African Integration

The ideas expressed by the early Pan-African thinkers have failed to become the road taken at present. In a sense the prevailing state of conflict in the continent is a mirror showing the cost of not taking an imaginative leap in the first place at the time of political decolonisation. As noted earlier, Nkrumah had argued for a continental integration at the time of the historical transition to political independence. Any honest theorisation of Pan-African integration must therefore revisit the thinking of its most courageous and intellectually far-sighted proponent – Kwame Nkrumah. Indeed, Nkrumah was a rare leader in Africa. He had written more books than he had time to govern Ghana. It is rare that leaders write with such foresight and creativity while they captain the ship of state. He is unique in having produced enormously original ideas such as the idea of a monetary union with one African currency of issue - a novel idea in the early 1960s.

A theory of Pan-Africanism should therefore begin by confirming the essential validity of much of the insight from the progressive leaders of the 1960s. The maximalist unitarian ideas so consistently espoused by Nkrumah and others have not been tried. Had these ideas been tried, Africa would still have experienced problems, but these would have been problems related to making the unity function and strengthen. The alternative trajectories based on the inherited 1885 Berlin Conference's colonial map of Africa - and some tentative moves towards regional integration have not worked. A theory of Pan-Africanism should also attempt to enrich the new optimism coming from South Africa, Libya and Nigeria for a grander vision to lift the continent from its present predicament.

A theory of Pan-Africanism should also identify how equality could be established in the context of recognition of differences, and how liberty can be forged amid differences in culture, religion and resource and ecological endowments. Such a theory should also forge a shared value and vision worthy enough to shape, mediate and put in place effective mechanisms for resolving intractable conflicts.

The African identity should provide the shared basis or focal imagination for building the African citizenship of all those living, working and constructing a future in Africa. A comprehensive civic education to foster the African identity of Africans across the continent should be part of the strategies for realising a Pan-African imagination.

African identity should not be defined or fixed biologically. It should be defined as a process of social construction and historical experience. If we bring genetics, race and biology into it, it will be difficult to compose unity. Social experience is much more dynamic and fluid while biological determinism is static. Social experience can accommodate a range of group types from any race - Arab, Jew, Gentile, Black, Caucasian, Brown or Yellow. There must be a home for each of these types in Africa as there is a place for any type of person in the USA, Israel and some of the multicultural European societies. If people make a home in Africa, bear children, work and contribute honestly to Africa's wealth and power, they should not be excluded because of their biological identity or because of the wrongs their ancestors inflicted on the majority of the African population.

Africaphone or Africa-philia is the same thing as having an African consciousness and it is the moral, political, intellectual and cultural minimum required to forge a Pan-African perspective. While the Pan-African movement should be a broad church reflecting spatial, regional, cultural, racial, linguistic and ethnic variations, diversities, varieties and creativities, its core must be built from the oppressed African majority. This will help to provide stability to the movement despite the problems relating to the time needed to shed completely Afrophobia notions inherited from an oppressive history.

A key issue for theorising about Pan-Africanism is to identify a founding principle that will give shape and substance to Africa's hopes and aspirations by rejecting the oppressive past. Such a theory must establish some principles for evolving a shared goal to pursue an African solidarity and union.

Africa's common challenge is its unmitigated oppression. This should be a crucial resource for evolving a shared sense of identity. From the reservoir and flow of Africa's liberation, the continent attains a moral stature of world significance.

Concluding Remarks

The current revival of Pan-Africanism presents an opportunity to re-frame it. Despite inevitable obstacles, Pan-Africanism seems to be the antidote to many of the problems currently confronting Africa. But it has to be re-thought not in terms of a union of Governments, but more as a shared goal and a vehicle for generating the political, social, economic and cultural resources that will bring peoples, economies, cultures and communities together. Instead of looking to the existing states to unite, it is helpful to think of how the unity of the peoples, regions, economies, learning systems and communities can be forged. States must be asked to facilitate this unity process and not become themselves barriers. Beyond this objective, it may not be wise or feasible to coerce states to unite when they are so diverse.

A continental approach to Africa's problems should be able to lay the foundation of a self-reliant and selective external intervention approach. This will impel Africans to put on the agenda their own issues and not the issues, which come with gifts, from the donors. The African Union should write an African Constitution embodying the principles of Africa's identity and aspirations. For this to happen, however, requires a re-thinking of the Africa Union.

References

Barratt-Brown, M. (1995) *Africa's Choices*, (London: Penguin Books).
Castells, M. (1999) *The End of the Millennium*, (Oxford: Blackwell).
ECA (1991) *African Alternative Framework to Structural Adjustment Programmes for Socio-Economic Recovery and Transformation*, Addis Ababa.
Loppes, L. (1995) "Enough is Enough: for an Alternative Diagnosis of the African Crises," *Discussion Paper 5*,)Scandinavian Institute of African Studies, Uppsala).
Muchie, M. (1999) "Problems of Sub-Saharan Development in the Era of Globalisation," *Working Paper no.70*, (DIR, Aalborg University).
Muchie, M. (2000) "Searching for Opportunities for Sub-Saharan Africa's Renewal," in *Futures*, Vol.32, no.2.
Mumford, L. (1944) *The Conditions of Man*, (New York: Harcourt, Brace and Company).
Nkrumah, N. (1963): *Africa Must Unite*, (London: Panaf).
OAU (1991) *The Abuja Treaty*, Addis Ababa.
Pan African News (1999) March, Kampala.
Third World Resurgence (1997) no. 103, Kuala Lumpur.
Washington Post and *New York Times* (1999)
Africa Research Bulletin
World Bank (1991): *Africa Recovery*, (September, Washington DC).
World Bank (1996): *World Development Report*, (Washington DC).

World Bank (1997) *World Poverty Indicators*, Washington DC.
http://www.hartford-hwp.com/archives/30/033.html (1998)

Endnotes

1.The CIA operative involved in planning and executing the coup in 1966 has now publicly admitted that they were involved actively to get rid of him; see John Stockwell (a former CIA officer), *In Search of Enemies*, published in 1978 which exposed CIA involvement in the overthrow of Nkrumah in Ghana and in the murdering Lumumba in the Congo. Also see the film, *Black Power*, shown by BBC2 during the Winter of 1992 where those involved admitted active US intervention to bring the downfall of Nkrumah. That this CIA operative, the US intelligence community and their Ghanaian associates can freely admit this and still move about freely shows how much they feel they can ignore Africans.

[2] Purchasing power parity index.

[3] Pan-Africanism evolved as an elite movement. The first four Pan-African conferences were organised by Du Bois from the Diaspora. It was at the 5th Pan-African Conference in 1945 in Manchester that some of the postcolonial leaders such as Kenyatta and Nkrumah were included. The first Pan African conference was held in 1919 organised by the American scholar Du Bois, who died at the age of 95 as a Ghanaian citizen.

4

The New Humanist Perspective on Pan-Africanism

Silvia Bercu

Africa finds itself today in a conundrum. On the one hand, it is trying to move away from the oppression of its recent colonial past, mainly under the European colonial powers. On the other hand, it sees its old masters as the model to follow in economic terms, in cultural terms and in existential terms. This antinomy of oppressor/model image of those who have left but still exert a tremendous power over the lives of ordinary people drives the search for identity and a new conundrum: should Africa remain divided and trading through the established lines of the old imperial routes? Or should it abandon altogether those remnants of its disempowerment and form a Regional Bloc both for trade and defence in order to relate to the rest of the world on equal terms?

This ambivalence towards Europe has opened the door to a new situation in which a type of neo-colonialism and neo-slavery is being practiced by a new World Empire, which has its epicentre in the political, military, financial and cultural institutions of the United States of America.

But who is this World Empire? What we call the World Empire, in spite of its apparent geographical concentration in the USA, is in fact a structure that stretches throughout the planet. It is interlinked with speculative financial institutions, arms dealers, secret services unanswerable to any elected body or government officials, most of whom do not represent the people but rather the interests of the big corporations that pay for their campaign, and sections of the media that masquerade as the voice of the people whilst in reality vying to dominate the subjective life of the population, for the sake of profit. This is the skeleton of the World Empire. The people who live in the area where the neo-Empire has accumulated most of its wealth are given, through nationalistic rhetoric, the illusion that they are also part of the power structure.

A very important tool used in the expansion of this World Empire has been the so-called "free" market. This is a form of fundamentalist capitalism, which allows unlimited movement of capital (be it for investment or for speculation) and goods (but not people) throughout the world. Under this, investment for rapid profit could be carried out without any commitment to production or to the people in the countries where speculation is taking place. It could be argued that the abolition of trade barriers and restrictions to investment could be a good idea if all the actors started from the same mark, that is, from a position of equality. However since the system favours the multinational corporations and the banking system already in place, free trade can only lead to increasing concentration towards the rich countries to the detriment of the worse off. Today the policies imposed by the World Trade Organisation supported by the World Bank and the International Monetary Fund in the name of "free" trade are draining poor countries in favour of richer ones, and producing massive unemployment in "emergent economies" already burdened by artificially inflated foreign debts contracted as a "favour" from the financial institutions of the Empire. This is the root of modern day neo-colonialism and the most important mechanism in the concentration of wealth and resources into increasingly fewer hands.

Wars fuelled by the arms trade and the disastrous consequences of imposed economic systems have produced huge movements of people. These uprooted peoples are sometimes called refugees when they are needed as shields to criticise the situation of their countries of origin. They are at other times called economic migrants to invalidate the justification of their immigration, or "bogus asylum seekers" to excite the hatred of the local population and scapegoat them for domestic problems such as unemployment and violence. These masses of migrant workers form a fundamental body in the economy of the "free" market philosophy. They are the neo-slaves of the neo-Empire. I shall examine briefly the way this neo-Empire has organised itself.

The West, Africa and New Humanism

- International economic policies agreed by the most powerful economies, the G8, and imposed on poor countries, give free reign to multinational corporations that move their production to where they can pay the least to the workforce. In this way they exploit the population of countries with high unemployment and low income. Then they sell the cheaply produced goods in the rich countries at prices that cannot be matched by production carried out utilising workers who receive reasonable salaries. More firms take their manufacturing base away to the third world, reinforcing in the process unemployment and negative attitudes of the workforce in the richer countries. As multinationals withdraw their profits from the poor countries and maximise their earnings with total disregard for environmental damage, they worsen the impoverishment of the countries and also accelerate migration of skilled but frustrated local workforce. Those who lose out the most in the present global capitalist economy are the countries that were also the most ravaged as colonies. Governments of ex-colonies tend to be "kleptocracies" (government by thieves), that is, those who join the political game in the hope of enriching themselves. This is, of course, not exclusive to the poor countries but the colonial structures left in place favour corruption. The system by which "loans" are agreed (for example, from the International Monetary Fund) favours the corruption of officials who are often the agents of the "lenders"- those in charge of making sure that their countries keep to the rules imposed on them, such as the shrinking of the state and privatisation, even if that leaves most of the population bereft of services, health and education.

- The "aid" from the ex-colonial powers imposes conditions that benefit mostly the lenders (mistakenly called "donors") and perpetuate the cycle of dependency and poverty. Typically an "aid" to build five schools may come with a "structural readjustment" conditionality that demands the shrinking of the public sector budget through privatisation, which will in turn lead to the closure of ten schools. Government officials in the "recipient" country will favour the loan and enforce the conditions imposed because they get financial rewards from doing so. Aid is always tied to certain conditions, for instance, to buy products from the "donor" countries.

- Developed nations make huge profits by selling weapons to the poor ones and benefit from their political instability. This is a manufacturing industry that tends to remain in the industrialised countries in order to keep the secrets regarding their production, otherwise there would be the risk of the poor countries becoming as militarily powerful as themselves. The armament industry is therefore one of the few industries that are not allowed to move abroad in search of cheap labour. It is promoted amongst the workforce as a source of jobs rather as a source of violence (even if it is obvious that keeping a healthy market for the weapons industry implies that there *must* be some wars around). Furthermore, the buying and selling of weapons features within what has been generically referred to as "issues of national security" which ensures a degree of secrecy not allowed to other areas of trade. In this way a great deal of shady money transfers can take place away from the sight of ordinary citizens in the countries involved.

- When workers in countries battered by persecution and poverty attempt to escape their plight by entering the industrialised nations they are qualified as "asylum seekers" and kept in legal limbo for long periods of time, during which they are forced to work in near-slavery conditions to survive. Much of the world economy is based on this mass of migrant workforce, which becomes also the focus of discrimination and scapegoating during political campaigning. The hatred promoted against migrants by those who fuel the belief that "they are coming to take our jobs" leads to the election of governments with a more extreme "free" market stance that tends to appeal to the silently racist sectors of the population by exciting their worst fears of foreigners. This in turn worsens the situation of the migrants, strengthening the slave-like conditions of their existence.

- Professionals in poor countries whose opportunities for employment and development are curtailed by reductions in public investment tend to migrate to the richer countries for further jobs or training. This "brain drain" reinforces the poor self-image of the most oppressed economies.

Potential benefits of globalisation

Instantaneous communication purveyed by globalisation could, if properly harnessed, promote a rich multicultural interchange among different socio-cultural groups. This will help local groups to link up to international networks capable of looking at the global picture to propose alternatives to present system challenges.

The anti-globalisation movement is completely dependent on globalisation for its very existence. Without travelling, the internet, a common language and international communications, it would not be possible to organise demonstrations that are synchronised throughout the world in order to protest against the effects of international trade regimes, and so forth.

Perhaps the most ominous quality of the new global empire is its success in conquering the minds of people far away from the centre. In previous times this would have been impossible, but Hollywood and television have done what invasions and annexations had never achieved before. Values and a lifestyle alien to communities far away from the centres of power have been the daily dose of brainwashing for billions of people living in the remotest corners of the Earth. Television has introduced the American (yes, a country appropriated the name of the whole continent!) way of life to all parts of the world. No wonder we can see people in jeans, trainers, baseball caps or people who drink Coke anywhere we go. Television has been presented many times as a vehicle for culture but as Quino, the Argentinean cartoonist, pointed out in his work *Mafalda*: "…if I were culture I would rather walk".

A particular malignant consequence of this domination of the media by the neo-Empire in Africa is an unwitting promotion of the stereotypic image of whites as being more capable or intelligent than the black population. Children in the African continent are conditioned by these images, which reinforces the beliefs left by the empire about foreign (racial) superiority. One of the most important impediments to

African development is therefore the lack of belief in the capacity of its own inhabitants.

Paying attention to the contamination and cultural destruction induced by the mass media in certain communities should not be confused with the choices that such communities make about technology and their future. It has become a feature of well meaning people in the developed world to romanticise traditional lifestyles and criticise those who bring technology to them. The important issue is one of choice. If the Masai community, for instance, decides that it is their choice to accept a lower life expectancy in order to continue traditional cultural practices that give them identity and meaning, then it is their decision. However to deny information about the advances that humanity has made such as in terms of overcoming illnesses in the name "preserving" the culture of an isolated community, is anti-progress. In other words, not offering good quality water to an isolated community that has all kinds of water-borne parasites and infections for "fear" that it will contaminate their culture is discriminatory. As the late Dr Salvatore Pulleda[1] pointed out at his conference on "Globalisation, a threat to cultural diversity?" there is a tendency to consider culture as something from the past, fixed and unselective, with particular stress on the primitive. But culture is also the future project that unites a community and the choices that that community makes of their past experiences. An example could be the Maoris in New Zealand, bringing their dances and language with them into their modern lives but leaving behind cannibalism. If there is a common African culture it does not necessarily have to be just based on tradition, but on its common future.

The art of story telling is probably as ancient as humanity itself. Stories by the campfire about the lives and accomplishments of the local heroes and role models were often seen as the best way of communicating to the new generations the values, norms and ethos of the society. Whilst animals carry only their living memory and experience, human beings, fables and folklores were also used in resolving psychological conflict through identification with different characters.

It is not always possible to be aware of the way we have been influenced by stereotypes. For example, on one occasion travelling by plane I was startled by the usual announcement, "This is the Captain speaking", delivered by a female voice. I saw then that in spite of my commitment to the liberation of my gender, I too had been successfully conditioned to see women in a stereotypical way, in this case not in the role of pilot in charge of a Jumbo Jet. Some time later, whilst reading Nelson Mandela's biography, *Long Walk to Freedom*, a passage reminded me of that experience. Young Nelson takes a plane. He's a little nervous and suddenly he realises with a startle that the pilot is *black.* And then he sees that he himself, in spite of his commitment to the struggle for the liberation of his people, has been somehow brainwashed. As he has never seen a black pilot either in real life or in films he is taken by surprise. So, we can see that unless we become aware of the insidious effects of propaganda and stereotypes, we will continue to recreate the society we are trying to change. In this way, it is healthy to realise that *we are all not just victims but also in our own little way agents* of the sick value judgements imprinted on our consciousness by the massive power of the present day campfire storytelling.

We have a choice then to continue living by the values and intentions of somebody else's dream or to start to wake up to the alternatives. This means to intentionally devise ways to change the social structures that surround us, at the same time that we change our own structures of thought and feeling. Neutralising the years of learning from the education system, hours and hours of uncritically absorbing the subtle messages in soap operas and Hollywood films, is absolutely necessary for the mental emancipation of the African.

Africa needs to wake up to its fundamental role in the world in a way that utilises its resources, natural and human, for the benefit of its own inhabitants. From the perspective of New Humanism, this should be a network of countries and peoples working for their common interests but always at the service of the human being. Money should not be worshipped. Maintaining the rich cultural diversity of the traditional African peoples while finding the common objectives and needs of the continent seems to be the only way that Africa could protect itself from the assault on its population and its resources.

Many people who despair of their conditions attempt to escape through the road of violence. Violence cannot be a tool to fight the prevailing system, not just because it is morally wrong, but also because it is the very methodology of the inhuman system in which we are submerged. To justify violence for one side is to justify it for anybody else, and so the system thrives on guerrilla movements, terrorism, popular violent uprisings and wars. With the justification of self-defence, the need to punish those responsible for atrocities or simply to "prevent" further violence leads to the inflation of military budgets and the by-passing of painfully achieved human rights legislations. True dissidents of the present brutal system do not play its violent game but make a void to its violence. To oppose the present violent system through the imitation of its methods is tantamount to maintaining it.

Many thinkers and analysts have already spoken and written volumes on the roots of the current crises in Africa. Some, like Kenneth Kaunda, are beginning to look at the humanist philosophy to inspire as a possible antidote to these crises.

One of the greatest challenges in Africa is education. Education must not be a mere access to scientific, historical or artistic data, but an integral formation that includes the consequences of international interactions. Qualitative education is also one of the best tools to reduce the crime and violence that often accompany the descent of an economy into the "Third World" bracket. One of the main problems in implementing strategies to reduce them is that there are vested interests that block the path, and we are not just talking about the arms industry but also forces that profit from the prevalence criminal violence in a particular country. Dr James Gilligan conducted a study at Massachusetts, which demonstrated that those violent offenders that completed a college degree whilst serving a sentence had a much reduced risk of re-offending than those who did not have access to such programmes. Unfortunately, the state governor considered that people would commit crimes in order to get an education and closed the programme!

Africa must not isolate itself, lest it lose its share of the intellectual and technological revolution taking place in the world today. We must not confuse the tool with the intention. Technology creates problems when it is applied with only profit in mind. Unfortunately this is the prevailing trend, but in rejecting it uncritically (as some suggest we should do), we risk losing more, and being left behind by the rest of the world.

In conclusion, from a New Humanist perspective, it is important for Africa to form a regional alliance that not only looks at its trading needs but also at its culture and technological needs. Above all, Africa needs to put its resources truly at the service of its population.

[1] Author of On *Being Human,* (New Humanism series, Latitude Press, San Diego), and professor of Chemistry and its applications to environmental protection at the University of Rome

5

Civil Society and Pan-Africanism

Mammo Muchie

If you can look into the seeds of time,
And say which grain will grow and which will not,
Speak then to me, who neither beg nor fear
Your favours nor your hate (Shakespeare, Macbeth, 1.358-61)

Introduction

Since the 1980s a global neo-liberal agenda has dominated the world's intellectual, political, moral space and vision. One of the consequences of this unalloyed and untrammelled liberal hegemony is the double and simultaneous global construction of the "failed" state and the assumption of "success" in favour of non-governmental organisations (NGOs) and the "vibrant" civil society. The state was demoted; civil society along with the market was promoted. State failure was decried while there was an unverified attribution of "some metaphysical benign goodness" to NGOs. As a consequence, many of the functions of the state were pushed into the sphere of civil society. Donor funding shifted from the state to civil society. The state was morally condemned. More of it was seen as a problem. Less of it was seen as necessary. The state was exhorted to be lean and minimal. The global discourse urged that the state reduce itself, maintain macro economic stability through balance of payment adjustment, promote the privatisation of the economy, come out of failure by learning to create state capacity through "good governance" and an enabling environment for private actors and civil society. How a failed state can do all these things is difficult to fathom.

Principally, the discourse of the "failed state" and the "successful civil society" has been globally constituted. The global constitution of "failure and success" betrays more an ideological preference than a real description of the reality on the ground. We will look at the factors considered for establishing a discourse of "failure and success" with respect to the state and civil society relationships in Africa. In addition the discourse of "failure and success" will be examined in relation to the need for establishing coherence and creative partnership between state and society in Africa.

We will try to examine the possible conflicts implicit in the global narratives of "failure and success" and the local development of civil society. Does the global influence distort the local evolution of partnership between civil society and the state? It appears that the description of the state as "failed" and by implication civil society as a potential social space for "success" by external actors introduces two problems. The first is the right of ownership to discourse formation: that is, it is related to the relative weight of internal and external contributions in framing the discourses. Is there a denial of the right to define this discourse by local actors, on the basis of their own knowledge and cultural assumptions? What is the proper domain and competence of the state and civil society spheres respectively? What is the relationship of the triad: state, civil society and the market? What is the relationship of a failed state, free market and successful NGOs? The second is the manufacturing of a new political economy through donor funding where state and civil society become engaged in tensions and conflicts rather than being able to promote partnership and social cohesion.

Donors bring in the funds and consultants to shape civil society according to their (donors) own image. Some international NGOs set up their own local offices that often threaten or undermine the local NGOs. NGO-dom in effect becomes something like a new social space for making a living. There may be thus a scramble to create NGOs for reasons of self-employment rather than promoting a social or cultural cause. Even within local NGOs, there appears to be those that are funded by western government and foundations and those that may not have this opportunity. People with the same qualifications but with different connections with Western Governments and foundations earn different salaries. This creates resentment and division among the local actors engaged in the NGO sector. A shared understanding is lost. Civil society becomes a terrain for the different articulation and validation of private interests with new enclosure and barriers for inclusion and communication amongst large swathes of civil groups occupying roughly the same social status and role. It turns into an arena of battles amongst similar groups who are divided by income and funding possibilities due to relations with foreign sources or otherwise.

The global mode of constituting civil society and state relations in terms of the frames, narratives, discourses, rhetoric and metaphors of "failure and success" needs to be questioned. Civil society itself, as constituted by the global discourse of donors, requires questioning.

An alternative development of civil society based on local definitions, knowledge and cultural assumptions ought to be explored. A strong partnership between civil society and developmental state provides a necessary framework for constructing social cohesion/coherence in Africa.

Thus, central to the argument of this paper is the need to construct a model of the African state-society dialectic and tension. The global constitution of the African state-society relation gives primacy to external actors to define and shape the connection. This may contribute to the construction of a relationship that may not sustain cooperation between state and society in relation to promoting democracy and development in Africa. A Pan-African constitution of the state and society nexus has the advantage of making Africa's interest at the centre of such a relationship. Pan-Africanism builds upon the knowledge and life worlds of Africa's pristine communities. It provides the shared anchorage of values for constructing ethically worthy and locally rooted and competent institutional arrangements that will promote the concept of free and self-reliant Africa.

Taming the Power of Discourse

Discourse has an intrinsic power to frame, set parameters, suggest agenda, help select policy options and legitimise outside intervention especially by those who are able and can manufacture, name and control the discourse. Throughout the post-war period, there have been a number of powerful discourses competing to control the normative content and related social practices regarding the way economic, social, political and economic changes can, do and should take place in Africa. These discourses were externally imposed and did not include the indigenous concepts and beliefs of Africans. They in fact tried to undermine and reject the core of native self-confidence.

In the nineteenth century colonialism brought the discourse of "civilising mission" and the "white man's burden" to shape Africa's political and economic future. In the post war period there were the discourses of "development", "the third world", and "democracy". Each, in its own way, has dominant discourse generators and discourse receivers showing clearly who has agency and who lacks it. The coloniser, the developed, the first world and the democratic have been made out to possess agency, the knowledge, the freedom and power to set the agenda and select the terms of intervention. The colonised, the underdeveloped, the non-western democratic arrangements have been defined as the objects of intervention and not the subject of history.

In the same vein, starting from the 1990s, "civil society" and "good governance" were included among the discourses to be promoted - along with globalisation, economic liberalisation and political democratisation in Africa. In the good governance discourse, civil society emerges as the key link between economic liberalisation and democratisation; it is both the locus of economic growth, vitality and the seedbed of democracy. The weakness of civil society in Africa is often blamed on the effects of the past development strategies of the post-colonial state. The centrality of the state is seen to have prevented the growth of autonomous organisations, which in turn enabled state officials in many countries to serve "their own interests without fear of being called into account" (World Bank, 1989:60). Civil society is therefore seen as a "countervailing power" to the state, a way of curbing authoritarian practices and corruption, hence the concern for strengthening or nurturing civil society" (Abraham's, 2000:52).

Civil society has become one of the most prominent global concepts that have been promoted by every spectrum of thinking and belief. It has become everything and nothing - a dusty old concept being brushed to provide legitimacy to all sorts of interest groups that are not core government and business actors. Ernest Gellner calls civil society a " dusty term, drawn from antiquated political theory, belonging to long, obscure and justly forgotten debates." Civil society is thus an old idea, which is now being repackaged as novel with a plethora of terms such as revival, renaissance and re-emergence in the last twenty years.

Its origin is traceable to Aristotle and seems to have been fully integrated in the political philosophy of Hegel (Cohen & Arato,1997:92). As a social domain, it refers to the life-world of actors that do not form the direct function/activity of the economy and the state. It also refers to the way actors understand their role in society outside the core economic (profit-making) and political (power-augmenting) spheres.

Is this old concept relevant to Africa? Will it be helpful to institutionalise democracy and development in Africa? Does the latest discourse on civil society accord agency to domestic political and social actors in Africa or do the global actors retain their monopoly of the framing of discourses on civil society and the terms of thinking and speaking about them in relation to the ambition of delivering social change in Africa? Is there a discourse continuum from colonialism to civil society in Africa or can civil society unlock local agency and free society from being constituted by the global discourse of social and political actors?

The aim is to find ways in, which civil society may encourage the voiceless to express their own voices, define their own problems and capture it as their own discourse. The advantage or disadvantage in using the language of civil society is ultimately interwoven with the project of creating free Africa. If it leads to the domination of Africa by others or continues the discourse of domination from earlier times, then civil society must be questioned. This questioning is essential. It can be a means of control or liberation and therefore matters how the concept is appropriated, by whom, and for whom.

Making sense of it all: A definition of Civil Society

Civil society is one of the most contested and controversial concepts in social theory. The diverse ways in which the exposition of the concept has evolved has not however prevented its wide diffusion throughout the world. Its spread in Africa via the agency of transnational actors makes it vulnerable to misuse, abuse and interpretation. Civil society has been taken as the sphere par excellence for habituating or embedding the ideas of development and democracy. In Africa it has been made to anchor the good governance agenda as well.

Civil Society for Free Africa

Can Africa claim the 21st century? Even the World Bank has asked this question recently in one of its reports. The millennium has given impetus to the search for meta-narratives to unlock the latent energy and inner resources of the continent to move it with the temper of the times for constructing a durable future. We are treated to a variety of upbeat metaphors such as the African Renaissance, Omega Plan, Millennium Africa Project (MAP) and the New African Initiative. Above all, the Rubicon has been crossed with the transformation of the OAU into the AU. Africa can be fully free if it is fully united. The key is to translate this idea into dynamic institutional arrangements capable of self-correction, learning, self-adjustment and self-reliant innovation.

The Concept of an African State

Historical Africa had empires and communities. *Enslaved* Africa had crumbling empires and communities mostly run by chiefs. *Colonial* Africa had been defined by the hyphenation of British, French, German, Portuguese, Belgian and Italian Africa. *Decolonised* Africa affirmed the divisions of the 1885 Berlin Treaty as the territorial basis of the independent state while rejecting the colonial rulers who casually tore up the continent.

The ensuing post-colonial state did all it could to create order and manufacture a fractional state-nation from the constituting nationalities. With time, it became more difficult to manufacture nations out of the divided African nationalities by using the mobilising ethos of the state. Governments have been largely run either as one party systems or as military and personalised dictatorships. Change of government was not orderly for the most part. It was often violent and unpredictable. Most of the states got their countries mixed up in the Cold War. The state became part of the problem unable to control the instability that was induced by superpower competition. Western powers selected loyal allies such as Mobutu by planning the murder of the duly and legally elected Pan-African national leader, Patrice Lumumba. This frightened African leaders and forced them to side with either the West or the East and, ironically not with AFRICA!

For example, those who murdered Lumumba and enthroned Mobutu were fully aware that destabilising the Congo basin is equal to administering a fatal heart attack to Africa. To paraphrase Fanon, Africa is like a revolver, and the Congo basin is the trigger. And whoever controls the trigger controls Africa. If Africa's detractors could not control the Congo for themselves, they spoil it for others, especially those they know are true Africans who stand for African interests and aspirations. That is why they stimulate through arms trade and export a situation of unending armed conflicts, thereby creating a permanent negative imposition on life, history, civil society, territory and above all, the African spirit.

African State Failure: A Self-Fulfilling Prophecy?

Most of the African states have joined the roll call of the hundreds of "failed states" that the CIA identified in 1994 by establishing the "State Failure Task Force". The latter had the mandate to carry out the "most comprehensive study of state failure". The Task Force identified 113 cases of state failure during 1957-1994. Most of these are from Africa. The factors supposed to trigger state failure, according to the task force, include inter-ethnic wars, genocide, and adverse or disruptive regime changes. If a state is integrated into the open world economy, if it is democratic and has lower mortality rates, it is assumed to contain possibilities to stem the tide of failure.

The US, the International Financial Institutions and other donors seem to follow a strategy of making the "failed" state to fail more rather than to emerge as a "successful" state. The state was forced to withdraw from the economy but was also entrusted to oversee the divestiture of public assets. It is seen as incompetent to manage the economy, but competent to select the buyer of public assets. By making the state withdraw from the economy, politics and economics were ruptured. The state was caught in a catch-22 time warp. It has to service its debts without shedding its responsibility to build roads, schools and clinics. It has no means to do the latter because all the revenues are tied to the former. Structural adjustment imposed an *export to pay debt* logic by expelling violently the ability of the state to pursue or carry out any worthy national development agenda. The state appeared to be rudderless, unable to support the population and losing the power of policy- making. Most of the state's functions, including security, have been contracted out or privatised to NGOs and the market. As Jeffrey

Sachs, the Harvard development economist who is reputedly behind "Russia shock therapy", remarked: "Failed states (are) seedbeds of violence, terrorism, international criminality, mass migration and refugee movements, drug trafficking, and disease." (Sachs, Summer 2001, pp.187-198). Impose shock therapy or structural adjustment and weaken the state and force it out of its public policy role.

The shock therapy seems to be:

- Create a policy vacuum; and blame the state when it fails to carry out any meaningful public action.
- Make the state to fail and blame it for failing.
- Abandon the state and make all those interested in Africa's developments to look elsewhere - to civil society and the market.
- Establish a new regime of NGO-dom and corporate power to do the job the "failed states" are said not to have been good at.

By using such zero morality and infinite cunning, donors fund the non-state actors by often withdrawing their loans and grants from the supposedly failed states. "Success" is assigned to NGOs and the market. "Failure" is put at the state's door. The discourse of success and failure completes the ideological and rhetorical circle in the moral condemnation of the state. With success assignment going to NGOs and other non-state actors, the attributes of "good governance, transparency, representation, participation, democracy and accountability" come with the recognition. A new triad consisting of patronising donors that assign definition such as failed states and successful NGOs occupies the African space in the domain of social or public policy formation. NGOs are constituted by donors as empowering and "clean" while the state is cast as "venal" and "unclean". Donors arrogate to themselves the power of controlling the discourse on the NGOs and the demotion of the State. African society and community is forced to become even more incoherent with the privatisation of the national developmental agenda. Over 2000 international NGOs and thousands of local NGOs criss-cross the continent.

The state becomes further eroded by the defection of civil servants to the more lucrative sphere of NGO-dom and civil society. Thus, those from the public sphere migrated in search of lucrative opportunities in the non-profit and profit-making sectors. The new opportunities led to the creation of a type of three-legged entrepreneur. With one leg a civil servant tries to accumulate grants by getting involved in NGOs. With another leg, his knowledge of the workings of the bureaucracy helps the accumulation of political capital. With the remaining leg, a business venture is run. The combination of resources from the civil, political and economic spheres in order to promote personal enrichment seems to have contributed to the complete loss of commitment to public institutions. Thus with the so-called failed states, for the most part, public interest disintegrates. And with it any coherent public spirit, public purpose, public ethics and public policy. The various failed states were too vulnerable, too fragmented, too tied to external powers, that they largely were unable to mount a credible national agenda for renewal and social innovation.

In all these, what is lost is working for, and attaining the appropriate social construction of the African state-society partnership.

State and Society in Africa

Africa has suffered from the backlash against the state - the developmental, the planning and interventionist states as a result of the ascendancy of neo- liberal policies in the 1980s and 1990s. The state retreat has been yoked with the revival of free-market ideology and civil society. According to the World Bank:

Economic liberalisation is expected to decentralise decision-making away from the state and multiply the centres of power. This in turn is assumed to lead to the development of a civil society capable of limiting the power of the state and providing the basis for liberal democratic politics. Democratic rights, on the other hand, are seen to safeguard property rights, which in turn create the security and incentives necessary for economic growth (World Bank, 1989: 60).

While the state, market and civil society relations reflect the interdependence and mutual shaping of political, economic and civil societies, the ascendancy of free market and civil society suggest ideologies of what Putman called "bowling alone!" Its merit lies in de-legitimising ideologically and rhetorically the regulative role of states over markets and civil society actors.

What Africa needs are strong developmental states that work equally with strong civil society and strong markets (and not free markets!). There is no such thing as a free market, as there is no such thing as free air outside the context of space and time. The market is always and universally embedded in societies and social-economic arrangements and structures. State or civil society strength does not lie in its confrontations with each other but in the social innovations for furthering their partnerships and co-operations. Strength is built on a public policy orientation founded on the bedrock of public purpose, public service and public ethics that stimulate solidarity amongst states, markets and societies in Africa. They are not built with policies that divide, confront or weaken the triad of state-market-society. Strength is not measured by how many states are adjusted to attract IMF-World Bank loans and grants by passing their dictations and conditions. It is measured by how much the state has developed public sense by being rooted in society and markets and by emerging from it to guide society and the market in turn. And it is measured also by how much it does this by becoming itself a community for promoting self-reliance by following independent policy trajectories. Instead of donors that appropriate to themselves the power to assign and define, free Africans should take over that power without delay. It means the political authority of the African state should not be undermined by the promotion of civil society.

The current global "failure-speak" is largely a false construct. It is not that existing African states are not problem-ridden and under-performing. They are full of problems and they under-perform. But the failed state discourse is rooted in the hypocrisy of the major trans-national system that brought conveniently "the failed state" rhetoric to deny culpability. The IMF and the World Bank are more implicated than the local states in Africa that tried to implement their policies. The rhetoric constitutes, as well as distances the responsibility of the global actors who contributed to the failure, ascribing all blame to the local actors, as if these were free actors from institutionalised dependency.

The successful state thrives on a successful civil society and equally successful market, not on free market, retreating state and "civil society gridlock" made possible by NGOs scrambling for donor handouts. The successful state can be constructed by challenging the global constitution of the failed state. If we wish to reject the donor role in this definition of failure, we can only do that by resisting the discourse of failure through an alternative discourse of success. Such a state must be unified and developmental, if it is to be capable of resisting donor ideological intrusion, discoursing and framing.

Remember that donors want to have their cake and eat it. They weaken the state in Africa and they blame it for being weak. They oppose the nationalist leaders and condemn their Pan-African national aspirations as utopian. Having made it impossible for an authentic African national project to take off, they continue to feel wary of any nationalist resurgence. Will Africans see through their hypocrisy and try to construct a nation-state from the local, sub- national, regional and continental levels with a clear self-reliant and developmental agenda? The crucial question will be whose agenda is the state following? If it follows a corporate-cum-local ruling elite agenda, the state, under such circumstances, will not be productive. What will make it productive is if the agenda is people-centred, African-centred, civil society-centred and market-centred. In this case, even if there is no all-African level national coordination, Africa will be on the move because African politics would have shared the same aspiration from the micro to the meta-level and vice versa.

The crucial question therefore is not the form of organisation and its procedural attributes. It is more a matter of anchoring all forms of government/organisational arrangements from the local to the continental on a distinctly Africa-nation agenda. The existing states can re-negotiate their internal arrangements to enter into an all African union framework. They do not have to break up to enter into the new arrangement. They must be willing to challenge their institutionalised dependency on transnational actors in order to enter the Africa-nation system. When all - from the micro to the continental - are guided by an overriding African interest and identity, the task of designing social arrangements that integrate individuals, communities, peoples, regions, nations, religions and states will be easier. There will be a shared common framework that can facilitate the negotiation for various forms of institutional arrangements. Thus, the convergence of spirit, sense and action will emerge in spite of the varieties of organisational arrangements that African polities wish to define, actualise or organise.

There is thus the need to find consensual mobilising ideas and practices for all to recognise an African meta- narrative that embodies a strong and successful co-ordination of African state-market and society. Such a meta narrative should displace the donor driven narrative or discourse. It can be made to assist and interact and even guide the local narratives of self-defining African communities. Pan-Africanism provides that meta-narrative and metaphysics for going beyond existing barriers whilst remaining rooted in African authentic communities.

Concluding Remarks

The Pan-African way can assist and guide Africa to reject donor power to shape, generate and inter-nationalise domestic political institutions, agendas and actors through money. For the donors, their money thinks, their money governs and their money defines or assigns. Free Africa can be born when it develops the power to reject donor dictation through money. The partnering of the state, society and market triad based on the concept of emancipated Africa can play a pivotal role in spreading forms of governance that promote true development. In fact, the crystallisation of the African concept for anchoring government opens huge possibilities for African communities to associate, organise, define and shape a dynamic state- market and society partnership. Such a partnership on an African scale should free African initiatives by promoting varied forms of combinations and self-realisations. It need not be confining and restrictive of freedom.

The opportunity cost of not creating the triad of African State, market and civil society on the basis of webs of solidarity, partnership and toleration will be a regime of violence.

It is the consequences of that failure to unite, which Nkrumah warned against, that the donors now describe as the "failed African State?" But is the failure of the post-colonial state the same thing as the failure of the African State? How can the latter fail before it is made. We think the African State, which is at once both developmental and strong, and in partnership with the market and civil society, is yet to be created. Such triadic creation will assist Africa to claim the 21st century. That is why one can say that Pan-Africanism is an ideal whose time has come.

References

Sachs, J., *Washington Quarterly*, vol.24. No.3, summer 2001

Gellner, E., 1994, *Condition of Liberty, Civil Society and its Rivals* (London :Hamish, Hamilton)

Cohen, L.J. & Arato, A., 1997: *Civil Society and Political Theory*, (The MIT Press, Cambridge (USA) and London)

World Bank, 1989, *Sub-Saharan Africa: From Crises to Sustainable Growth*, (World Bank, Washington D.C).

Abrahamsen, R., 2000, *Disciplining Democracy: Development Discourse and Good Governance in Africa*, (Zed Books: London & New York)

6

Pan-Africanism and the Second Liberation Struggle for a United New Africa

Chen Chimutengwende

Africa is the only region of the world with most of its countries going backwards in terms of their socio-economic development. Africa's marginalisation in the international system has also become depressingly total and has reached frightening proportions. It is apparent that the ideologies of unplanned and uncontrolled market forces, foreign dictated and rushed privatisations as well as economic dependence on the West have all driven Africa to this catastrophic situation.

Most African countries continue to regress in terms of development indicators. The United Nations Economic Commission for Africa in its 2002 economic report on Africa stated that: "Africa will not achieve any of the Millennium Development goals set by the United Nations at its Millennium Summit. In Africa, levels of poverty, endemic diseases and unemployment are continuously and rapidly worsening. The availability and quality of social services have been greatly reduced. Social conflicts, often leading to ethnic or national hostilities, are on the increase. Political direction is faltering. External manipulation and interference is at its highest level.

The West finds it easy to manipulate and dominate Africa because of Africa's political orientation and fragmentation into mini-states, many of which cannot ever be viable in their present forms. After independence, the West created - and has to this very day expanded and maintained a deadly network of puppets and collaborators among the African leaders through whom it implements its exploitative schemes in Africa. Apart from the West, this network is a beneficiary of such schemes and that is part of the essence of neo-colonialism.

This situation must be reversed if Africa is to survive and prosper. The only real way to reverse this situation properly and thoroughly is through what may best be called the second liberation of Africa based on the principles of Pan-Africanism and economic egalitarianism which will bring about Africa's re-awakening, unification, anti-neo-colonialism, independence, self-reliance, democratisation and sustainable development. This second liberation struggle has already started as the only process, which can defeat the forces of neo-colonialism and stop the re-colonisation of Africa.

The origin and impetus of the second liberation of Africa is both local and international. Progressive internal and external forces are now spearheading this second liberation, which is bound to take Africa deep into the twenty-first century. It must be recognised that liberation itself is not an event, but a permanent process, which moves in stages or phases. The first stage was therefore the African independence struggle, and the second stage is the second liberation struggle against neo-colonialism and imperialism, and for the unification of Africa, its democratisation and development.

The first liberation struggle led to the independence of most African countries in the 1960s and 1970s. During these two decades, the ideas of Pan-Africanism and hope had gained ascendancy. This new historical epoch was aimed at the achievement and consolidation of Africa's independence and for its development. The first liberation struggle of Africa against European colonialism was highly successful in terms of its objectives.

The most incisive, and the greatest Pan-Africanist of that time, President Kwame Nkrumah of Ghana, had warned against the dangers of internal and external negative forces combining their efforts to reverse the gains of African independence. He said that in order to prevent this, Africa needed to be totally united, mass-oriented and fully committed to economic independence and a human-centred development process. He strongly advocated for a socialist, vigilant, totally united, and consistently and permanently anti-neo-colonialist Africa.

Without creating a strong, democratic, independent, anti-imperialist and self-reliant United New Africa, (sometimes referred to as the United States of Africa), Africa will remain an easy victim of the western imperialist tactics of divide and rule, marginalisation, manipulation, exploitation, neo-colonialism and even re-colonisation. This, as we have seen, is largely responsible for Africa's continuous, sickening and worsening political crises, poverty and negative socio-economic development. It is true, therefore, that if united, Africa will stand; but if it continues to be divided, it will continue to fall.

Since the 1980s, the gains of African independence and the reality of independence itself have been seriously eroded in many African countries. The achievements of Africa's first liberation struggle have been found to be difficult to consolidate in many parts of the continent. Vigilance, unity, anti-neo-colonialism, commitment and vision have been more than lacking on the part of some African leaders. Such leaders have turned out to be oppressors and/or western collaborators against their own people for their own benefit, and that of the West, which helps to keep them in power. In countries under such leadership, there is massive corruption, economic mismanagement and naked abuse of power, which became rampant just after independence and still continue today.

Right from the beginning, there have always been a collaborationist, moderate, unclear, inconsistent, vacillating, unprincipled and cunning elements in the leadership of the nationalist movement. Such elements were, and are still not motivated by the principles of socio-economic democracy, justice, anti-imperialism and development. It is also not unusual that some genuine and committed nationalists can degenerate to despicable proportions. This is proved by their post-independence practice as government leaders. It is now one of the major tasks of the second liberation of Africa to replace such leaders and defeat their horribly selfish, decadent and evil ideas and policies. The proposed United New Africa, by its very nature, will have no place for such oppressive, dictatorial and corrupt leaders.

After independence, the differences between such reactionary leaders and imperialists quickly vanished. Their differences had been temporary anyway. The two sides became allies and partners politically and financially after independence. It is true that the nationalism of the oppressed is progressive and liberationist, and the nationalism of the oppressor is retrogressive, oppressive and also racist. Nationalism of the oppressed on its own has a limited but positive role in the liberation of a people.

Nationalism could be dynamic, and even revolutionary, if it can incorporate ideals of socio-economic democracy, human rights, Pan-Africanism and anti-imperialism; and, if it could also be developed into an integral part of the progressive and democratic internationalism. Otherwise mere nationalism on its own, after its initial success, often relapses into a negative and reactionary force. It is not a consistent, reliable, lasting and guiding philosophy for running the affairs of any country. A progressive country needs a national philosophy or ideology, which is higher than mere nationalism and capitalism.

But since independence, there have always been some progressive nationalist African leaders and governments who have managed to sustain the resistance against neo-colonialism and re-colonisation. These progressive African leaders were, and are still engaged in this struggle in different ways, at different levels and their pace is also not the same. Such forward-looking governments and leaders must be supported and encouraged to continue, widen and intensify the fight for a United New Africa through the African Union (AU).*

The present situation of the post-colonial period should now be made to be a fast passing phase of African history. It is a period in which Africa has been trying to consolidate its independence and push for its own socio-economic agenda. The balkanisation of Africa was meant to be for the benefit of Western Europe and still serves that purpose. But post-colonial Africa has failed to reverse it for its own good. Without the total unification of Africa, the continent will remain permanently weak and vulnerable to western machinations and exploitation. The creation of a vast African common market and the opening up of African economies to each other is a prerequisite for Africa's development and survival. It must, therefore, be re-emphasised here that Africa either unites or perishes, and there is no other choice.

The establishment of the African Union is part of the second liberation process. At the same time, the African Union will need to effectively lead this process with the strong support of Pan-Africanist non-governmental organisations working for a United New Africa. The second liberation proponents must be inspired by the ideas, principles and strategies which were well articulated and/or applied by Africa's liberation heroes who, among others include: Kwame Nkrumah,

Marcus Garvey, Malcolm X, Gamal Abdul Nasser, William E B Du Bois, Patrice Lumumba, Franz Fanon, Julius Nyerere, Ahmed Ben Bella, Bob Marley, Sekou Toure, Modibo Keita, Samora Machel, Walter Rodney, Kwame Toure (Stokely Carmichael) Martin Luther King Jr, Edward Wilmot Blyden and Louis Troissant. The views, objectives and strategies of these heroes are still as valid as ever. Without such ideas, the second liberation of Africa would be meaningless.

Like the first liberation, the second liberation of Africa should be fully backed by the African Diaspora and the anti-racist progressive forces worldwide. Their contribution was highly crucial and commendable in the first liberation struggle. It must also be unequivocally stated that the freedom, dignity and security of the African Diaspora is essentially linked-up with the condition of the African continent itself. Africa is their base in this world of racism and imperialism.

African Diaspora means all Africans including African descendents permanently or temporarily living outside Africa. Their relationship with the African Union and the United New Africa is inseparably intertwined. Their maximum involvement in all the programmes and activities of the AU is essential. During the past few decades, their capacity to contribute has also increased tremendously. A high level of co-ordination and inter-dependency between them and the progressive forces of Africa is essential for the speedy success of the second liberation struggle. The African Diaspora should therefore be directly represented in all the organs of the AU especially the Pan-African parliament and they should be given citizenship on request.

This second phase, or second liberation struggle of Africa, is emerging with a better vision, more experience and stronger determination than ever before. The aim of the second liberation is a United New Africa which will be engaged effectively and systematically in a movement for the speedy reduction, and eventual elimination of mass poverty, squalor, HIV/AIDS and other endemic diseases, illiteracy, unemployment, injustice, corruption, ethnic wars, rural neglect and all other problems of under-development.

The United New Africa that is envisaged here would be based on the principles of Pan-Africanism, Afro-Arab unity, Third World Solidarity; South-South co-operation; the democratisation of international relations including its institutions and international trading regimes; progressive and democratic internationalism; socio-economic democracy; open debate on all public issues; and, maximum mass participation in the decision-making processes. This kind of Africa would also be based on people-oriented and environmentally sustainable development; collective self-reliance; economic and social human rights, women's rights, children's rights, minority rights; responsible and accountable freedom of the press and association; probity and accountability; transparency in both the public and private sectors; pluralism in matters of politics and religion; a permanent liberation process; and checks and balances in the socio-economic system.

The satisfaction of basic human needs for all would be given a priority in such a United New Africa. Production and development would be based mainly on domestic demand. Growth models that are exclusively designed by the indigenous people would be given a chance. Orienting the continent to living within its own means would be taken as a starting point. In a United New Africa, the movement against corruption, nepotism, regionalism, ethnic chauvinism and the foreign domination of African economies, cultures and values, together with the struggle for socio-economic democracy and human-centred development, would be recognised, promoted and led by the state as a permanent process. United New Africa would, at both local and continental levels, have a permanent and effective mechanism for conflict prevention, management and resolution.

As a genuinely independent entity, United New Africa would, by its very nature, have the capability to make a decisive contribution to world peace and to the re-structuring and democratisation of the current and unjust international relations system, including its institutions and international trading regimes. Another major task of the second liberation struggle is to make the Western former colonial powers pay massive reparations to Africa and black people internationally for slavery, colonialism and neo-colonialism. United New Africa's solidarity with the poor, oppressed, those discriminated against and all other disadvantaged peoples internationally would also be unwavering and uncompromising.

The African Condition

Much has been written about what has gone wrong with the post-colonial period in Africa. This period has resulted in the present African condition, which has been a major disappointment in terms of Africa's economic development and the progress of its democratisation process. Both the pace and the results have been dismal in many countries. The post-colonial period has been dominated by serious myths and illusions. Some essential elements have clearly been either weak or missing. The achievement of independence has often been seen as the end of history. Liberation has not been seen as a continuous process, which has no end. The independence leaders, structures and state procedures have also often been treated as permanent and sacrosanct.

Absolute power, lack of a system of checks and balances, the absence of democratic and practical possibilities for change and foreign machinations caused many leaders to lose touch with reality and the people. It made them insensitive, complacent and hence blunderous and dictatorial. At the same time the international dependency system has maintained an almost unshakeable grip on most of Africa, through the machinations and neo-colonialist policies of western governments and international financial institutions like the World Bank, IMF, WTO, and the multinational corporations. It has, therefore, been easy for the clock to be turned back by these retrogressive forces, which operate with the full connivance of Western interests and their local allies.

It must be emphasised that there is an orientation and attitude problem with many African people in both Africa and the Diaspora, especially the educated, which has to be reversed. This is the problem of mental colonisation and brainwashing by the West. It results in self-hatred, inferiority complex and lack of confidence. This problem must be addressed as one of the starting points in the development of the African Union, both in Africa and in the Diaspora. It must be reversed through a process of mental de-colonisation so that Africans can be positive about themselves both as individuals and as a community. That process should make them committed and optimistic about Africa's future as a united continent.

The second liberation of Africa needs to be thoroughly decisive in taking care of mental de-colonisation once and for all. This process of mental de-colonisation requires massive re-education campaigns among black people and others globally through the educational systems, mass communications media, conferences, and other forms of encounter and inter-personal communication. The African Union must create its own pro-African and patriotic mass communication system, which it should fully finance and control without western involvement. The Pan-African media should propagate and champion the views and interests of Pan-Africanism, anti-imperialism, anti-capitalism, the African Union and the United New Africa. More than 70 per cent of people in Africa live on less than one US dollar a day, while a cow is subsidised to the tune of two and half US dollars per day.

It is important here to briefly show in figures and discuss how far the African condition has deteriorated into a political and economic catastrophe, and how the present contradictions have grown to uncontrollable proportions. Africa has over 800 million people, which is 13 per cent of the world's population, but its contribution to the world's GNP is one per cent and also produces one per cent of the world's manufactured goods.

Out of every three children, one goes without any primary school education. Out of every eight children, one is badly disabled. The number of malnourished children is over a third of the total child population. One child in every six dies before the age of five, that is, more than four million African children die every year before they reach the age of five. Africa has the highest infant mortality rate in the world, at 108 per 1,000. The world's average is 63 per 1,000. The figure for the developed world is 12 per 1,000. Life expectancy in Africa has dropped to 47 years and is still dropping. It used to be well over 60 years. Only three per cent of students in Africa are able to go to university. The most frightening and distressing factor is that these figures are continuously getting worse and the process is being dramatically exacerbated by HIV/AIDS.

HIV/AIDS, malaria, tuberculosis and other poverty-related and endemic diseases are increasing fast in Africa. Of the 3.1 million people who were estimated by UNAIDS and WHO to have died of AIDS in the world in 2002, 70 per cent of them were in Sub-Saharan Africa. Better treatment and prevention of HIV and AIDS related diseases should cost about US $15 billion a year by 2007, which is not likely to come from anywhere. In Africa, over 50 per cent of the population has no ready access to health services, and this figure is increasing. Over one-third of Africa's high-powered experts and professionals have left the continent for greener pastures in the industrialised countries or because of repression or non-recognition.

Africa is losing more than three million hectares of fertile land every year because of desertification. Poverty leads to deforestation, land degradation, desertification and diseases. Three-quarters of all cultivatable land in Africa is now badly affected by soil erosion. Only a tenth of arable land is under cultivation. Many rural areas are over crowded because of unfair land distribution policies and practices. Real wages have dropped drastically. Unemployment in urban areas of many African countries is now between 40 and 80 per cent in many countries.

The West insists on a regular devaluation of Africa's currencies, which leads to more poverty. It even goes to the extent of bribing some leaders to devalue their currencies regularly. The main reason is for the West to be able to pay peanuts for African properties, commodities and services. It also insists on the continuous lowering of prices of Africa's raw materials while continuously raising prices of manufactured goods from the West. It also puts tariff barriers against manufactured goods from developing countries.

The West insists that there must be free trade; meaning goods from the West must be exported to developing countries without any barriers. But exports from developing countries must have limited quotas and face other tough restrictions to enter the West. The West achieves its goals, as stated earlier, with the co-operation of some African governments and through the machinations of such institutions as the World Bank, IMF and WTO. All this is part of the re-colonisation process. The issue is: how can Africa achieve any real economic development under such neo-colonialist exploitation? It is, therefore, not surprising that sub-Saharan Africa's share of total world trade has dropped from four to one per cent. Some 70 per cent of this is accounted for by South Africa and North Africa.

In order to pay for its imports and to service its debts, Africa is forced to sell more and more of its raw materials, and yet, the prices for these raw materials continue to fall. The volume of Africa's exports is therefore always increasing while their value is always dropping as determined by the West. Africa and the rest of the developing countries have hardly any say in determining the prices of their exports and imports. Clearly, Africa's trade relations with the West are based on naked exploitation. This is well supported by the nature of the globalisation system, which is undemocratically controlled by the industrialised countries for their own benefit.

As a result, more than 20 sub-Saharan countries had debts in excess of their GNP since the early 1990s. Out of the world's 20 poorest nations, 16 are in Africa. It is also the only region in the world where it is almost certain that poverty will increase during the next ten years unless circumstances change. Essentially, Africa is undergoing a period of rapid negative development and de-industrialisation with no end in sight. The financial outflow from Africa to the West is astronomical. For every one US dollar put into Africa, the West receives back ten. That is how the West designed and controls the nature of its relationship with Africa and other areas of the developing world.

During the last 30 years, the gap between the richest and the poorest in Africa has dramatically increased. The richest fifth now gets 180 times more income than the poorest fifth. These depressing statistics and facts, which are expected to continue getting worse, are far from being exhausted here. Africa is actually being destroyed! The West, through the IMF and World Bank, insists that Africa should cut down expenditure on social services and welfare programmes. This has been their policy for the past 30 years. They have now been trying to revise this policy after having caused so much untold misery in Africa. The ruling elite in most African countries has always been ready to co-operate with this because it does not affect them. They have their own private transport, schools, hospitals, and so forth. Cutting down on public expenditure for the poorest majority has been easy because they are politically powerless. The situation is more than pathetic: It is, in fact, explosive!

This African condition – that is, mainly mass poverty and the ever-widening gap between the rich and the poor, has become worse than a catastrophe. The West even owns most of the processing plants and other resources of Africa. In some African countries, all that Africans own are their parliaments and the power to legalise and facilitate the exploitation of their own people and their resources for the benefit of the West and a handful of some well-placed and powerful local Africans. This is why it is important to emphasise the need to indigenise African economies far beyond this elite, and the economic empowerment of the poor, including women and the youth.

It is not difficult to find out why the economies of many African countries are in shambles. As has been stated earlier, economic mismanagement and corruption have reached unimaginable proportions and there is a fast deepening leadership crisis in most African states. Some African countries have been put in a situation where they are almost at a point of no return. They can only borrow more and more, and yet get poorer and poorer. The state machinery is collapsing or has totally collapsed in some countries.

Most of the African leaders have lost vision and no longer talk about the type of society for which they are supposed to be striving. They now only talk about the survival of their countries. They are just hopelessly trying to manage the crises. The number of civil wars and other political upheavals is increasing. Africa has more countries in a state of war or near war situation than any other region in the world. The reasons are as much internally as they are externally caused. Such crises and conflicts can only be resolved through the second liberation of Africa and the establishment of a United New Africa. This is why the establishment of the African Union must be fully supported as an important first step towards this direction.

Re-colonisation of Africa

The re-colonisation of Africa means the extreme political and economic control of Africa by the West for the benefit of the West. In this case, the West does not have to put in place its own colonial administration as it did in the past. Re-colonisation takes place through either forced or willing co-operation of certain sections of the African leadership. It is more extreme than neo-colonialism.

Africa's internal and external progressive forces are no longer in the ascendancy in African politics. Negative and exploitative forces have clearly become dominant and they call the shots. Africa has emerged, in socio-economic terms, as the most backward, divided and foreign-dominated continent in the world today. In fact, Africa is now being re-colonised through privatisations, structural adjustment programmes, the international trading regime and globalisation which are all unfairly controlled by the West for its own benefit.

Africa is even losing its sovereignty, which it gained at independence. Re-colonisation is taking place through the nature of Africa's relations with the West and western-controlled multi-national corporations and international agencies like the World Bank, International Monetary Fund and the World Trade Organisation. These international agencies, especially the IMF and the World Bank, are there to control and supervise the economies of Third World countries. They ensure that Third World countries have no choice but to adopt and follow policies, which facilitate the smooth exploitation of their economies. Africa is moving from neo-colonialism to re-colonisation.

Re-colonisation is also being done in the name of freedom and democracy, which is a complete distortion of these concepts because, in reality, it does not mean the socio-economic advancement and the true freedom of Africa and its peoples. It means the continued control and robbery of Africa's resources by, and for the West. The West also describes such a state of affairs as inter-dependence or globalisation or partnership or international co-operation, which, in this case, are euphemisms for dependency, westernisation, de-humanisation, and re-colonisation of Africa and its peoples, both in Africa and the Diaspora. The liberal elements in the ruling classes of the West believe that while there should be continued democratisation in the West for their people, there should be some form of democracy in developing countries which will, at the same time, allow the West to derive maximum profits.

During colonialism, western governments, as the colonisers, were openly opposed to human rights and democracy in the colonies. The colonial peoples had to fight for the basic right to vote. But now they insist on democracy, which they really do not mean. It is just a change of tactics while the main objectives remain the same, that is, the exploitation of African resources. This is why at the international level, they unequivocally and consistently oppose democracy. Their attitude to the democratisation of the UN and other international institutions is a good example of this. America and its allies, for instance, can defy the UN but will not allow other countries, which are not its allies, to do the same.

Contrary to what the West would like the world to believe; western imperialism and neo-colonialism still exist. What prevails in the world today is a temporary defeat of the progressive forces, which has resulted in a temporary and false global unity and consensus led by the

US for the benefit of the global (western) capitalism. This is why when one talks of the international community one means the West, that is, North America and Europe. The developing countries are not regarded as part of this so-called international community.

The invasion and occupation of Iraq by the US and British forces clearly proves that the imperialist West has not changed its colours. The objective of the invasion was to weaken the Arab countries, strengthen its ally Israel, and to politically and economically control and exploit Iraq. Were Iraq and Afghanistan immediately democratised after their so-called liberation by the US led forces? Why not? Were any weapons of mass destruction found in Iraq by the occupying forces? It is feared that the US and its allies are now busy trying to secretly bring the weapons of mass destruction into Iraq so that they can say they found them there and thus justify their invasion.

It therefore follows that the reason for invading Iraq was neither the issue of democracy nor weapons of mass destruction. But in any case, why should the right to possess the weapons of mass destruction be restricted to the US and countries that are approved by the US alone? What kind of democracy is that? The invaders of Iraq are now like any colonial power. They have appointed a US Administrator, Mr Paul Bremer, who in reality is the Governor of the colony of Iraq. The US will sooner or later after a period of nationalist resistance, yield and allow the indigenous peoples to have a government to be voted into power through a one person one vote based election. But they will try to ensure that they leave behind a neo-colonialist government in charge as was done in Africa and other former colonies in the rest of the world.

New Partnership for Africa's Development

The African Union certainly needs a socio-economic development programme. It is essential for Africa's development. There are many and important socio-economic projects that are required at regional and continental levels, which should be planned, implemented and co-ordinated at continental level. This is why the idea of a New Partnership for Africa's Development (NEPAD) must be supported. But the current NEPAD basic document has an orientation problem. It needs to be re-designed and re-focused to make it a self-reliant continental development programme, with a clear anti-neo-colonialist orientation.

NEPAD should not be dependent on the West for its success as suggested in the present NEPAD basic document and by the regular meetings of African leaders and the G8 leaders where NEPAD is discussed. NEPAD should not seek to worsen Africa's dependency on the West. It should not have been designed in such a way that the West can easily take advantage of it and be able to use it for its own benefit and at Africa's expense. In its present form, it is easy for the West to use it as another instrument for neo-colonialism or even re-colonisation. In a re-designed and re-focused NEPAD, the name of the programme would have to drop the word "partnership" and the role of the West would have to be de-emphasised. There can never be a genuine partnership for development between Africa and its western exploiters.

What the West means by partnership with Africa has never changed. It was clearly stated in the late 1950s by Sir Roy Welensky, the Prime Minister of the Federation of Rhodesia and Nyasaland, when he said that his new policy of "partnership" between black and white was the same kind of partnership one finds between "a rider and a horse". This Federation was made up of countries which are now called Zimbabwe, Zambia and Malawi and it was dissolved in the early 1960s. Sir Roy Welensky could not understand how any sensible and modern person would fail to support his new policy which he thought was more modern and not cruel like the old colonial system. Indeed this is still the nature of the relationship or partnership between the industrialised West and the developing countries, especially those in Africa.

The West, going by its history, current practice, strategies and objectives will not finance Africa to a point where Africa becomes a real competitor and therefore a threat to its interests or to a point were Africa will no longer be amenable to manipulation. The West knows that if Africa is united and also given a chance, it would become a dangerous economic giant, which it would no longer be able to control and exploit. The West prefers Africa to remain completely divided and dependent on it as its backyard. This is why the leaders of the G8 countries have qualified their support for NEPAD by insisting that their support should not be taken to mean a Marshall Plan for Africa. If the West were a real genuine partner, it would be interested in a Marshall Plan.

In reality, after the failure of its structural adjustment programmes at the country level, the West now hopes that NEPAD will be another IMF and World Bank economic structural adjustment programme at the continental level. As stated earlier, Africa needs a self-reliant socio-economic development programme, which would be an effective instrument against neo-colonialism and imperialism. Such a programme must give maximum support to agricultural productivity, mining, tourism, industrialisation and women's emancipation and participation. It should not try to move Africa deeper into western dependency. The present NEPAD document does not take this approach.

United New Africa's support organisations

As history teaches us, whenever there is injustice or oppression, there will be, sooner or later, a resistance. This resistance almost always starts small and weak but inevitably grows, and in the end, it becomes unconquerable and victorious. As the saying goes, "a long journey has to start with a single step". Africa's internal and external progressive forces have already started re-grouping, networking and strategising for the second phase of the liberation process. This re-grouping and networking must surely grow into a victorious movement just like the first liberation struggle. What motivated the people of Africa to rise up against colonialism will motivate them to fight against neo-colonialism, re-colonisation and imperialism.

More and more organisations or structures are needed for the purpose of serving as instruments, voices and channels for research, mass communication work and action in support of the African Union and for a United New Africa. They are needed both locally and internationally, so that they can combine their efforts and hasten the victory of the liberation struggle in Africa.

Such instruments of action and channels of communication, which have been, or are being formed, are necessary in order to make up a solid and indomitable international mass movement for the second liberation of Africa. They must be as numerous as possible for tactical reasons. The task is too formidable and the geographical area is too vast for one or just a few organisations alone. The more, the better. The more numerous they are, the more scope there would be for practically involving as many people as possible. This is also good for the purpose of making the maximum impact that is required. It also helps to strengthen the uncontrollability element, which is essential for such a world-wide movement in support of the African Union and a United New Africa.

The strategy should be: one struggle, many fronts and different levels. There has to be a combination of efforts. The organisations and groups for a United New Africa should avoid sectarianism and factionalism. There is always an unhealthy tendency by some revolutionaries to want to specialise on attacking other revolutionaries whom they regard as not quite good enough and therefore part of the enemy. This is sectarianism and makes the real enemy more than delighted. True and advanced revolutionaries do not insist on ideological purity but on the defeat of the main enemy. The concept of the 'United Front' is once again most appropriate in the second liberation struggle of Africa. What is needed initially is a broad-based movement. Wrong ideas can always be effectively corrected without personally antagonising the holders of such ideas.

The strategy of such instruments or organisations should be based on a clear understanding and the ability to distinguish primary from secondary contradictions, and primary from secondary enemies. They should re-define from time to time and at every stage, who the main enemy is and then unite with all those who can be united with, against the main enemy and isolate, divide, neutralise or destroy Africa's enemies one by one. Both temporary and long-term alliances are essential. It is tactically fatal for the movement for the second liberation to put all its enemies on one side; and itself, on the other.

The United New Africa support organisations, groups and centres should carry out research, disseminate information, maximally use the mass media, network, campaign, mobilise and take action in support of a United New Africa. Such United Africa support organisations should effectively, systematically and in a highly co-ordinated manner support and popularise the Africa Union. The New Africa International Network (NAIN) is meant to be one of such organisations. It links up with, and helps to co-ordinate organisations, centres, groups or individuals with similar objectives and concerns internationally.

NAIN was established as a Pan-Africanist, non-governmental, independent and international organisation for research, mass dissemination of information, networking, campaigning, mobilising, and for social action for the purpose of consolidation and developing the African Union into a strong, anti-neo-colonialist, independent, self-reliant and democratic United New Africa. NAIN therefore aims at vigorously promoting the speedy growth of the African Union.

In order to consolidate and develop the African Union, NAIN works, as a priority, for South-South co-operation, third world solidarity and the re-structuring and democratisation of the current system of international relations, including its institutions and the international trading regime. NAIN believes that as a system, this so-called New World Order (or globalisation), which is controlled by the West and for the benefit of the West, is undemocratic and exploitative of the developing countries mainly in Africa, Asia and Latin America. The real democratic is the New International Economic Order and the New World Information and Communication Order as advocated by countries known as the Group of 77.

The aims and objectives of NAIN, if it can be used as one of the models for the United New Africa support organisations, are as follows: -

1. To promote, publicise, defend, network and campaign for a strong, democratic, independent and self-reliant African Union leading to a United New Africa as the base for all Africa's peoples, including the African Diaspora.

2. To re-educate the peoples of Africa in order for them to wipe out the neo-colonial mentality which helps to perpetuate neo-colonialism, racist domination and the manipulation of Africa and its peoples globally.

3. To articulate, defend and champion the cause of Pan-Africanism and the interests, aspirations, rights and image of Africa and its peoples both in Africa and the Diaspora; and, to mobilise Pan-Africanist support internationally for the African Union.

4. To communicate to the people of Africa the benefits of a strong, democratic, independent and self-reliant African union; and, to promote unity and maximum mass involvement in the

development of the African Union which must lead to a United New Africa.

5.   To disseminate locally and internationally, popular and technical/scientific information, publications and electronic programmes originating from NAIN or any other sources which promote the speedy development of the African Union.

6.   To establish and/or support any programmes and projects for Pan-Africanist education and mass mobilisation of the African people in Africa, in the African Diaspora and of any other friends of Africa internationally; and, in support of the African Union and a United New Africa.

7.   To counteract, in both the local and the international media any anti-African propaganda and misrepresentation of facts on Africa and the movement for Pan-Africanist unity and sustainable development.

8.   To campaign for the democratisation of the international relations system, including institutions and the international trading regime. This also means to continuously expose and act on any iniquitous aspects of North-South relations.

9.   To defend, give solidarity and champion the rights of media practitioners, writers and intellectuals committed to Pan-Africanism, anti-neo-colonialist and democratic change in Africa and globally.

10. To conduct research and to carry out advocacy work on African and international conflict issues affecting African countries and the peoples of Africa internationally, with the objective of bringing about just and durable peace in Africa and internationally.

11. To establish Associate Branches of NAIN, and or to support and work with similar supportive organisations in Africa and internationally in order to build a strong global mass movement for the African Union. This also means the

resuscitation and maintenance of strong linkages and facilitating the continuous re-definition of common objectives among Pan-Africanists and revolutionary internationalists all over the world.

12. To operate not only as a Pan-African global think-tank on the future of Africa and that of its peoples globally but, also to serve as an organisation of activists implementing ideas, programmes and projects and undertaking campaigns and other appropriate actions for the consolidation of the African Union.

The headquarters of NAIN is in Harare, Zimbabwe, where it is registered as an international, non-profit and non-governmental organisation. It has a 50-member Board of Governors and two Patrons. These are all outstanding Pan-Africanists from different parts of Africa and the African Diaspora. NAIN aims at becoming a very powerful and truly global network for Pan-Africanist unity and the progress of Africa and its peoples globally. NAIN runs a website, which is meant to be a powerful forum for Pan-Africanists internationally in support of the African Union and the United New Africa. It will be interactive in due course in order to further promote debate internationally on how to swiftly develop the African Union leading to a United New Africa.

It must be re-emphasised that the organisations that carry out tasks like NAIN's need to co-ordinate their activities closely in order to build a powerful and effective global Pan-Africanist movement. In the development of any such struggle, the mass dissemination of information and the spread of ideas, at both popular and scientific levels, are crucial. Research, publishing, broadcasting and any other mass communication work have an essential role to play in the conscientisation and mobilisation of the people.

The Pan-Africanist global movement, which includes all the United New Africa support organisations like NAIN, should be part of the international movement against imperialism and for socio-economic democracy. This movement should continuously define what egalitarianism and socio-economic democracy means in the present day-world of western controlled globalisation. The result should be a rejuvenated, dynamic and undogmatic socialism. This rejuvenated socialism thus becomes the only valid alternative force for the true liberation of Africa and the world.

References

Greene, Felix: The enemy – What Every American Should Know About Imperialism (New York, Random House, 1970).

Addo, Berb, et al: *Development as Social Transformation* (Tokyo. The United Nations University, 1985).

Africa Alternative Framework to the Structural Adjustment Programme for Socio-economic Transformation-popular version-(Addis Ababa, United Nations Economic Commission for Africa, April, 1991).

Africa Recovery (Newsletter from the United Nations Department of Public Information, New York, with support from UNDP and UNICEF, 1993-5).

Chimutengwende, C: "Zimbabwe and White-Ruled Africa", a chapter in the book: *New Revolutionaries*, edited by Tariq Ali (London, Peter Owen Publishers, 1969).

Chimutengwende, C: 'The role of communication education in the development and democratisation of African society' (Nairobi, *African Media Review,* Vol. 2. No. 2. 1987, African and Msasa Publications, 1997).

Nyangoni, W. W: *The Western Media and the Third World* (Massachusetts, USA – Msasa Publications, 1992).

Chimutengwende, C: *South Africa – the press and the politics of liberation* (London, Barbican Books, 1978).

Nyangoni, W. W: *Development and Underdevelopment: the political economy of exploitation in North-South relations* (Marlborough, USA – the centre for Development and Global studies and Msasa Publications, 1995).

Nyangoni, W. W: *Global Capitalism and the Developing World* (Marlborough, USA-the Centre for Global Studies

Green, R.H. and Seidman, A: *Unity or poverty: the economics of Pan-Africanism,* (Harmondsworth, UK, Penguin Books, 1968).

Haq, Mahbub ul: *Reflections on Human Development* (New York, Oxford University Press, 1995).

Onimode, Bade (ed): *The IMF, The world Bank and the African Debt: the social and political impact* (London, Zed Books and the Institute of African Alternatives, 1991).

Rodney, Walter: *How Europe Underdeveloped Africa* (Washington D.C., Howard University Press, 1992).

Sawyer, Akilagpa: *The Political Dimension of Structural Adjustment Programmes in Sub-Saharan Africa* (Accra, Ghana University Press, 1990).

The State and the Crisis In Africa: In Search of a Second Liberation, (Proceedings of the conference held at Mweya, Uganda, 12-17 May, 1992 , Uppsala, Dag Hammerskjold Foundation, 1992).

Nkrumah, Kwame: *Neo-colonialism-The last Stage of Imperialism* (New York, International Publishers, 1965).

Fanon, Franz: *Wretched of the Earth* (London, Penguin Books, 1972).

Stiglitz, Joseph: *Globalisation and its Discontents* (London, Penguin Group, 2002).

Blums, Williams: *Rogue state* (South Africa, Spearhead, 2002).

Human Development 2002 (New York, Oxford University Press – published for the UNDP).

Winning the War Against Humiliation (Report of the independent commission on Africa and the challenges of the third millennium sponsored by UNDP and headed by Albert Tevoedjre, published by the UNDP, 2002).

Bamford, James: *Body of secrets – anatomy of the ultra-secret National Security Agency* (New York, Anchor Books, a Division of Random House, 2002).

Icke, David: *Alice in Wonderland and the World Trade Centre Disaster-Why the official story of 9/11 is a monumental lie* (Mildwood, Missouri, USA – Bridge of Love Publications, 2002).

---

* The African Union was launched by African Heads of State as a successor to the Organisation of African Unity (OAU) on July 9, 2002 in Durban, South Africa. (The website address of the African Union is: http://www.Africa-union.org)

7

From Colonialism to Elitism: An Enquiry into the African Imbroglio

Messay Kebede

Africans tend to ascribe the numerous impediments to the continent's development to colonialism and neo-colonial policies. Ranging from the persistence of poverty to the ravages of ethnic conflicts, these impediments are perceived as the main cause of the African failure to modernise. A good number of Western scholars, however, attribute these impediments essentially to the persistence of traditional views and methods and to the lack of reforms radical enough to uphold a sustained process of modernisation. My position attempts a rapprochement: it connects many of these impediments to elitism and argues that it originates from a socio-cultural condition that implicates colonial as well as African legacies.

The Internalisation of the Colonial Discourse

The understanding of elitism as a characteristic effect of colonial rule is not hard to establish. Surprising, as it may seem, the first scholar who drew attention to the phenomenon of elitism in Africa is a Western missionary by the name of Placide Tempels. In his controversial book, *Bantu Philosophy*, written in 1945, he defends the revolutionary idea that the Bantu people have a rationally constructed philosophy. Tempels's recognition of Bantu philosophy was indeed a direct blow to the justification of colonialism as a civilising mission. Besides refuting the colonial allegation of irrational and immature peoples, Tempels has reflected on the harmful results of denying philosophy to indigenous peoples. A major consequence of the indiscriminate smear of the African cultural legacy is the belief that unless the African mind is emptied of its irrational and absurd beliefs it will not be fit for Western ideas. One of the consequences of this line of reasoning is that instead of encouraging learning through dialogue and the exchange of ideas, acculturation, which was aimed at uprooting African peoples, was promoted. So dehumanising and decentring was this colonial method that Tempels does not hesitate to write that "in condemning the whole gamut of their supposed 'childish and savage customs' by the judgment 'this is stupid and bad', we [missionaries] have taken our share of the responsibility for having killed 'the man' in the Bantu."[1]

The characteristic result of this inhuman method is, according to Tempels, the *évolués* - a French term to characterise those 'natives who supposedly evolved into civilised Africans', as a result of colonial education. Tempels has no kind words to describe the *évolués*. He calls them *"déracinés* and "degenerates,"[2] as well as "empty and unsatisfied souls – would be Europeans – and as such, negations of civilised beings."[3] All these severe flaws suggest that these uprooted indigenous peoples have so internalised the colonial attitude that they ended up nurturing contempt for their own peoples. To show that colonial education produces people with a colonial mindset, Tempels stresses that the *évolués* "have no longer any respect for their old institutions, or for the usages and customs which, nevertheless, by their profound significance, form the basis of the practical application in Bantu life of natural law."[4] Since their primary function is to serve as a local instrument of colonial rule, their teaching, training, and mode of life dispose them to construe the dislike of their own legacy as a norm of civilised behaviour.

In particular, partly reproducing the colonial greed and partly expressing their irreparable loss of commitment, these imitators of the colonisers are obsessed with money: "money is their one and only ideal, their end and the supreme ultimate norm regulating their actions,"[5] writes Tempels. This obsession with money is how they display the cynicism, which invades them as a result of their rejection by the colonial society despite the fact that they themselves have rejected their own cultures and peoples. In a word, these would-be Europeans internalised all the vices of the coloniser without assimilating any of the positive aspects of modernity. That is why he defines them as "profoundly distrustful or embittered," by the obvious lack of "recognition of and respect for their full value as men by the Whites."[6] Accordingly, the torment of a deep humiliation so dominates these people that they even succumb to manifestations of eccentricity and megalomania just for the sake of appeasing their need to impress the coloniser at all costs. This is to say that the opposition of the *évolués* to colonial rule hides deeper emotional disorders of the kind pushing them toward negative and destructive behaviours. In this respect, the error has been to take at face value the rebellious stand of the *évolués*. While their role has been decisive in the struggle for independence, their overall attitude did not implicate an independent turn of mind. To overlook this point is to miss the extent to which the perpetuation of the colonial rule under the guise of independence remains the appalling reality of Africa.

In effect, African elitism is born of the entitlement to an uncontested leadership inferred from the privilege of being exposed to modern education. The inference singles out the *évolués* as heirs to the civilising mission. It is as though Westernisation passes on to local elites the right to rule, that is, to continue the unfinished business of colonialism. In other words, to rule is still a civilising mission, with the difference being that the "natives" rescued from primitiveness, assumed it. The entitlement to rule maintains the belief that Africans are indeed primitive, and so calls for methods of government similar to the colonial rule. Native rulers who think and act like the former colonisers make up the substance of African elitism. Of course, no African leader will openly admit that he/she perceives Africans through the eyes of the coloniser. But what matters here is less what African leaders say than what they practically do. Basil Davidson has described well the hidden substitution thus:

> …the regimes installed at independence became rapidly subject to upsets and uproars. Striving to contain these, the multi-party parliamentary systems gave way increasingly, whether in theory or practice, to one-party system. Most of these one-party systems at this stage, perhaps all of them, decayed into no-party systems as their ruling elements became fully bureaucratised. Politics came to an end; mere administration took its place, reproducing colonial

autocracy as the new 'beneficiaries' took the place of the old governors.[7]

This confirms that colonialism remains the major source of hindrance not so much by its plunders and destructions as by its ideological legacy. While all the rest is reparable, the colossal human wreckage caused by the internalisation of the colonial discourse and so aptly personified by the *évolués* is how Africa was handed over to psychopathic personalities.

Take the characteristic opposition on the basis of which theories of modernisation are constructed, to wit, the opposition between tradition and modernity. It scarcely needs to be pointed out that the rejection of tradition exactly reproduces the colonial attitude toward the African legacy. On top of ruling out the presentation of modernity as an extension, a continuation of tradition, "the static binary opposition between tradition and modernity,"[8] turns tradition into a major obstacle to modernisation. No less than the new science of anthropology established that the disparity between European modernity and African traditions rises to the level of a radical antagonism, the very one opposing the rational to the irrational, the civilised to the primitive, the good to the bad, the dynamic to the static. So presented, the disparity could not but implant a desire for a conversion to Western views and methods deep down into the African soul. Make no mistake: this conversion has nothing to do with becoming modern; rather, it is how Africans are conditioned to play a subordinate role in the colonial order. The absorption of the anthropological discourse produces the *évolué* as the one who, having a foot in both the modern and traditional worlds, best promotes the hierarchical order of colonialism by serving as a reliable liaison between the colonised and the colonisers.

The acquiescence of Africans to this colonial description of African tradition is what nurtures the elitist mentality by reviving the *évolué* sleeping in every "educated" African. It causes a characteristic blur assimilating the use of colonial conceptions and methods to an enlightened and positive approach. As a result of this mix-up,

...the native societies of Africa will be not so much transformed as replaced by modern, secular societies; and the key agents of this process will be native elites, including business elites or capitalists,

106

conceived of as bearers of the necessary universal values of global modernity.[9]

As substitutes for the colonisers, the *évolués* resolve on a condescending and paternalistic attitude, which, however far it falls short of being racist, is nevertheless an entitlement to privilege and uncontested leadership.   V. Y. Mudimbe gives a striking illustration of the mentality of the *évolué* in the person of Samuel Ajayi Crowther, a former slave and native of Yorubaland in Nigeria. Educated first in Sierra Leone and then in England, Crowther became in 1864 "the first Anglican bishop of 'the territories of Western Equatorial Africa beyond the Queen's Dominions'."[10] In one of his missions, he is reported to have asked, "'whether the inhabitants of Gomkoi were Pagans or Mohammedans'," if "'the males wore some sort of cloth around their loins'," even if "'they were cannibals'."[11] In other words, he had so internalised the Western discourse on Africa that he became unable to clear his mind of the images of "paganism, nakedness, and cannibalism"[12] inherited from the colonial discourse. Rather than being the learning of modern methods and concepts, acculturation is thus essentially how indigenous peoples learn to adhere to their allotted inferior rank and marginality through the depreciation of themselves and their legacy.

According to Mudimbe, the deconstruction of Western discourse is the only appropriate weapon against this induced self-debasement. Nothing genuinely African and good can be realised without the radical extirpation of the internalised colonial discourse. The deconstruction of the Western paradigm must include the rejection of the antinomy between modernity and tradition. Since colonial reading deforms the African past, there is no reason to endorse the alleged opposition between tradition and modernity. The main mistake of those African scholars who give their consent to the Western dichotomy in the name of modernisation is that they fail to realise that their idea of modernity only confirms Eurocentrism in its pretensions to be a model.

The other African scholar who, in addition to providing a tight and impressive criticism of African elitism, has gone further by linking it with entitlement to power is Niamkey Koffi. According to him, the rejection of African tradition is not an innocent academic view; it is an ideology of power legitimation and conquest. It is how traditional values and thoughts are discredited as unscientific and uncritical popular views. This view endorses the Western discourse on Africa, and in so doing, it advances the position of African educated elites. By vouching for the opposition between tradition and modernity, these elites play the game of the West and promote assimilation. But more yet, by opting for a discontinuous process of modernisation, they confer on themselves the exclusive right to rule, there being no doubt that the ultimate intention of the valorisation of modernity at the expense of tradition is to initiate a struggle for power by taking all legitimacy away from tradition and its representatives. In the words of Koffi, the rejection of tradition "reveals a secret struggle for power," and expresses "the will of the carriers of knowledge to overthrow the authority of the alleged carriers of false knowledge."[13] Such a position is not in line with the real interest of Africa and its search for freedom, since it implies the depreciation of one's legacy. But the riddle is solved if we read into the support for the colonial description a justification for the political ambition of the African intelligentsia. It is how African intellectuals present themselves, in the words of Davidson,

> ...as those who were to be the instruments of applying the European model to Africa, and therefore as the saviours of the continent. Being sure of the values of their Western education, they were convinced of their superiority over their vast majority: who but they, after all, possessed the keys to the powerhouse of knowledge whence European technology and conquest had flowed?[14]

Unsurprisingly, the would-be savours of Africa turned out to be its plunderers and a complete disillusionment took hold of Africans. Economic crises, perpetual political instability, social tensions, in addition to rampant corruption and nepotism, became the defining features of Africa. If anything, the depravity and predatory nature of the postcolonial elite testify to the complete loss of its sense of accountability to society. One explanation is uprootedness: because it dilutes respect and commitment, uprootedness takes away the sense of obligation to the people from the political elite. Stated otherwise, when perceived as essentially inadequate, society is likened to a raw material that must be fashioned at will; it inspires no obligation to its demiurges. This is to say that, as a result of the educated elite ceasing to belong to their native society on account of its Western education, it gives itself over to elitism whose conspicuous result is the collapse of all ethical relationship with the social community.

To sum up, the elitist attitude echoes the colonial mentality, meaning that the moral bankruptcy of the educated elite is a direct consequence of the endorsement of the idea of primitive Africa. The act by which Africans welcome Western education is the act by which they acquiesce to the colonial discourse on Africa: the one is inseparable from the other. As a result, the contempt – mostly unconscious, that educated Africans feel for Africanness disturbs their ethical relationships with themselves and their original society. Disdain and non-accountability appear to them as the only way by which they can demonstrate their complete emancipation from their discredited legacy. Imperative, therefore, is the recognition as a major explanation of African numerous impediments the fact that modern African states have simply replaced the colonial states. Because "Africans replaced the Europeans officials right to the to top of the bureaucracy"[15] without the prior dismantling of the colonial state and methods, especially without a far-reaching decolonisation of the educated and political elites, small wonder the same structure and turn of mind lead to similar results.

Tradition at the Service of Elitism

The rise of elitism through the internalisation of the colonial discourse does not seem to include those African scholars and political leaders who defend the value of African traditions. The rehabilitation of African traditions suggests an orientation that should ward off elitism: instead of imposing the imitation of an external model, the thinking should be committed to building modernity on African realities and centrality. In effect, most of these scholars and leaders, for instance Léopold Sedar Senghor, Kwame Nkrumah, Julius Nyerere, to name but the most influential of them, have referred the future of Africa to the idea of African socialism. Besides implying the inadequacy of the Western model, the reference pledges to rehabilitate "the traditional social order and to seek salvation in the pristine values of our [African] ancestors."[16] Since the Western model is inadequate, Africans must return to their sources, all the more so as the search for authenticity provides a solution to African failure by suggesting that the path to socialist development alone is suitable for African personality. Above all, the revival of tradition and the reconnection of Africans with the idea of a free pre-colonial Africa are perceived as the best ways to decolonise the African mind. Decolonisation is impossible so long as Africans do not rediscover and reconcile themselves with the idea of a free Africa.

Positive though they may be, these inspirations do not fully warrant the escape of the defenders of African traditions from the ascendancy of the colonial discourse. The case of Negritude ascribing emotion to Africa and rationality to Europe is a case in point. Instead of viewing the colonial idea of Africa as an invented and detrimental notion, the tendency to amplify it only reveals the readiness to accept marginality, and hence to act as an auxiliary of Western hegemony. Moreover, by insisting on the great divide between Africans and Westerners, the position talks Africans into self-denial and the desire of Westernisation. When, without any critical reservation, and in perfect agreement with racist views, Senghor "takes negative Eurocentric descriptions and presents them as positive Negrocentric manifestations,"[17] a greater desperation with the subsequent desire to escape Africanity at all cost is all that he achieves.

But there is more. On top of shunning the criticism of Western descriptions of Africa, the African endorsement of the racist view panders to a rosy description of the African past. It speaks of a return to the source without making sure that the unearthing of the past does not hamper the number one priority of Africa: modernisation. In advocating an uncritical return to the past, the defence of tradition turns into an elitist position. Indeed, one of the basic methods of elitism is to inspire lofty ideals whose interpretation and implementation requires the unchallenged leadership of the few, which often deteriorates into the dictatorship of one individual. Accordingly, the hidden purpose of the rehabilitation of tradition is to ban criticism and contest in favour of what an African philosopher called "unanimism."[18] For every time tradition is hailed, the alignment of the people behind the uncontested chief is presented as a normative attitude and a genuine African characteristic. Thanks to the "myth of unanimity,"[19] the individual view soars high above any critical examination and demands the mere capitulation of dissident positions in the name of authentic Africanness. It springs to mind that this apology of unanimism is a justification for dictatorial regimes and undemocratic methods of ruling. The ideology of the one-party system, the rejection of individualism as unAfrican, the praise of the collective, the suppression of dissident views, all work toward the goal of consecrating absolute power as an African virtue.

More often than not, the myth of unanimity rests on the inheritance of the debilitating notion of race from the colonial discourse. The notion is responsible for illusory conceptions of unity that lose sight of African social, tribal, and cultural diversity. From the alleged racial unity, it is easily deduced that all Africans think alike. In the name of this racial unanimity, African despots have stifled differences and initiatives: all that was dynamic, plural, and democratic was stigmatised as unAfrican. Take the idea of African socialism. It appeals to strong racial presuppositions, as it is said that Africans are socialist by nature. Communalism, in the strong sense of implicating the absence of acquisitiveness and individualism, is therefore their inborn characteristics. As a result, class differentiations and conflicts should be considered as alien and superficial. Thus, rejecting the Marxist interpretation of class struggle, Nyerere speaks of African socialism as being "opposed to doctrinaire socialism which seeks to build its happy society on a philosophy of inevitable conflict between man and man."[20] According to him, the revival of the former pre-colonial attitude of mind is enough to dissolve all the acquired capitalist attitudes whose exclusive birthplace is the West.

Interestingly, the discovery of this ideal and normative Africa confers on Western educated Africans a messianic role, a historic mission which feeds on the elitist image of rescuer. Dragged from their natural inclination and confounded by an alien situation, Africans need nothing more than a tutorial leadership that puts them back into their natural socialist milieu. The spectacle of Nkrumah, for instance, forcefully implementing African socialism on a people that he otherwise declared to be socialist by tradition gives a good evidence of elitism. His elitist slip clearly transpires when he makes the success of anti-colonial struggle dependent on the intervention of those who control knowledge. He remarks that "this triumph must be accompanied by knowledge,"[21] which means that "it must be socialist in form and content and be embraced by a mass party."[22] Clearly, the imperative of a mass party guided by the enlightened few is how power and knowledge fall into the same hands and government, thus armed with a regenerative ideology, changes into tutorship.

The other muddled goal that the racialisation of Africans has inspired is the idea of Pan-Africanism. I am not denying the great merit of African continental unity. The common history of slavery and colonialism and the added syndrome of prolonged marginality give Africans enough reason to stake a common cause. Also, there is no doubt that the idea of continental unity works against dispersion: unity being force, Africans have a better chance of combating marginality and poverty if they unite. The argument according to which the political unity of the African continent will favour peace by solving the problems of divided tribes and arbitrary borders is also worth considering.

However positive all these attributes of unity may be, they still do not change the fact that Pan-Africanism remains an endorsement of the colonial discourse. More than the common experience of domination, the idea of Africans belonging to the same race, sharing common physical and cultural traits cements the ideology of Pan-Africanism. To show that Pan-Africanism echoes the colonial racialisation of Africans, Franz Fanon reminds that for the colonist, the Negro was neither an Angolan nor a Nigerian, he simply spoke of "the Negro".[23] Nothing evinces better the internalisation of the colonial discourse than this propensity of African educated elites to echo racist definitions. Repulsed by the idea of national cultures and states, in perfect accord with racism, Africans too speak of African culture only, and place the future of Africans in the hands of the Negro continent and the Negro state. This puts a severe strain on existing African states by taking away their legitimacy. Emphasising the particularity of African nationalism, Nyerere writes that "the African national State is an instrument for the unification of Africa, and not for dividing Africa, that African nationalism is meaningless, is dangerous, is anachronistic if it is not at the same time pan-Africanism".[24] Already stigmatised as artificial entities imposed by external colonial forces, the existing African states lose the little legitimacy they had in the face of the racial state of Pan-Africanism, all the more regrettably as it is not clear why Africans would obtain better results in a larger unit than in smaller ones.

It is no surprise if the branding of African states by the elitist discourse of Pan-Africanism easily shifts to the no less elitist discourse of ethnicity. This is to say that Pan-Africanism, as much as ethnic separatism, flows from the same traditionalist and colonialist discourses. What connects the two ideologies is the fact that the way Pan-Africanism removes legitimacy from existing African states is also how it encourages the rise of ethnic politics. Not only is there a direct passage from race to ethnicity, but also the promotion of ethnicity joins the main stream of African elitism. First, the uncritical return to the past rediscovers and re-values ethnic membership. Second, the tendency to base union and solidarity on relatedness easily yields to ethnic calling because, in agreement with the Pan-Africanist moment, it thinks that blood and kinship favours a better and more cohesive social life and organisation.

Fanon gives a good illustration of the logical connection between race and ethnicity. Elaborating on his warning that the mere replacement of colonial rulers by African ruling classes will only lead to a dependent policy reproducing the syndromes of colonial governments, he notes that "we observe a falling back toward old tribal attitudes, and, furious and sick at heart, we perceive that race feeling in its most exacerbated form is triumphing."[25] Fanon analyses the rise of ethnicity as a bourgeois inspired ideology; inherited from colonial mentality, which is nothing more than an exasperated racism. It is a cheap racism, racism in the African style. It is definitely an expression of colonised mentality in that it classifies, separates, excludes peoples on the basis of natural characteristics. Above all, ethnicity is the weapon of the dependent bourgeoisie: unable to accomplish its national historic mission, it finds no other means to hold on to power than through the politics of division and exclusion, which exclusion, in turn, feeds on the ethnicity of the excluded. To show that ethnic politics reproduces the principle of colonial rule, Fanon reminds us that "by its very structure, colonialism is separatist and regionalist. Colonialism does not simply state the existence of tribes; it also reinforces it and separates them."[26] The support that ethnicity finds among some Western academic and political circles today confirms its revival in neo-colonial practices.

The elitist content of ethnicity becomes particularly glaring when we pay attention to the manner it justifies power. Scholars have been struck by the modernist language of ethnicity: it speaks in terms of justice, democracy and self-determination.

Educated groups are among its most ardent supporters and leaders. Because of this modern content, many scholars rightly warn against any identification of ethnicity with tribalism. Even so, behind the modern and democratic language, there looms an ascriptive entitlement to power. As one scholar notes, "the rigidity of ascriptive characteristics that define ethnicity compared to the fluidity of alternative bases of identity (especially class) accounts for the comparative advantage of ethnicity in sustaining group solidarity."[27] In going back to the past, elites discover a new form of entitlement: the ascriptive right of kinship. According to this principle, the representatives of ethnic groups have, or exercise power as a matter of natural right, from belonging to the same natural group. They are the natural representatives of the group; their entitlement is in the blood, in the ethnic belonging. No other people have the right to represent them: others are precisely outsiders. Nor is there a more compelling principle of unity than natural solidarity; it even transcends classes and common economic interests. Class mobilisation maintains the entrenched disadvantages by subordinating particular interests to common interests when what excluded groups need is the defence of their particularity. Because the alleged common interests usually favour the dominant ethnic groups, minority groups prefer ethnic mobilisation to class unity.

But then, ethnicity is where the ideology of unanimity achieves its perfect expression. Indeed, the ethnic group is the embodiment of unanimism: in addition to having common characteristics and history, members of an ethnic group are supposed to think alike and have common interests beyond class and status divisions. Most of all, ethnic solidarity is presented as a normative behaviour with the assumption that kith and kin are the best possible representatives of the ethnic group. No better way exists to deliver a whole people in the hands of elitism than to brandish the possibility of a breakaway ethnic state or a state functioning on the basis of ethnic solidarity. The logic that pushes Nkrumah to argue in favour of the one-party system - that it "is better able to express and satisfy the common aspirations of a nation as whole, than a multiple-party parliamentary system, which is in fact only a ruse for perpetuating, and covers up, the inherent struggle between the 'haves' and the 'haves-nots'"[28] works beautifully well for ethnicist politician, whose basic credo is the origination of common aspirations from ethnic membership. Not only does ethnic solidarity replace class solidarity, the dividing line here is between the ethnically related and the alien; diversity is then believed to be detrimental to the struggle. The same enthronement of the enlightened few, who alone illuminate the road to freedom, follows as a matter of course. The ideology of the return to the source gives them a messianic stature and turns them into deliverers from ethnic oppression. Once ethnic solidarity becomes the principal rule, it stifles all dissident views by authorising the characterisation of all internal opposition as a betrayal of common interests. It exactly institutes unanimity around the leadership canonised as the sole interpreter of the interests of the ethnic group.

This analysis of ethnicity must not be interpreted as a total condemnation of ethnic politics in Africa. The fact that an excluded group organises itself, and fights the exclusion, cannot be rejected without going against democratisation. Moreover, the inclusion of pluralism strongly favours the development of modern values by stimulating openness and competition. What is adverse, however, is the tendency of ethnic politics to harbour a separatist spirit by identifying the nation with the ethnic group. The use of ethnicity to break up the state confuses what is essentially a problem of democratisation with the emergence of a new ethnic state whose democratisation is yet to come. Because ethnically related people now control the state, issues pertaining to democratisation and modernisation are not done with yet. On the contrary, the ideology of relatedness can even get tougher to democratise inasmuch as it is not very amenable to the impersonalisation of the state. The question is then to know to what extent the defence of the ascriptive rights of ethnicity is compatible with the principle of modernity, decreeing the dependence of the status and place of individuals on their achievement. Unless the entitlement promoted by ethnicity is reconciled with the competitive principle, the style of household politics will prevail to the detriment of public accountability and democratic rules.

Power as Tutorship

It seems that we have now enough elements to define better the phenomenon of elitism. Take the case of Fanon. We saw how pertinent his critiques of the racialisation of Africans were, and yet he himself personifies elitism to the highest degree. Quite rightly D. A. Masolo writes that Fanon considered elitism to have a key role in the revolutionary process. The intellectual and political elites must exist and unite to give leadership to the masses. For him, as much as the masses need to be led into political activism as an uncompromising revolutionary force, they also need to be educated about the proper political and cultural awareness.[29]

What produces elitism is precisely this normative union of knowledge and power, this assumption that those who get involved in intellectual work should also rule. Behind this entitlement to rule, we find the ethos of the *évolués* who, having internalised the Western discourse, take on the task of rescuing their society from barbarism and ignorance. It is because modernisation is perceived as a passage from savagery to civilisation that knowledge and enlightenment entitles one to power.

This entitlement completely redefines the role of the state. According to the influential liberal theory, modern states implicate a contract of citizens among themselves, and with the government, as a result of which the latter becomes accountable to the former. Classical Marxist theory insists that the contract does not involve the working people, there being no doubt that governments protect the interests of ruling classes. The attribution of a modernising role to the state adds a civilising mission to the normal administrative and political functions of the state. In other words, following the colonial paradigm, from representative of social forces the state grows into a tutor. And who can direct this state if not those indigenous peoples who had access to Western knowledge? Since civilisation must come from outside, power must become tutorship. This equation produces elitism in all its various forms.

As yet, the most influential and thoroughgoing model of the unification of power and knowledge has been Leninism. In his book, *What Is To Be Done*, V. I. Lenin develops the principle that intellectuals, going beyond their normal role as bureaucrats, technicians, researchers, educators, and critics, should also become political leaders. His argument that power and knowledge must come into the same hands is all based on his assumption that, left to itself, the working class would only develop a trade-union consciousness. Let us listen to Lenin:

> We said that *there could not yet* be Social-Democratic consciousness among the workers. This consciousness could only be brought to them from without. The history of all countries shows that the working class, exclusively by its own effort, is able to develop only trade union consciousness . . . the theory of socialism, however, grew out of the philosophic, historical and economic theories that

were elaborated by the educated representatives of the propertied classes, the intellectuals . . . Similarly, in Russia, the theoretical doctrine of Social-Democracy arose quite independently of the spontaneous growth of the labour movement; it arose as a natural and inevitable outcome of the development of ideas among the revolutionary socialist intelligentsia.[30]

Other Marxist intellectuals (Antonio Gramsci, Mao Tse-tung, Fanon, etc.) have added their voices, turning the conjunction of power and knowledge into a credo of revolutionary movements in Third World countries. Incidentally, the Leninist principle is little in agreement with the original ideas of Karl Marx, who did not think that intellectuals should have a special role, still less a dominant role in the transition to socialism. He assumed that socialism being what the working class creates as its struggle unfolds, there was no need for external organisers or leaders. The subject, the maker of the process remained the working class, and this excludes the idea that socialism could be a process imposed from outside.

Be that as it may, many African thinkers and African leftist movements in general have fully adopted the Leninist principle. All agreed that unless the struggle of the people is organised and radicalised by committed intellectuals, it will have no positive outcome, in particular it will not steer toward socialism. Thus, after contesting the capacity of the peasantry, urban petit bourgeois social formations and workers to wage a revolutionary struggle, Amilcar Cabral focused on the "the need for a revolutionary (as opposed to simply nationalist) vanguard party led by a politically conscious elite."[31] In a chapter of his book, *Revolution in Guinea*, characteristically titled "The Weapon of Theory," Cabral goes so far as to define the unique historical role of members of this elite by their propensity to "committing suicide as a class in order to be reborn as revolutionary workers, completely identified with the deepest aspirations of the people to which they belong."[32] Needless to say, the myth of an elite entirely committed to the cause of the people would not have been possible without the suggestion that the possession of a revolutionary theory is the reason for its transfiguration.

The flourishing of the Leninist principle, first in backward Russia and then in Third World countries, reveals the social condition that feeds on elitism. It is a condition of perceived social impasse where in the name of a class or a large section of the people, believed to be unfit to conquer political hegemony, an enlightened group aspires to or seizes power. It claims to have the mandate for tutorship until the class or the people become mature enough to assume the task of self-government. To have an idea of the shift of the role of intellectuals in Third World countries, recall the position of European intellectuals fighting the feudal order. When one reads the political writings of Jean Jacques Rousseau, Voltaire, John Locke, etc., other than the purpose of enlightenment and the suggestion of alternative social organisation and evolution, no goal to seize power in the name of a class or a people suffuse their works. On the contrary, they thought that the new emerging bourgeois class, once properly enlightened and armed with alternative views, is perfectly able to establish a new and progressive social order.

Significantly different is the belief of Leninism or elitism: it is based on the assumption that underdeveloped societies are so perturbed that they are devoid of progressive social forces. Being in a deadlock, such societies call for outsiders, saviours (intellectuals, military officers) from outside traditional sectors as well as from modernised sectors of production. For these outsiders to appear as saviours, to acquire the entitlement to rule, there is need for a theory of history from which they draw the calling, the mission. The purpose of the theory is to establish and explain the deadlock. Once more the case of Lenin gives a perfect example of such a theory. In defining imperialism as the stage of "parasitism and decay of capitalism,"[33]his theory announces the exhaustion of bourgeois forces and revolution. In particular, the hegemony of this parasitic capitalism on peripheral societies prevents the rise of regenerative social forces, thereby investing intellectuals with the historic mission of guiding the liberation movements. This historic role legitimises elitism as the self-appointed delegate of the people. The clear impact of imperialism is the paralysis of the inner process of evolution while generating a small but active enlightened sector; this social impasse passes on to the enlightened few the role usually ascribed to classes.

Because politics thus shifts from administration to domestication, elitism is unthinkable without the assignment to modernise. This is to say that modernisation is itself couched in terms of snatching the ignorant masses from traditionality. The conflict between tradition and modernity is, we know, the main leitmotif of modernisation theories, be they liberal, socialist, or Marxist. Entirely based on the colonial paradigm of civilising mission, these theories assert that, in light of the larger society being immobilised by centuries of apathy, fatalism, and barbarism, salvation must come from outside, from the enlightened few. When leading Marxist intellectuals, in unison, insist on the revolutionary role of organised intellectuals, little do they realise that they are advocating a revamped version of the colonial rule. What prevents these scholars from seeing the colonial inspiration of theories of modernisation is the illusion of possessing the science of social evolution. Here, African scholars are clearly victims of false promises created since the Enlightenment according to which "it is possible to formulate perfect social and economic models, and that society can be 'engineered''[34]

This analysis equally applies to the other elitist drift that promoters of ethnicity incarnate. First of all, facts indicate that among the promoters of ethnicity many were at one point Marxist so that ethnicity is for them a substitute for the now outmoded theory of class struggle. Add to this the fact that the organisation and mobilisation of people around ethnic issues is a political option that justifies elite ascendancy. Just as in the case of class interest, it is believed that, left to themselves, people are unable to fight consistently for their ethnic identity and interests. The political leadership of intellectuals is necessary to turn the ethnic group into a self-sufficient, free, and self-governing movement. Only when intellectuals assume the leadership can the group change from mere entity into subject. The secessionist alternative is only an exasperated form of the resolution of local elites to claim the exclusive right to represent a group of people. We find the same Leninist idea that positive developments cannot emerge from the people themselves so that those who are conscious and organised must exercise the necessary tutelage to bring the ethnic group round to the idea of its distinct identity and interests.

Evidently then, in all the considered cases, whatever the chosen path, a decisive role is accorded to intellectuals because they appear necessary to impose a development that cannot originate from within the social life. In line with the colonial reasoning, development must come from outside and must be imposed on the people. If it is accepted that the latter are unable to realise it by themselves, it becomes clear that the difference between the colonial paradigm and the elitist model boils down to the burden of the white man becoming the burden of the native intellectuals, of the *évolués*. It is essential to understand that it is the social condition of the intellectual that constantly feeds on elitism. African intellectuals cannot reflect one moment on themselves and the backwardness of their society without thinking that they incarnate freedom and emancipation while all the rest is in darkness. Thus, whether they like it or not, they think of themselves as liberators, thereby developing what we can call the demiurge complex. Everything conspires to nurture this belief, for it is inscribed in their modern education. Being Western educated is how they see themselves in a sea of ignorance and barbarism. They cannot give credence to their modern education without secretly acquiescing to the image of primitive Africa.

But this paternalistic model is doomed to failure for the simple reason that it cannot internalise the colonial contempt and yet give birth to a positive outcome. The truth is that it leans toward negative policies because both its inspiration and methods draw on flawed assumptions. It only originates such recurring and detrimental practices as the liquidation of democracy, the institution of absolute and dictatorial powers, the spread of ethnic conflicts, the mismanagement of the economy through nationalisation, centralisation, and household management style, to say nothing of rampant bribe and corruption. These detrimental practices have one thing in common: all are designed to take initiative away from the people following the assumption that they are completely inept. If so, the blame for the African failure lies directly or indirectly with the internalisation of the colonial discourse as a result of which political power became entrusted with the mission to domesticate Africans.

References

1. Placide Tempels, *Bantu Philosophy* (Paris: Présence Africaine, 1952), p.20.

2. Ibid, p.19.

3. Ibid., p.117.

4. Ibid., p.118.

5. Ibid.

6. Ibid., p.116.

7. Basil Davidson, *Let Freedom Come* (Boston: An Atlantic Monthly Press Book, 1978), p.298.

8. V. Y. Mudimbe, *The Invention of Africa* (Bloomington: Indiana University Press, 1988), p.189.

9. Bruce J. Berman, "African Capitalism and the Paradigm of Modernity: Culture, Technology, and the State," in *African Capitalists in African Development* (Boulder: Lynne Reinner Publishers, 1994). p. 237.

10. Mudimbe, *The Invention of Africa*, p. 49.

11. Ibid.

12. Ibid.

13. Niamkey Koffi, "L'impense de Towa et de Hountondji,"*Actes du Seminaire sur la philosophie africaine*, edite par Claude Sumner (Addis Ababa: Chamber Printing House, 1980), p.167. My translation.

14. Davidson, *Let Freedom Come*, p.148.

15. Berman, *African Capitalists in African Development*, pp. 250-251.

16. P. O. Bodunrin, "The Question of African Philosophy," *African Philosophy*, edited by Richard A. Wright (Lanham: University Press of America, 1984), p. 5.

17. Tsenay Serequeberhan, *The Hermeneutics of African Philosophy* (New York: Routledge, 1994), p. 47.

18. Hountondji, *African Philosophy: Myth and Reality* (Bloomington: Indiana University Press, 1983), p.174.

19. Ibid., p. 61.

20. J. K. Nyerere, *Ujamaa-Essays on Socialism* (London: Oxford University Press, 1971), p. 12.

21. Kwame Nkrumah, *Consciencism* (New York: Monthly Review Press, 1964), p.104.

22. Ibid., p.105.

23. Franz Fanon, *The Wretched of the Earth* (New York: Grove Press, Inc., 1982), p, 211.

24. Cited by Rupert Emerson, "Pan-Africanism," *African Politics and Society*, ed. Irving Leonard Markovitz (New York: The Free Press, 1970), p. 458.

25. Fanon, *The Wretched of the Earth*, p. 158.

26. Ibid., p. 94.

27. Shaheen Mozaffar, "The Institutional Logic of Ethnic Politics: A Prologomenon,"*Ethnic Conflict and Democratisation in Africa*, ed.Harvey Glickman (Atlanta, Georgia: The African Studies Association Press, 1995), p. 37.

28. Nkrumah, *Consciencism*, pp.100-101.

29. D. A. Masolo, *African Philosophy in Search of Identity* (Bloomington: Indiana University Press, 1994), pp.36-37.

30. V.I. Lenin, "What Is To Be Done," *Selected Works*, (New York: International Publishers, 19), vol. 2, p. 53.

31. Patrick Chabal, *Amilcar Cabral* (Cambridge: Cambridge University Press, 1983), p.178.

32. Amilcar Cabral, *Revolution in Guinea* (New York: Monthly Review Press, 1972), p.110.

33. Lenin, *Imperialism the Highest Stage of Capitalism* (New York: International Publishers, 1972), p. 99.

34. Daniel Chirot, *Modern Tyrants* (Princeton, New Jersey: Princeton University Press, 1996), p. 22.

PART III

Africa-Nation, Pan-Africanism and the African Renaissance: Issues, Challenges and Prospects

<u>8</u>

African Renaissance: Frankly, it's up to "us"[1]

David Abdulai

Introduction

The future is in Africa. The future is Africa. Such bold statements by this author to many are an anathema. To some, it is heresy, wishful thinking from the mind of a daydreamer. But is it? Definitely not. Before anyone starts by shrugging these views aside as rubbish, it is wise to recall the pronouncements of Galileo Galilei, the 16th century Italian astronomer, who dared to proclaim that the earth revolves around the sun (*Eppur si mouve*). Many were those in his day who regarded his proclamation as rubbish. Today, it is obvious that Galileo was right. In the case of Africa, no one can deny the fact that the Africa of yesterday is different from the Africa of today. In the Africa of today, 80 per cent of Africans are fighting and winning the war on poverty. Economic growth is taking hold in most of the countries that have undertaken reforms. Political systems are more open than they were years ago, the press is freer than it was ten years ago, countries in the region are ridding themselves of outdated solutions, whilst drawing on the wealth of their cultural traditions. Furthermore, regional institutions are growing stronger and private investment in Africa is picking up, to mention just a few.[2] Thus, the fact that Africa is going to witness its renaissance is no longer the question. What is now important is when and how. This chapter subscribes to the view of Africa attaining its renaissance. The first section of this chapter would start out by debating the naysayers who hold the opposite view for Africa.

It will draw on history, using concrete examples to show why the naysayers are wrong. The chapter will then point to some of the reasons why there is hope for an African renaissance, drawing from current economic data and other tangible examples. Next, the chapter will look at the challenges or hurdles that Africa has to overcome to attain its renaissance. After offering some solutions to some of these challenges, I shall conclude, upholding the view that if Africa were to witness its renaissance, it would require effort on the part of Africans.

Africa and the naysayers

Raise the issue of Africa and its developmental efforts, or current socio-political events in the region at most international forums and what you hear is a litany of problems, ranging from wars, drought, famine, corruption, beggarly states and governments who do not work, amongst others. Others have consistently depicted Africa negatively in print and in the media claiming that "Africa has no future"[3]. Even the *Economist*, a current affairs magazine out of London, in its May 13th issue of 2000 labelled Africa "The Hopeless Continent".[4] Lester Thurow, an economist at Massachusetts Institute of Technology (MIT), in his book, *Creating Wealth: The New Rules for Individuals, Companies and Countries in a Knowledge-Based Economy*, describes Africa as an "economic desert."[5] Victoria Brittain in the *New Statesmen and Society* painted a negative picture of Africa in her article "Africa, the lost continent".[6] There are so many of these pronouncements by these prophets of doom and gloom of Africa to mention here. In fact, this author had a discussion with a high official in one of the renowned international organisations about Africa a couple of years ago. This official remarked that if Africa fell off the face of the earth, nobody would notice. If one had to go by all these negative pronouncements, then it would be easy to write-off Africa as incapable of growth and development. But the "smart" peoples of the world know better than these "self-appointed apostles" of Africa, for most of them, their only knowledge of Africa is as deep as the casual impressions of tourists. The irony is that these are the same people who write about Africa with authority, speaking in numerous fora, in the media and in books about Africa, proclaiming to know Africa better than Africans. It is true that Africa has its share of problems just like any developing region of the world but to continue to paint a negative picture of the continent, making sweeping generalisations and off-the-cuff statements based upon a few incidents is disingenuous. The effect of such negative depiction of Africa on the psyche of Africans, on foreign direct investment and on the continent's efforts at growth and development cannot be emphasised enough.

Psychologically, the continuous negative portrayal of Africa and Africans could leave an indelible mark on their psyche, making them believe that they are indeed the "wretched of the earth". The continuous portrayal of Africans in such negativity could also become a self-fulfilling prophecy, dampening their enthusiasm and self-esteem. It could result in their ending up in not believing in themselves. Furthermore, such negative portrayal of Africa in the media has a negative impact on capital inflows to the region. For example, reference to Foreign Direct Investment (FDI) outflows from developed to developing countries since 1995 show that $90 billion in FDI has gone to developing countries like China, Singapore, Indonesia, Malaysia, Mexico, Brazil and Argentina.[7] In all, 52 per cent of all FDI go to East Asia, 29 per cent go to the whole of sub-Saharan Africa.[8] It would be safe to say that the continued negative portrayal of Africa as unstable, violent and a corrupt environment, have contributed to less capital flows to the region.

Why the naysayers are wrong

The current negative portrayal of Africa by many who insist that it is incapable of development[9] has been visited by most countries in Asia. Today, these countries are held out as economic success stories. For example, over thirty years ago, much of the world's misery was in Asia. During that time, India and Pakistan fought three wars, the Korean War was in 1950, as were many wars in Indochina. During this same time, Vietnam and Indonesia saw violent upheavals and internal instability; Thailand, Malaysia, Burma and the Philippines saw a lot of guerrilla insurrections, China under Chairman Mao Zedong saw brutality under the Red Guards in the mid-1960s, and in Cambodia, the Khmer Rouge, which is synonymous with "Killing Fields" wiped out over 20 per cent of the population of the country.[10] Why is such a reminder of Asia's instability over thirty years ago important? This is because, one can spot a similar trend in Africa and it is the political instability in some African countries that has given the naysayers a *carte blanche* so to speak, and to make sweeping generalisations about the future of Africa. Thus if the Asia of today has progressed from being regarded as an unstable region to an economically successful and stable region, then the naysayers are advised to consult history and to take into consideration Asia's experience before writing off Africa. Africa would also be able to shed its image as unstable and would prosper like Asia.

Economically, another interesting example we can draw from Asia is that around the 1950s and 1960s, there was nothing compelling about the economies in this region. They looked rather bleak with least promise. In fact, the economies in this region were written off as incapable of development. A Swedish author, Haken Hedberg, writing about Korea and its prospects for development at that time said it has "no future, full stop".[11] Hedberg's observation was circumscribed by his view of the economy of Korea and others in Asia at that time. For example, around 1969, Japan had a GDP per head of $380, South Korea in 1962 had a GDP per head of $110, Taiwan has a GDP per head of $160 and China in 1962 had a GDP per head of $60.[12] Today, before the Asian Financial Crisis of 1997-98, most economies in the region witnessed growth rates of over seven per cent with a high GDP per head. These high growth economies suddenly became "darlings" and were referred to as "Tiger Economies", "High Performing Asian Economies", "Newly Industrialised Countries", to mention just a few. These economies were written off a little over three decades ago just like how the Africa of today has been written off by the naysayers and so called "experts". The "Hedberg's" of today who consistently write off Africa as incapable of development and maintaining that it has no future are cautioned to consult history and to draw from Asia's experience. Africa is far more endowed than Asia and has the capability to grow and prosper more than Asia.

Besides, if economic history is anything to go by, the argument can be made that the economic performance of nations operate in cycles, so to speak. There are periods when nations can stagnate, regress or progress. For example, the early 20th Century saw none of the countries in Asia regarded amongst the top ten of the world's wealthiest. Britain at that time was the wealthiest in the world. At the end of the 20th century, three Asian countries were in this list. These included Singapore and Hong Kong that were all ahead of Britain- their colonial master. Singapore was second and Britain was 17th. Also, in 1955, Japan produced about 30,000 cars and the US seven million. By 1980, Japan had increased its wealth by eightfold through the export of cars and electronic products. Thus when Japan was prospering, America was in a recession. America's decline at that time elicited damning books by some of the Japanese elite. One of the most talked about at that time was a book titled: *The Japan That Can Say No*[13]. The book was basically bragging about the economic prosperity of Japan at that time and heaping scorn on America's decline. Ten years later, Japan fell into a recession, which continues even at the time of this writing. In 1999, Japan was third from the bottom of the OECD's table of growth in industrialised economies, registering a mere 0.2 per cent growth.[14] Today, the tables have been turned. America is prospering and Japan is mired in a spiral recession. It is also worth noting that at the beginning of the 20th century, China was definitely in a decline. Its economy was in a decline and around 1950, it had one of the worst living standards. Towards the end of the 20th century to the beginning of the 21st, it increased its per-capita GDP by about six times.[15] The importance of such an observation is to point to the fact that because Africa's socio-economic picture was not bright during the 20th century does not hold true that it would be the same in the 21st century. In fact, current signs and data from Africa indicate that the region is poised for its renaissance. Some of the fastest growing economies in the world today are in the region. Most of the countries in the region are undertaking the requisite reforms, which are turning their economies around. Stability is taking root as Africans find solutions to their own problems. From these numerous promises, there is reason to hope for Africa, that it would attain its renaissance. If such is the case, then the naysayers who claim that "Africa has no future" are wrong. They only need to open their eyes to the constant changes in the African landscape as it pertains to socio-economic and political renewals. Comparing current changes in Africa to its previous state of affairs, point to tremendous changes. Hence there is reason to hope for Africa's renaissance.

Reasons for hope

Today, the truth is that Africa is a region that is witnessing an upturn and Africans are taking their destiny into their own hands, charting the roads to their successful future and shattering old stereotypes by the Afro-pessimists. Barber B. Conable, a former President of the World Bank, addressing the 27th Session of the OAU in Abuja in Nigeria on June 4, 1991, pointed to some important reasons why there is hope for Africa in realising its renaissance. The first is that most countries in the region were barely a generation away from independence. Second, their colonial rulers bequeathed to them neither strong institutions nor educated citizenry, critical capacities for development. Despite such deficiencies, Africa has attained a lot in this short time. Africans have changed their attitude and approach towards economic policy making. This has led to the increase in productivity and growth in most countries in the region.[16] This gives reasons to hope.

Economically, African countries registered impressive growth rates in the 1990s. Several countries in the region attained and sustained double-digit growth. Real GDP growth in Africa in the second half of the 1990s averaged 4 per cent per year. This exceeded the continent's population growth of 2.8 per cent a year. Export growth doubled to 80 per cent a year and real GDP grew by 2.3 per cent in 1999, up from 3.1 per cent in 1998. No country in the region experienced a negative GDP growth in 1999 and only one posted a growth rate of less than 1 per cent. In 1999, 19 countries had growth rates between zero and 2.9 per cent, another 17 clustered between 3 and 4.9 per cent, and 12 had growth rates of between 5 per cent and 6.9 per cent (Table 1)[17]. Mozambique and Equatorial Guinea recorded the highest growth rates: 10 per cent. East and Southern Africa, which together account for 45 per cent of the region's population and 37 per cent of GDP enjoyed a faster growth in 1999 (Table 2). These promising economic data are reasons to hope for Africa.

Table 1: Distribution of African Countries by real GDP growth 1995-99
(number of countries)

Growth rate (Per cent)	1995	1996	1997	1998	1999
Negative	6	2	4	2	0
0-2.9	11	12	12	13	19
3-4.9	23	28	25	28	17
5-6.9	6	9	10	8	12
7 and above	7	2	2	2	5
Total	53	53	53	53	53

Source: Economic Commission for Africa

From the above table, one can see a gradual growth in African economies from six countries, which had a negative growth in 1995 to zero with a negative growth rate in 1999. It is equally striking that in 1995, only six countries in the region had a growth rate of 5-6.9 per cent. In contrast, 12 had such a growth rate in 1999. The point worth making here is that the economies in the region are on the mend and offers a reason for hope.

Table 2: Economic growth in Africa by region, 1998 and 1999

	Mean	Standard Deviation	Med	Mean	Standard Deviation	Med
North	4.4	2.1	4.5	3.6	1.8	2.6
West	3.6	1.4	4.5	3.3	1.8	4.5
Central	5.0	4.2	5.5	4.5	2.7	4.8
East	2.6	2.2	3.0	4.1	2.4	3.0
Southern	1.7	2.4	4.5	2.2	3.0	4.0
Africa	3.1	2.5	4.0	3.2	2.3	4.0

Source: Economic Commission for Africa

Another reason to hope for Africa is exemplified by GDP growth of a landlocked country like Botswana. Botswana's GDP has risen from $350 per capita in 1981 to $3,350 today. Botswana can thus be said to be richer than some countries in South East Asia like the Philippines, Thailand or Indonesia. Between 1970 and 1995 for example, Botswana's average annual growth rate was 7.3 per cent.[18] Furthermore, Southern Africa, once a war-torn area is now also enjoying significant growth. Since 1996, all the countries in the Southern African Development Community (SADC) saw an average growth in their GDP of over 6 per cent. Such GDP growth would not have been heard of right after independence. These promising growth rates are all reasons to hope.

Furthermore, the new thinking emerging in Africa today amongst its new leadership, as it pertains to concerted effort and the willingness to confront their own problems and find workable solutions to them, is refreshing. Indeed the commonly held view amongst the African leadership of today is that Africans must find African solutions to African problems. President Yoweri Museveni of Uganda put it best when he said, "Africans must liberate themselves from themselves."[19] The arrival of Africans at such a view in itself is a milestone. It used to be that major decisions about the continent were made for them in capitals far away as Moscow, Washington, D.C., London, Brussels or Paris. This was more pronounced during the era of the Cold War when the Cold War combatants divided African countries into spheres of influence. The end of the Cold War has culminated with the abandonment of Africa, politically and economically, so to speak. Suddenly, issues and problems of former client states were no longer of immediate importance. In fact, they became a burden. Any talk about aiding Africa is met with frowns and degrading remarks and an attitude of disconnect.[20] It has made Africans to realise that no one, no matter how well intentioned, would like Africans more than they like themselves, and would do for them what they should be doing for themselves. Hence this new willingness to "do for themselves". Such a change in perception in itself is a paradigm shift from the "beggar" mentality that most countries in the region had been known for.

A good example of such African self-help is the intervention of the ECOWAS Cease-fire Monitoring Group (ECOMOG) to halt the crises in Liberia (1989-1998) and Sierra Leone (1991-1999). Later with the help of United Nations troops deplored alongside ECOMOG troops, peace has been brought to Sierra Leone.[21] Elsewhere, when Guinea Bissau was in crises, the Community of Lusophone Countries (CPLP) and the Economic Community of West African States (ECOWAS) came together to broker a successful cease-fire between the parties to the conflict and brought peace back to Guinea Bissau on July 27, 1998. It proves the capability of Africans finding lasting solutions to African problems. It offers hope and the belief that Africans can find lasting solutions to the problems of instability on the continent. Early efforts in this vein were when Tanzania sent troops into Uganda to stop the brutality and mayhem of Idi Amin in 1979. Also, it was with the help of military and financial support from Uganda and Rwanda that the Alliance of Democratic Forces for the Liberation of the Congo under the leadership of the late Laurent Kabila that the long-time dictator of the former Zaire, Mobutu Sese Seko was removed from power.[22] There are of course those who may argue that African countries have no right to intervene in the affairs of other sovereign African countries. Such "non-interference" was outlined in the charter of the former Organisation of the African Unity (OAU). But one can argue that African countries have the right and moral imperative to intervene to quell crises in neighbouring countries when they see it as a just cause. No one can argue against the fact that when instability arises in one African country that the numerous refugees it creates usually find refuge in neighbouring African countries. The ensuing consequence and cost to those neighbouring countries, politically, economically, socially cannot be emphasised enough. For example, most of the refugees caused by the instability in Sierra Leone and Liberia sought refuge in Guinea and in other neighbouring West African countries. Similarly, most of the refugees from the prolonged war in Angola found refuge in other South African Development Community countries.

There are so many examples that point to why there are so many reasons to hope for Africa's renaissance. Two more examples will suffice. The protracted war in Mozambique brought so much suffering and destruction to the people of the country. In fact, at one point, Mozambique was one of the poorest countries in the world and was written off as another African basket case. Today, the war is over and the government has been able to absorb over 95,000 demobilised soldiers and over five million refugees into the society.[23] The Economist Intelligent Unit, a sister company of the *Economist* magazine, reported that Mozambique was the fastest growing economy in the world in 2000.[24] Mozambique's economy grew at an astonishing rate of 12 per cent in 1998 and nine per cent in 1999. Growth of money slowed in the country from over 70 per cent in 1992 to less than 17 per cent in 1998.

Sound monetary policies introduced have helped to lower inflation in the country from 50 per cent in 1998 to less than two per cent in 1999. Despite the devastating floods that hit the country in February and March of 2000, the economic forecast still looks good. The economy is projected to grow again to about 10 per cent in 2001/02 and to an average of six per cent through 2005.[25]

Finally, the most important reason to hope in an African renaissance is depicted by the experience of South Africa. For all purposes and from the predictions of the prophets of doom and gloom, particularly those harping on the demise of Africa; South Africa would have descended into chaos under black majority role. It was also predicted that the black majority would seek revenge against the white South Africans who ruled them oppressively for many years. Many were those who predicted that Nelson Mandela who was jailed for 23 years by the apartheid regime of South Africa would seek revenge by directing his rage at the white South Africans when he took over power as the first black president. Such a negative picture and alarmist predictions forced many white South Africans to flee the country in fear. When the black majority won the first multiracial elections in the country, Nelson Mandela did not seek revenge as was predicted; neither did the black South Africans seek revenge on their fellow white South Africans. Instead a government of national unity was formed and Bishop Desmond Tutu's Truth and Reconciliation Commission offered amnesty to all South Africans who came forward to tell the truth about their actions during the apartheid years. This is now copied all over the world, especially in other areas that had a violent and painful past of human suffering, and man's inhumanity to man. The example of South Africa, as a beacon of hope for racial harmony in the world speaks for the African renaissance. It is a reason to hope for Africa, that despite the loud negative pronouncements by the naysayers, Africa will witness its renaissance.

African Renaissance: Challenges

The recent positive developments, economically and politically on the continent point to an emerging Africa, an Africa that is going to realise its renaissance. We are seeing renewed efforts to move to popularly elected democratic governments in most African countries. At the time of this writing, most of the countries in Africa have reverted to democratically elected governments after decades of rule by the military or by totalitarian governments. Even though there have been complaints that point to the imperfection of some of the multiparty elections on the continent, the mere fact that majority of the countries now see that as a way of choosing their leaders is a step in the right direction[26].

Economically, most of the economies in Africa are on the rebound after years of stagnation as already pointed out in this paper. Despite external shocks that are beyond the control of most of the economies in the region, the signs that point to the potential for economic growth in these countries are huge. Most importantly, there is the arrival on the African political scene of a new breed of leaders, who are different from the post-colonial leaders/crooks and tyrants like Mobutu Sese Seko, Idi Amin, Marcias Ngeuma, Jean Bedel Bokassa, and many of their ilk commonly referred to by Basil Davidson as "Pirates in Power".[27] This new leadership, which I would call *Nouveau Dirigeant* (New Directors), are questioning Africa's own role in its underdevelopment, and breaking away from unworkable formulas as well as the culture of blame to charting a sustainable future for Africa.

With all these positive signs showing that Africa is witnessing a renaissance, the question some may ask is whether all the countries in Africa would witness this renaissance at the same time? The answer is not far-fetched. At the macro-level, African countries realise that to survive in a continuous global environment that they must change. The new leadership also realises that they cannot fight today's battles with yesterday's weapons. Thus, they have no choice but to change. At the micro-level, some African countries would realise their renaissance earlier than others. As in Asia, not all the countries in the region witness the "miracle" at the same time. Countries like Indonesia, Philippines, Vietnam, and Cambodia to mention a few are latecomers. In Africa, just as in Asia, there are going to be first, second and third wave countries arriving at the finishing line.

Despite the optimism expressed in this chapter for the African renaissance, there are numerous challenges that need to be overcome for such a renaissance to be attained and sustained. First, the new African leadership and the African people in general must unite. Three aspects of such unity are envisioned. The first is unity in vision. African people and their leaders must have a clear vision of where they want their countries to be in the future, say the year 2050 for example, a farsighted vision for the type of development they seek for themselves. Such a vision would serve as a road map, so to speak, that would help in the development of specific goals and plans for the development of their individual countries and the continent. A complimentary component of a unified vision is having the requisite political will to conceive and develop effective policies and sticking with them when they are implemented to reach desired goals. Waffling, withdrawing well-thought-out policy plans due to pressure from one ethnic group or a privileged class within the country, should be a thing of the past. That there is the need for some amount of flexibility when policies are developed and implemented are understandable. If the requisite policies are for the common good, then the new leadership in Africa should not compromise or give in to any opposition from a vocal but privileged minority.

The second challenge is that of a unified economic vision. More than 45 years has passed since the first African country attained its political independence. Yet, their economic independence eludes them. Africans and their leaders must develop a unified economic vision to move their people up from "mat to mattresses". Such an economic vision should take the form of developing a continental African market by eliminating all trade barriers amongst African countries. There should be an effort to move towards the use of a single currency for trade amongst African countries. Such a currency should be different from their local currencies. This single currency should be convertible to any of the local currencies and its management should be under the control of an African Central Bank (ACB), a central bank to all the central banks in all the African countries. It could take the form of the European Central Bank but with an African focus and ideal. For example, the European System of Central Banks (ESCB) is composed of the European Central Bank (ECB) and the national central banks of all the 15 European Union member states. The national central banks who have not adopted the Euro, however are members of the ESCB with a special status, thus while they are allowed to conduct their respective national monetary policies, they do not take part in decision-making with regard to the single monetary policies of the community. The basic tasks to be carried out by the ECB are: to define and implement the monetary policy of the Euro area; to conduct foreign exchange operations; to hold and manage the official foreign reserves of the member states; and to promote the smooth operation of payments systems.[28] The establishment of an ACB would help expand trade between African countries, which is currently at a very low level. There must also be a unified economic vision to diversify their economies. A concerted effort must be made to move away from the sole reliance on the export of primary products and mineral resources. The danger of such reliance is because of the fluctuations in the prices of such products on the world market. It does make it difficult to come up with realistic budgets to undertake development projects. Thus these countries must diversify their economies to include non-traditional goods, manufactures, value-added goods and services as part of their export mix. This would help them counteract depressed prices for their primary products and declining revenues for their principal exports.

But a unified vision to diversify the economy alone is not enough. Africans and the new leadership must also develop a unified vision of undertaking and implementing effective macroeconomic reforms. These would include a concerted effort to reduce fiscal deficits, current account and capital expenditure imbalances, exchange rate stabilisation, the elimination of price controls and distortions as well as the reduction in inflation. Such macroeconomic reforms would help stabilise African economies and help them to be more responsive to constantly changing conditions in today's global economy.

Finally, the important challenge is that of the vision of a politically unified Africa. It is true that most African countries have attained their political independence, but to be able to survive and prosper in an increasingly globalised world, where strong alliances are now the order of the day, no single independent African country, no matter how well endowed, is versatile enough to go it alone. Kwame Nkrumah, the first president of Ghana, trumpeted this important challenge to Africa's economic development. In one of his speeches as a seminal voice on this issue to his fellow African leaders, he said:

> I can see no security for African states unless African leaders, like us, have realised beyond all doubt that salvation for Africa lies in unity . . . for in unity lies strength, and as I see it, African states must unite or sell themselves to imperialist and colonialist exploiters for a mess of pottage, or disintegrate individually.[29]

Why is such a call by Nkrumah important? It is because the economic and political independence of Africa lie in its economic and political unity. Africans would be unable to attain their economic progress without political unity and vice versa. According to Nkrumah, if Africa's "economic unity is going to be effective, it must be accompanied by political unity. The two are inseparable, each necessary for the future greatness of our continent and the full development of our resources."[30] This call by Nkrumah is important if one can draw briefly from the European Union as an example. The European Union owes its evolution to developments in Europe right after World War II, as a result of a revulsion against national rivalries and parochial loyalties. The idea of a united Europe grew out of such revulsion, but also it was believed that a united Europe was the best way to prevent another war and the best way to strengthen European security. Thus in 1950, Robert Schuman, the French foreign minister at that time, proposed that the coal and steel industries of France and West Germany be put together under a single supranational authority. In 1952, Belgium, Luxembourg, the Netherlands and Italy joined to form the ECSC. Later the European Community (EC) (informally known as the Common Market in 1980s) and the European Atomic Energy Community (EURATOM) were established in 1958. The Brussels Treaty of 1965 saw the merger of these organisations into what became known as the EC. In November 1993 in Maastricht, the Netherlands, the Treaty of the European Union or the Maastricht Treaty to form the European Community (EC) was signed. The European Union is now an economic and political confederation of European nations, and other organisations that are responsible for a common foreign and security policy and for co-operation on justice and home affairs.[31]

A unified political vision for Africa would entail several diversified fronts. The first would be the establishment of a unified military and defence strategy. This will entail the combining of the military resources of the various countries to enable Africa provide a united front against a common enemy. Nkrumah had earlier called for the establishment of an African High Command as a way for Africans to develop a unified military front. I suggest that today, any such unified defence and military strategy fall under the umbrella of an African Security and Defence Initiative (ASDI). This proposed ASDI's mandate should include peace-building and peacekeeping operations in the region, rapid response to external attacks, joint military interventions in trouble spots in Africa, security consultation and training amongst others[32]. A unified African political vision would also have as one of its strategies the establishment of a unified foreign and diplomatic policy. It will enable Africans speak with one voice in global fora. The current cacophony of voices by African countries with divergent views and interest at international fora do not in anyway benefit the region. Without a unified voice, it is much easier to squash the views of each individual country at such fora as unimportant. At the end of the day, the whole of Africa loses.

All such goals and ideals for the African renaissance are fleeting if we pay just lip service to them. Holding conferences to exchange views and engaging in dialogue on the way forward for Africa are laudable. However, when such ideas, speeches and decisions agreed on at these conferences, workshops, or whatever they are called are not implemented, they become just "talk shops." Furthermore, if the numerous reports generated from these fora are not applied, they become just another report to be filed and put away on a library shelve as a reference item, the African renaissance would be an illusion. We must see to it that African policy makers implement some of the progressive decisions that come out of these conferences and workshops[33]. By implementing them, we can learn from our successes and failures and that in itself is the way forward. We would make sure not to repeat those mistakes again.

It's up to us

At the end of the day, when all is said and done, others may sympathise and empathise and even drop us a few crumbs, euphemistically speaking, but they cannot do for Africa what it can do for itself. To earn our place in the sun and our renaissance, we must toil; to sweet, we must sweat. The words of Frederick Douglas, an African-American abolitionist, are poignant here our destiny is largely in our hands. If we find we shall have to seek. If we succeed in the race for life it must be by our own energies, and our own exertions. Others may clear the road, but we must go forward or be left behind in the race for life. If we remain poor and dependent, the wealth of others will not avail us. If we are ignorant, the intelligence of others will do but little for us. If we are wasteful of our time and money, the economy of others will only make destitution the more disgraceful.[34]

Similarly, the destiny of Africa and its renaissance is in the hand of Africans, if Africans are to find they must seek. If they are going to succeed, it must be through their own sweat and toil. To believe that others would toil for us is an illusion. Yes, other countries might lend a helping here and there, but we must be willing to take advantage of any such help or it shall never come again. If we continue to waste our meagre resources on petty issues and battles without any concrete developmental trajectory, we shall reap a harvest of pain and suffering. Fredrick Douglas again says it best, "the history of civilisations show that no people can well rise to a high degree of mental or even moral excellence without wealth. A people uniformly poor and compelled to struggle for barely a physical existence will be dependent and despised by their neighbours and will finally despise themselves." Frankly therefore, if Africa is to attain its renaissance, it is solely up to us. So what should Africans do?

The first place to begin is to examine our attitudes. Our attitudes would determine our developmental attitudes. But there is overwhelming evidence to support the premise that the success of any people results more from certain mental traits and personality characteristics that are commonly known as attitudes. Attitudes are the result of choices we make, these include decisions about what to believe or disbelieve with respect to our lives. From the foregoing, it can be safely said that the achiever is not born but is self-made.[35] Similarly, great and prosperous nations of today were not born; they evolved through concerted effort and struggle. Africa can realise its renaissance, that it becomes a reality is entirely up to us. We must develop new attitudes, those that are ambitious and devoid of backward thinking. We must subscribe to Nkrumah's dictum of "forward ever and backwards never". The suffocating attitudes of greed, the siphoning of Africa's meagre resources into Swiss and foreign bank accounts, without putting it to good use for the benefit of the people must be a thing of the past. The billions of dollars looted by the late Sani Abacha of Nigeria and stashed in foreign banks is a case in point. The current government of Nigeria is frustrated in efforts to repatriate these monies from western banks[36]. The attitude of petty squabbling, wars and an eye for an eye has kept Africa blind for decades, resulting in it missing numerous developmental opportunities. These should be a thing of the past.

For Africa to realise its renaissance, it must think big. Such big thinking must be accompanied by "a can do" attitude and the willingness of most countries in the region to move out of their comfort zones. Such cannot happen if Africans continue to fear and see themselves in a negative and inferior light. The story of the scared mouse is worth recounting here. Once, a mouse scurried near the house of a magician. This mouse, because of its constant fear of a cat, was always in distress. The magician took pity on the mouse and turned it into a cat. Just as soon as it was turned into a cat, it started suffering from the fear of a dog. The magician again took pity and turned it into a dog. Then it began to suffer from the fear of a tiger. It was then turned into a tiger and it started to suffer from the fear of a hunter. The magician turned it back into a mouse in disgust[37]. The rationale of this story is that as long as Africans think small and act small, fear and are afraid to bite the bullet and take their destiny into their hands, so to speak, and stand up and be counted, they would forever act small. Metaphorically, the actions of Africans and African countries should speak with pride and dignity for Africans. If not, they would be regarded as such - less important in the scheme of global affairs.

The next is the need to have a sense of purpose. Africans must spell out concisely, what the region, each country, leader and politician, and individuals hope and aspire for. That hope and purpose would create the enthusiasm that would drive them to attain the necessary goals. Without enthusiasm, nothing can be attained. This should be coupled with honesty and trust. For Africa to attain its renaissance, honest and trust must prevail amongst its people, between its people and leaders, between different ethnic groups and between Africans and other peoples of the world. Honesty and trust is the glue that holds every block in the development puzzle together. It is the basis for successful businesses and enterprises as well as for sustainable relations. Writing on the importance of trust in his book, *Trust: The Social Virtues and the Creation of Prosperity*, Francis Fukuyama argues that it is only in those societies with a high degree of social trust which will be able to create flexible, large-scale business organisations needed to be able to successfully compete in a global economy[38].

We must also begin to develop our own economic power base just like how other regions and countries around the world have done. Until we do that, there is no compelling reason why others should deal with us as equals. The current talk about China and its potential role as an economic giant is a case in point. This writer remembers vividly a little over a decade ago, goods from China were regarded as inferior; today nobody talks about that. The same applied to Korea and Japan. A superpower like America is forced to deal with these countries because of their economic muscle. One of the ways of building an African economic muscle is to develop a Capital Market Strategy, where Africa Inc. should be developed to buy huge shares in some of the large companies around the world. It would offer Africans say in the way they are run and would shape how these companies affect African interest. If this proposed Africa Inc. were to own majority shares in such companies, it would be able to help bring about the transfer of technologies to African countries and affect the way these companies deal with other countries. This strategy can also be pursued by the different economic groupings in the region or by individual countries. For example, the purchase of Lotus by the government of Malaysia enabled the country to develop its own national automobile, the Proton. Technology transfer from Lotus has contributed to this effort.

Finally, for Africa to find its place in the sun and to realise its renaissance, we must dare to invent the future, Africa's future that is. According to the late Thomas Sankara of Burkina Faso, we must have the courage to turn our backs on old formulas that have not worked. To do that, "we have to work at decolonising our mentality and achieving happiness within the limits of sacrifices we should be willing to make[39]." To dare to invent Africa's future is not going to be an easy task. The going will be rough and friends are going to be few. Furthermore, mistakes are going to be made and there would be the wish that we never started on such a tough journey. But as Nkrumah said in his *Motion of Destiny* speech:

"doubtless, we shall make mistakes as has all other nations. We are human beings and hence fallible. But we can try also to learn from the mistakes of others so that we may avoid the deepest pitfalls into which they have fallen. Moreover, the mistakes we may make will be our own mistakes, and it will be our responsibility to put them right. As long as we are ruled by others we shall lay our mistakes at their door, and our sense of responsibility will remain dulled. Freedom brings responsibilities and our experience can be enriched only by the acceptance of these responsibilities."[40]

Despite the hurdles and obstacles ahead, Africans must persist in their efforts to attain their renaissance. It is only persistence that is going to serve as a bulwark against failure. President Calvin Coolidge, the 30th president of the United States remark about persistence is worth recounting here: "nothing in the world can take the place of persistence. Talent will not; nothing is more common than unsuccessful men with talent. Genius will not; unrewarded genius is almost a proverb. Education will not; the world is full of educated derelicts. Persistence, determination and hard work alone make the difference." It is therefore up to us to realise the African renaissance, Africans must persist against all odds.

Conclusion

Africa has come a long way. It has survived colonial domination, to post-colonial misrule and now a new era of the *Nouveau Dirigeant*. Most countries in the region have undertaken macroeconomic reforms and the economies are looking up. There is generally a feeling of hope amongst the people of Africa, a hope in an African renaissance. This feeling has not been talked about or written about enough. This chapter hopes to add to the minority voices in this area. Yet, the chapter holds no illusion that the attainment of the African renaissance is going to be a breeze. Far from that, it would require tremendous effort and the willingness to learn from the past and the mistakes made in the past. The chapter has also pointed out that there are going to be hurdles on the way of Africa attaining its renaissance. It is the current willingness on the part of Africans and the *Nouveau Dirigeant* that gives a reason for hope in the African renaissance.

This chapter shares the same optimism of the African renaissance and has offered tangible and visible signs in the region that point to such. It has thus shown why the naysayers, who are preoccupied with the doom and gloom of Africa are wrong. The chapter has also pointed to some of the challenges that Africa would face as it moves towards it renaissance and have offered some solutions to some of these challenges. The major concern of this author is that if Africans stand in their own way, it would be hard to attain the renaissance. Henry David Thoreau once said that, "if a man stands in his way, everything seems to be in his way." Africans can stand in their own way with petty squabbles, instability, myopic thinking, lack of vision and effort, and all that has been mentioned in the latter part of this chapter. We must therefore not stand in our own way, we must be willing to embrace change, employ effort, committed to creating a better future for the next generation of Africans. No one is going to do that for us. If Africa is to realise its renaissance, frankly it is totally and entirely up to us.

References

"A Survey of Asia,"in *The Economist*, October 30, 1993, p.6

Abdulai, David N. *African Renaissance: Challenges, Solutions and the Road Ahead*, (London: ASEAN Academic Press, 2001)

----------------------, "Rawlings 'wins' Ghana's presidential elections: Establishing a new constitutional order," *Africa Today*, Vol. 41, No.3, pp. 66-71

Bleakley, Fred., "Developing world gets more investments," *Wall Street Journal*, December 15, 1995, p.A12

Brittain, Victoria., "Africa the lost continent," *New Statesmen and Society*, April 8, 1994, pp. 20-22

Davidson, Basil., *The Black Man's Burden: Africa and the Curse of the Nation-State*, (New York: Times Books, 1991)

Diamond, Larry., "The new wind," in *Africa Report*, September-October 1994, p.51

Economic Commission for Africa, *Transforming Africa's Economies: Overview*, (Addis Ababa, Ethiopia: Economic Commission for Africa, 2001)

"European Union: Evolution,"(see the website below)

http//:www.encyclopedia.com/articles/04281Evolution.html

"Foreign direct Investment in Africa is lagging, despite good returns, U.N. Report says," *Wall Street Journal*, July 14, 1995

French, Howard., "Africa takes care of crisis on its own once again," *New York Times*, June 9, 1997, p.A6

Fukuyama, Francis., *Trust: The Social Virtues and the Creation of Prosperity*, (New York: The Free Press, 1995)

Gourevitch, Philip., "Letter from the Congo: A Continental Shift," *The New Yorker*, August 4, 1997, pp. 44-52

Kimboro, Dennis P. and Napolean Hill, *Think and Grow Rich: A Black Choice*, (New York: Fawcett Crest, 1992)

----------------------, *What Makes the Great Great*, (New York: Doubleday, 1997)

"Lions 3, tigers 1," The *Economist*, January 22, 2000, p.75

Madavo, Callisto., "Stand back and take a more positive look at Africa," *International Herald Tribune*, June 6, 2000, p.8

McGeary, Johanna and Marguerite Michaels, "Africa Rising," *Time*, March 30, 1998, pp. 34-46

----------------------, "African for Africa," *Time*, September 1, 1997, pp.36-40

Morita, Akio., and Shintaro Ishihara., *The Japan that Can Say "No"*, (Washington, D.C.: The Jefferson Educational Foundation, 1990)

Morias, Richard C., "Africa: the untold story," *Forbes*, November 17, 1997, p.88

Naipul, V.S., "Africa has no future," *New York Times Book Review*, May 15, 1997, p.36

Nkrumah, Kwame., *Africa Must Unite*, (New York: Frederick Praeger, 1964)

----------------------, *Neo-Colonialism: The Last Stage of Imperialism*, (London: Heinemann, 1965)

----------------------, "The Motion of Destiny" Speech, delivered by Kwame Nkrumah before the Gold Coast (Ghana) House of Assembly, July 10, 1953

Ong, Timothy., "Back to the future," *Asia-Inc.*, August 2001, p.4

"Organisation of the European System of Central Banks,"

http://www.ecb.int/about/escb.htm

Robinson, Randall., *Defending the Spirit: A Black Life in America*, (New York: Dutton, 1998)

"The Hopeless Continent," The *Economist*, May 13-19, 2000, pp. Cover, 15, 20-22

Thomas Sankara Speaks, (New York: Pathfinder Press, 1988)

Thurow, Lester: *Creating Wealth: The New Rules for Individuals, Companies and Countries in a Knowledge-Based Economy*, (London: Nicholas Brealey, 1999)

"Western banks still keep Abacha's billions," *New African*, November 2001, pp.10-11

Woronoff, Jon., *Korea's Economy: Man-Made Miracle*, (Seoul, Korea: Si-Sa-Yong-o-sa Publications, 1983)

Seidman, Ann., and Frederick Anang., *Twenty-First-Century Africa: Towards a New Vision of Self-Sustainable Development*, (Trenton, New Jersey: Africa World Press, 1992)

Endnotes

[1] "Us" as used here refers to Africans, Africans in the Diaspora, and people of African descent, Africanists and friends of Africa.

[2] Callisto Madavo, "Stand back and take a more positive look at Africa," *International Herald Tribune*, June 6, 2000, p.8

[3] V.S. Naipul, "Africa has no future," *New York Times Book Review*, May 15, 1979, p.36

[4] "The Hopeless Continent," The *Economist*, May 13-19, 2000, pp. Cover, 15, 20-22

[5] Lester Thurow, *Creating Wealth: The New Rules for Individuals, Companies and Countries in a Knowledge-Based Economy* (London: Nicholas Brealey Publishing, 1999), p. 35

[6] Victoria Brittain, "Africa, the lost continent," *New Statesmen and Society*, April 8, 1994, pp. 20-22

[7] Fred Bleakley, "Developing world gets more investments," *Wall Street Journal*, December 15, 1995, p. A12a

[8] "Foreign direct investment in Africa is lagging, despite good returns, U.N. report says," *Wall Street Journal*, July 14, 1995

[9] For more on this issue, see, "Africa has no future?," in David N. Abdulai, *African Renaissance: Challenges, Solutions and the Road Ahead*, (London: ASEAN Academic Press, 2001), pp. 25-33

[10] "A Survey of Asia," The *Economist*, October 30, 1993, p.6

[11] Jon Woronoff, *Korea's Economy: Man-Made Miracle* (Seoul, Korea: Si-Sa-Yong-O-Sa Publishers, 1983) p.12

[12] Ibid, "A Survey of Asia."

[13] Akio Morita and Shintaro Ishihara, *The Japan That Can Say "NO"*, (Washington, D.C.: The Jefferson Educational Foundation, 1990)

[14] Timothy Ong, "Back to the future," *Asia-Inc*, August 2001, p.4

[15] Ibid

[16] David N. Abdulai, *African Renaissance: Challenges, Solutions and the Road Ahead*, (London: ASEAN Academic Press, 2001), p.3

[17] Economic Commission for Africa, *Transforming Africa's Economies:Overview*, (Addis Ababa, Ethiopia: ECA, 2001), pp.1-3

[18] Richard C. Morias, "Africa: the untold story," *Forbes*, November 17, 1997, p.88

[19] Johanna McGeary, "African for Africa," *Time*, September 1, 1997, pp.36-40

[20] Randall Robinson, *Defending the Spirit: A Black Life in America* (New York: Dutton, 1998)

[21] Howard W. French, "Africa takes care of crisis on its own once again," *New York Times*, June 9, 1997, p.A6

[22] Philip Gourevitch, "Letter from the Congo: A continental Shift," *The New Yorker*, August 4, 1997, pp. 42-52

23 Johanna McGeary and Marguerite Michaels. "Africa Rising," *Time*, March 30, 1998, pp.34-46

24 "Lions 3, tigers 1," The *Economist*, January 22, 2000, p.75

25 Ibid, *Transforming Africa's Economies: Overview*, p.3

26 David Abdulai, "Rawlings 'wins' Ghana's presidential elections: Establishing a new constitutional order," *Africa Today*, Vol. 41, No. 3, pp. 66-71; Also see, Larry Diamond, "The new wind," *Africa Report*, September-October 1994, p.51

27 Basil Davidson, *The Black Man's Burden: Africa and the Curse of the Nation-State*, (New York: Times Books, 1991), pp. 243-265

28 "Organisation of the European System of Central Banks," http://www.ecb.int/about/escb.htm

29 Kwame Nkrumah, *Africa Must Unite* (New York: Frederick Praeger, 1964), p. 145

30 Kwame Nkrumah, *Neo-Colonialism: The Last Stage of Imperialism*, (London: Heinemann, 1965), p. 30

31 "European Union: Evolution," http://www.encyclopedia.com/articles/04281Evolution.html

32 Ibid, *African Renaissance: Challenges, Solutions and the Road Ahead*, p. 132

33 Ann Seidman and Frederick Anang, *Twenty-First-Century Africa: Towards a New Vision of Self-Sustainable Development*, (Trenton, New Jersey: Africa World Press, 1992), pp. 1-4

34 Cited in Dennis P. Kimbro and Napolean Hill, *Think and Grow Rich: A Black Choice* (New York: Fawcett Crest, 1992), pp. 185-6

35 Dennis P. Kimbro, *What Makes the Great Great*, (New York: Doubleday, 1997), p.19

36 "Western banks still keep Abacha's billions," *New African*, November 2001, pp.10-11

37 Ibid, p.97

38 Francis Fukuyama, *Trust: The Social Virtues and the Creation of Prosperity* (New York: The Free Press, 1995).

39 *Thomas Sankara Speaks*, (New York: Pathfinder Press, 1988), p.117

40 Kwame Nkrumah, "The Motion of Destiny," From a speech by Kwame Nkrumah arguing for independence for the Gold Coast (Ghana) before the Gold Coast House of Assembly, July 10, 1953.

9

The Power of Logo:
The implication of the Chinese
Revolution for Pan-Africanism

Xing Li

Introduction

China and Africa

In the 1840s, the Sino-British Opium Wars ended with China's defeat. The *Treaty of Nanjing* forced China to pay a huge indemnity to Britain for the cost of the war and imposed on China a tariff on all imported goods. The Chinese civilisation was greatly contested and challenged when the static Chinese feudal system gradually collapsed. Unlike the downfall of previous dynasties, which did not inflict any obvious damage to the Chinese way of life and the identity of Chinese culture, the decline of the Manchus Dynasty had the whole civilisation facing collapse. The causes of the decline were both multiple and complex. There were certainly a number of domestic socio-economic factors as well as external forces, which contributed to this state of affairs.

The consequences of the Opium War to China were very damaging: Traditional tributaries were taken away; concessions to foreign privileges were made; the authority of the emperor, upon which the Chinese order was based, was ended; the hand-labour-based industries on which the Chinese economy depended upon were destroyed; and the favourable balance of trade, which existed until 1830 and which had brought an uninterrupted flow of silver from the outside, became lopsided (Kapur,1987:2). Indeed, China became an international colony. The traditional social structure was finally broken down. China's customs and post offices were largely controlled by Westerners. Western ships were permitted to navigate freely on its waters, and even to demolish some of its coastal defence; many Western troops were stationed at a number of points on a permanent basis; pieces of territory in various parts of the country were taken over as concessions. China was thus divided by Western powers as "spheres of interest" and was "carved up like a melon." This situation was very similar to what colonialism had once done to Africa.

Since the beginning of the 20th century, never before in history, had the Chinese society been so radically transformed in so short time. China underwent more thorough and dramatic changes than any other country in the world. Its state and society transformed were from an imperial monarchy to a short-lived republic; from a weak and decentralised warlord authoritarianism to a centralised revolutionary socialist state. Economically it went from a state-led industrialisation based on planned economy and socialist egalitarianism to an all-round structural reform based on market mechanisms. The economy underwent repeated shift from crisis and failure to very rapid growth and modernisation. Politically the Chinese society and people experienced imperialism and warlordism as well as dictatorship and class struggle. Ideologically the Chinese value systems underwent transformations from feudalism to socialism and from collectivism to individualism. For more than a century, generations of Chinese revolutionaries have been striving to find answers to the dazzling puzzles of war and peace, national liberation and independence, development of productive forces and human capacities, self-reliance and equality.

The search to ensure its existence as a prosperous, strong nation and political entity has been a key concern in China's modern history. Seeking a way for the transformation and revival of the Chinese nation, Mao Zedong and the Chinese Communist Party eventually found elements of an answer in Marxist philosophy and revolutionary worldview to deal with the scope of the challenge and the pressures from internal and external forces. Depending on how one assesses its successes and failures, China was characterised as historically unique experiment to skip over the stage of capitalism and to bring about a socialist transformation of both the social structure and the consciousness of the people (Li, 1998).

Today, China is struggling to probe its own way to find an industrialisation path to develop the nation into a prosperous great power while adjusting the Chinese society strategically and practically to the existing capitalist world. A difficult task facing the Chinese people is how to promote wealth-creating aspects of the market economy while restraining its socially polarising tendencies as well as its ecological destruction (Li, 1999).

If we take the case of continental Africa, one can argue Africa and Africans have not so far "developed". Contemporary Africa is beset with difficulties rooted in its inability to unite territorially, politically and economically. The consequences have been national economies incapable of developing because of geographical, economic and political reasons. Africa has been constantly beset with underdevelopment, poverty, diseases, endless border wars, economic domination and the dictatorship of the IMF and the World Bank.

Today, the continent is the most oppressed and exploited, the most marginalised and debt-ridden, the most impoverished and war-worn, and the most corrupt and diseased one in the world. Despite its abundant resources not only is Africa considered to be the least industrialised of all the developing regions, it also accounts for more than half of the world's economic and war refugees. The African socio-political landscape has been widely described or perceived to be one full of political oppressions, human rights abuses, continuous ethnic, racial, regional and religious conflicts, endless military coups, and high illiteracy. After all, it is doomed to be a "hopeless continent" (*The Economist*, May 13, 2000). As one scholar describes:

The fact is that over the decades that Africa became independent, none of its languages, literatures, institutions, religions and systems of thought have had any impact on the social, political, economic and technological experience imposed on the continent. Islam and Christianity are recognised as religions in all Constitutions, but no African religion gets that place since anthropologists have long since reduced African religion to folklore. (Alvares, 1995:5-6)

The continent's economic situation is claimed to be the worst in the whole world. The $300 billion, which African countries owe to foreign creditors, represents a serious burden, which fundamentally hampers progress in every sector. Africa's debt burdens, says Jesse Jackson, "are the new economy's chains of slavery" (*Los Angeles Times*, September 29, 1998). But 33 of the 41 countries identified by the World Bank as "Heavily Indebted Poor Countries" in sub-Saharan Africa spend more on debt repayments than on health care and education combined. Sub-Saharan African governments owe foreign creditors an average of almost $400 for every man, woman and child on a continent where the average annual wage for most countries is less than $400 per person. Africa carries 11% of the developing world's debt, with only 5% of the developing world's income.

In terms of social well-being, over half of Africa's population is without safe drinking water and two-thirds lack access to adequate sanitation. Africa, with about 12% of the world's population, accounts for 80% of the world's deaths due to AIDS and almost 90% of the world's deaths due to malaria.

Pan-Africanism

Historically, one of the strongest social and intellectual movements to resolve Africa's dilemma and bring new hope to its people has been the Pan-African movement. It became a positive force after two conventions in London and America in the early 1900s with great inspirations from Jamaican Marcus Garvey. In the 1950s, the movement was dominated by Jomo Kenyatta, Kwame Nkrumah, and the "father of Pan-Africanism" - W. E. B. Du Bois. In 1963, in Addis Ababa, 32 independent African nations founded the Organisation of African Unity, by which time Pan-Africanism had moved from being an ideal to practical politics.

Philosophically and theoretically, Pan-Africanism is based on the belief that African people share common bonds and objectives. Politically, Pan-Africanism has been expressed as the construction of a Pan-African identity through the development of a shared goal and social and historical experience of struggling to lift up Africa from its untenable status as a marginal, oppressed and largely written-off continent.... It is a process which comes by a sustained fostering of communication, conversation, deliberation, dialogue, coordination, cooperation and solidarity amongst the population in Africa as equal and different African citizens based on a sustained development of a shared African identity, consciousness and interest irrespective of colour, creed, racial origin, nationality, region and so on. (Mammo, 2000:1)

Still today, Pan-Africanism represents a strong political will to transform the African continent. It implies the essential elements of a social-political revolution aiming to bring about fundamental changes to all spheres of the continent. Recently, some scholars even proposed an African defence and security system, which adds a new dimension into Pan-African integration (Mammo 2001).

Pan-Africanism has been conceived in varying ways. Given the common assumption that life began on the African continent, it has been applied to all black African people and people of black African descent; to all people on the African continent, including non-black people or to all states on the African continent. As one scholar put it, it is the "acceptance of a oneness of all African people and a commitment for the betterment of all people of African descent" (Kodjoe, 1986: 368).

These broad concepts of Pan-Africanism contain strong political connotations on the basis that "African people all over the world could exert sufficient political clout toward liberation from slavery in the Americas and from colonialism on the African continent" (Fosu, 1999:7-8). It is the belief that "all people of African descent have common interests and should work together to conquer prejudice and oppression worldwide" (Sharp, 2000: 33). Pan-Africanism has been used as a general term for various movements in Africa that have their common goal in the unity of Africans and in the elimination of colonialism and white supremacy from the continent.

However, on the concrete scope and meaning of Pan-Africanism, especially regarding such matters as leadership, political orientation, and national as opposed to regional interests, one notices sharp differences. Is Pan-Africanism purely a wishful ideal or is it a realisable project? Are there any lessons in the world history of social transformations, which Pan-Africanism can draw some inspirations and strength from?

Objectives

The overall objective of this chapter is to establish a theoretical discourse between the way Marxism, Mao Zedong's thought, and the Chinese Revolution emerged, developed, and succeeded and the on-going struggle of the Pan-African movement. It emphasises the role of consciousness (politics, goals, desires, skills, knowledge) and ideological conviction as an approach to understanding the Pan-African movement as a "continental political project." In other words, it intends to argue that political discourses and ideological or the conscious elements in social-political life can be the driving-force for societal transformations and for a specific socio-political project. It is not intended to provide *the answers*; rather, it aims at constructing a framework for understanding Pan-Africanism and the complexities of such a movement on the basis of historical forms of political, social and ideological relations.

Methodological considerations

This contribution attempts to take a novel approach to the study of discourse and its effect on the macro-context of social, political and cultural structure. It offers an empirically and historically applicable framework of concepts and methods to analyse its applicability on the new Pan-African social-political movement, on the politics of Pan-African identity as well as on ideologies and social imageries that structure Pan-Africanism.

The method is an open-end discussion on the Pan-African movement based on the framework of *discourse* analysis. According to Alexander:

> (discourse) refers to modes of argument that are more consistently generalised and speculative than normal scientific discussion. … It focuses on the process of reasoning rather than the results of immediate experience, and it becomes significant where there is no plain and evident truth. Discourse seeks persuasion through argument rather than prediction. Its persuasiveness is based on such qualities as logical coherence, expansiveness of scope, interpretive insight, value relevance, rhetorical force, beauty, and texture of argument. (Alexander, 1988: 80)

Discourse is often expressed in the form of theories. And theories are constructed to generate assumptions entailing empirical facts so as to legitimise and generalise discourses. Discourse theories intend to offer a particular type of explanations that are constructed to generate assumptions to legitimise certain political and ideological ideas and conceptualisations. Discourse theories are often established at both epistemological and ontological levels.

Discourse is related to the study of important concepts such as argument, identity, relation/relationship, conflict, power, dominance and inequality, the role of the state or state institutions, and the processes of societal, cultural and ideological *reconstruction* or *reproduction*. Discourse represents both knowledge and power.

Knowledge and power

Francis Bacon's "knowledge is power" is known to most people. However, the reverse principle "power is knowledge" is equally true but less known. Yes, knowledge does produce power. For centuries the Western world has apparently been both a powerful producer of ideas and knowledge and a dominant enforcer and promoter of a vast corpus of knowledge about nature, human beings, societies, the rest of the world as well as itself. Less discussed is the fact that power, whether physical and non-physical, decides and defines knowledge.

Power can decide whether a certain system of knowledge is universal, scientific, creative, economic, rational, or whether it is primitive, local, irrational and backward. Over the last several centuries, knowledge, based on assumptions or empiricism, becomes so imposing and de-culturalised that the West has dominated the power to decide and define everything. Not only are Western modern sciences dominant, its entire social sciences and humanities are so universalised that they become non-deniable and non-negotiable beyond any culture, creed, class and colour. It is commonly accepted that the driving force of motivation promoting continued progress of human beings is to be found in the self-propelled, inherent dynamism of the West. One of the West's key universalised explanation systems to make sense of the real world and life is economic rationality (the econocentric approach) with theological principles seen as guidelines for human behaviour and societal development.

Discourse theories: econocentrism and logocentricism[1]

Econocentrism

In its specific form, econocentrism refers to a belief that the economic mode of production absolutely determines a society's social, political and intellectual life. It sees to the primacy of economics as a point of departure in the production and reproduction of social life due to human "rationality". In other words, it is an ideology that views economics as the key factor determining the course of human history.

Today, the econocentric worldview dominates every part of our everyday life. All theories of rational choice: major theories in politics, sociology, international political economy, international relations, development studies are constructed based on the premises of economic analysis or within the framework of economic thinking as their primary paradigm of interpretation (Li, 2001). Most concepts which we deal with daily, such as "culture", "ideology", "nationalism", "democracy" and so forth, are used to serve either as residues or supplements to econocentric models. It is generally accepted that economic structure determines all aspects of human activities and social relations and economic dominance lead to political and ideological leadership.

One of the consequences of the econocentric model is *methodological individualism* in which politics is perceived as a process that "objectifies private and individual wants and desires in the form of social needs and priorities according to distributive schedules and alternative possibilities" (Apter and Saich, 1994). It can only survive in the environment of private property, individual profit-searching, innovation and entrepreneurship. The understanding of power under the econocentric systems of explanation (discourses) is associated with rationality - bargaining and compromising forms of politics in which interests prevail over principles and negotiations over confrontations.

Thus, it is obvious that Pan-Africanism can never be constructed under the norms and values of econocentrism. It will only bind Africa with the existing capitalist world system defined and run by imperial powers and institutions like the WTO, the World Bank and IMF. It also ties Africa with certain types of social relations and political systems promoting civil society and liberal democracy, which in turn will be an effective way for US-led Western powers to promote *polyarchy* in the Third World in order to complement neoliberal economic restructuring and facilitate the US global hegemonic role (Robinson. 1996).

Logocentrism

The word *logo* originated from the Greek language meaning word and speech. In its general form, logo is short for logogram and logotype, which refers to "a name, symbol, or trademark designed for easy and definite recognition...."[2]

Logocentrism, philosophically, is a concept used in critical theory aiming to designate the way thought systems are organised around fundamental assumptions about reality and truth. It is a key term in the thinking of Jacques Derrida (1983, 1974, 1978) and the deconstruction theory. It argues that language in terms of explanations and interpretations is composed of elements which combine with each other to produce linguistic signs which are accorded meaning (logos and symbols). Since language and texts are always tied to experience, the use of language contains perception, conceptualisation, power and position.

Logocentrism implies a process of deconstruction and reconstruction and its final aim is to reconstruct a worldview, a new interpretation of the truth and reality in order to find alternative possibilities. It is a strategy applied to writing generally and to literature in particular, whereby systems of thought and concepts are dismantled in such a way as to expose the divisions, which lie at the heart of meaning itself.

Politically, logocentrism can be applied to display an alternative view of the world, including the search for other perspectives, for what is present, for what can be brought to light, for what can be signified and for the narrative structure of new explanations. Narratives can become the new totalising logos, which, in turn, gather multiple narratives for practical purposes

Hence, political power may be generated through *logo* (language and symbol), i.e. through both power *behind* discourse and power *in* discourse. It is concerned less with available choices than with *projections* on the basis of some convincing definition of necessity that specifies its own rules, theoretical principles and logic (Apter and Saich, ibid.). Its central goal is to re-establish social order based on a redefined and projected equity. It looks into the conscious part of human beings and emphasises learning and education as the key to power, and knowledge and wisdom as a form of truth. Power is identified with logos (discourses) with proto-religious characteristics intertwined in a secular theory of politics (Apter and Saich, 1994).

The logocentric strength of such an emphasis on political discourse and symbolic capital is that it can unleash potential energy to create a political community under conditions of virtual chaos and disintegration. The construction of alternative discourses can transcend randomness and create order so that the condition of disorder itself became the condition of transition and even transformation. The logocentric discourse approach cultivates a common interpretation of shared history and experiences. It offers people the idea of liberation and transformation in order to think a way out of their current predicaments, no matter how hopeless these seem to be. By reinterpretation it attempts to resolve the contradictions of historical legacy in their own favour in order to pave the way for great economic, social and cultural transformations

Logocentricism and the Chinese Revolution

The Chinese logocentricism explains the way Maoism and the Chinese Revolution emerged, developed and succeeded. The dynamic strength of logocentricism in the context of the Chinese revolution lies in its effort to generate power through an *inversionary discourse* (inversing the econocentric discourse and social order) based on its own language of conviction, together with ideological, ethnic and linguistic strands. The Chinese logocentricism can be analysed as follows:

1) *To change people's worldview through reinterpretation of history and narrative reconstruction of reality in order to think one's way out of current predicaments*

The Maoist Marxism related China's underdevelopment to the outcome of a historical process caused by the Western colonial-imperialist expansion rather than to the "stage of development" by the modernisation school or to the consequences of a specific mode of production caused by cultural barriers.[3] In the light of this view, underdevelopment is not an inborn characteristic of pre-industrial societies but a consequence of a specific historical process. It argues that even though imperialist penetration did bring elements of modern economy to China, the impact was geographically confined and sectorally skewed to serve foreign interest (Esherick as quoted in White, 1982: 114).

After numerous failures in resisting Western imperialist challenges since the Sino-British Opium War in the 1840s, Confucianism as a state ideology and as ethical and political traditions obviously proved to have lost its viability during a time when China urgently needed a new analytical framework. Marxism, and especially Lenin's theory of capitalist imperialism, provided Chinese intellectuals with a partial theoretical framework as well as a psychological answer to their difficulties, in finding the proper explanations and theories to the failures of traditional Chinese culture and for the humiliation suffered at the hands of the West (Peck, 1975: 73).

At the time when Confucianism failed to function as a state ideology, Marxism-Leninism made the Chinese intellectuals more open-minded and internationally-oriented in conceptualising and analysing the world from different perspectives. China, as they saw, was no longer an isolated centre of globe surrounded by barbarians, but a part of the world full of different forces and ideas. The Chinese view on its role in international affairs had changed from regarding itself as the center of the world and universal authority, to seeing China's problem as part of the world problems and Chinese revolution was relevant to the outside world. The attraction of Marxism-Leninism to the Chinese was that, as Kapur observed:

> It was an effective ploy to criticise the West from a Western point of view; b) it gave the Chinese a new methodological framework to understand their own past and foresee the contours of their future; c) it offered a conceptualised view of international reality. Lastly, it amply proved its anti-imperialist credentials - an important source of attraction after the 1917 Bolshevik Revolution when the Soviet leaders denounced imperialism, unilaterally abolishing unequal treaties and relinquishing many privileges of tsarist Russia including extraterritoriality as well as their share of Boxer indemnities. (1987:3)

2) *To unite people based on collective individualism and social, political and economic divide*

It persuaded people to associate their private narratives and personal interpretations to the collective. It called for individual contribution but emphasised collective consequences. Such a strategy was to analyse society from the lens of a politico-economic and sociocultural *divide(s)* (class divisions) which perceives human morality and consciousness in close relation to the superstructure of society. In a society in which people (human beings) are divided into different classes, all men possess certain class interests and relations. All realms relating to human beings, such as values, rights, dignity, liberty, freedom, love and hatred, humanity and inhumanity, and so forth can only be correctly understood and explained through concrete historical and class analysis (Chen, 1984: 41-44). It persuades people to think in this way that all political conflicts can be interpreted in terms of this *divide*. Its power is established when the majority of members of all social strata interpret politics and participate in the struggle in terms of this divide.

The failure of Sun Yat-sen's Republic Revolution and the destructions of the First World War together with Japanese imperialist intention tore up Chinese admiration of the West and Japan. So, if Western constitutional monarchy and republicanism, as well as Japanese militarist culture could not be imitated as alternatives to save China, then what else could be an option? Early Chinese Marxists Li Dazhao and Chen Duxiu argued that with or without a strong state the establishment of Chinese capitalism would eventually become the agent of Western capitalism and would not solve China's poverty and backwardness. The most forceful and comprehensive argument was put forward by Li:

> .... although China itself has not yet undergone a process of capitalist economic development such as occurred in Europe, America, and Japan, the common people (of China) still indirectly suffer from capitalist economic oppression in a way that is even more bitter than the direct capitalist oppression

suffered by the working class of the various (capitalist) nations....

If we look again at the international position of China today, (we see) that other nations have already passed from free competition to the necessary socialist-cooperative position, while we are still juveniles; others have walked a thousand *li*, while we are still taking the first step... I fear that we will be unable to succeed unless we take double steps and unite into a socially cooperative organisation. Therefore, if we want to develop industry in China, we must organise a government made up purely of producers in order to eliminate the exploiting classes within the country, to resist world capitalism, and to follow (the path of) industrialisation organised upon a socialist basis (Li as quoted in Kung, 1975: 259)

Li's argument identified China as a "proletarian nation" although it lacked a strong proletarian working class. He associated the potential of a Chinese proletarian revolution to the worldwide proletarian movement against international capitalism and imperialism. His far-reaching and insightful analytical worldview paved the way for the establishment of a populist tradition within the Chinese Communist Party, which was further developed by his disciple, Mao Zedong.

Armed by an inversionary discourse based on the conceptual power of class divisions, the Chinese Communist Party transformed Chinese people from being "a piece of blank paper"[4] to being ideologically and politically conscious. Being a member of this inversionary revolution, one feels becoming a member of decision-makers, an activist of social transformation, a master of his/her own fate, rather than a consciousless wanderer and a passive victim.

3) *To project a future based on structural transformations rather than evolutionary modifications*

The immediate context of logocentrism is *conflict* and *chaos*, *war* and *revolution* (not reformism or evolutionism). It rejects what the current *reality* or *truth* is, and it intends to project what is to be realised. It attempts to constitute a new hegemonic project - a *moral* economy, not a political economy, which is inversionary in object and transformational in consequence.

The reason why China was able to industrialise more rapidly since 1949 was because the "Communist revolution decisively broke the ties that chained China to the imperialist system" (Mould as quoted in White, ibid.: 114). In other words, China went straight to the roots of its historical problems and made thorough structural transformations - unique experiments to skip over the stage of capitalism and to bring about a socialist transformation in terms of both society and consciousness of the people.

For almost a half-century many Chinese truly felt China to be at a disadvantage and some of them even were ready to admit its culture to be inferior to that of the West. But with the rise of Chinese Communism with its logocentric mobilisation together with armed struggle, this view was changed. Many later believed that the Communist party represented the progressive side of contemporary human society. Although it was a fact that not all Chinese supported the Communist party, some were even strongly anti-Communist, they could not avoid being impressed by the achievements the Chinese Communist Party had made, and that China once again started to wield an undeniable influence in world affairs, which it had not enjoyed for many, many years. Some Chinese might wish that such a result had not come about under Communist leadership, but whatever they might prefer they could not but admire the result.

4) To continue the logocentric tradition and bring "uninterrupted revolution" into postwar development

After the communist victory in 1949 and with the successful development of the socialist economy and transformation in the early 1950s, few people in the communist leadership thought of a continuous revolution through a prolonged period of contention and struggle. Revolution was mainly regarded as the act of seizing power, whereas the building of a new economy and society would require a different method. But the next three decades was to see the continuation of the Chinese revolution through a progression of several mass movements, such as the *Great Leap Forward* in the 1950s, *Anti-rightist Movement* and the *Great Proletarian Cultural Revolution* in the 1960s. Mao's theory of uninterrupted revolution was practiced in these experiences and it maintained that even under socialist development the revolution must continue. Among those experiments, the Cultural Revolution was perhaps the most dramatic example of a nation in search of a development strategy that would avoid the shackles of the "old," resolve continuous contradictions and pursue an independent self-reliant development.

The meaning of "uninterrupted revolution" should be understood as referring to the preservation of some important logocentric continuities in Mao's thoughts and practices. As Selden summaries:

> They include the fierce commitment to eliminate exploitation and property-based inequality; the emphasis on political mobilisation, class struggle, and political and ideological transformation and their relationship to economic development; the proclivity to replace the market and the household economy by large cooperative, collective, and state institution; and the emphasis on self-reliance and the suspicion of intellectuals and technical personnel. (Selden, 1989: 54-55)

In order to fully utilise human-beings as the decisive factor in the socialist development strategy, Mao found it important to establish a worldview in which one thinks of part, in the context of the whole. It aimed at broadening the concept of the "whole," which had been narrowed to imply loyalty to one's family, village, clan, to the consciousness of the class, the nation and beyond. The goal was to form in society a *Gong*-oriented (collective, public and broaden) outlook in contrast to the *Si*-oriented one (selfish, individual and narrow). Mao firmly believed that only collective socialism could save China and build a strong nation, and in order to adopt such a worldview one needed an uncompromisingly ethical and moralistic revolution. He very often referred to the Cultural Revolution as a movement to establish the moral foundation of socialism - collectivity, which was advocated not only in terms of public ownership as a socialist ideology but also in terms of devotion and selflessness in the behavioural sense. *Gong* implied that socialist economic development was a process based on collective effort rather than based on *Si*, individualistic self-oriented motivation. Hence, one of his purposes in launching the Cultural Revolution was aimed at eliminating the consciousness and motivation of the old semi-capitalist society and establishing a just socialist consciousness and motivation in conformity with the new socialist economic base. It was an attempt to substitute egotistical motives (*Si*) with moral impulses (*Gong*) as incentives to increase production and development. The wage policy attempting to bridge income differences at that time reflected such incentives. In urban industries, wage differences were under control and encouraged to reduce, whereas in the people's communes, income through allotting working points was based not only on the individual physical contribution to production, but also on the level of his/her political consciousness and socialist devotion.

Implications for Pan-Africanism: the need of logocentrism

The above discussions of the Chinese Revolution are not recommending the application of the same process to various global and regional Pan-African movements. Rather, it attempts to inquire whether some of its logocentric powers can be generated in the Pan-African movements. If Pan-Africanism is to be seen as, first of all, a transformative political project, the most important element is, as shown by the success of the Chinese Revolution, is how to dismantle the structural and ideological "hegemony" in the domestic and international system and especially to overcome the dominant discourses of contemporary mythology. The effectiveness of the Chinese Revolution was its devotion to inventing a nationwide logo - common concepts, metaphors, ideologies, narratives and myths.

For Pan-Africanism to achieve similar objectives, the construction of an overriding identity of a united and emancipated Africa is the first step of such an ambitious hegemonic project. For example, a logocentric Pan-Africanism can be generated under the common glorious history of the most ancient civilisation in the world history as well as the collective historical and social experiences as an oppressed people since 1500 (Mammo, 2001:1-35). The success of the Pan-African movement depends not only strategic methods but also the unity of a broad ontology.

A shared logo

Pan-African logocentrism can conceptually be identified as a project of constructing shared logos. First, a shared logo refers to a unified "African" metaphysics without which it is not possible to achieve a united front and to sustain the spirit of solidarity. It also refers to common narratives which cover everyone who shares the African continent including those whose ancestors had left the continent in the enforced exile of the slave trade. As one scholar rightly points out:

> A shared African value and vision worthy enough to shape, mediate and put in place effective mechanisms for resolving intractable conflicts and stimulate and inspire the capabilities of citizens and communities is necessary in order to achieve harmony consistent with a shared conception of an African identity. (Mammo, 2001: 30)

There will continue to be ideological and intellectual crises in the African world until Africans understand Pan-Africanism, its value and benefits, and apply it to their many problems. The flaws of econocentric and polyarchic approaches to Pan-Africanism are to pluralise and individualise the understanding of Africa and its problems.

A shared history

A shared logo means the common colonial history: the disruption of natural processes of nation-state and class formation; the deformation, distortion, and disarticulation of the native African ethnical and social formations; the imposition of capitalist social relations - production and accumulation patterns; the imposition of alien tastes and values; and the incorporation of Africa into a metropolitan dominated and controlled global capitalist order. These experiences require an ideological response and political will to challenge the established econocentric discourse on the development of underdevelopment of Africa. This is where the African independent movement was betrayed: the failure to fundamentally challenge imperialism, and reconstruct an African logo - the socio-political and economic landscape to reflect popular realities and aspirations, and this is where the Chinese Revolution fundamentally succeeded. Political decolonisation did not automatically include the decolonisation of cultural and ideological domination and did not unconsciously generate Africa's own logo of identity - a fundamental basis for real self-determination.

The historical relationship between Africa and the world (especially the Western world)

The historical relationship between Africa and the rest of the world especially the West is very unequal: many people from Africa went to the rest of the world as slaves, conscripts, maids, servants, attendants, soldiers, cheap labours, refugees, students, skilled Africans (fuelling the brain drain) and some as migrants in search of new opportunities. The rest of world people came to Africa are "explorers", missionaries, slave traders and raiders, imperial "civilisers", aid workers, humanitarian relief workers, investors, project contractors, consultants, settlers, tourist and so forth. It is important for all Africans to remember that this historical narrative is a *common* rather than an individual legacy.

The above shared historical heritage can be a valuable source for the promotion of Pan-Africanism. A "cultural Africa" and a "continental Africa"[5] can be the logos for broad identity and unity. As Mammo sharply points out:

> The key to a theory of Pan-Africanism is to forge a shared value and vision worthy enough to shape, mediate and put in place effective mechanisms for resolving intractable conflicts and stimulate and inspire the capabilities of citizens and communities in order to achieve harmony consistent with a shared conception of an African identity. A shared conception of an African identity should be a universal value which is not detained by partial interests, cultural particularisms, state-nationisms, ethnic primordial loyalties, racial classifications and other desultory practices, capable of commanding moral and political authority, much like Christ, Mohammed and Buddha commanded religious authority. (Mammo, 2000:23)

In the context of modern China, the Chinese logo embedded in the century-long experiences of humiliation brought by Western imperialism, has been one of the key elements which have kept China from disintegration. Today, Hong Kong and Maokau have been handed over to China, and despite the unwillingness of the Taiwan regime to reunite with Mainland China, it feels powerless to revoke the "one China" concept, that is the "Chinese nation" and "cultural China".

Conclusion

The reason why China was able to industrialise more rapidly to become a global power since 1949 was that the Communist revolution "decisively broke the ties that chained China to the imperialist system" (Mould in White, 1982: 114) and also broke a variety of complicated domestic confinements, such as localism, provincialism and warlordism. A new and efficient take-off could only be realised by cutting the roots of these social diseases and re-establishing an independent social, political, economic and cultural foundation.

Many people tried to study the history of the Chinese Revolution in a non-logocentric approach, but they all ended up with a dilemma. As Dirlik describes it, "students of Chinese Communism in the West, the majority of whom do not share a similar conviction in Marxism's truths, have nevertheless found in China's circumstances variegated reasons for radicals' attraction to Marxism and consequently turning to Communist politics, as the only means to resolve the problems of Chinese society" (Dirlik, 1989: 255). Therefore, to understand the transformation of China one has to understand the nature of the Chinese communist revolution and its entire discourse.

Seen from some lessons of the Chinese Revolution, it is argued here that in order to transform the idea of Pan-Africanism into a reality, a second wave of decolonisation is a must. In the first wave of decolonisation, most African states stood up and achieved political independence. However, the very questions can be addressed directly to challenge the fundamental nature of "African states": are African states African? Are African states states? These questions imply that Africa has not fully achieved real "independence". It needs further decolonisation in order to build such a hegemonic project that represents a real independent Africa.

Gramsci's "war of position"[6] is believed to be a decisive strategy to the success of Pan-Africanism. Although Africa consists of vast differences in culture, language, religion and race, and despite the fact that race, nation and metaphysics do not necessarily enforce an identity, Africa can still choose, on the basis of historical experiences, and political and economic realities, what is important for Africans both now and in the future. The triumph of Pan-Africanism, the only way Africans can survive the foreign onslaught and live as a truly liberated people, will come out of the sweat and blood of the African people themselves.

References

Alexander, Jeffrey C. (1988) "The New Theoretical Movement", *Handbook of Sociology*, ed. by Neil J. Smelser, (California: SAGE Publications).

Alvares, Claude (1995) "Resisting the West's Intellectual Discourse", in *Dominance of the West over the Rest*, (Kuala Lumpur: Just World Trust).

Apter, David E. and Saich, Tony (1994): *Revolutionary Discourse in Mao's Republic*, (Cambridge: Harvard University Press).

Chen, Zhishang (1984) "What is the Difference between Bourgeois Humanism and Socialist Humanism?", in *Red Flag* (Beijing), No. 3, February.

Derrida, Jacques
- *Speech and Phenomena* (trans. 1973),
- *Of Grammatology* (trans. 1974), and
- *Writing and Difference* (trans. 1978).

Dirlik, Arif (1989): *The Origins of Chinese Communism*, (New York: Oxford University Press).

Dirlik, Arif and Meisner, Maurice (ed.). (1989), *Marxism and the Chinese Experience*, (New York: M.E. Sharpe, Inc.)

Fosu, Augustin Kwasi (1999) "An economic theory of Pan-Africanism", *The Review of Black Political Economy*, 27 (2): 7-12.

Gramsci, Antonio (1971), *Selections from the Prison Notebooks*, Quintin Hoare and Geoffrey Nowell Smith (ed.), (London: Lawrence &Wishart; New York: International Publisher).

Kapur, Harish (ed.), (1987) *As China Sees the World*, (London: Frances Pinter Publisher).

Kodjoe, Ofuatey W. (1986) *Pan-Africanism: New Directions in Strategy*, (Lanham: University Press of America).

Kung, Chungwu (1975) "Cultural Revolution in Modern Chinese History", in Victor Nee and James Peck (ed.), *China's Uninterrupted Revolution from 1840 to the Present*, (New York: Random House).

Li, Xing (1998) The Yin and Yang behind China's Transformation: a dialectical assessment of the Chinese revolutions from Mao and Deng.

Research Centre on Development and International Relations, Department of Development and Planning, Aalborg University.

(1999) "The Transformation of Ideology from Mao to Deng: Impact on China's Social Welfare Outcome", *International Journal of Social Welfare*, Vol. 8, No. 2.

(2001) "The Market-Democracy Conundrum", *Journal of Political Ideologies*, Vol. 6, No. 1.

Muchie, Mammo (2000) "Towards a Theory for Re-framing Pan-African Integration: An Idea Whose Time Has Come" *Development Research Series*, Working Paper No. 96 (Department of History, International Studies and Social Relations, Aalborg University, Denmark).

---- (2001) "African Union – forward ever, backward never", *New African*, September.

Peck, James (1975) "Revolution Versus Modernisation and Revisionism: A Two-Front Struggle", in Victor Nee and James Peck (ed.), *China's Uninterrupted Revolution from 1840 to the Present*, (New York: Random House).

Robinson, William I. (1996) *Promoting Polyarchy: Globalisation, US Intervention, and Hegemony*. (New York: Cambridge University Press).

Selden, Mark (1989) "Mao Zedong and the Political Economy of Chinese Development", in Arif Dirlik and Maurice Meisner (ed.), *Marxism and the Chinese Experience*, (New York: M.E. Sharpe, Inc.).

Sharp, Anne Wallace (2000) "The Pan-African movement", *Cobblestone*, 21 (2): 33-35.

Weber, Max [1904] (1976) *The Protestant Ethic and the Spirit of Capitalism*, London: Allen & Unwin.

White, Gordon (1982) "Why Did China Fail to Follow the Japanese Road?", in Manfred Bienefeld and Martin Godfrey (ed.), *The Struggle for Development, National Strategies in an International Context*, (New York: John Wiley & Sons Limited).

Endnotes

---

[1] See Apter, David E. and Saich, Tony (1994), *Revolutionary Discourse in Mao's Republic*, Cambridge: Harvard University Press.

[2] Source: *The American Heritage® Dictionary of the English Language*, Third Edition

[3] Friedrich Hegel, in comparing with Western consciousness of the world, which created revolutionary history, placed China in the "childhood" of history. Even Karl Marx, whose theories and insights inspired the Chinese Revolution, described China as a society "vegetating in the teeth of time", and discovered in the Great Wall of China a metaphor for the universal resistance of non-European societies to change. See A. Dirlik and M. Meisner (1989), p. 17.
Max Weber also considered Chinese culture (Confucianism) and social pattern (family relations) as structural barriers to the rise of capitalism. See Max Weber [1904] (1976).

[4] This is part of Mao's understanding of power in which ignorance and illiteracy can be a source of power. It also means that poverty and underdevelopment can be a driving force for societal transformation.

[5] "Cultural Africa" constitutes all Africans including those in the Diaspora outside the continent. "Continental Africa" includes those settled in Africa from various parts of the world despite their origins.

[6] "War of position" refers to the struggle to receive broad unification of various social forces and groups under the general consent of a political ideology (Gramsci, 1971).

10

The role of the African media in promoting African integration

Baffour Ankomah

"During times of universal deceit, telling the truth becomes a revolutionary act." - George Orwell

"The only way to express ourselves in the new world is by being together. I don't like to be a colony. If we do not get together, we will disappear from world history." - Romani Prodi, president of the European Commission, speaking in London on 16 February 2001 on the need for European unity.

(For the purpose of this chapter, I am going to use media as a singular noun whenever and wherever I am distinguishing between the "Western media" and the "African media", or the "British media" and the "Ghanaian media", etc).

Preamble

For those who are not journalists and who may have underestimated the power of the media, let me start by quoting the African-American writer and Egyptologist, Anthony Browder: "Everything you see," he said recently, "whether it is on a billboard, a movie, video or commercial, has been designed by a person. So every image is there for a reason."

Browder was speaking in an interview with The Voice, the London-based weekly newspaper. To him, "the media are the most powerful forms of communication ever devised by man. If you are not conscious of that, then you won't know how to protect yourself from negative images projected through the media." Browder is not alone. In a recent leader comment on the sale of the British daily, The Express, the paper's competitor, The Guardian, wrote:

"The Daily Express was once a paper whose journalism thundered out across country and Empire. For more than 15 years, it sold more than four million copies a day. Its proprietor, Lord Beaverbrook, liked to think of his main paper as a weapon. 'When skilfully employed,' he wrote, "no politician of any party can resist it. It is a flaming sword, which will cut through any political armour. Many newspapers are harmless because they do not know how to strike or when to strike... But teach the man behind them how to load and what to shoot at, and they become deadly'."

Anybody reading this essay should please read it with Lord Beaverbrook's remarks at the back of their minds. "Many newspapers are harmless," he said, "because they do not know how to strike or when to strike. But teach the man behind them how to load and what to shoot at, and they become deadly... When skilfully employed, no politician of any party can resist it. It is a flaming sword [that] will cut through any political armour." To better understand what the African media can do to promote African integration - the central theme of this essay - we must first understand the dynamics driving the global media (especially the Western media) and Africa's place in it. I am going to explain it in three simple steps:

First, I will review the current state of the world media, pointing out the dynamics and agendas that drive them and how they impact on Africa, its journalists and the coverage of the continent. Second, I will show how the African media unwittingly add to the bad reporting of the continent, and the pessimism that flows from it. Third, I will show how the African media can change all this. And then, lastly, I will make some recommendations on how the African media can help promote African integration.

We may not like it, but the truth is that it is the Western media that today sets the agenda and tenor of what makes news and how it is reported across the world (including the slant, the pitch, how it is played and so forth). The African media is sadly caught up in this web, and having been so bamboozled, we are reduced to only mimicking what the Western media puts out about our continent, the world and us. Thus, all that we do is simply follow the lead set by the Western media. Why this is so is partly due to the training we get in the journalism schools of Africa and elsewhere. "You are what you know", says one of the catchphrases being used by the CNN in recent months to advertise its programmes. To me, nothing can better that. We are what we know. All of us are! Throughout our days as trainee-journalists, we are made to believe that there is something called "the free press" in the West. This "free press", we are additionally told, is free to publish whatever is the truth, fairly, accurately and without favour. We are never told what Lord Beaverbrook tells his editors and journalists at The Express: That a newspaper (or the media) is a "weapon, a flaming sword" that must "know how to strike and when to strike". That, for the men and women "behind" this "flaming sword" to "become deadly", they must know "how to load [the weapon] and what to shoot at."

This is a very important lesson we never teach in African journalism. Rather, we feed ourselves with notions of this mythical free press that doesn't exist anywhere. On the wings of this deceit, we set forth to reproduce this "free press" in Africa often with catastrophic results. "Publish and be damned" then becomes a code to die for. It makes us feel good if we are seen to "uphold" press freedom by being truculently hostile to our governments whether what we seek to reveal harms national interest or not. In fact, many times we are not even conscious that we are harming national interest. For example, we have all read recent articles by Zimbabwean journalists who, because they want President Robert Mugabe out of office, thunder about how ordinary Zimbabweans "want jobs, not land".

It may be so, but these journalists are simply refusing to look at the broader national interest issues involved. In a country where agriculture (reduced to its simplest denominator, land) is the major foreign exchange earner, it is suicidal for Zimbabwe to continue to leave the control of land in the hands of only 4,500 commercial farmers, almost all of whom happen to come from one ethnic minority group.

Jobs are very important; they make the world go round. But the Zimbabweans who want "jobs" now, not land" are looking (some would say selfishly) at the short term only, and not thinking about their future generations. What will their future generations inherit? Jobs, of course, but not the control of their country and its destiny, because without land you have no country.

If we compare the attitude of these Zimbabweans with the Palestinians in Gaza and the West Bank, a sad dividing line emerges. The Palestinians have "jobs" in Israel all right. They commute every morning to their jobs in Israel, yet they are fighting and dying for land. They already have jobs, the Israelis would be happy to give them all the jobs they want, so what is the point in getting killed in a struggle for land? The Palestinians know that jobs are not enough without the control of their own land and their own country! They are thinking not only about themselves today, but also about their future generations!

Zimbabweans should think (or be made to think) in the same way. Land is an important issue of national-interest that no Zimbabwean, whether a journalist or a commoner, should belittle. After all, without land there will be no jobs. A factory is built on land, an office block stands on land, airports, roads, railways are built on land, you cannot have a home without land, and even democracy thrives on land. There is no parliament house that doesn't stand on land. And if that piece of land on which you want to build your parliament house is owned by a man who doesn't want to sell it, or wants an arm and a leg for it, what do you do? Even land can be exchanged for money to start a business and create jobs. Land, again, is accepted worldwide as collateral for bank loans. You don't necessarily have to farm the land. You can put it up as collateral for a loan to be invested in a business to create jobs. For any country (not only Zimbabwe), land is crucial. When the Europeans "discovered" America, they went first for the land by wiping out the native population in a deliberate act of genocide. The Mayflower pioneers knew that with land they could create whatever jobs they wanted. Today America, the only economic and military superpower in the world, is testament to that land policy (we may call it a genocidal policy) of their forebears. The Europeans did the same thing in Canada, Latin America, Australia and in New Zealand. They went first for the land, and if that meant annihilating the native populations, so be it. Today we all know who owns the land in America, Canada, Australia, New Zealand, and Latin America. It is certainly not the descendants of the natives. And Zimbabwean journalists cannot see beyond their noses?

The free press

This is one myth that we should all spend the rest of our lives exploding, because it has caused a lot of trouble to Africa. There is NOTHING like a "free press" anywhere in the world! Not in Britain. Not in America. Not in France. Not in Germany. Not anywhere! And I challenge anybody who knows, or has ever met, this "Mr Free Press" to kindly introduce me to him because I would want to have dinner with him and ask him some searching questions. What is true (and you don't get it in any textbook) is that the "freedom" of the Western media is restricted by national laws and the various agendas that influence their reporting of the news. As Tony Benn, the Labour MP, who retired after 50 years in British parliament, once put it: "If I had rescued a child from drowning, the national press would no doubt have headlined the story: 'Benn grabs child'."

But why "Benn grabs child"? Why not "Benn saves child"? The answer is found in Tony Benn's background. He is (or was) seen to be on the "hard left" of British politics. As a result, the British "national press" (especially the Tory Press) considers him a "loony". The last time I checked the word in my dictionary, it meant "dangerous, can open the eyes of the masses". To the uninitiated, Britain has a free press. But if "free" means the ability to report whatever is the truth, fairly, accurately and without favour, why would they (hypothetically) report Tony Benn as having "grabbed a child", when he had "saved a child" from drowning? The answer is simple: The agendas that drive the British media, like its counterparts elsewhere in the West, restrict its freedom to report freely. In effect, the British media is not free to report freely.

Britain has perhaps the most laws on its statute book restricting press freedom in the whole world. That British journalists are not routinely harassed or dragged before the court by the government is testament to the journalists' religious observance of the restrictive laws and not to any democratic inclinations of the British state or government. This is something African journalists must learn - and fast. The continent gets a bad press internationally because of the agendas driving the Western media. A confident Africa, able to fight for itself and its interests, squarely and fairly, is not what the metropolitan powers really want, in spite of all their assurances.

Remember that part of the reasons put forward in 1974 by Henry Kissinger and his friends in the then American government, for the control of world population as published in the infamous National Security Study Memorandum 200 (NSSM 200), was that if the populations of the less developed countries (which means Africa and the so-called Third World) were allowed to grow unchecked, it would adversely affect the supply and the prices of raw materials from our countries to the developed world. And they didn't want that. You don't have to take my word for it here. Read it from the Kissinger-commissioned document - the NSSM 200. Paragraphs 8 and 9 (under the heading: 'Minerals and Fuels') say:

> "The world is increasingly dependent on mineral supplies from developing countries, and if rapid population frustrates their prospects for economic development and social progress, the resulting instability may undermine the conditions for expanded output and sustained flows of such resources... "Imports for fuel and other minerals will cause grave problems which could impinge on the US, both through the need to supply greater financial support in LDC [less developed countries] efforts to obtain better terms of trade through higher prices for exports."

In effect, it is bad for the national interests of America and the developed world for Africa and the other LDCs to "obtain better terms of trade through higher prices for exports". As a result, measures were put in place to keep our populations in check. American national interest, according to the NSSM 200, wanted the world population "stabilised" at "8 billion" by the year 2000 instead of the "13 billion or more" that was feared might happen if nothing was done at all. In the end, Kissinger and his friends did much better! The world population today is 6.5 billion - even lower than the "lower target" of 8 billion that the NSSM 200 recommended in 1974. And what were the measures used to control our populations? Don't ask Kissinger or his friends because they won't tell you!

What one needs to bear in mind is that, as proven by the NSSM 200, an Africa able to fight for its rights, including better terms of trade, is not what the developed world wants, contrary to their many pronouncements of goodwill. And a strong Africa can only come with a united Africa. This is why African unity has always been seen in the North as a threat, and attempts have been made in the past (and even today) to scupper it. Unity means that the divide and rule tactics used by the metropolitan powers to safeguard their interests in Africa will be dead and buried.

Read it in the NSSM 200: "The United States has become increasingly dependent on mineral imports from developing countries in recent decades, and this trend is likely to continue. The location of known reserves of higher-grade ores of most minerals favours increasing dependence of all industrialised regions on imports from less developed countries. The real problems of mineral supplies lie, not in basic physical sufficiency, but in the politico-economic issues of access, terms for exploration and exploitation, and division of the benefits among producers, consumers, and host country governments."

The above paragraph was written in 1974, but nothing has changed since. Africa is still home to most of the minerals and raw materials that make the world to round. Africa is still the world's largest producer of the "strategic" mineral, uranium (in South Africa, Namibia and DR Congo in order of volume). The uranium in the atomic bombs dropped by the Americans on Hiroshima and Nagasaki during World War II, came from Congo's Shinkolobwe mine in Katanga. Congo was for a long time the world's largest producer of uranium. That is why the Americans kept the corrupt Mobutu Sese Seko in power for all those 32 years. He was to guarantee Western access to Congo's huge reserves of uranium, cobalt and the other strategic minerals.

The metropolitan powers have always known and feared (and still fear) that if a United Africa is allowed to emerge, and it decides not to sell its uranium or even merely controls its supply and prices to suit its strategic and continental interests, the world's ability to generate electricity from its nuclear power plants, will be seriously compromised. And where will the Western world be without electricity? So, like Tony Benn, Africa must be pushed down or prevented from seeing or using the power it holds in its hands. And all sorts of excuses and sophistry are used to keep Africa down. In modern times, the ugly messenger happy to carry the message across the oceans has been the Western media at so huge a cost to Africa and its future generations. For example, an investor planning to expand his business abroad gets a copy of The Economist with a front cover headline

Baffour Ankomah

saying, "Africa, The Hopeless Continent - (and The Economist and its sister-paper, The Financial Times are taken seriously by investors; The Economist's editor-in-chief, Bill Eammott, even says: "We are the house journal of globalisation; we advocate it and report it in all its aspects") - the investor's immediate reaction will be: "No, I can't possibly put my money in a hopeless continent". And that's it for Africa. He takes his money elsewhere. Africa loses!

You can imagine how many investors have felt this way, and how many zillions of dollars of investment and tourism revenue Africa has lost through the relentless negative portrayal of the continent by the Western media. In effect, the efforts being made by Western governments and their lending institutions to help Africa are undermined by the Western media's negative portrayal of Africa, which drives away business from the continent. This is where the African media should take a stand and help educate our people. Sadly, our journalists don't even see the agendas being pushed by the Western media, and as a result, Africa has not, as yet, developed any counter measures.

How the Western media works

In general, the Western media (and I am going to focus on the British media here) is guided by what I call "a five-point unwritten code".
* National interest
* Government lead
* Ideological leaning
* Historical baggage
* Advertisers/Readers' power
Besides the "Big Five" above, there are other minor factors that inform the bad reporting of Africa, such as: (A) the lack of adequate manpower; (B) the sheer ignorance about Africa; and (C) the disrespect and contempt for Africa, its cultures and institutions. Let's first take (B) and (C) above. The Western media loves to run stories about "half-naked" Africans walking about in the towns and villages oblivious of their state of half-nakedness. What they don't add is the context: which is that, these "half naked" Africans live in temperatures so hot that they necessarily have to take some of their clothes off. In summer, when the weather is hot and "the living is easy" in Europe, it is normal to see some Europeans walk about in town "half naked". But we don't see any

demeaning articles published about them. It is even considered "fashionable" to expose some flesh in summer. It brings delight to all, especially the male species. So then, what is news about Africans who live all-year round in temperatures even hotter than the European summer, walking "half naked" in their villages and trying to get a tan (if not delighting their male species like the European women do?)

Lack of adequate manpower

To the average Westerner, Africa is just one country where everybody knows everybody. In fact that is the impression you get from the size of Africa on an average world map. Though Africa is said to be the "second largest continent" in the world and the most variegated, it looks so small on the world map in comparison to the other continents. USA and Canada together actually look bigger on the map than Africa! How this is possible is explained away by a colleague who traces it to the colonial construct that seeks to make the metropolitan powers look bigger than the colonies they controlled. However you look at the world map, you can always excuse the average Westerner (including the new American president, George Bush, the Son) for his inability to pick his Nigeria from Ethiopia on the map.

But you can't excuse the Western media because it is not run by average Westerners. Their treatment of Africa, huge as it is, as a small, unimportant place deserving to be covered by just one correspondent, or at best two, is inexcusable. In the past, these "Africa correspondents" were based in Nairobi, Kenya, and lately in Johannesburg, South Africa. But how can one correspondent cover the 53 countries of Africa and do the job well? Can one correspondent even cover Denmark, small as it is, and do the job well?

And if you think that Congo alone is bigger than 12 European countries put together - yes, I have checked my atlas, Congo is bigger than Britain, Germany, France, Spain, Portugal, Italy, Denmark, Belgium, the Netherlands, the Republic of Ireland, Switzerland and Croatia all put together, and you still have four million square miles of Congolese territory to give away to the descendants of King Leopold. And Congo is not even the largest country in Africa, Sudan is! Imagine what one correspondent can do if he is assigned to cover Britain, Germany, France, Spain, Portugal, Italy, Denmark, Belgium, Netherlands, Ireland, Switzerland and Croatia. And this correspondent is based in the Irish capital, Dublin, in the far west of Europe. What quality of work will he or she produce on these 12 countries? Yet in terms of Africa, these 12 countries translate into just one country - Congo! Imagine, therefore, the quality of work *The Times* correspondent is producing about the 53 countries of Africa from his base in Johannesburg.

Historical Baggage

Of the "Big Five" factors informing the bad reporting of Africa by the Western media, historical baggage distresses me the most. As therapy for my depression, I always go back to an article in The Guardian (8 January 1998), written by George Alagiah, the BBC's former African correspondent. Returning to base in London, after his tour of duty in Africa, Alagiah exhorted his Western colleagues to change the way they report Africa. Alagiah is of Asian origin but spent part of his childhood in Africa. His article is so pregnant that it deserves to be quoted here extensively for those who didn't see. He wrote: "For most people who get their view of the world from TV, Africa is a faraway place where good people go hungry, bad people run government, and chaos and anarchy are the norm. "My job is to give a fuller picture. [But] I have a gnawing regret that, as a foreign correspondent, I have done Africa a disservice, too often showing the continent at its worst and too rarely showing it in full flower. "There is an awful lot of historical baggage to cut through when reporting Africa: the 20th century view of the continent is, even now, infected with the prevailing wisdom of the 19th century. "Take this description of an African from a speech given by the explorer John Hanning Speke in the 1860s:

'As his father did, so does he. He works his wife, sells his children, enslaves all he can lay his hands upon and unless fighting for the lands of others, contents himself with drinking, singing, and dancing like a baboon, to drive dull care away.' "It's an ugly thought but I would bet one of my new suits that there are many out there for whom these words still have resonance..."I take this personally because I spent part of my childhood in Africa. After Britain, Africa is probably the place I feel most at home. I know it to be a place of great passion and variety. Above all, it is a place where the outsider is forever welcome. In the hardest of times and in the most desolate of places, I have been greeted with a warm hand and an open heart. "I had reason to remember this when reporting from Albania recently. I am no expert on European affairs, and it came as a shock that there was somewhere as poor as Albania in [Europe]. "But what I found more surprising and disturbing [in Albania] was the lack of joie de vivre. Whereas even in the most poverty-stricken and politically oppressed corner of Africa, there is an irrepressible vein of hope and humour that bubbles to the surface. "Perhaps this is what Ben Okri had in mind in his poem, An African Elegy:

'We are the miracles that God made/To taste the bitter fruit of time/We are precious/And one day our suffering/Will turn into the wonders of the earth.' "It is a noble sentiment but not one you will easily glean from my reporting [of Africa]. There has been too much of Africans as victims and not enough showing their daily triumphs against impossible odds..." Anybody who knows Africa will readily agree with every sentiment in Alagiah's article. Yet, The Guardian, in its infinite mercy, chose to headline Alagiah's article: "New light on the Dark Continent". There you have it! Alagiah is pleading that the Western media should drop the "historical baggage" nonsense. And yet The Guardian insists on calling Africa "the Dark Continent" in the very headline of the very article in which Alagiah is asking for the very "Dark Continent" nonsense to be dropped!

In a major series, which started in the New African in April 2001, Milton Allimadi, an Ugandan who edits his own paper in New York, has shown why the Western media cannot let go the "historical baggage". Because, he says, they inherited it from an earlier generation of Western writers "whose hearts were full of darkness" rather than Africa being the "dark continent".

The phenomenon goes back "as early as the 5th century BC, when Herodotus wrote The Histories," says Allimadi. "Europeans regarded the African continent as backward and inhabited by at worst savages and at best unintelligent and cruel people. "Much later, in the 18th and 19th centuries, the journals of the European travellers became the main medium of disseminating this stereotypical image of Africa. "In the early part of the 20th century, negative characterisations of Africa were pervasive in American publications such as The New York Times, National Geographic, Time, Newsweek, The New Yorker and many European newspapers and magazines."

In 1959, when The New York Times sent Homer William Bigart (a Pulitzer Prize winner) to cover events in West Africa at the start of the decolonisation period, he went with a suitcase full of "historical baggage" by his side. Bigart was soon writing back to his foreign news editor, Emmanuel Freedman, after visiting Ghana and Nigeria, in these words:

"I'm afraid I cannot work up any enthusiasm for the emerging republics. The politicians are either crooks or mystics. Dr Nkrumah [who was then the president of Ghana] is a Henry Wallace in burnt cork. I vastly prefer the primitive bush people. After all, cannibalism may be the logical antidote to this population explosion everyone talks about."

When The New York Times foreign news editor, Freedman, received those reports, he was so thrilled that he sent this note back to Bigart:

"This is just a note to say hello and to tell you how much your peerless prose from the badlands is continuing to give us and your public. By now you must be American journalism's leading expert on sorcery, witchcraft, cannibalism and all the other exotic phenomena indigenous to darkest Africa. All this and nationalism too! Where else but in The New York Times can you get all this for a nickel?" Where else, indeed! But wait for this one from Bigart in 1960, written four weeks to Congo's independence. He complained to Freedman in a letter from Kinshasa (then Leopoldville), thus: "I had hoped to find pygmies voting and interview them on the meaning of independence but they were all in the woods. I did see several lions, however, and from Usumbura I sent a long mailer about the Watutsi giants."

Poor Bigot (sorry Bigart). Having failed to see any pygmies voting, he chose to dig deep into his suitcase of "historical baggage" and came out with even a winner that thrilled the folks at The New York Times. It was printed on 5 June 1960 under the headline "Magic of Freedom Enchants Congolese". Bigart, our Pulitzer Prize-winning journalist (and remember the Pulitzer Prize is still American journalism's highest honour), wrote from Leopoldville:

"As the hour of freedom from Belgian rule nears, 'in-de-pen-dence' is being chanted by Congolese all over this immense land, even by pygmies in the forest. Independence is an abstraction not easily grasped by the Congolese and they are seeking concrete interpretations. To the forest pygmy, independence means a little more salt, a little more beer."

How foreign news editor Freedman must have enjoyed it! He it was who four years earlier, on 25 July 1956, had written to the then

New York Times Africa correspondent, Leonard Ingalls, in these words:

"We read that in Black Africa, where the principle of the wheel was scarcely known a generation or two ago, there is now a great demand for bicycles, a trend is underway toward two-bicycle families. Is there a light economic air-mail feature in the increasing mobility of the aborigines? Where do they buy their bikes? What do they cost? How long does it take a man to earn enough money to buy one? Is his status advanced? Does he have roads or bicycle tracks, or does he ride through the bush? What is the usual biking costume - robe, breach-cloth, animal skin or birthday suit? How is the bicycle business? Are dealers getting rich? Are there bicycle garages in the bush? What social effects is the bicycle having?"

Freedman's mindset still rules the newsrooms of the West. Nothing has changed. After the recent assassination of President Laurent Kabila in Congo, British newspapers could find no appropriate headline than rush back to the tired, old one: "In the heart of darkness". Alex Duval Smith, a woman journalist (usually women know better) who writes for the British daily, The Independent, filed this report from her "African base" in Johannesburg, South Africa:

"The heart of darkness was never darker. President Laurent Kabila, the latest in an uninterrupted line of pillagers of a territory the size of Western Europe is dead. Now the vultures are massing for the next round of Africa's First World War."

What has "darkness", you may like to ask, got to do with assassinating a president? If Alex Duval Smith were covering the assassination of President J.F. Kennedy in Dallas, USA (and more than one Kennedy has been assassinated by the Americans), she would never had dared to describe it in those "dark" tones. Yet when it comes to assassinations, the Americans lead the Congolese by a good mile. From the Kennedys to the Martin Luther Kings and the Malcolm Xs! But nobody describes America as a "dark" place. It is a "goodland" as against Freedman's "badlands" of Africa. In effect, this is what you get when "historical baggage" rules the roost in Western newsrooms.

National Interest

By far, national interest is the most important factor that drives the Western media and determines whether a story is printed or spiked, whether it is on the front page or buried inside. African journalism schools tend to put too much premium on fair and impartial reporting, and less on national interest. I don't remember myself ever being told by my journalism lecturers in Accra, Ghana, about national interest. It is simply not in the curriculum. Of course, what do you expect? - the textbooks are all written by Westerners.

But my 16 years as a practising journalist in Britain have taught me how important the role national interest plays in the reporting of news. As Ronald Spark, former chief lead writer of The Sun, one of Britain's largest circulation newspapers, put it in 1991: "Truth is sacred, but a newspaper that tells only part of the truth is a million times preferable to one that tells the truth to harm his country."

Interestingly, you don't get Mr Spark's frank-parler in any textbook. Hence, African journalism students come out of school with our heads full of the idea, which was so succinctly put recently by Nana Kofi Coomson, editor of The Ghanaian Chronicle in Accra. "The true professional journalist anywhere in the world," he told a media conference, "will tell you that the relationship between government and the press should of necessity be adversarial."

Well, by that score, "the true professional" Western journalist is not yet born. Because the relationship between, for example, the British media and the government is not, and has never been, adversarial throughout the centuries. Rather, there is a thick layer of complementarity between them. The one supports the other. In fact, they feed on each other for the betterment of the British nation as a whole.

The thread that binds them together is national interest. Any story that risks harming the interests of Britain is treated with utmost care, and many times such a story finds a comfortable place in the dustbin. Conversely, any story that enhances Britain's national interest is given a big play. "Adversarial relationship"? You bet.

A recent example of how national interest works in the reporting of news was demonstrated in an article by Audrey Gillan (The Guardian, 21 August 2000). Her article, about the Kosovo War (under the headline, "The Propaganda War") came complete with this rather interesting "introduction": "It was obvious to anyone there that facts and figures were being manipulated in Kosovo to suit the West".

Let me quote here portions of the article:

"It is now clear," she wrote, "that the number of ethnic Albanians massacred in Kosovo was way short of Nato's claims. It seems that the figure of 100,000 dead will be slimmed down to 3,000, following the exhumation of bodies from graves. The original numbers were used to justify [Nato] intervention, and talk of indiscriminate killings to excuse our killing.

"As this difficult truth emerges, it needs to be said that it was possible to get the real picture much earlier... Truth could be scarce at the Blace border and in the camps dotting around Macedonia, but you were not allowed to say that during the [Kosovo] war, just as you were not allowed to doubt atrocity. But it was clear that there were exaggerations for very calculated ends.

"There was no real evidence for what was being said. Western journalists accepted details without question. Almost every day, the world's media jostled for stories in Macedonia, straining to find figures that didn't exist. In the absence of any testimony, many reported what some agency or other had told them...

"The things you come to know as a journalist do not march in single file. Facts are often renegade. But among the rape victims arriving in Macedonia, nobody spoke of anything like the camps the British foreign secretary, Robin Cook, referred to. [Cook had told the world: 'Young women are being separated from the refugee columns and forced to undergo systematic rape in an army camp. We have evidence form many refugees who have managed to escape...']

"But a senior OSCE source told me that Robin Cook's rape camp was an attempt to get the British public behind the bombing. And wasn't all this a lesson in how propaganda works in modern war? "Watching the television images and listening to the newscasters thunder about further reports of Serb massacres and of genocide, I felt uneasy about saying that they had very little to go on. But the story at home was different from the one that appeared to be happening on the ground." So then, where is the "adversarial relationship" between the Western media and their governments?

According to Audrey, "the truth" about Serb atrocities in Kosovo was known by the Western media at the time of the war, "but you were not allowed to say that during the war, just as you were not allowed to doubt atrocity". Yet the Western media is said to be free - free to report whatever is the truth. The question arising is: Who was not "allowing" the truth to be reported? The Guardian's "introduction" to Audrey's article said it all: "It was obvious to anyone there that facts and figures were being manipulated in Kosovo to suit the West."

In short, the guy who was not allowing the truth about Kosovo to be reported was the "West" - or if you like, Western interest. But if you think that the Western media only did it in Kosovo in the year 2000, wait for this: George Orwell, the famous novelist, was so appalled by the reporting of the Spanish Civil War (1936-39) that he was moved to say in 1939: "Early in life, I had noticed that no event is correctly reported in newspapers, but in Spain, for the first time, I saw newspaper reports which did not bear any relation to the facts, not even the relationship which is implied in an ordinary lie."

This all fit so well with what is known in Britain as the "Wolf's Law of Journalism", which says unashamedly: "You cannot hope to bribe or twist, thank God, the British journalist. But, seeing what the man will do unbribed, there is no occasion to." In fact, it is not only the British journalist who is guilty of this crime, his American counterpart is equally as bad.

The American version

On 19 February 2001, William Rees Mogg, writing in The Times (of London) under the headline, "When Uncle Sam was a drugs runner", provided a damning example of how national interest rules American journalism. Rees-Mogg told of how the "the biggest scandal in modern American history" - the Meana Airport Scandal in Arkansas - was not published by the big newspapers, magazines and TV networks of America because of national interest concerns. The scandal involved "the wholesale route of cocaine importation into the US in the 1980s," Rees-Mogg writes. "The cocaine was turned into crack; the crack epidemic ravaged the black districts of the big American cities as badly as Aids ravaged the homosexual communities in the same period."

At the time, the man who later became the president of America, William Jefferson Clinton, was the governor of Arkansas. Somehow, the state government that Clinton headed allowed (or just played blind to) planes loaded with guns from the Meana Airport flying to South

America, and returning with drugs that found their way into the black neighbourhoods of America, all under the watchful eyes of agents of the US Drug Enforcement Agency (DEA). The operation, according to Rees-Mogg, was spearheaded by one Barry Seal (since deceased) who "flew the weapons in violation of US foreign policy and, in return, the US federal government secretly allowed Seal to smuggle drugs back into the US... Seal was [later] murdered by Colombian gunmen while in federal custody." When the Arkansas Congressman, Bill Alexander, ("at the time the Democratic whip in the House of Representatives in Washington DC, and the senior Democrat of the House Appropriations Committee!") tried to investigate the Meana Scandal, "his inquiry was sidetracked both in Arkansas and in Washington".

After Seal's murder, his friend Jerry Parks, a private detective in Little Rock, Arkansas, became Governor Clinton's security chief in Little Rock, during the 1992 American presidential election campaign. Later Parks confessed that "Vince Voster - Bill Clinton's lawyer - paid him $1,000 in cash for each [drugs] trip". In 1993, Parks was murdered by two gunmen, who to the best of my knowledge still remain unidentified. Later Vince Voster himself was found dead in a park in Virginia.

"There were then, and there are now good grounds for a full inquiry into Meana, an inquiry such as Congressman Alexander was asking for," says Ress-Mogg. "There is evidence that the Arkansas State Police protected the smugglers; there were several suspicious deaths connected to Meana; money from Meana can be traced through Jerry Parks as far as Vince Voster; though both Parks and Voster are long since dead, there is evidence of money laundering." Ress-Mogg adds that "there is no evidence which takes the money trail beyond Forster to Clinton himself or to his campaign funds. The criticism of Clinton is not that he was directly involved, but that he did not respond to the concerns that were expressed to him, by Congressman Alexander and others... He allowed a catastrophic event to happen." Yet nobody in authority in America wants to talk about Meana. "The Republican silence is explained by the fact that Meana was connected to the Iran-Contra affair; indeed Congressman Alexander's letter sees Meana as a Republican scandal", says Rees-Mogg.

The big question here is: What did the "free press" of America do with the Meana story? Remember, national interest was at stake. So, although some little newspapers ran bits of the story in April 1988,

September 1991, and April 1992, America's finest and heavyweight newspapers, magazines and the main TV networks such as The New York Times, The Washington Post, Time magazine, Newsweek, CBS, ABC and CNN all refused to investigate the story for publication. "It is the US press which should most blame itself," Ress-Mogg says, adding: "Where were The New York Times, The Washington Post, Time, Newsweek, or the main television networks of that period? Virtually silent." "In 1994," Ress-Mogg continues, "I remember reading a thorough Meana investigation by two American journalists prepared for The Washington Post; that was never published... In the years, when Clinton was still a candidate, Meana was not included by The New York Times among 'All the News That's Fit to Print'", Ress Mogg sadly ends his piece. You may like to ask why?

More American examples

In their book, The CIA And The Cult of Intelligence (published in 1974), Victor Marchetti and John D. Marks also tell how national interest affects the American media's coverage of news. The revelations in their book are so telling that, in the interest of Africa and African journalism, I am going to crave everybody's indulgence to quote them here extensively. They tell it better than I can possibly do. And every African journalist, especially those who still believe that the relationship between the government and the media must of necessity be adversarial, should read the following extracts very slowly and study them line by line: Marchetti and Marks wrote (remember they are writing in 1974):

"In a recent interview, a nationally syndicated columnist with close ties to the CIA was asked how he would have reacted in 1961 if he had uncovered advance information that the Agency was going to launch the Bay of Pigs invasion of Cuba. "He replied somewhat wistfully, 'The trouble with the Establishment is that I would have gone to one of my friends in the government, and he would have told me why I shouldn't write the story. And I probably wouldn't have written the story'. "It was rather fitting that this columnist, when queried about exposing a CIA operation, should have put his answer in terms of the 'Establishment' (of which he is a recognised member), since much of what the American people have learned - or have not learned - about the Agency has been filtered through an 'old-boy network' of journalists friendly to the CIA.

"There have been exceptions, but by and large, the CIA has attempted to discourage, alter, and even suppress independent investigative inquiries into agency activities... "For example, on 23 September 1970, syndicated columnist Charles Bartlett was handed, by a Washington-based official of ITT, an internal ITT report sent in by the company's two representatives in Chile, Hal Hendrix and Robert Berrellez.

"This eight-page document - marked PERSONAL AND CONFIDENTIAL - said that the American ambassador to Chile had received the 'green light to move in the name of President Nixon...[with] maximum authority to do all possible - short of a Dominican Republic-type action - to keep Allende from taking power'. "It stated that the Chilean army 'has been assured full material and financial assistance by the US military establishment' to the anti-Allende forces. The document also included a lengthy rundown of the political situation in Chile.

"With the material for an expose in his hands, Bartlett did not launch an immediate investigation. Instead, he did exactly what ITT hoped he would do: He wrote a column about the dangers of a 'classic Communist-style assumption of power' in Chile. He did see some hope that 'Chile will find a way to avert the inauguration of Salvador Allende... He did not inform his readers that he had documentary evidence indicating that Chilean politics were being left to the CIA and ITT. "Asked why he did not write more, Bartlett replied in a 1973 telephone interview: 'I was only interested in the political analysis. I didn't take seriously the Washington stuff - the description of machinations within the US government.' "Yet, by Bartlett's own admission, his 28 September column was based on the ITT report - in places, to the point of paraphrase... Most reporters will not use material of this sort unless they can check it out with an independent source, so Bartlett was showing extraordinary faith in the reliability of his informants. But he used their material selectively - to write an anti-Allende scare piece, not to blow the whistle on the CIA and ITT. "An ITT official gave the same report to Time's Pentagon correspondent, John Mulliken. Mulliken covered neither the CIA nor Chile as part of his regular beat, and he sent the ITT document to Time's headquarters in New York for possible action. As far as he knows, Time never followed up on the story...

"Thus, the public did not learn what the US government and ITT were up to in Chile until the spring of 1972, when columnist Jack Anderson published scores of ITT internal documents concerning Chile. Included in the Anderson papers, as one of the most important exhibits, was the very same document that had been given 18 months earlier to Bartlett and Time magazine...

"Former Deputy Director of Intelligence, Robert Amory, was speaking for most of his colleagues when in a 26 February 1967 television interview, he said that press disclosures of CIA funding of the National Student Association and other private groups were 'a commentary of the immaturity of our society'. "With the pronounced Anglophile bias and envy of Britain's Official Secrets Act so common among high CIA officials, Amory compared the situation to our 'free motherland in England' where if a similar situation comes up, 'everybody shushes up in the interest of national security and...what they think is the interest of the free world civilisation".

"To be sure, there was a CIA press office, but it was not a very important part of the Agency's organisation... The press office was largely bypassed by Director Allen Dulles and a few of his chief aides who maintained contact with certain influential reporters. "Dulles often met his 'friends' of the press on a background basis... An ex-CIA official who worked closely with the Clandestine Services chief, Frank Wisner... recalls Dulles and Wisner frequently telling subordinates, in effect: 'Try to do a better job in influencing the press through friendly intermediaries'... "Reporters were not inclined to write unfavourable or revealing stories about the CIA, and the Agency, for its part, received a good deal of useful information from friendly newsmen. "Reporters like Joseph Alsop, Drew Pearson, Harrison Salisbury, and scores of others regularly sat down with CIA experts to be debriefed after they returned from foreign travels. These newsmen in no way worked for the Agency, but they were glad to provide the incidental information that a traveller might have observed...

"The Agency's Intelligence Directorate routinely conducted these debriefings of reporters, as it does today. "Selected newsmen, however, participated in a second debriefing conducted by the Clandestine Services. In these, the emphasis was on the personalities of the foreign officials encountered by the newsmen (as part of the unending probe for vulnerabilities) and the operation of the internal-security systems in the countries visited. "At the same time the CIA was debriefing newsmen, it was looking for possible recruits in the press corps or hoping to place a CIA operator under 'deep cover' with a reputable media outlet.

"The identities of these bogus 'reporters' were (and are) closely guarded secrets. As late as November 1973, according to Oswald Johnston's Washington Star-News report (confirmed by other papers), there were still about 40 full-time reporters and freelancers on the CIA payroll. Johnson reported that CIA Director Colby had decided to cut the 'five full-time staff correspondents with general-circulation news organisations', but that the other 35 or so 'stringers' and workers for trade publications would be retained...

"Before the CIA's successful armed invasion of Guatemala in 1954, a Time reporter dropped off the staff to participate, by his own admission, in the Agency's paramilitary operations in that country. After the Guatemalan government had been overthrown, he returned to the Time offices in New York and asked for his old job back... "The Dulles years ended with two disasters for the CIA that newspapers learned of in advance but refused to share fully with their readers.

"First came the shooting down of the U-2 spy plane over the Soviet Union in 1960. Chalmers Roberts, long the Washington Post's diplomatic correspondent, confirms in his book, 'First Rough Draft', that he and 'some other newsmen' knew about the U-2 flights in the late 1950s and 'remained silent'. "Roberts explains: 'Retrospectively, it seems a close question as to whether this was the right decision, but I think it probably was. We took the position that the NATIONAL INTEREST [caps Baffour's] came before the story because we knew the United States very much needed to discover the secrets of Soviet missilery'... "The whole U-2 incident may well have been a watershed event. For much of the American press and public, it was the first indication that their government lied, and it was the opening wedge in what would grow during the Vietnam years into the 'credibility gap'...

"As the date for the [Bay of Pigs] invasion [of Cuba in 1961] approached, the New Republic obtained a comprehensive account of the preparations for the operation, but the liberal magazine's editor-in-chief, Gilbert Harrison, became wary of the security implications and submitted the article to President Kennedy for his advice. Kennedy asked that it not be printed, and Harrison, a friend of the President, complied.

"At about the same time, The New York Times reporter Tad Szulc uncovered nearly the complete story, and the [paper] made preparations to carry it on 7 April 1961, under a four-column headline. But [the paper's] publisher, Orvil Dryfoos, and Washington bureau chief, James Reston, both objected to the article on NATIONAL-SECURITY grounds [caps Baffour's], and it was edited to eliminate all mention of CIA involvement or an 'imminent' invasion.

"The truncated story, which mentioned only that 5,000 to 6,000 Cubans were being trained in the United States and Central America 'for the liberation of Cuba', no longer merited a banner headline and was reduced to a single column on the front page. The New York Times editor, Clifton Daniel, later explained that Dryfoos had ordered the story toned down 'above all [out of] concern for the safety of the men who were preparing to offer their lives on the beaches of Cuba'. "The New York Times reporter Szulc states that he was not consulted about the heavy editing of his article, and he mentions that President Kennedy made a personal appeal to publisher Dryfoos not to run the story. "Yet, less than a month after the invasion, at a meeting where he was urging newspaper editors not to print security information, Kennedy was able to say to The New York Times' Catledge: 'If you had printed more about the [Bay of Pigs] operation, you would have saved us from a colossal mistake'.

"The failure of the Bay of Pigs cost CIA Director Dulles his job, and he was succeeded in November 1961 by John McCone... In McCone's first weeks at the Agency, The New York Times got wind of the fact that the CIA was training Tibetans in paramilitary techniques at an agency base in Colorado, but, according to David Wise's account in 'The Politics of Lying', the Office of the Secretary of Defence 'pleaded' with The New York Times to kill the story, which it did.

"In the Cuban missile crisis of 1962, President Kennedy again prevailed upon The New York Times not to print a story - this time, the news that Soviet missiles had been installed in Cuba, which the [paper] had learned of at least a day before the President made his announcement to the country.

"According to the [paper's] Max Frankel, writing in the winter 1973 of Columbia Forum, there was still a feeling that the paper had been 'remiss' in withholding information on the Bay of Pigs, so The New

York Times extracted a promise from President Kennedy that while the paper remained silent, he would 'shed no blood and start no war'. "Frankel notes that 'no such bargain was ever struck again, though many officials made overtures. The essential ingredient was trust, and that was lost somewhere between Dallas and Tonkin'.

"Then, in 1964, McCone was faced with the problem of how to deal with an upcoming book about the CIA, and his response was an attempt to do violence to the First Amendment. "The book was 'The Invisible Government', by reporters David Wise of the New York Herald Tribune and Thomas Ross of the Chicago Sun-Times. Their work provided an example of the kind of reporting of the Agency that other journalists might have done but had failed to do. In short, it was an example of investigative reporting at its best and, perhaps as a result, it infuriated the CIA. "McCone and his deputy, Lt-Gen Marshall Carter, both personally telephoned Wise and Ross's publisher, Random House, to raise their strong objections to the publication of the book. Then a CIA official offered to buy up the entire first printing of over 15,000 books. Calling this action 'laughable', Random House's president, Bennett Cerf, agreed to sell to the Agency as many books as it wanted, but stated that additional printing would be made for the public.

"The Agency also approached Look magazine, which had planned to run excerpts from the book, and, according to a spokesman, 'asked that some changes be made - things they considered to be inaccuracies. We made a number of changes but do not consider that they were significant'. "When Richard Helms took over the Agency in 1966, press relations changed noticeably. Helms himself had been a reporter with United Press in Germany before World War II, and he thought of himself as an accomplished journalist. He would tell his subordinates, when the subject of the press came up in the Agency's inner councils, that he understood reporters' problems, how their minds worked, what the CIA could and could not do with them...

"So Helms began to cultivate the press. He started a series of breakfasts, lunches, and occasional cocktail and dinner parties for individual reporters and groups of them. On days when he was entertaining a gathering of journalists, he would often devote part of his morning staff meeting to a discussion of the seating arrangements and make suggestions as to which CIA official would be the most compatible eating partner for which reporter.

"While a few senior clandestine personnel were invited to these affairs, Helms made sure that the majority came from the CIA's analytical and technical branches. As always, he was trying to portray the Agency as a predominantly non-clandestine organisation. "Helms' invitations were not for every reporter. He concentrated on what The New York Times' John Finney calls, the 'double-domes - the bureau chiefs, columnists, and other opinion makers'.

"David Wise, who headed the New York Herald Tribune's Washington staff, has a similar impression: 'In almost every Washington bureau, there is one guy who has access to the [CIA] on a much higher level than the press officer. Other reporters who call up get the run-around'. "Finney states that Helms and his assistants would 'work with flattery on the prestige of' these key journalists. CBS News' Marvin Kalb, who attended several of Helms' sessions with the press (and who was recently bugged by the Nixon administration), recalls that Helms 'had the capacity for astonishing candour but told you no more than he wanted to give you. He had this marvellous way of talking, of suggesting things with his eyes. Yet, he usually didn't tell you anything'. "Helms' frequent contact with reporters was not a sinister thing. He was not trying to recruit them into nefarious schemes for the CIA. Rather, he was making a concerted effort to get his and his agency's point of view across to the press and, through them, to the American public - a common activity among government officials...

"The source of a news leak is not usually revealed in the newspapers. Yet when Helms, or any other government official, gives a 'not-for-attribution' briefing to reporters, he always has a reason for doing so - which is not necessarily based on a desire to get the truth out to the American people. He may leak to promote or block a particular policy, to protect a bureaucratic flank, to launch a 'trial balloon', to pass a message to a foreign government, or simply to embarrass or damage an individual. "Most reporters are aware that government officials play these games; nevertheless, the CIA plays them more assiduously, since it virtually never releases any information overtly. The New York Times' Washington bureau chief, Clifton Daniel, notes that although the Agency issues no press releases, it leaks information 'to support its own case and to serve its own purposes...' "Daniel says, however, that they 'would accept material not-for-attribution if the past reliability of the source is good. But you have to be awfully careful that you are not being used'.

"In early 1968, Time magazine reporters were doing research on a cover story on the Soviet navy. According to Time's Pentagon correspondent John Mulliken, neither the White House nor the State Department would provide information on the subject for fear of giving the Soviets the impression that the US government was behind a move to play up the threat posed by the Soviet fleet.

"Mulliken says that, with Helms' authorisation, CIA experts provided Time with virtually all the data it needed... [But Mulliken] never did find out exactly why Helms wanted that information to come out at that particular time when other government agencies did not; nor, of course, did Time's readers, who did not even know that the CIA was the source of much of the article which appeared on 23 February 1968.

"From the days of Henry Luce and Allen Dulles, Time had always had close relations with the CIA. In more recent years, the magazine's chief Washington correspondent, Hugh Sidey, relates: "With McCone and Helms, we had a set-up that when the magazine was doing something on the CIA, we went to them and put it before them... We were never misled'. "Similarly, when Newsweek decided in the fall of 1971 to do a cover story on Richard Helms and 'The New Espionage', the magazine, according to a Newsweek staffer, went directly to the CIA for much of its information. And the article, published on 22 November 1971, generally reflected the line that Helms was trying so hard to sell... "Newsweek did uncover several previously unpublished anecdotes about past covert operations (which made the CIA look good) and published at least one completely untrue statement concerning the multi-billion-dollar technical espionage programme...

"The CIA has also used the American press more directly in its efforts against the KGB... The CIA has often made communist defectors available to selected reporters so news stories can be written (and propaganda victories gained). "David Wise remembers an incident at the New York Herald Tribune in the mid-1960s when the CIA called the paper's top officials and arranged to have a Chinese defector made available to reporters. According to Wise, CIA officials 'brought him down from Langley [for the interview] and then put him back on ice'... "The CIA is perfectly ready to reward its friends. Besides provision of big newsbreaks such as defector stories, selected reporters may receive 'exclusive' on everything from US government foreign policy to Soviet intentions. "Hal Hendrix, described by three different Washington reporters as a known 'friend' of the [CIA], won a Pulitzer Prize for his 1962 Miami Daily News reporting of the Cuban missile crisis. Much of this 'inside story' was truly inside: it was based on CIA leaks. This is the same Hendrix who later joined ITT and sent the memo saying President Nixon had given the 'green light' for covert US intervention in Chile."

The British example

I hope nobody is fooled by the "ancient-ness" of Victor Marchetti and John D. Marks' revelations above. True, 1974 is a long time ago, but nothing has changed. Next time you read a Newsweek or Time expose on your country or president, look beneath the article, and see whose fingers are there, and what agenda they are pushing. The close relationship between the Western media and their governments/intelligence agencies should make us all take some of their "exclusive" exposes and insights with loads of salt, not a pinch. What is good and should be emulated by the African media is that the American (and by extension, the Western) media work together with their governments and intelligence agencies to protect national interests. This is irrespective of the "fact" that they "have" a "free press" in the West.

To prove that nothing has changed, please let me introduce the British journalist, David Leigh. Writing in the June 2000 issue of the British Journalism Review, Leigh provides a British balance to what pertains in America; a valuable insight into how British journalism is still manipulated by the intelligence agencies, MI5 and M16. (Again, it is important that I quote Leigh directly and liberally here to help African journalists who don't already know, get to know the real world of journalism). Leigh wrote: (Remember he is writing in June 2000):

"British journalists - and British journals - are being manipulated by the secret intelligence agencies, and I think we ought to try and put a stop to it. ...... "The manipulation takes three forms. The first is the attempt to recruit journalists to spy on other people, or to go themselves under journalistic 'cover'. This occurs today and it has gone on for years. It is dangerous, not only for the journalist concerned, but also for other journalists who get tarred with the espionage brush..... "The second form of manipulation that worries me is when intelligence officers are allowed to pose as journalists in order to write tendentious articles under false names. Evidence of this only rarely comes to light, but two examples have surfaced recently, mainly because of the whistle-blowing activities of a couple of renegade officers - David Shayler from MI5 and Richard Tomlinson from MI6... "The third sort of manipulation is the most insidious - when intelligence agency propaganda stories are planted on willing journalists, who disguise their origin from readers. .. "There is - or has been until recently - a very active programme by the secret agencies to colour what appears in the British press, called, if publications by various defectors can be believed, 'Information Operations' or 'I/Ops'. I am - unusually - in a position to provide some information about these operations."

Leigh went on to show that "false information where the source is disguised" by the press has been a tool of British intelligence since World War II. He gave examples of stories planted by the intelligence agencies in various British papers, including The News of the World, The Observer, The Sunday Telegraph and The Spectator in which the "sources were members of the MI6".

"This was not an isolated example of recent MI6 I/Ops," Leigh continued. "In August 1997, the present foreign editor of The Independent [of London] was also in contact with the MI6 while he was at his previous post at The Observer. I know, because I became involved in an MI6-inspired story as a result... "We were supplied with a mass of apparently high-quality intelligence from MI6, including surveillance details of a meeting in an Istanbul hotel between a pizza merchant [who lived in Glasgow, Scotland] and men involved in Iranian nuclear procurement. "I should make clear that we did not publish merely on the say-so of MI6. We travelled to Glasgow, confronted the pizza merchant, and only when he admitted that he had been dealing with representatives of the nuclear industry in Iran did we publish the article. In the story we made it plain that our target had been watched by Western intelligence. "Nevertheless, I felt uneasy, and vowed never to take part in such an exercise again. Although all parties, from the foreign editor [of The Observer] down, behaved scrupulously, we had been obliged to conceal from our readers the full facts and had ended up, in effect, acting as government agents."

Leigh now believes that the "cause of honest journalism is best served by candour. We all ought to come clean about these approaches, and devise some ethics to deal with them. In our vanity, we imagine that we control these sources. But the truth is that they are deliberately seeking to control us. "The practice whereby the British press allows "spies to write under false names" also worries Leigh. He reveals that "two articles appeared in the Spectator in early 1994 under the byline Kenneth Rogers. They were datelined Sarajevo, and Roberts was described as having been working with the UN in Bosnia as an adviser. In fact, he was an MI6 officer whose local cover was as a civilian 'attached' to the British military unit's Balkan secretariat." "There is no reason," Leigh says, "to believe that the then editor of the Spectator did anything improper at all... But, as an editor, wittingly or not, it must be a bad idea to end up in a position where an MI6 officer is writing for your publication on matters of political controversy, under a false name. To Leigh, "the most dismaying" thing about it all is when journalists agree to be recruited as spies while still working as journalists. "This is an old crime," he says. "Kim Philby, former foreign correspondent of The Observer would have plenty of stories to tell about that. But it should be exposed and stopped."

Kim Philby was stationed in the Middle East as foreign correspondent of The Observer (of London). But that was only a cover. He was an MI6 agent and also worked for the Soviet KGB at the same time. He finally jumped and went to live in Moscow before the MI6 could get him after his treble life of journalist, MI6 agent and KGB agent was discovered.

Now, what does all this amount to? Very simple. It shows that when it comes to national interest, the so-called "free press" of the West is prepared to throw every journalistic principle out the window and work with the government and its agents for the general good of their countries. If African integration can be achieved, African journalists will have to borrow a thing or two here.

Government lead

Contrary to the "fiercely independent" image of the Western media, it often follows the lead set by their home governments. For example, if the British or American government targets a particular country or its leader, and bestows good or bad accolades on it or him, the Western media obediently follows the lead set by the government, irrespective of the facts on the ground. A good example is Saddam Hussein and

Iraq. In the 1980s, when it served Western interests to use Saddam as a check on Ayatollah Khomeni's Iran, Saddam was a "good guy" beloved by the West. Britain, America and their Western allies supplied Saddam's every military need. From the pages and TV screens of the Western media, dripped fawning articles about Saddam the good guy.

After the Iran-Iraqi War, when the West had no more need of Saddam, the same Western governments pronounced him a bad guy. And like sheep, the media followed the lead set by their governments. Today, the evidence is there for all to see. The same thing happens in Africa. During the 1960s, pan-Africanist leaders such as Kwame Nkrumah of Ghana, Lumumba of Congo, Sekou Toure of Guinea and others were pronounced bad guys by Western governments, and the media dutifully followed the lead set by the governments. Today, Presidents Mugabe of Zimbabwe and Charles Taylor of Liberia have become Africa's top-shelf "bad guys" merely on the say-so of the US and British governments. As expected, the Western media is slavishly following the lead set by the governments and is reporting Mugabe and Taylor in the most negative terms. In contrast, the media's current treatment of Presidents Museveni of Uganda and Paul Kagame of Rwanda as "new breed African leaders" is also a reflection of the lead set by the Western governments. On 18 January 2001, two days after President Kabila's assassination, The Independent [of London] reported that Rwanda "is secretly funded by the CIA", and as a result, Rwanda "has military operations [in the Congo] far above its means. [It] has 10,000 troops in [the Congo]."

What the paper refused to add is that America has a military base in the Bugesera district of Rwanda ostensibly to train the Rwandan army. But why is America still training an army that has 10,000 troops fighting in a neighbouring country? At the time of writing this essay, the American and the British governments were desperately trying to get United Nations Security Council to impose sanctions on Liberia for "supporting the RUF rebels" in Sierra Leone. At least, among all its sins, Liberia has not been said to have troops in Sierra Leone, yet America and Britain who are supporting Rwanda and Uganda with funds, military material and political support in the war in Congo, are still wanting to impose trade and other sanctions on Liberia, for "supporting the RUF rebels" in Sierra Leone. It doesn't add up, does it? The excuse is that the Liberian president, Charles Taylor, "handles" conflict diamonds and arms for the RUF. But that is exactly what Uganda and Rwanda are doing for the Congolese rebels - handling "conflict diamonds and gold" and arms for the rebels, under the noses of their American and British supporters.

On 19 January 2001, Chris McCreal of the *The Guardian* [of London] reported that the "foreign forces on the rebel side [in Congo - i.e. Uganda, Rwanda and Burundi] have also been 'self-financing' their intervention, and making a tidy profit, too. Uganda's gold exports have risen almost ten-fold since its involvement in Congo, and its £400m trade deficit has been erased." Yet no sanctions are being sought against Uganda and Rwanda. And the "free press" of the West is happy to play along.

In August 2000, the African-American Congresswoman for Georgia, Cynthia Mckinney, attacked the American government for the dirty tricks in Congo. She told the East African newspaper based in Kenya:

"It is unfortunate that US policy in Africa has been such an abysmal failure. It is true that Bill Clinton is the friendliest US president to Africa in several generations, but how can someone so friendly end up with such an outrageous, atrocious, horrible policy that assists perpetrators of crimes against humanity, inflicting damages on innocent African peoples? The whole world knows that Uganda and Rwanda are allies of the United States and that they have been given a carte blanche for whatever reason to wreck havoc in the Congo."

Western NGOs have recently estimated that about 1.7 million Congolese have been killed in the past three years. But to the Western media, that does not pass for news so long as the killing is being done by the "good guys" supported by America and its Western allies.

Ideological leaning

Within the Western media are political and ideological divisions that also influence the reporting of the news. In Britain, the media is split into two ideological halves. One is called "The Tory Press" and the other "The Leftwing Press". The Tory Press brings together all the conservative newspapers, magazines, radio and TV stations etc. Prominent titles in this group include The Times, The Economist, Financial Times, The Daily Telegraph, The Sun (since moved towards

Tony Blair's New Labour), The Daily Mail, Spectator, The Express, News Of The World, etc. These papers and magazines have always supported the Conservative (or Tory) Party, the Old Establishment and right-wing views. Thus, the treatment of stories and the slant put on them by this group are pro-Tory/the Old Establishment. Broadly, the readers of this group vote Tory, and many of them would not touch The Guardian with a long pole.

The Leftwing Press, on the other hand, groups the ideologically left-leaning papers such as The Guardian, The Mirror, The Daily Star, etc, who have always supported the Labour Party and leftwing or liberal ideas such as gay rights, feminism such like. In the main, these papers are broadly anti-Establishment. Thus, the slant and treatment of stories by this group is pro-Labour and pro-Left. Their readers, in the main, vote Labour and will not take The Times, for example, even if given free. On domestic matters, both The Tory Press and The Leftwing Press behave according to their respective ideological/government leanings. And this affects the choice of words, the space given to the stories, the tone, the photos and cartoons that come as illustration, etc.

For example, while The Times would use an anti-Labour story big and on the front page with a wicked slant on it, The Guardian might use it on the front page but would choose its words so carefully that the sting would be taken out of the story, in effect, making it look not too bad. But when it comes to international issues that affect British national interests, or Western interests and values, both The Tory Press and The Labour Press stick up like glue and sing from the same hymnbook. Ideological differences and political party sympathies go out the window, and a united front is erected to "bat for Britain" or the West. That explains why there is a broad tone in the critical reporting of the Zimbabwe land issue and the demonising of President Mugabe by the British and the Western media at large. Then, when election time arrives in Britain, The Tory Press recoils and goes back to supporting the Conservative Party, while The Leftwing Press returns to the Labour fold.

In 1991, when Prime Minister John Major led the Tories to that year's election victory, The Sun (a tabloid and the largest circulating paper in Britain, with 4 million copies a day), famously ran a headline saying it won the elections for the Tories. Most British commentators agreed. So, before the May 1997 elections, Tony Blair, leader of the

Labour Party, had to go all the way to Australia to court The Sun's owner, Rupert Murdoch, in a desperate attempt to get the tabloid, a traditional Tory paper, on Labour's side. Murdoch obliged. The Sun moved towards Labour. And Tony Blair became prime minister. So much for "press impartiality". So much for "adversarial relationship". It only exists in African journalism and explains why African journalists often fall into trouble with their governments. In America, the ideological divisions within the media were clearly demonstrated during the coverage of the disputed presidential election results that pitted George W. Bush against Vice President Al Gore. Time and Newsweek did not hide their Republican leanings when on in their 4 December 2000 issues, the two magazines ran almost identical front covers with Al Gore hiding behind Bush. This was during a time that the election result was a hot potato in the courts. But Time and Newsweek had designed their covers in such a way that George Bush was dominant and Al Gore pushed into the background - meaning he was the loser. This was four whole weeks before the US Supreme Court finally ruled 5-4 in favour of Bush. Newsweek even had Bush in colour on the 4 December cover, and Al Gore in black and white. And they say the media should be impartial in such matters.

Advertisers/readers' power

The behind the scenes string pulling by advertisers and readers, and hence the power they exercise over the Western media, is hardly seen by people outside the industry. Advertisers routinely remove or stop their advertisements or simply refuse to advertise in a particular newspaper, radio or TV station if unhappy with the paper's reporting of certain events. Since every newspaper survives mainly on advertisement revenue, editors are careful not to upset the principal advertisers. Readers, too, cut their subscriptions or stop buying a particular newspaper if unhappy with the coverage of news. Readers are a vital component of the media industry and editors pander to their every whim to keep them on side. Without readers, there will be no advertisers. Without advertisers, there will be no newspapers. As a result, readers occupy a tender place in the heart of the media. If a newspaper is looking for the now increasingly powerful homosexual readership, it cannot afford to print anti-gay stories.

The Laws

Britain, as stated earlier, is by far the most secretive of all the Western democracies, and it has the most laws restricting press freedom. I will not even touch the libel laws in this essay, and again, Britain has the worst libel laws in the game. I will instead dwell at length on the maze of sinister laws restricting press freedom, which the ordinary people don't even know exist. Britain has scores of these laws, yet British journalists are hardly caught by these laws, because they obey them to the letter even as they put up brave faces to the outside world that they are "free" to publish as they please. Not true.

At last count, Britain had five Official Secrets Acts in force - the 1889 Act, the 1911 Act, the 1920 Act, the 1939 Act and the 1989 Act. The 1889 Act was replaced by the 1911 Act, which was supplemented by the 1920, 1939 and 1989 Acts. The 1889 Act was originally called the Official Secrets Bill. It was enacted to prevent civil servants from leaking information to the press and other unauthorised recipients. When the bill was brought parliament, the then attorney general Sir Richard Webster told the house that the bill's main objective was "to punish the offence of obtaining information and communicating it against the interests of the state". But there was a loophole in the 1889 Act. It had no provisions for the punishment of recipients of information (except proven spies). A civil servant could be charged, but no action could be taken against the journalist or newspaper that received his information. The loophole was to be filled by the 1911 Act which is the central law governing this field today. Interestingly the bill passed into law in a mere 30 minutes, and occupied less than eight columns in the parliamentary record, Hansard.

"To understand how this came about," writes John Bunyan in his excellent book, The History and Practice of the Political Police in Britain (published in 1977), "it is necessary to go back to 1909. It was in this year that the Committee for Imperial Defence [which later became the Ministry of Defence in 1964] decided to set up a small unit (MI5, then known as MO5) under Captain Vernon Kell, to collect information on German spying activities in Britain.

"Kell found evidence of holidaying German officers gathering information on harbour plans and the like. However, he soon realised that the 1889 Official Secrets Act was quite insufficient to deal with these German spies and raised the matter with Sir Henry Wilson, the director of military operations... The question was referred to a sub-committee of the Committee of Imperial Defence, which drafted a new bill with the aid of the various intelligence services, the War Ministry, the Admiralty and the Home Office." Because "national interest" was at stake, the bill was passed in just 30 minutes by parliament. A year later, in 1912, the Act was supplemented by the introduction of the Admiralty, War Office and Press Committee to "advise" (a misnomer in all its ramifications) the press on sensitive matters of state. This committee is now known as the Services, Press and Broadcasting Committee, or, more popularly, the "D-Notice Committee". It is made up of senior civil servants, government officials and media executives, including editors. It is supposed to be "a voluntary system of self-censorship whereby editors agree not to publish information about subjects relating to defence and the activities of the security and intelligence agencies".

But in reality, the media break the supposedly benign D-Notice rules at their peril. So every editor toes the line. The D-Notice Committee issues from time to time notices to editors of all national, regional and local media (radio, TV and print) "requesting" them not to publish this or that, in the "interest of national security". Because of these D-Notice "requests", it was not until fairly recently (in the late 1990s) that the British media was able to publish such a mundane thing as the photograph and name of the head of MI5 and MI6, or their buildings in Theobalds Road in Holborn, central London. The strange thing was that the "enemies", the Russians, had for decades known the names of the various heads of the MI5 and MI6. In fact foreign newspapers had published the names for years, but no British paper dared to print them in Britain! Free press, you bet.

Today, the regime is a lot more relaxed in Britain because the authorities cannot help it as the advent of new technology has made it impossible to keep a tight lid on "secret Britain". As The Guardian wrote on 27 January 2000: "The rules about secrecy, about what we are allowed to see and publish, have been left trailing behind as commercial organisations exploit great leaps of technology. A pillar of 'national security' and the long-standing system of protecting Britain's most sensitive sites, appears to be crumbling before our eyes... The defence and security establishment now realises that past attempts to control what we can and cannot see are doomed to failure in the light of new and increasingly available technology. This fact is being recognised by Nick Wilkinson, a retired admiral and the new secretary of the D-Notice Committee."

Until 1992, about 50 secret sites in Britain (a good number of them American military bases and listening posts) were covered by "D-Notices" and no British editor could publish anything about them. With the new improvements, it is now common to see British TV reporters standing in front of the new MI6 headquarters on the Thames River at Vauxhall Cross, central London, and using it as a backdrop to their stories. Ten years ago, no paper and no TV station could do that and live in peace. In fact, they would not (and could not) do it in the first place! Records show that the two central Official Secrets Acts - 1911 and 1920 - were both passed in haste by parliament at the behest of the intelligence agencies. Despite its small size at the time, MI5 (which came into existence on 28 August 1909) was the instigator of the 1911 Act. And the British media, despite the loud talk of being free, dared not go against the Acts.

Section One of the 1911 Act, for example, opens with the statement: "If any person for any purpose prejudicial to the safety or interests of the state..." In 1964, the House of Lords (the highest court in Britain) ruled that "the national interests of the state" were "defined by the government of the day and not the courts." Under the 1911 Act, "official information" is defined as "anything which relates to or is used in a prohibited place" or which is entrusted to a state employee. Sir Martin Furnival-Jones, when head of MI5 told the Franks Committee set up by parliament, that: "It is an official secret if it is in an official file." Section 3 of the Act defines a "prohibited place" as every building which the state chooses to define as such." In addition to the Official Secrets Acts, Britain (and almost all the so-called Western democracies) has the Public Records Act which ensures that public records are kept closed (classified is the technical term) for 30, 40 or 100 years at the discretion of the government. The question arising here is: Why does Britain need all these laws? The answer is simple: The state, like every individual person, needs to keep some secrets to survive. And the laws help in the achievement of this goal for the general good. For African journalists intoxicated on the mythical "free press", it should be a salutary lesson for us all. There is even the Treason Felony Act of 1848 that stipulates that anyone imagining or publishing anything which might lead to the British monarch's downfall should be deported for life. These countries take themselves seriously, and their journalists take their countries seriously. For African integration to be achieved, African journalists will have to learn to take our countries seriously.

African lessons: Now what is the role of the African media in all this?

Because of the kind of education we get in the African journalism schools, (which rely too much on Western textbooks), our minds and therefore our Eurocentric outlook and output are shaped early from school. Strangely, in mimicking the Western media, we yet fail to copy their fierce protection of national interest, and the patriotism that makes them "bat for Britain" or the West.

To think that we can have a "free press" in Africa, when it doesn't exist anywhere in the world, is a bad mistake. We should move to correct it - and fast! For years, African journalists ourselves have added to the bad reporting of Africa by just repeating what the Western media puts out about the continent. We use the same words, the same style and the same doom and gloom stories! That must change - and fast! In fact, we think that once it is on the BBC or in the Newsweek, it must have come from the Son of God himself. As Mr Alpha Lebbie, a Gambian freelance journalist, wrote in criticising my July/August 2000 article on Reporting Africa: "And frankly," he wrote, "every journalist needs to know that it is bad news that sells, in as far as news connotes the bad and ugly." That, in fact, is the BBC definition of news - the bad and ugly.

Promoting African integration

I now come to the central theme of this essay. If the African media can help promote African integration, the following must be done. It is not an exhaustive list, merely the essential:

(A) African journalists should become more knowledgeable by reading more and beyond the spoon-feeding that we receive at school and from the Western media. As Anthony Browder says: "We should appreciate knowledge, not just for its own sake, but so it can also be applied". Knowledge is power and it comes only by pushing oneself to find it. Sometimes you may not find it in any textbook, (like the things I am writing here) but that should not stop us from wanting to know more.

(B) We should cultivate the habit of reading between the lines, be more alert and analytical. We should not just accept what Time or Newsweek or The Economist has said, we should respect their views but never take them as coming from the Son of God. We should always be alert to their omissions. For example, after Kabila's assassination, all the reporting on Congo by the British media poignantly refused to mention the uranium mines and deposits in the country, even though all the other harmless minerals such as gold, diamond and copper were routinely mentioned. Some of the papers even went as far as publishing maps showing where these minerals are mined in Congo. But never uranium! The question African journalists should be asking is: why the omission?

(C) It is desperately important (I can't emphasise it enough) that we know what our national interests are. There must be some good in it for the BBC World Service (both radio and television) to be funded (they don't say controlled) by the Foreign Office as against the BBC Domestic Service getting its funds from TV licences and government subvention. Though the BBC will tell you that it is free, yet its freedom ends where national interests begin. The head of the BBC World Service, for example, go to the Foreign Office to have routine briefings and debriefings. And they don't discuss fish and chips at the Foreign Office.

(D) To quote Romani Prodi, president of the European Commission: "The only way to express ourselves in the new world is by being together. I don't like to be a colony. If we [Europe] do not get together, we will disappear from world history." If even Europe needs to "come together" to survive, it is even more imperative for Africa to do the same. Our countries and economies are far weaker than Europe's. Our first generation of leaders failed to achieve African unity in the 1960s because they allowed themselves to be divided, and thus, ruled by the same outside forces who are today uniting to gain strength. Today Europe is building its Rapid Response Army to deal with European emergencies. Europe has its common currency, its common agricultural policy, its common market, and is moving towards a common European foreign policy. When Nkrumah wanted Africa to have a "High Command" (a Rapid Response Army) and a common African foreign policy, he did not have support from both the African politicians and the media. We allowed the outside forces to again divide us and shoot Nkrumah down. Forty years on, Europe is implementing every one of Nkrumah's 11-point agenda for African unity. And Africa is still sleeping. This is the time the African media should wake up the continent, by being alerting to the internal and external factors and obstacles still militating against the African union project.

(E) The African media should be street-wise. When we see an African leader under assault by the Western media and governments, we should be slow in joining the bandwagon and quick in investigating the matter. The agendas the Western media push are not always in Africa's interest.

(F) Very important: We should begin to do as the Western media does. They respect and obey their laws restricting press freedom, they "bat for Britain" and for the West where and when necessary, they network even though they claim to be competing with one another, they don't have 'adversarial relationships' with their governments, they work closely with their intelligence agencies for the good of their countries and people, and they work for the preservation and propagation of Western values. To help in achieving the above, African governments should make the laws clearer and more intelligible to the African journalists. Though our countries inherited the same laws from the colonial masters (for example, the British Official Secrets Acts were inherited by all the former British colonies in Africa), journalists are not consciously made aware of them. So we have a grey area where anything goes. There is no D-Notice Committee in Ghana, for example, to point the way to journalists. I was not taught at the journalism school in Accra about any Official Secrets Acts of Ghana, or any other law for that matter restricting what can be published and what cannot, (apart from the laws of libel which are essentially British laws bequeathed to Ghana). There is no shame in getting these laws in place. Even the so-called Western democracies have them.

(G) African journalists must read more authentic African history and publish more stories on African history. There is still a lot of merit in George Orwell's assertion: "He who controls the past, controls the future. He who controls the future, controls the present." Without our history as a guide, Africa will go nowhere.

The colonial construct that African history started with the arrival of the Europeans should be deconstructed, and the African media has an important role here.

Above all, we should not let ourselves as journalists, nor our people and continent be pushed down by pessimism. "No greater tragedy," Martin Luther King said, "can befall a people than to be circumscribed to the dark chambers of pessimism. Pessimism is a chronic disease that dries up the red corpuscles of hope and slow down the powerful heartbeat of positive action."

Africa shall rise from the depths to which we have fallen!

References

Anthony Browder, interview in *The Voice*, 27 November 2000

Lord Beavebrook, Leader Comment, *The Guardian*, 24 November 2000

George Alagiah, article in *The Guardian* (London), 8 January 1999, headlined: "New Light on the Dark Continent".

Milton Allimadi: *The Hearts of Darkness - How White Writers Created the Racist Image of Africa*. This was initially written as an article for *New African*, but later self-published as a book in 2003

Alex Duval Smith, reporting the death of the DRCongo president, Laurent Kabila, *The Independent* (London), 17 January 2000.

Audrey Gillan, article in *The Guardian* (London), 21 August 2000

William Ress Mogg, article in *The Times* (London), 19 February 2000

Victor Marchetti and John D. Marks in *The C1A and the Cult of Intelligence*, published in 1974

David Leigh, article in the *British Journalism Review*, June 2000

Cynthia Mckinney, Interview published in August 2000 by an East African newspaper, based in Nairobi, Kenya. Later re-published by *New African* magazine, London, September 2000.

John Bunyan, *The History and Practice of the Political Police in Britain*, published in 1977

Alpha Lebbie, letter to the editor, *New African* magazine, November 2000

Roman Prodi as reported by *The Independent*, 17 February 2000.

11

Language in the construction of Afrikan unity: past, present and policy

Kimani Nehusi

We have been handed down a vision of a slave man roaming the desert sand – a perfect image of our hollowed chiefs today. Language he had not, not ours, and not his own. It had been voided out of him, his tongue cut out *from his mouth.*
Ayi Kwei Armah: **Two Thousand Seasons**, p.7.

Every generation must, out of its relative obscurity, discovers its mission, fulfils it, or betrays it.
Franz Fanon

Introduction

The Afrikan mind is the last great frontier to be retaken in the struggle for real freedom for all the peoples of the world. The physical departure of European administrators and other enforcers of European rule at the end of formal colonialism did not solve the most fundamental problem of the European presence in Afrika. That departure demonstrated that the end of formal political domination does not end cultural penetration, mental enslavement and economic servitude. The systems and patterns of deep domination erected and enforced by many generations of formal colonial presence did not disappear with the withdrawal of those who were its direct administrators on the spot. The ways of thinking and behaving engendered by the colonial system, as well as the institutional arrangement that continually reproduces them, were left intact. The domination of Afrikan communities and society by European languages and by the language of the Arabs is a central factor in the continuing domination of Afrikans by Arabs and Europeans and the accompanying stultification of the development of Afrikan languages, Afrikan culture, Afrikan people and Afrikan society. The restoration of Afrikan languages to a position of centrality in the conduct of all Afrikan affairs: political, economic, legal, social, educational, etc. is therefore critical to the restoration of Afrikan cultural autonomy, of the Afrikan personality, Afrikan self-confidence, Afrikan creativity and sustained Afrikan development. Thus the liberation and development of Afrikan languages is a central aspect of the project of Afrikan liberation, the construction of Afrikan unity and building the Afrika- nation.

Frantz Fanon has observed that "To speak ... [a] language ... means above all to assume a culture, to support the weight of a civilisation" (Fanon, 1967, pp. 17-18) and, again, "To speak a language is to take on a world, a culture." (Ibid, p.38). Ahmed Sheikh has been no less instructive on this issue: "In speech are embedded, like fossils, the sum total of a people's values, attitudes, habits, aptitudes, in short a people's world view." (Ahmed Sheikh, 1992, p.30). Kwesi Prah articulates a similar observation in modern technological parlance: "Language is the dominant feature in any culture. More than any other aspect of culture, it is in language that the whole cultural heritage of any people is registered and catalogued. ... Language is the root directory of the culture of a speech community." (Prah, 2000b, p.49). These relationships among language, culture and history are not unknown to non-Afrikans. For example, it is almost a century ago that Ferdinand de Saussure, later widely regarded as a foremost authority and seminal influence on the study of linguistics, concluded that " [t]he culture of a nation exerts an influence on its language, and the language ... is largely responsible for the nation." (de Saussure, 1915,1966, p. 20). Further, de Saussure also notes the influence upon language of important historical events, political history and "all sorts of institutions" such as the church, schools, courts, national academies, etc. Significantly, he cites colonisation as an example of such political history. (Ibid, pp. 20 – 21).

Every language has at its very basis a value system upon which rests both the individual and collective personalities of its users. It is this value system that orders the minds of the users, determines the way in which they perceive reality, the attitudes they adopt to that reality, and therefore the behaviour patterns they will display. To speak is to think aloud, and every individual thinks in language, mostly her/his mother tongue. Hence language frames the very genesis of perception and thought, that is, the cognitive structure of its users. Language is the medium through which reality is perceived and thoughts are conceived, vocalised, and expressed in other ways, for example in writing, song, dance and in poetry. Language, then, is the instrument of perception, of thought and of the way in which the human mind is ordered and in which humans, in turn, order their world. Further, language reflects the social history and cultural traditions of its users. Language is a profoundly powerful possession.

Since each language expresses a world view and language is the medium through which deep thought or "philosophy", world view and culture are born in the human mind, implanted into the human consciousness (as well as the human unconscious), reinforced, clarified and validated, Arab and European languages, and therefore Arab and European value systems, culture and worldview, mediate between Afrikans and the reality of Afrikans at this very deep level. Foreign languages institutionalise non-Afrikan values and worldviews and therefore hijack the cognitive and psychological structure of Afrikans. This mediating presence of Arabia and Europe in Afrika is an entrapping, limiting and dangerous presence that ultimately prevents the development of Afrikan people, Afrikan communities and Afrikan society.

Historically, foreign languages and therefore foreign value systems and foreign ways of thinking and perceiving were imposed upon Afrika in the context of the *Maafa*: the Arab and European holocaust of Afrika, the single most important factor affecting the lives of Afrikan people to this very day. The *Maafa* has impacted and continues to impact massively and negatively upon every aspect of Afrikan existence – cultural, psychological, social, economic, spiritual.

The current language situation in Afrika is that Arabic and European languages are the predominant languages in which Afrikan national business is conducted. These are mostly the languages of the legislature, the judiciary, administration and education and training.

Many Afrikan countries received their flags and anthems at about the same time as some Asian countries like Singapore and Malaysia. But while the Asian countries have been able to transform their flags and anthems into real independence, Afrikan countries remain mired in underdevelopment. Asian countries have developed their own languages and culture and nowhere in Asia is the language of a former coloniser the national language. In Europe the Académie Française guards the French language and French culture from outside influence; the Real Academica de la Lingua Españiola guards the Spanish language and Spanish culture. Similar arrangements are in place in many other European countries. Afrikans are the converse wherever they exist in the world. They have remained subjected by Europe and Arabia and the languages of Europe and Arabia remain the official languages throughout the Afrikan world. Ebonics, a beautiful language created by Afrikan ancestors in the greatest depths of European barbarism, is today despised and misnamed Creole, broken English, broken French, patois, and so forth. This is a central factor in the continuing dominance of the cultural values and models of Arabia and Europe among Afrikan people.

The Afrikan elite is hardly Afrikan in the most fundamental of ways. Culturally, they are mostly Arab or European. Their foreign oppressors are the major sources of their values, their religion, their fashion, their idols, their models, their ideas and ideals. They invent nothing, for those who spend their lives imitating their oppressors cannot create anything. They are mostly not in favour of any fundamental change in the system that delivers some power and privilege to them and death and destruction to the great majority of Afrikans. They are content to be the managers of neo-colonial enterprises, including state structures, set up by others in the interests of others but in the lands and lives of the Afrikan people. This condition has been more or less so from since the time of Arab invasion and the time of European invasion of Afrika and the Afrikan mind.

The common denominator in most of the afflictions of the Afrikan people is powerlessness: the failure to influence, much less determine, their own perceptions and representations of reality from their own historical and cultural perspectives and in their own interests. Mentally imprisoned by foreign oppressors' notions of reality, their very perceptions of themselves and their world predetermined by foreign value systems, Afrikans have been therefore powerless to dictate changes or organise that reality to their own collective advantage.

The need to imagine a new, different and vastly better Afrika then set about boldly constructing it has been the task of all Afrikans in every generation from the inception of the *Maafa*. It remains the primary task of every Afrikan today. Today, with Afrikans everywhere on this planet apparently gripped by a seemingly permanent downward spiral marked by crisis after crisis – AIDS, desertification, famine, cultural and economic bondage, poverty, racism, internal strife - this task must be clearer and more urgent than ever. That is why those important observations of Ayi Kwei Armah and Frantz Fanon are planted at the head of this chapter.

Afrika and Unity

A viable Afrikan language policy can best be articulated and be most effective only in the wider context of a comprehensive plan for the total liberation and transformation of the Afrikan reality by the masses, the great majority of the Afrikan people, and in their own interests. Such a project must therefore cover every aspect of the Afrikan reality, because language is merely one aspect of that reality, one area – though a very strategic and therefore a critical one - through which foreign domination has been imposed and is continually reproduced. It is in this regard that there is a fair sign that the drive for unity is part of the current political context. The foremost thinkers and doers on behalf of the vast majority of Afrikans, including Marcus Garvey, Kwame Nkrumah, Amilcar Cabral, Malcolm X, Walter Rodney and others, have agreed that Pan Afrikanist unity is a prerequisite for real liberation of the people and continent of Afrika. Kwame Nkrumah declared that the independence of Ghana "is meaningless unless it is linked up with the total independence of the African continent" (Nkrumah, 1980, p.121). Cheikh Anta Diop presented plans for a federated state of Afrika (Diop, 1987). Ultimately it is Afrikans who must assume responsibility for the direction of change in Afrika. History, as well as the present, shows clearly that anything else will amount to the continuation of foreign domination and the increasingly desperate condition of the vast majority of the Afrikan people.

In the past there was the much-lamented Organisation of African Unity (OAU); now the African Union (AU) has emerged from the dust of the OAU and many are wondering what has changed beyond the name. Previous conceptions of Afrikan unity were failures partly because there was no clear recognition that just as the underdevelopment of Afrikan languages and Afrikan culture were key factors in the underdevelopment of Afrika, the converse is also true: that the development of Afrikan languages and Afrikan culture are vital components in the realisation of Afrikan liberation, Afrikan unity and Afrikan development (Cabral, 1980, pp.138-154; Nehusi and Nani-Kofi, 1999, pp. 14–18; Prah. 1998, pp.85-86; Nehusi, 2001, pp. 56-122). The acquisition of the correct perspective on the role of culture in Afrikan unity and Afrikan development raises the significance of identity and worldview in the debate.

It is here that is located the urgent and long outstanding necessity to repair the Afrikan personality through proper relocation in Afrikan history, Afrikan cultural values, attitudes and behaviours, i.e. an Afrikan centred orientation, which is the only proper basis of consistent and sustained action for Afrikan liberation and development. This leads, logically, to the realisation that the definition of the Afrikan has always been central to the great issues of Pan Afrikanism, Afrikan liberation and Afrikan development. Afrikans must be clear about their own identity and unite with themselves before Afrikans can associate successfully (i.e. with benefits to Afrikans) with any other people in any way.

Placing Afrikan culture at the centre of the definition of the Afrikan is not merely logical and consistent. It also places the role of the Arabs and Europeans in the *Maafa* in stark relief, for the cultural genocide of Afrikans, as an inescapable prerequisite to domination, oppression and exploitation, has been a major objective of Arabs and Europeans from the inception of these two foreign presences in Afrika. The continuing effects of cultural genocide still imprison the minds of most Afrikans today. Afrikan culture remains central to Afrikan liberation, Afrikan development and Afrikan unity.

Pan Afrikanism offers a number of advantages to the Afrikan people, which are not offered by continentalism and other forms of neo colonialism. In a Pan Afrikan arrangement the individual can belong simultaneously to a clan, 'tribe', state and nation without any contradiction. Thus someone can be Yoruba, Nigerian and Afrikan at the same time without any contradiction or neurosis or trauma. Pan Afrikanism urges the (re)definition of self as part of a large entity with its corresponding psychological, social, economic, cultural and political security. Pan Afrikanism offers a secure context in which every Afrikan can be herself/himself and develop all her/his potential to the fullest while simultaneously contributing towards the development of the Afrikan nation in its widest sense. This is the securest context in which to settle conflicts, since it substantially removes the circumstances in which Afrikans define themselves in mutually antagonistic terms that emphasise difference and consider other Afrikans as strangers, total outsiders, people with whom they have nothing in common. Further, Pan Afrikanism offers a way out of this mess because it presents both the basis and the compelling necessity for negotiating an integrated and united Afrika based upon a clear recognition of and respect for the lines along which Afrikan people developed naturally. This understanding of Pan-Afrikanism does not seek to negate differences or variations in the Afrikan cultural experience or in its expression. It does not seek to coerce Afrikans into some notion of sameness. It emphasises commonalties of language and culture, common values, a shared ancestry, a shared history, a recognised Afrikan world community of interests and a common understanding of all this, which in turn could be articulated and perpetuated through common and or mutually intelligible Afrikan terminology - a Pan Afrikan terminology to describe and represent this shared vision and objective of the Afrikan world.

The converse of this vision is the currently dominant reality of increasingly irrational attachment to increasingly anachronistic and dysfunctional 'states' that were set up by foreigners in the interests of foreigners without consultation with Afrikans. Today it is increasingly clear that the neo-colonial state and its apparatus, inherited from colonialism, cannot meet all the needs of all the Afrikan people. These states and their apparatuses were not designed by Afrikans in the traditions of Afrika for the benefit of Afrikans. Consequently, they do not function for the benefit of the vast majority of Afrikans. They were designed by Arabs and Europeans mainly for the economic benefits of Arabs and Europeans, and they continue to play this role, for they are firmly integrated into the global system of exploitation in which the World Trade Organisation (WTO), the International Monetary Fund (IMF), the World Bank and some Non Government Organisations

(NGOs) are important instruments of continuing Afrikan underdevelopment. Neo-colonial states do not and cannot meet the needs of the vast majority of their peoples because they were not designed to do so; they normally meet the perceived needs only of the elite, who are mostly collaborators with the dominant system that exploits and impoverishes the great mass of the Afrikan people. For these reasons both the elite and the neo-colonial states they control are increasingly challenged by their own people on issues of resource allocation and other forms of sovereignty, as is illustrated in Somalia, Nigeria, South Afrika and elsewhere. After more than forty wasted years of neo-colonial "independence" it is becoming clearer that most Afrikans received only flags and anthems from this process. The people versus the state is the plainest statement of this great contradiction in many parts of the continent.

The experience of Kwame Nkrumah, the great Pan Afrikanist leader of 'independent' Ghana, shows just how dangerously limiting are these imposed structures (Nkrumah, 1969). Pan Afrikan language initiatives must therefore mean acting across foreign imposed 'borders' and against the interests of the neo-colonial state structures, for co-operation across boundaries imposed by non-Afrikans is needed for standardisation and harmonisation of orthographies, the general development of Afrikan languages and the advancement of the Pan Afrikan project. The audience of each language is, by this imposed definition of nationality, trans national, so literatures produced for the Afrikan masses must be trans national also(Prah, 2000b, p.70). It is the same with any other viable cultural or economic or political initiative. Afrikans must liberate Afrikan minds, Afrikan languages and every other aspect of the Afrikan reality from the still living boundaries imposed by foreign conquerors long ago.

The Afrikan Heritage of Language and Writing

Any appropriate language policy for Afrika must be culturally and historically sensitive and relevant. Such a policy must therefore consider the questions raised by both the past and the current language realities of the Afrikan people. The institutionalised lies and distortions put out by Arab and European sources disaffected and continue to distort every area of Afrikan reality, including language. Today it can no longer be denied that Afrikans were the first humans. That means that Afrikans invented language, for language is simultaneously both an attribute and an inescapable indicator of humanity. The common precursor of modern Afrikan languages, the 'predialectal mother tongue, the common predialectal language' (Obenga, 1992, p. 107) was therefore the first language in the world. It is one of the tasks of Afrikan linguists to reconstruct and explain this ancestor language, showing its genetic links to all subsequent Afrikan languages. (see for example, Obenga, ibid., pp.105-141, Diop, 1977, Nehusi, 2001).

In an era in which the dominant forces of the world often misrepresent Afrika as essentially an oral culture in which underdevelopment is inherent, it is especially important to note that the Afrikan language and development heritage stretches back to the very first language and the very first writing, which were fundamentals of the very first massive, consciously organised and sustained developmental process and civilisation in the history of this planet. But even the invention of language and writing does not describe the full Afrikan heritage of language and writing – or the full Afrikan communications tradition. Afrikans can and must claim and understand much more, for Afrikans have invented many more scripts, including the Meroetic script of ancient Nubia, the script used to write Ge'ez, Amharic and Tigrinya in Ethiopia, the Manding script in Senegal and Mali, the Vai script in Liberia, the Mende script in Sierra Leone, the Bamoun script in Cameroon, the Nsibidi and Edo scripts in Nigeria, the Afaka script in Suriname, Tifinagh, the now disused Berber script and Osmania, a Somali script. It may also be possible and necessary to speak of an Adinkra script employed by the Akan people of Ghana/Côte d'Ivoire. (Nehusi, 2001, p.60; Prah, 2000b, p.53; Thompson, 1984, pp. 228-229).

Afrikans have therefore invented language and have also invented writing as a way of harmonising and standardising their written communication. The conceptual leap from pre writing to writing resulted in a very powerful tool in planning and organisation for national development. Moreover, Afrikans have made this leap many times in the different time/spaces that they have invented scripts, including in Afrikan communities abroad.

The fact that Afrika is the birthplace of language and civilisation is a source of example, knowledge and inspiration which are all necessary for the project of Pan Afrikan unity and liberation, which in turn is so imperative for the salvation of Afrika and the Afrikan people. This

216

heritage is not generally known throughout Afrika because the system of development, publication and distribution of knowledge, as well as the (mis)education system it supports, are organised and function against the interests of the great majority of Afrikans. The knowledge that the ancestors of Afrikans invented both language and writing, as well as science, etc., indeed civilisation, ought to be a source of pride as well as the confidence that Afrikans can do again what they did many times before and must so obviously do now.

There is a vulgar contradiction between the linguistic and scribal heritage of Afrika and the current Afrikan reality. That contradiction has been imposed, and is mediated, by foreign cultural and language domination.

Language is an unfailing witness to and record of social history. The languages through which the social history of the last 1400 years of Afrika has been articulated are deeply marked by, and yield much evidence of that history. This is true for both Afrikan and non-Afrikan languages. The former have been deliberately underdeveloped as a policy objective of colonialism and the systems that continuously deliver that underdevelopment have been continued under neo colonialism. The languages of the colonisers and despoilers of Afrika, chiefly Arabic and the European languages of English, French, Spanish, Portuguese and German, and the knowledge industry conducted in these languages, are marked by a deeply racist value system that sustains centuries of lies and distortions that were necessary for the Arab and European project to subjugate and exploit Afrika and its people.

The many variations of this fragmented, disunited, weak and very distorted vision and version of Afrika and Afrikans have been codified into a number of myths and distortions. These myths and distortions are based upon a value system that consistently posits Arabs and Europeans as inherently superior and Afrikans as inherently inferior. These basic and dominant lies have been repeated in many forms, resulting in myriad ramifications in every area of knowledge. They include such myths as the tower of Babel: the alleged vast multiplicity of Afrikan languages as well as the myth of Caliban and Prospero. Together, all of these constitute another level of domination that is continuously reinforced and perpetuated through alien ideologies in alien terminology in alien languages. These foreign viewpoints are upheld, reinforced and perpetuated through the functioning of the major institutions, which are based upon this racist value system, which in turn has been unknowingly internalised by many Afrikans. The result is that the perceptions, attitudes and behaviours of the Afrikan believers in this value system have been determined by their oppressors.

Today a dominant feature of Afrika is the balkanisation of language, of culture, of land and so, most importantly, of the masses of the Afrikan people. The languages, borders, systems of administration and so forth imposed by Arab and European despoilers divide Afrika and Afrikans into small and often mutually antagonistic and economically unviable parts, which prevent the free interaction of Afrikans and therefore exist against the interests of Afrikans.

The most fundamental damage remains the balkanisation of the Afrikan mind, for Afrikans remain shut up behind these barriers to unity and strength. Linguistic balkanisation has to be overcome if Afrikans are to achieve political union. Afrikans cannot remain in Anglophone, Dutch-Afrikaans, Francophone, Hispanophone and Lusophone prisons and even hope to be members of any Afrikan union worthy of that name.

Linguistic, cultural, territorial, social, political, economic and psychological balkanisation derailed the historical evolution of Afrikans towards the unity of Afrikan people and therefore towards Pan Afrikan authorities which represent the vested interests of Afrikans in each of these areas. By fragmenting Afrika into small pieces the policy of balkanisation sharply increased the potential for mutual antagonisms, both because it increased the chances of conflict by increasing the number of separate units, each with its own, real or imagined interests and each of which is by itself weaker than a united Afrika, and because it increased the chances of foreign intervention and domination, which could play off weak units and weak leaders against each other and against the common interests of the vast majority of Afrikans. The forced migration of Afrikans through the Arab and European trade in enslaved Afrikans, and more historically recently the flight of increasing numbers of Afrikans from the appalling conditions created and maintained by foreign control and exploitation of their homelands, have created substantial Afrikan communities abroad.

This question of language is therefore also important for the Afrikan communities abroad. It must be made clear here that the continent of the ancestors of all Afrikans is also of the greatest importance to every Afrikan abroad – not only to Afrikans in the homeland. The converse is also true, for Afrikans abroad constitute a pool of talent, training, experience and insights which will prove valuable for the necessary processes of repairing the entire Afrikan people and their world. This is not only a psychological or even a romantic involvement with the notion of Afrika. The concrete conditions of Afrikans abroad are deeply influenced by the very forces that control the continent and for the same reasons – and the fate of Afrikans abroad will ultimately be determined by what transpires on the continent. The notion of Afrika must therefore include both the continent and the communities abroad.

The language situation in Afrikan communities abroad is very similar to the situation on the continent. Afrikans abroad are subjected to imposed foreign languages, again mainly Arab and European languages, which are the official languages of the countries in which they live. Ebonics, their own Afrikan language, is not even recognised as a language in most of these countries (Crawford, 2001). The full understanding and recognition of Ebonics as an Afrikan language that is intimately related to other Afrikan languages is an important step in promoting the unity of the Afrikan continent and its communities abroad and therefore beginning the process of repairing centuries of separation, trauma and mutual weakness (Nehusi, 2001, p. 78). The necessity for standardisation and harmonisation of the different varieties of Ebonics along lines similar to the work of The Centre for Advanced Studies of African Society (CASAS) is still evident, though there have been some steps in this general direction.

The languages imposed on Afrikans in the processes of Arab and European colonisations have functioned and continue to function as languages of dis-empowerment and exclusion. By this arrangement the mass of Afrikan people are permanently locked out of the developmental processes

It is for these reasons, as well as for the very additional reasons of pride and appearance, that no self-respecting people will allow their affairs to be conducted in the language of their oppressors. For to do so amounts to the most fundamental kind of surrender; that is, the surrender of the mind of the oppressed to be constructed and directed by their oppressors, and their actions predetermined by the interests of the latter.

Towards An Afrikan Language Policy

The imperative of development is a natural drive among any healthy people. Development must be defined as the sustained all round ability of a people to meet the challenges of their environment to fulfil the basic needs for food, clothing, shelter, defence and renewal, recreation and entertainment, more or less independently of any other people and on their own terms: that is, according to and in fulfilment of their own cultural traditions and historical mission. The application of science and technology to both human organisation and motivation and to industrial processes is the true basis of the sustained development and maintenance of the production process, making it more and more efficient so that both production (volume) and productivity (volume in relation to inputs) are increased continually year over year. The capacity to be creative or inventive, even if this is only at the level of application, is therefore critical to continuous scientific and technological renewal. But the only real secure basis of sustained and independent creative thought and action is a people's own language and culture. These prerequisites to real independence are negated by foreign linguistic dominance. Thus the centrality of language and culture to sustained development is encountered once again. Language is central to culture, and culture is central to identity, which in turn determines worldview, interests and goals and provides the basis for a programme of self-fulfilling action.

For there to be development, people as well as ideas and materials are necessary. But it is not just any people who are necessary. The experience of the Japanese, Chinese and the so called Asian Tiger economies and societies demonstrate that an essential aspect of sustained development is the ability to acquire knowledge, skills, technique and materials from outside their own environment and indigenise these without compromising their own cultural identity; that is, without becoming cultural orphans or the cultural step children of others. This is exactly what European countries have also been doing over the last six hundred years with materials and ideas largely looted from people and lands they dominate, chiefly Afrika.

From this perspective humans emerge as the most important resource of all the elements in the developmental process. But this does not mean that it is enough merely to have humans. The orientation and motivation of those humans is critical. The supreme and securest form of orientation and motivation is a retention of and location within one's own language, culture and identity. There can be no sustained development worth its name in Afrika and Afrikan communities abroad without the development of Afrikan languages and culture. For all Afrikans this can mean only Reparations, the recovery of history, of culture, of a correct view of self; the repair of self and so a positive view of the future informed by an accurate understanding of the past.

There exists today, and has always existed, the very real bases for a common language policy in Afrika and among Afrikans the world over. These constitute, too, part of the considerable bases for Pan Afrikan unity. Those bases are to be found all over the Afrikan world in the genetic relationship among Afrikan languages, a common communications tradition, as well as the common origin in and belonging to a single cultural complex that unites Afrikans across space and time. The recognition of this important fact prompted Cheikh Anta Diop, the great Afrikan intellectual worker, to entitle his book devoted to part of that subject, *The Cultural Unity of Black Africa.* (Diop,1963,1989). It is clear that Afrikans possess a common core of cultural values, institutions, attitudes, behaviours and a common world-view.

These terms and their variants, which exist in Afrikan languages, demonstrate more than the linguistic and cultural unity of Afrika. If properly understood within their semantic context they also indicate the classical Afrikan world-view, one constructed by Afrikans for the benefit of Afrikans, one that consequently served Afrikans very well for millennia before the *Maafa*. In the present context of the search for unity Afrikans will do no better if they look to their own linguistic tradition, the oldest one on the planet, to find concepts upon which to construct that unity, and if they search for the Afrikan linguistic terms to express those concepts. This is the only logical step because language is never neutral and terminology articulates ideology. The creative deployment of Afrikan terminology, including inventions where necessary, is an important step towards bringing to life, once again, throughout all strata of Afrikan society, the world-view traditional to Afrika. This is the only good practice and the best psychology for Afrikans.

To try to articulate and represent Afrikan retrieval of heritage, of vision, and Afrikan renewal in terms taken from non-Afrikan languages, as some have attempted, is really to try to represent Afrikan possessions, inventions and processes by non-Afrikan concepts and ultimately through non-Afrikan eyes. The term *renaissance* reached the consciousness of Afrikans from its origins in the French language, sometimes via other European languages. Grounded in the experience of Europeans, it is a European linguistic and therefore a European cultural item that inculcates and expresses the viewpoint of Europeans.

The continued employment of such terms, and ultimately the foreign languages out of which they are taken, represents a fundamental contradiction to the very notion of Afrikan development, for it negates the sustained retrieval, development and deployment of Afrikan terminologies and so of Afrikan languages; the Afrikan worldview and the Afrikan aesthetic, it minimises and stifles opportunities for the creative mental processes in Afrikan languages, and so condemns Afrikans to be uncreative recipients of values, ideas, concepts, ideals and materials originated by others. In such a context Afrikan society may increase in size of population, in volume of consumption of this or that commodity it does not manufacture, but it will not develop, for mimicry and imitation have never been the bases of development. Rather, this condition of permanent dependency at the most fundamental level is a recipe for permanent underdevelopment.

Similarly, the notion of "Black Afrika" raises the unvoiced notions of "Arab" Afrika and "White" Afrika. Such terms are contradictory and opportunistic, since culture and history are the major determinants of who is an Afrikan. Terminology articulates ideology: the values and worldview that imprison the mind and determine perception, attitudes and patterned behaviour. Foreign terminologies articulate foreign ideologies and ultimately safeguard existing structures of power that oppress Afrikans.

Quite apart from the dissonance, or worse, which arises as a cross cultural issue here, such a way of proceeding is surely the worst sacrilege, the clearest form of cultural suicide. For to try to represent processes indigenous to one culture by the terminology of another culture, especially an historically oppressive one, is not merely to misrepresent or distort the processes in question; it is also to acquiesce to domination at the deepest level, the level of perception and representation, of ideology and the mind. It is to elect - consciously or not - for continued mental enslavement, the most fundamental form of bondage. It is therefore not possible to conceive or argue or undertake in any way real Afrikan development in non-Afrikan terms.

It is clear that the Afrikans, as part of their cultural revival, face the task of reconstructing a system of perception and representation of reality from the Afrikan perspectives, a fully functional Afrikan aesthetic that must once again become the common possession of all Afrikans. It is this system which must become the basis of the standards Afrikans obtain in all their conceptions and representations of reality; the basis of the cultural tastes, orientations and standards that rule the Afrikan creative imagination as well as the built environment of the Afrikan. Afrikans must control the representation of Afrika – at least among themselves in the first instance. One aspect of this aesthetic must of necessity be terminology as a representation of Afrikan ideology. The invasion and colonisation of Afrika was not merely a physical act; it was fundamentally a process with deep spiritual, cultural, psychological and mental ramifications that still reverberate in the Afrikan consciousness and so in the Afrikan reality today. Hence both Afrika and counter Afrika exist in language, myths, legends, history and ideology. Employing terminology from oppressive languages upholds the ideology of oppression; employing the terminology of Afrikan languages upholds the Afrikan cultural perception and tradition and validates and reaffirms Afrikan values. This is the ideology of liberation.

The Sankofa tradition for instance is represented graphically by the Sankofa Bird with its beak in its feathers, looking backwards, recognising that it is not taboo to retrieve the past. Sankofa is at once a metaphor for this reclamation and a challenge to do so whenever necessary. But Sankofa is not an indiscriminate regurgitation of the past or an inordinate desire to remain there. Although it has the potential to retrieve the entire past, the Sankofa bird retrieves only those aspects that are useful to the current challenges and tasks and it is to the present and the future that these are applied. Sankofa must connote an engagement with the missing part of a solution, the crucial piece of knowledge necessary to complete a task. That is why the Sankofa bird sometimes has an egg in its beak. This egg symbolises something valuable, a treasure. It also symbolises creation, fertility, renewal or rebirth and resurrection.

The egg has long symbolised these concepts in Afrikan tradition. In Kemet the egg is symbolic of beginnings and the very origins of the primeval world. A Kimetu myth represents the first divinity coming into being from an egg of a goose divinity known as the 'great Cackler'. The Afrikans of Kemet also represented Ptah, their creator divinity, fashioning the first egg on a potter's wheel. It is in this very way that they represented Khnum, another divinity, fashioning humans from clay. In the Late Period of Kemet egg shaped amulets were placed in tombs to symbolise a new afterlife. (Wilkinson, 1992, 1998, p. 97).

Sankofa, therefore, represents excavation, reclamation and re-examination of meaningful experience within a context of periodic interrogation and re-interrogation of experience for the purpose of continuous renewal. Sankofa proclaims that Afrikans must continuously re-tool and re-invent themselves as necessary, but upon the same basic cultural principles that their ancestors invented, developed, and handed down to them as the very basis of the Afrikan cultural heritage. This principle of effective choice, of separating the useful from the useless or potentially damaging and limiting, is also represented in another aspect of Akan Afrikan tradition: Odomankoma Kyerema, the Ashanti Divine Drummer, relays only truthful information.

The etymology of the term Sankofa lies in the Twi words *san* = "to return, to retrace one's steps, to return to the roots"; *ko* = "to go" and *fa* = "to take", "to seize" (Willis, 1998, p. 189). For Willis, this term means, ultimately, "… a realisation of self and spirit. It represents the concepts of self-identity, redefinition, and vision. It symbolises an understanding of one's destiny and the collective identity of the larger cultural group." (Willis, 1998, p. 189). Willis reminds us that "Though the concept may seem new, it is an old tradition that links a people to the discovery of their past, which is a fundamental building block for the future." (Willis, 1998, p. 189) Willis does not say exactly how old this tradition is, but in the history of the Afrikan people the Kemites or ancient Egyptians invented the notion of *whm msw* long before the Akan, who are one of the successor groups of the Kemitew.

The story of the Sankofa and other Adrinka symbols, terminology and thus ideology may be read as symbolic of the experience of almost all Afrikan people. In the communities abroad many of the symbols were placed in wooden furniture. But as time went by they were passed on and inherited from generation to generation as mere decoration. No one understood these messages from Afrikan ancestors any longer; the things they tried to tell in this and many other ways were lost. These graphic messages were erased from the Afrikan overseas environment when metal furniture of a new style and another aesthetic replaced the wooden traditional furniture, announcing the greater dominance of another culture. But all is far from lost. Afrikan communities abroad are now increasingly re-familiarising themselves with Sankofa and other Afrikan concepts such as Kwanzaa, Afrikan Liberation Day, Libation, the Council of the Elders, Naming Ceremony and Afrikan Names. These are all aspects of a growing movement of reclamation and restoration of Afrikan identity, which in turn is part of the Reparation movement.

Afrikan concepts ground Afrikans in Afrikan reality, for they are born out of that reality and express it faithfully, in every nuance, and do it so beautifully as no other language and culture can do. In this way *Sankofa, Weheme Mesu*, and so forth are opposed to "renaissance" which is a concept native to European attempts to reborn themselves in a certain historical era after an image that was at least partly derived from Afrikans, but which nevertheless does not and cannot accurately capture and articulate the Afrikan reality. A logical consequence of all this is that Afrikans will continue to be mentally enslaved if they do not apply their own languages, terminology and ultimately their own ideology to the description and analysis of their own lives. Doubtless appropriate terms also exist in other Afrikan languages.

The Objectives of an Afrikan Language Policy

In the struggle for liberation one of the last great frontiers to be retaken by Afrikans is the mind of Afrika, imprisoned by racist and demeaning terminology, by myths and distortions and consequently locked away in alien worldviews that are integral aspects of languages imposed by the enemies of Afrika. A major objective of a relevant language policy for Afrika must therefore be to move from alien languages of exclusion, dis-empowerment, oppression and domination to Afrikan languages that respect, include empower and will ultimately liberate and help to develop Afrikans because these are their own languages that belong to and express faithfully their own traditions, identity and worldview. In a context of a genuine search for unity and liberation from centuries of foreign domination and the resulting cultural and material poverty, powerlessness and dependency in which foreign languages envelope the thought processes of many Afrikans like a shroud, the reliance on their own Afrikan languages will help to inculcate habits of proud self confidence so essential for self reliant, empowered, democratic, self sustaining and liberated communities.

It is clear that the deployment of Afrikan languages at all levels will enable the vast majority of Afrikan people to embark upon the process of their own development. Employment of the mother tongue will break the vicious downward spiral, banish insulting and inaccurate images of the self so assiduously perpetuated by foreign languages, resulting in the disablement so common among Afrikans as a direct result of foreign domination.

MOTHER TONGUE	IMPOSED FOREIGN LANGUAGE
1. Understanding of and dealing efficiently, effectively and comfortably with a variety of language situations; very few areas of society, if any, inaccessible.	1. Unfamiliarity with and imperfect understanding of foreign language lead to inadequate communication discomfort in situations in which the foreign language is mandatory, alienation and exclusion.
2. Internalisation, understanding and practical deployment of concepts through perceiving and thinking in a totally familiar language, based upon a positive value system, with totally familiar and relatively easily accessible idioms and concepts that may have no exact equivalents in imposed foreign languages. Creative potential unfettered. Culturally confident, self-confident and self-sustaining individuals and society assured.	2. Dissonance and difference between two cultures result in difficulty or limitation in communication. The subject is forced to think and create in an imposed foreign language, which may contain inaccurate and demeaning values and representations as well as unfamiliar and only partially accessible idioms and concepts. Severe limitations or block on creative process occur, resulting in a real strategic threat to self-confident, fully independent and self-sustaining individuals and society.
3. Empowering, enabling and liberating language, resulting in individual enhancement and group dynamism.	3. Hijacked cognitive structures, imprisoned minds, disempowering and disabling language, resulting in enfeeblement and helplessness – and less dynamic or even relatively static individuals and society.

3.a. Positive value system initiates and continuously reinforces positive self-image and positive self concept	3.a. Imposition of negative value system undermines and destroys positive self-image and positive self-concept and installs and continuously reinforces negative self-image and negative self-concept.
3. b. Highly motivated individuals and dynamic society.	3.b. Demotivated individuals and undynamic society.
3. c. High goals are set at both individual and group levels.	3.c. Low/no goals are set at both individual and group levels.
3.d. High achievement levels, productivity, strong individuals and society	3.d. No/low attainment level, weak individuals and weak collective
4. A wider community of interest is engaged; unity promoted	4. Narrow interest groups serviced, fissiparous tendencies reinforced
5. Positive affirmation of group identity continuously reinforced at all levels of society	5. Continuous disruption, assassination and negation of identity through denial, erosion, undermining of mother tongue or vernacular.
6. Permanent mobilisation	6. Permanent demobilisation
7. Stimulus for other (related) cultural institutions, which function in an integrated way	7. Cultural institutions penetrated, distorted, isolated, do not function in an integrated manner and may be dysfunctional in many other respects
8. Social tradition of enthusiasm and full democratic participation promoted and maintained	8. Apathy and non-participation, or only limited participation, with associated attitudes, become the tradition
9. Democracy and other forms of inclusion and empowerment.	9. Colonisation, neo-colonialism and other forms of exclusion and domination.
Development	Underdevelopment

For Afrikans everywhere, on the continent as well as in the Afrikan communities abroad, there is no viable alternative to the mother tongue. All thought about anything, and all relations among people: cultural, economic, political, educational and so forth are conducted through language. To attempt to engage even in private thought or to try to conduct these relations in an imposed foreign language is to undermine and exclude the majority, a profoundly undemocratic process that limits or prevents participation in society. It therefore

227

limits freedom and imposes severe consequences upon the individual and society by undermining the culture and identity of those forced to use the imposed foreign language.

On the other hand, to conduct relations in a mother tongue and or an acquired Afrikan language is to engage in a deeply creative and enriching process, for all Afrikan languages belong to the same communications tradition, share the same world view and belong to the same culture complex, so dissonance and alienation will be erased or minimised and genuine unity can be propagated.

Mother tongue development will help to engender a shift in the centre of gravity of Afrikan society. The major source of creative energy is the masses, the vast majority of the people. When the social, political, economic and cultural processes of a society are conducted in the mother tongue, the language of the people, then the people own these processes, their full creative potential is released, and they embark upon processes of sustained self development, both as individuals and as families, clans, communities and so on. If, on the other hand, these relations are conducted in a foreign tongue then people remain partially or fully locked out of participation in the processes that shape society, locked out of development and dominated in the deepest way by foreigners. For creativity is stymied when conceptual tools are devised and articulated in foreign and not totally understood idioms. Clearly, development of the mother tongue is a potent way of owning, valuing and creating a dynamic and self-sustaining self, identity, community and society.

The validation of the Afrikan language family and the Afrikan linguistic and communications traditions in the popular and official practice of the Afrikan people is really the validation of the Afrikan world-view and orientation and ultimately validation of Afrikan identity. It is the validation of the Afrikan self by the Afrikan self. Raising the status of Afrikan languages is equal to raising the status, self-image and self-concept of Afrikan masses. A people's mother tongue is ultimately a tool for development, as it is critical for assuring inclusion, cultural and psychological security, creativity, self-confidence and higher work rates.

Mother tongue development as part of a relevant language policy will empower Afrikans and enable them to communicate freely and easily with each other wherever they may be located.

The Afrikan linguistic heritage and the Afrikan heritage in general are not fully known by most Afrikans because the system of the production (i.e. research), publication, distribution and consumption of knowledge in Afrika as well as about Afrika has remained substantially the same as in the period of formal colonialism. It does not concern itself with Afrika and Afrikans from the points of view of Afrika and Afrikans. Another part of the context of a proper language policy in Afrika must therefore be the replacement of the continuing system of misinformation and deliberate misinterpretation of Afrikan phenomena erected by oppressors in the interests of oppressors. A new system must be erected. This must serve the interests of the vast majority of the Afrikan people.

Afrikan scholars must begin to operate in the service of the vast majority of Afrikans. Since the inception of the Arab and European presence the dominant pedagogic practice in Afrika and among Afrikans abroad has been concerned mainly with promoting the retreat and death of Afrikan languages and the advance of Arabic and European languages. It is now time for Afrikan scholars and teachers to address the question of Afrikan revival.

The fact of a single linguistic system, based upon common origins and the inheritance of a common communication heritage anchored in a common worldview, ought to be accepted as the only real basis of a worthwhile language policy that will serve the needs of a modern Afrika, that is, an Afrika in a technological age. It will destroy the basis and fact of a fragmented Afrika, deeply divided and weakened, most strategically in the minds of the Afrikan people because of the way they have been made to perceive and articulate their own selves and their own reality wherever they are on the planet.

Most Afrikans speak two or more languages, a situation found both at home and abroad. This fact of bi- and multi-lingualism among Afrikans ought to be part of the basis of language policy as well as the construction of the best strategies and methodologies for language acquisition.

The appropriate language policy must also address the issue of the current knowledge and expertise in foreign languages in Afrika. Such knowledge, and especially the system used to reproduce it, may very well constitute a potentially valuable resource that can be re-deployed for the benefit of Afrika. The objective here must be to reproduce this knowledge in a culturally relevant context, one in which Afrikan languages and the Afrikan value system correctly predominate as the mother tongues and foreign languages are learnt as foreign languages, that is, additional to the main languages employed in the daily life of the vast majority of Afrikans.

Afrikan languages must become central in the education of future generations of Afrikans. Mother tongues must be instituted and so validated from the ground up: in Afrikan names, rituals, local, regional and Pan Afrikan government, the law, the legislature and all official business. The people's business must be conducted in the people's language.

Conclusion

Language is a bearer of cultural values and a reflector of history and tradition. Language is therefore a very strategic resource that is crucial to the preservation of Afrikan self-worth and is located at the very centre of the notion of Afrikan consciousness, mobilisation, development and nation building. Hence if there is to be any development of Afrikans and their families, communities and societies, language must be treated like any other strategic resource. Its value must be recognised, it must be developed, and all its possibilities fully exploited in a common project in which all will participate for both the individual and the common good. The idea of deliberately fashioning a future that is based upon a commonly shared vision is an idea whose time has long come. Such a vision must in turn be constructed upon a sober view of the common Afrikan past and the commonalties of Afrikan culture. A positive concept of the Afrikan self is an important prerequisite for a secure Afrikan future. It is an idea, which must be preserved and employed to preserve the self-worth of Afrikans and ensure Afrikan development.

These proposals therefore constitute a part of the necessary discussion aimed at ending foreign domination of the mind, perceptions, actions and resources of Afrika. They are made in the context and spirit of the search for concrete Pan Afrikanist unity, strength and development of, and for the vast majority of Afrikans. The precondition for a viable language policy in Afrika must be Afrikans standing upon their own Afrikan feet (self reliance) and looking at the world through their own Afrikan eyes.

The concept of Pan Afrikanism must, if it is to be worthwhile, grow out of Afrikans' own understanding of the Afrikan reality, rest securely upon the commonalties and continuities of Afrikan culture, and have an Afrikan linguistic system to articulate it. Afrikan language policy can only be argued and articulated in terms of Afrikan centeredness, concepts, terminology, ideology; Afrikan ways of thinking and of being, traditions and a world view that will guarantee Afrikan self-confidence, Afrikan self-reliance and recognise, respect, include, empower and even celebrate Afrika.

The damage done by centuries of emphases on division, promotion of disunity and disrespect of Afrikan culture and institutions has been promoted in a great part through imposed foreign languages of disrespect, dis-empowerment, exclusion, domination and exploitation to Afrikan languages. A viable Afrikan language policy will promote and institutionalise respect, inclusion and empowerment through the mother tongues of the speakers, which articulate their traditions, culture and worldview. If Afrikans wish to transform their reality Afrikans must be willing to first transform themselves. Language has been a key site of the oppression of Afrikans and the destruction of Afrika. Yet language can be an important aspect of the (re)construction of the new Afrika that is so obviously needed.

References

Anderson, S. E. (1995) *The Black Holocaust For Beginners* (New York and London, Writers and Readers Publishing, Inc)

Armah, Ayi Kwei. (1973): *Two Thousand Seasons* (London, Heinemann. Berkeley, California: Unesco and Heinemann).

Banda, Felix et al (2001) *A Unified Standard Orthography for South-Central Africa Languages: Malawi, Mozambique and Zambia* (CASAS Monograph Series No. 11. Cape Town, South Africa: CASAS).

Bekerie, Ayele (1995/96): "The History and Principles of the Ethiopic Writing System" *Ankh: Revue d'égyptologie et des civilisations africaines*, Nos. 4/5

Cabral, Amilcar. (1980): *Unity and Struggle* (London, Heinemann)

Crawford, Clinton (1996): *Recasting Ancient Egypt in the African Context*

------------------ (ed.) (2001): *Ebonics and Language Education of African Ancestry Students* (New York and London: Sankofa World Press).

de Saussure, Ferdinand (1915, 1966): *Course in General Linguistics* (New York: Mc Graw-Hill Book Company).

Diop, C. A. (1963, 1989): *The Cultural Unity of Black Africa: The domains of Matriarchy and of Patriarchy in Classical Antiquity* (London, Karnak House, first published 1963 Paris: Présence Africaine).

..............(1974, 1978, 1987). *Black Africa: The Economic and Cultural Basis for A Federated State* (Westport, CT and Trenton, NJ: Lawrence Hill and Co. and Africa World Press, Inc).

.... (1990,1996): *Towards The African Renaissance: Essays in Culture and Development* (London, Karnak House. First published 1990 as *Alerte Sous Les Tropiques.* Paris: The Estate of C. A. Diop and Présence Africaine).

.... (1977): *Parenté Génétique De L'Egyptien Pharaonique Et des langues Négro-Africaines* (Dakar, Institut Fondamental D'Afrique Noire).

Fanon, Frantz. (1967): *Black Skin, White Masks* (New York, Grove Press, Inc.)

Jahn, Janheinz (1961): *Muntu: An Outline of the New African Culture* (New York: Grove Press. Translated by M. Grene. First published in 1958 by Eugene Diederichs Verlag, Düsseldorf).

KaBaRa, Ayoola (1997): *African Origins of Creoles.* (London, Katsina Press).

Nani Kofi, Explo and Kimani Nehusi (1999): " Culture and the Afrikan Liberation Struggle" in *Kilombo* (Volume I, Issue 3, April-September, 1999).

Nehusi, Kimani (2000): "From Medew Netjer to Ebonics" in C. Crawford (ed.) *Ebonics and Language Education of African Ancestry Student* (New York and London: Sankofa World Publishers).

---------------- (2002) "Mental Enslavement" in D. Grainger (ed.) *Emancipation* (Georgetown, Guyana)

Ngubane, Jordan K. (1979): *Conflict of Minds: Changing Power Dispositions in South Africa* (New York: Books In Focus, Inc.)

Nkrumah, Kwame. (1962): *I Speak of Freedom: A Statement of African Ideology* (London: Mercury Books).

.... (1973, 1980): *Revolutionary Path* (London: Panaf Books Ltd.)

.....................(1965, 1966, 1969): *Neo-Colonialism: The Last Stage of Imperialism* (New York: International Publishers).

Oliver, Roland (1999): *The African Experience: From Olduvai Gorge to the 21st century.* London: Weidenfeld & Nicolson.

Prah, Kwesi Kwaa. (2002a) "Education, Mother-Tongue Instruction, Christianity and Development of an African National Culture" *Paper presented to the International Conference on Visionen für das berufliche Bildungssystem in Africa."* (*Loccum,* Germany. 13th – 15th February).

........................(2002b) "Language, the African Development Challenge" *TRIcontinental* (Year 36, Number 150).

.... (2000a) *Mother Tongue for Scientific and Technological Development in Africa.* (Cape Town, South Africa: CASAS. Previously published: Bonn: DSE, 1993, 1995).

........................(2000b) *African Languages for the Mass Education of Africans (Cape* Town, South Africa: The Centre for Advanced Studies of African Society (CASAS). First Published: Bonn: DSE, 1995)

........................(1998) *Beyond The Colour Line: Pan-Africanist Disputations, Selected Sketches, Letters, Papers and Reviews* (Trenton, New Jersey and Asmara, Eriteria: Africa World Press, Inc.)

.... and Yvonne King (eds.) (1998): *In Tongues: African Languages and the Challenges of Development* (Cape Town, South Africa: CASAS).

Sheikh, Ahmed. (May-October, 1992): "Watch Your Mouth: The Politics of Language" *Africa World Review* (London: Africa Research and Information Bureau).

Thompson, R. F. (1983, 1984): *Flash of the Spirit: African and Afro-American Art and Philosophy* (New York: Vintage Books).

Willis, Bruce W. (1998): *The Adinkra Dictionary: A Visual primer on the Language of Adrinka* (Washington, DC: The Pyramid Complex).

12

AGREEING TO DIFFER: African Democracy - Its Obstacles and Prospects

Steven Friedman

Decades ago, Rene Dumont's *False Start in Africa* (1988) lamented post-colonial Africa's failure to yield development. Today, a similar judgement might be passed on the first post-independence wave of democratisation's failure to produce substantive and sustainable democratic institutions.

If we use electoral contest as a measure, the 1990s, despite signs of authoritarian recidivism, have been a period of democratic renewal (Bratton and van de Walle, 1997). But it has become trite to point to the "fallacy of electoralism" (Schmitter and Karl, 1991) - the assumption that elections are a sufficient measure of democracy. If we see democracy as a system which institutionalises universal adult participation in public decision-making, civil liberties, and the resolution of conflicts within a common political space by peaceful political contest and accommodation, Africa's formal democratisation has, as Richard Joseph (1988) has argued in most cases proved illusory: popular participation in decision-making and control over elected officials is very weak, while in many cases, rulers present a facade of democracy while denying their opponents and dissenting citizens civil liberties. Autocrats old and new have proved adept at using electoral contest to legitimise undemocratic regimes. Nor has conflict resolution made significant progress, as another round of debilitating confrontation in the Democratic Republic of Congo, Lesotho and Angola attest. Some of these conflicts, while generated by internal inabilities to resolve differences, show a tendency to spill across borders, and to attract the engagement of other countries, promoting dire predictions of a trans-continental war.

This critique is not a utopian lament - debates which rage in parts of the North on the degree to which liberal democratic form has yielded the required substance have far less resonance in Africa, where the demands of the time are more fundamental. Given the centrality of conflict and state collapse in the production of misery, democratic states capable of resolving conflicts between contending elites and of providing citizens with basic rights to hold office holders to account and to make claims against the state would in itself be a major advance. The charge against the current wave of democratisation is not that it has failed to achieve idyllic political communities, but that, in more than a few cases, it has not performed its most basic function of protecting the ruled from the predations - and the conflicts - of rulers.

The casualties are not only fragile African polities: current trends also indict the frailties of northern countries' Africa policies - including, or some might say, especially, that of the United States.

The role of external powers in the current wave of surface democratisation is open to debate. While Michael Bratton and Nicolas van de Walle (1997) have marshalled an array of data to demonstrate that formal democracy is largely a response to domestic protest mobilisation, Joseph avoids the crude view that reforms were purely implemented on donor instructions, but stresses the external dimension, arguing that African oligarchs rely on the international system to secure the resources needed to retain power and that they have largely succeeded in manipulating their relations with it to ensure a continued flow by assuming a "presentable" appearance which belies the substance of their regimes.

Whatever weight we assign to American and European influence, it is clear that official conceptions in these countries of African democracy and the strategies required to induce or sustain it rarely move beyond an attempt to ensure that African countries adopt a plausible surface imitation of the political and economic institutions of the West - and a vain search for Northern-style liberal democrats who will perform the required transformation. A State Department desk officer probably came closer to the truth than many US policy-makers care to admit when, in a recent discussion, she described US policy as a matter of identifying and supporting the "good guys" in their struggle against the bad ones. At worst, this resurrects a new version of the Cold War paradigm. At best, it reduces Africa to an analogy of the Eastern European morality play in which good democrats do constant battle against bad authoritarians.

Imposed or induced democratisation might, as in post-World War II Germany and Japan, yield results - but only with a Marshall-sized aid package to buttress it and domestic traditions and institutions on which to build. Imposing on African countries the expectation of formal democratisation without either the domestic resources or the political traditions with which to sustain it was an inevitable recipe for illusion.

Yet, while it is easy to caricature the "ugly American" blundering over a continent he or she dimly understands in search of unlikely redeemers, the often false dawn of the 1990s poses challenges too to those who recognise the complexity of a continent in which "good guys" with the capacity to act on their virtue to lay lasting foundations of democracy and prosperity in much of sub-Saharan Africa are in short supply.

For millions of television viewers in the North (or the white suburbs of South Africa), the reason for formal democratisation's failure is as simple as it is unpalatable: it lies in the inability of Africans to govern themselves in a democratic manner. This assumption is, in some cases, dignified or implicitly reinforced by scholars who adduce pseudo-anthropological notions such as the "politics of the belly" (Bayart, 1989) to -wittingly or unwittingly - confirm the notion of Africa as a place marching to a more primitive, indeed primordial, rhythm.

For those who reject the notion of African atavism, much work remains to offer an alternative - to superficiality as well as racial or geographic determinism. If one flaw of the morality play theory is that the "good guys" often behave much like the bad ones the moment they achieve electoral victory, we need to move beyond explanations, which stress only the venality of post-colonial elites. And if the chief flaw of "Afro-pessimism" is that it fails to understand the degree to which failure is reversible, we need to do more to investigate the preconditions of reversal. The acknowledgement that the form of liberal democracy is not enough demands a renewed attempt, in the light of the experiences of the past few years as well as those which preceded them, to identify the elements of genuine renewal.

This article will not attempt definitive answers to these questions: it will, rather, seek to identify some of the broad directions which such a search may need to engage, both intellectually and in political practice.

And it will seek to do so partly by examining perhaps the most interesting contemporary African case study, South Africa - an exception in the view of its own elites, anything but that in the view of many members of the African intelligentsia (see for example Mamdani, 1995). The example is apposite, for both South Africa's similarities with and differences from the rest of sub-Saharan Africa may enable a diagnosis of pathologies - and illuminate some potential remedies.

African Specificity: Pitfalls and Possibilities

Perhaps the first task is to sharpen debate on what democracy in Africa may or may not be.

More is at stake than a scholastic search for definition. An oft-heard critique of Western analysis and action is that its brand of democratisation seeks to impose on Africa something alien (Ake, 1993). The complaint is not new: the context in which it is now voiced is novel. Traditionally, the appeal to cultural specificity has been a weapon in the hands of self-justifying elites: African despots long anticipated Lee Kwan Yew or the current Chinese elites by insisting that democracy is a stalking horse for a new colonialism. Today, the complaint is usually voiced by a new breed of African democrats (whose preference for democracy as a key element of state- and nation-building is itself an important phenomenon) rather than despots, and for the reasons implied above. The rulers are now often preoccupied with simulating democracy in the hope of attracting aid and trade, not with rationalising its absence. The critics insist that Western approbation for many of the quasi-democrats lies not only in an inability or unwillingness to see beyond liberal democratic form to the substance beneath, but in the form itself. Understandably unwilling to conclude that Africa is not good enough for liberal democracy, they assert rather that liberal democracy is not good enough for Africa.

Is this appeal to specificity any more plausible than when it was used as a rationale for avoiding democracy? No and yes. No, in the sense that there are features of democracy, which are not culturally specific and whose abrogation inevitably produces tyranny: accountable government, the right to decide, speak and organise are essential to free political expression, whether the site is Oregon or Ouagadougou. Where African tradition is invoked to dilute or deny pluralism, the outcome is tyranny, however ornate its indigenous cultural form. Yes, because we know that liberal democratic parliamentary forms are capable of capture by oligarchs - and that, by contrast, in Botswana, a "pre-democratic" institution such as the chieftaincy can coexist with democracy and, some analyses would suggest, strengthen it. Or that, in Mauritius, a complex electoral system, which allocates parliamentary seats partly on ethnic criteria, has sustained a functioning democracy for decades.

The Botswana and Mauritius cases highlight, perhaps, a key flaw in Northern recipes - and the degree to which they reinforce the pretensions of African political elites. In both cases, identities - which in Africa often assume an ethnic or quasi-ethnic form - or traditional authority are recognised as potential democratic elements rather than as pre-modern obstacles. For many Northern recipes seemingly oblivious to the persistence, at least for now, of a venerable European democracy in which a house of traditional leaders persists alongside democratic institutions - the United Kingdom - both identities and tradition are vestigial symptoms of pre-democratic polities. African elites share the prejudice and much of the venality of post-independence leadership has, therefore, been clothed in the language of modernisation and integrative nation building. In most cases, the result has been to commit one of democratic theory's cardinal sins - to suppress difference.

It has become almost trite to point out that most African states are entities cobbled together by colonial powers to serve administrative demands and that one consequence is that very different identities are invariably housed in a single state. There is also some evidence that the traditional unit of African politics is the local. And that, whether as cause or consequence of the failure of the post-colonial state, traditional authority has in some cases proved more pervasive than indigenous modernising elites had expected. The common theme is difference: African states inherited a political space inhabited by people harbouring differing identities, loyalties and concepts of the appropriate source of authority. And almost invariably, the response of the post-independence polity was to respond by portraying difference as divisive or "tribalistic". In a few cases - Botswana, Zambia under Kaunda - the attempt to build that common sense of nationhood, which is, in the view of Dankwart Rustow (197), essential to democracy succeeded (albeit, in the latter case, not under democratic conditions). In most cases, the attempt proved, over time, a recipe for a level of conflict far more ghastly than anything, which the nation-building attempt had sought to prevent.

The assumption that democratic modernity requires the obliteration of traditional identities and authority is not restricted to predatory politicians - it is a pervasive tenet of much of an African intelligentsia firmly committed to democracy. Indeed, in the view of one of the continent's foremost scholars, it is the failure to break the power of rural elites - whose claims to authority are said to stem more from the preferences of colonisers than in authentic tradition - that lies at the heart of democratic failure (Mamdani, 1995). There is more than a touch of Barrington Moore lurking beneath the surface of the argument: in essence, the complaint indicts a failure to achieve modernity. On one level, the charge is clearly accurate - if modernity is understood here as the capacity to generate the preconditions for active and independent citizens' participation in public decision-making. On another, it may ignore the potential for incorporating differences, in which elements of tradition must be included, in democratic institutions. While there clearly are important elements of tradition which are incompatible with full democratic citizenship - patriarchy, for one - it could be argued that a formal democracy which is incapable of accommodating those elements of tradition and the identities which it generates which are compatible with notions of full and equal citizenship is inadequate. Indeed, the ability to ensure that traditional authority and loyalty to it are expressed within democratic norms could be a key source of the system's strength in Africa.

But, while the question of tradition is perhaps the identity issue most uncomfortable to intellectuals, it is, as implied above, only part of a larger story. If the suppression of difference was a key feature of African authoritarianism, the same desire perhaps surfaces again in the current context.

On the one hand, some governing elites use the polarising potential of identities as rationales to abridge democratic form. One ill-fated attempt was the Nigerian junta's creation of two parties - one nominally right, the other putatively left, of centre - in an apparent attempt to prevent parties becoming ethnic vehicles. Another is Ugandan president Yoweri Museveni's "no party" democracy, [1] portrayed as a viable experiment in non-western democratic form, but, for at least one analysis, a potentially unstable one party state with a human face. (Landsberg, Kabemba and Cornwell, 1997:14) There is scant evidence in either case that suppressing the organisational form of difference wishes it away - the effect is simply to narrow democratic space.

The liberal democratic form of post-authoritarian African polities by definition acknowledge difference by sanctioning pluralism. But the difference which is conceded arguably assumes a sameness - the assumption that a national legislature elected in regular electoral contest can, on its own, produce democratic outcomes may assume a society in which, a la Rustow, the essential identity differences have been dissolved in a common notion of the political community. But if, as well may be the case, the result is simply to establish which identity - and thus which notion of the community - is dominant and to ratify its hegemony over the others, then the source of decades of conflict is merely reconstituted.

The test for new African democracies - and the prognosis for democracy's survival and sustenance - rests therefore on the degree to which the new democratic systems can recognise, perhaps even celebrate, difference in institutional forms which respect democratic essentials: both Botswana and Mauritius may well show that these forms would deviate from the Northern ideal types in important ways. The key to African democracy may be not only the recognition of the right to difference but institutions which reward co-operation between political leaderships, which articulate it. (see for example Cruise O'Brien, 1999).

Similarly, because difference often manifests itself at the local level, political elites have tended - and often still do tend - to rely on centralisation to obliterate it. The result has often been to heighten, not to diminish, conflict - and to suppress the most accessible forms of democratic government for the poorly resourced. If one of democracy's properties were its ability to accommodate difference, then the African reality would seem to argue for vigorous decentralisation so that multiple identities and loyalties can find expression in democratic representation. While decentralisation would hardly be a novel or Africa-specific form of representation, it might, if allowed to take root, take on distinctively African shapes.

None of this is intended to argue that democracy's limited success in Africa - and its prospects - can be reduced to institutional design faults. While a mindset among both Northern policy-makers and African elites which judges African democracy by its ability to suppress difference in service of a Platonic European or Northern American ideal not always realised in its countries of origin contributes to some contemporary *cul de sacs*, democracy's dismal African past can also be traced back to - and its uncertain future might prove to depend on - deeply-rooted structural features in African polities which produce unconvertible realities and dilemmas.

The Gordian Knot: Civil Society, the Market and Economic Development

The global resurgence of civil society as a proposed guarantor of democracy has not left diagnoses of the African democratic malaise untouched: appropriately so, if the preceding analysis is accurate, for the democratic expression of difference is civil society's prime *raison d'être*.

Scholars of widely differing persuasions seem agreed on the weakness of African civil society, even if some disagree with the current conventional wisdom among donor country strategists, Northern intellectuals - and many African activists - that civil society is a prerequisite of democracy. Debate on and investigation of the degree to which classic notions of civil society are appropriate, and currently possible, in Africa are a necessary ingredient of a plausible democratic prognosis for the continent.

But none of the differing strains would surely disagree with the claim that oligarchy has managed to survive the current democratisation wave because the forces arrayed against it in most African societies are unable to constrain or depose it. Opposition parties and forces are often led by figures who once played a role in authoritarian elites but fell out of favour (Bratton and van de Walle, 1997:8), suggesting that they may be vehicles for one section of the elite to claw back positions and power it lost to another; they are also on occasions vulnerable to purchase and co-option by governments, implying that the thirst for personal advantage is sometimes as strong among the seeming opponents of authoritarianism as among those they seek to replace. All these realities testify that most African societies are unable to generate a new and different leadership willing and able to abolish oligarchy - rather than to merely replace the oligarchs with similar substitutes.

The African new wave may thus have produced "virtual democracies" (Joseph, 1998) because its polities have virtual oppositions and civil societies. Recourse to classical texts suggests that the reason is as economic as it is political - that it lies in the weakness of African market economies. Independently acquired resources provide the means to resist - or to organise voluntary associations - the demands of the market produce the motive. As long as the majority in Africa remain beyond the reach of formal economic institutions, so too may the capacity to generate sufficient domestic pressure to achieve and sustain democracy remain limited and narrow.

At first glance, this proposition is at odds with an important strain of Northern theorising, which posits civil society as a normative antidote to the pervasiveness of the market. (Barber, 1998, Etzioni, 1998). But there is no necessary contradiction between arguing that the existence of institutions which allow the accumulation of private resources is a necessary condition of civil society's emergence and the proposition that, in some or all Northern societies, voluntary associations can provide citizens with centres of solidarity, reciprocity and collective action which limit the market's reach. The notion - implicit to the Northern theories discussed here - that the market needs to be civilised assumes that there is a market in the first place. This is not always the case in Africa whose task is, perhaps, to develop the institutions, which need to be curbed so that the vehicle, which is indispensable to the curbing, can begin to emerge.

But how is civil society - or an opposition with the means and motive to achieve democracy - to emerge? For those enthused with the spirit of Northern missionary zeal, it must be created: donor strategies are often devoted to this end. But, if the hypothesis presented here is accepted, this is a task beyond the capacity of even the most well resourced donor programme. Progress requires precisely that economic development which authoritarianism and its bedfellows, personalism and patronage, constrain in Africa. If donor nations really seek a thorough African democratisation, the spirit of George Marshall may be a more appropriate guide than the theories of Robert Putnam.

The Primacy of State and Stability

Yet, to identify economic development as a key is to beg yet another set of questions - its preconditions. Even before troubles in world financial markets became a catalyst for a return to forgotten truisms, the 1997 World Bank *World Development Report* forced the reality that state capacity has underpinned every economic advance in twentieth century societies again into the mainstream.

Nowhere is this more necessary than in Africa, and this for two reasons. First, the dominant state form on the continent has been inimical to all sustainable accumulation except that which takes place outside the rules and institutions which underpin the market: most of Africa's economic success stories occur outside the reach of the state (Simone, 1994; McGaffey, 1997; Tripp, 1997). In consequence, their effect on general living standards is negligible. And they remain remarkable because they are such exceptions: in most cases, the patronage state acts as a break on independent economic activity. To posit economic development as a key to political progress is to confront the reality that it is constrained by one of political weaknesses' most conspicuous effects: the incapacity of most African states.

As important as "objectively" weak capacity is its consequence, expressed in the response of many Africans to state failure - withdrawal or, in some contexts, antipathy. Wealth accumulation outside the state is not the only or, indeed, the most pervasive symptom. Forced to cope with states which fail to offer the possibility of democratic citizenship and which, from the oil shock of the 1970s, have proved increasingly unable to distribute material resources, citizens have often adopted the most rational route: withdrawal. Rather than seeking to challenge or change the state, they have fallen back on their own resources and defence mechanisms: in these cases, forms of social life which are not only outside the state but designed to insulate society from it become the norm (Simone, 1995). The trend should not be overstated: as Bratton and van de Walle show, citizens do at times choose to engage with the state by mobilising protest. But, if recent events in the Democratic Republic of the Congo are a guide, the engagement is often guided by a deep hostility not only to incumbent politicians, but also to the institutions of the state, which are seen as almost inherently predatory. This finds its corollary in a pervasive cynicism towards newly democratised regimes among many intellectuals. These forms of social life and attitudes are, of course, the product of lived experiences; but they illustrate the depth of the crisis of the African state.

Further, economic failure is not the proximate cause of Africa's malaise. Not only are the consequences, measured in quality of life, of a failure to produce economic "take off" dwarfed by Africa's prime bane, inter- and intra-state conflict (Landsberg, Kabemba and Cornwell, 1998:

12-16). Only a cessation of violence would free Africans to pursue the possibility of economic advance and create the conditions in which this may be possible. The conventional wisdom that African poverty is a consequence of "inappropriate" economic policies ignores the extent to which political conflict has been responsible for far more impoverishment in Africa than any number of tariff barriers or state-run industries - and the degree to which the accumulation of capital requires a stable political foundation which conflict destroys: the link between the ability to resolve conflict through political accommodation and adequate economic performance finds empirical support in recent research, which includes much data from African polities and economies (Rodrik, 1999).

It is far easier to express the need for effective and stable states than to spell out their preconditions. What must be asserted is the primacy of political stability to any attempt to ensure liveable African societies, let alone functioning democracies. The preconditions for state formation effective enough to resolve conflict remain elusive - searching for them an urgent intellectual task.

In some respects, the "good guy-bad guy" approach derided at the outset is entitled to some rehabilitation here: effective leadership can reduce conflict potential - witness Seretse Khama's role in Botswana or Nelson Mandela's in South Africa. But in both cases, leadership proved decisive at the birth of a democratic state: whether it can play as formative a role in states which have suffered deep-rooted decay over decades is open to question for, while individual capacities may suffice to maintain a state amidst change, they may prove inadequate to the task of reconstituting states.

We may encounter a paradox here. Effective conflict resolution requires states strong enough to achieve it, but decades of conflict - and more generalised state decline - have ensured that few are in evidence. But any investigation of the necessary elements of African democratisation will need to understand the preconditions for reconstituting effective states capable at the very least of protecting the persons of their citizens.

The (un)Democratic Paradox

In principle, a state does not need to be democratic to resolve conflict and provide the framework for growth. It requires, rather, some features which, while they are usually associated with democracies, are in principle and in some cases practice (*vide* Singapore or Taiwan) not restricted to them. Some key elements of a state capable of providing the conditions for economic accumulation are: the ability to maintain stability; the capacity and will to limit corruption; maintenance of a legal framework conducive to implementing the law of contract; and significant ability to extract citizens' compliance with public obligations. (Bernstein, Berger, Godsell, 1996:16)

Given this, the quasi-democratic route would seem at first glance most appropriate since it purports to prioritise the elements of state-building. It is in this context that enthusiasm for the "new Africans" - Museveni, Rwanda's Kagame, Eritrea's Aferworki, Ethiopia's Zenawi - must be understood. (Ottaway, 1999) All are said to be serious about effective and honest governance as well as market-led growth, although clearly not about liberal democracy, and some seemingly impressive growth figures would seem to confirm the hypothesis.

But how new are the "new Africans"? The question is not only apposite because the Ethiopian-Eritrean war, Rwanda's aggressive militarism and Uganda's taste for foreign adventures suggest that enthusiasm for the prescriptions of international financial institutions is not necessarily matched by equal eagerness to resolve transnational differences peacefully. In what ways do their new states differ from the old ones? If a recent impressionistic analysis of Uganda is a guide, (Landsberg, Kabemba, Cornwell 1998:14) they may be more fragile and prone to the old ills - such as recourse to patronage and weak links to society - than their admirers acknowledge. And it is the few African democracies who have proved far greater guarantors of stability than their authoritarian alternatives.

This is not accidental. Given the context sketched earlier, any progress towards state-building will require more than administrative technique: democracy, whatever its institutional form, seems an essential precondition not only for liberty, but also for state-building and thus for stability and economic development too. If it is agreed that respect for difference, and the inclusion of varying identities and loyalties, is a prerequisite of African state-building, then it is difficult to see how this might be institutionalised in any non-democratic form. Wise leaders with secure social bases might, in theory, prove far-sighted and magnanimous enough to preside over polities which incorporate diverse traditions and identities on terms which reduce or eliminate alienation. Whether these leaders can be expected in a context in which the putative bond between citizen and state posited by social contract theory has been ruptured by fundamental breaches of trust is another matter. It seems more plausible to presume that the task of enticing citizens back into the state will need to be central to African state-building and that, while the ability to maintain macro-economic balance as well as to provide social services or even basic infrastructure may be part of that attempt, the promise of real representation will need to become as - or more - important.

This raises in principle the uncomfortable possibility that a further paradox confronts African state building: effective governance is a more urgent requirement than democracy, but is impossible without it. The question is raised not to counsel a lapse into despair, but to propose a more fundamental line of enquiry than the search for democratic preconditions: a re-examination of the fundamental requirements of viable African states. If the problem is indeed one of weak states and strong societies, (Migdal, 1988) then a fairly venerable school of Africanist scholarship requires revisiting in an attempt to determine, in the light of contemporary developments, the requirements of African state-building.

South Africa: Exception To The Rule?

The preceding argument, in its search for generalisation, may have created the impression that this analysis, like many others, ignores the specificity of particular African societies. It ought, therefore, to be stressed that differences between states are a key African reality which must be recognised in any analysis of patterns and prospects.[2] This seems an appropriate reason for introducing the South African case which is instructive not only because its transition from racial oligarchy has attracted far more international interest than the attempted democratisation of other African states but because its surface uniqueness in the sub-Saharan African context provides an illuminating test of some of the ideas proposed here.

Whether South Africa is substantially different is, as noted at the outset, a matter of some debate. The country's new elite - intellectual as well as political - tends to assume a qualitative difference from the rest of the sub-Saharan continent. African intellectuals tend often to assume a sameness, an assumption which finds scholarly form in the writing of

Mahmood Mamdani. They are, ironically, supported by many white South Africans who share, for perhaps obvious reasons, the view that the country will prove unable to escape the malaise, which has afflicted most states to the North. Despite a vast gulf in perspective, the argument ends in much the same place: assumptions that South Africa's ruling elite is different to its counterparts elsewhere are misguided.[3]

The debate is of some importance to our argument. South Africa does appear to posses, albeit in limited form, some of the key elements posited here as preconditions for progress: a robust civil society, or at least organised groups with sufficient independence to constrain state power, a "usable" state[4] and a functioning market economy, prompting Mamdani to acknowledge it as "an African country with specific differences" (Mamdani, 1995:27). In contrast to many other African polities, the nature of its transition from *apartheid* has bequeathed democratic government an important resource: a high degree of goodwill towards the state and democratic institutions among most citizens. If these elements cannot produce a viable democracy, Afro-pessimism's assumptions appear to have been vindicated and this makes the stakes in South Africa unusually high.

An examination of South Africa's dynamic reveals that democratic prospects are indeed uncertain. But, if the South African experiment does seem less secure than its admirers believe, the reason may lie not in the inapplicability of some of the preconditions posited here, but of their relative absence in the polity and society. South Africa's vulnerabilities are, therefore, more similar to those elsewhere on the continent than a surface examination might suggest. Both its strengths and weaknesses are explicable by the analyses proposed here: this makes it an important laboratory for the future of African democracy.

Preconditions for Compromise

The most obvious difference between South Africa and much of the rest of the continent is its negotiated transition to democracy which remains a perhaps unique African example of conflict-resolving compromise. The history of the transition is well known (Friedman, 1993; Friedman and Atkinson, 1995) and will not be repeated here. Rather, some elements relevant to the issues raised in this article will be discussed.

In some respects, there were features of the compromise which could obtain in any African country: prime among these is foreign intervention, which played a more significant role in shaping the outcome than is often acknowledged (Landsberg, 1995: 276-300). But intervention did not create the settlement: it built on South African processes and sought to influence and shape them. South Africa thus provides at least one key pointer to the preconditions for fruitful international support. It has become conventional wisdom to note that both main protagonists, the African National Congress and the (then ruling) National Party concluded, accurately, that the costs of continued conflict outweighed those of the compromises entailed by settlement (Sisk, 1995). Thus, however sophisticated the techniques employed, external attempts are likely to be of little effect unless the antagonists perceive the need to compromise. William Zartman's term "mutually hurting stalemate" (1989) has become something of a cliché among students and practitioners of conflict resolution but it remains a useful means of understanding the preconditions of negotiated settlements to protracted conflicts.

There are current cases in which these preconditions are absent in African conflicts: Angola is a clear example, the Democratic Republic of the Congo, despite the apparent imminence of a settlement, may be another. In these countries, conflict resolution seems destined for failure until a mutual perception between antagonists of the need for compromise emerges. Former Tanzanian president Julius Nyerere's attempt to mediate a solution to the Burundi conflict may tell us whether these conditions now pertain in that country. But some key features of the South African process may identify some prerequisites for antagonists to conclude that compromise is a necessary option.

While both sides did conduct cost-benefit calculations which impelled them to settlement, this reality begs a more fundamental question: why? Antagonists in Ireland, Bosnia, Angola or Rwanda have also been immersed in conflicts in which the prospect of final victory by either side was not feasible: yet they avoided compromise until all other avenues were exhausted - or continue to avoid it. In South Africa, the answer lies in a political culture too complex and contradictory to allow for detailed analysis here (Friedman, 1995). But one of its consequences was that both sides were sufficiently loyal to the notion of a common state to believe that its survival merited significant compromise.

Part of the answer lies in a feature difficult to replicate in other societies: a peculiar sense of common national identity even amid deep-rooted divisions - in contrast to many Southern African countries, the liberation movement leadership never seriously contemplated changing the name of the country. This is not to say that South Africa is an exception to the point made earlier - that differing identities are extremely important in African societies. But, in South Africa, for complex historical reasons, the notion of a common political space has far greater resonance than elsewhere on the continent. The concrete effect is both a party politics in which identities are central, and unusual popular enthusiasm for democracy (which may also, of course, be heightened by the fact that black South Africans were denied the franchise in a polity in which whites did vote; this may prompt many to value it more than citizens of countries in which the vote was not available to a racial minority).

While at variance with some of the continental trends described earlier, this confirms the degree to which intangibles - such as identities and loyalties - matter in determining the fate of new African democracies. Instrumental theories of democracy - the notion, assiduously promoted by rational choice theory (see for example Downs, 1957), that citizens vote or participate in democratic activity purely to maximise their material interests, is unlikely to provide a basis for democratisation in Africa (or, it might be argued, anywhere else).

The point is perhaps best illustrated in the negative, by a brief examination of mainstream understandings of the 1999 South African election. Post-election media analysis of the second universal franchise poll was informed in the main by assumptions which are at once bizarre and ideological, since they insist on treating the electorate as if it were an ideal type of rationality maximising citizens of Peoria, Illinois. Phenomena such as traditional authority, or the liberation ethos which had spurred majority politics for at least eight decades, were simply ignored as explanations of voting behaviour in favour of accounts which stressed the effectiveness of campaigns or the ability of the winners to highlight "issues" such as crime and job creation.

A brief look at the context illustrates the absurdity of this paradigm. In one of the planet's most crime-ridden societies, which, despite government promises of ever-expanding employment, has shed tens of thousands of jobs over the past two years, the victimised and the unemployed flocked to the polls to give the governing party a larger majority than it enjoyed in 1994 - just on two-thirds of the vote. Suburban mythology would have it that they did this because they were driven by an atavistic "call to the blood", that most black African voters have not yet reached the exalted stage at which they vote their interests rather than their identities. In reality, the outcome was as rational as it was explicable: voters trusted the majority party not for its management skill but because it reflected their identity.

This is not to say that issues such as personal safety or employment are irrelevant to black voters: if surveys are to be believed, however, they have greater confidence in the governing ANC's ability to address these issues than in that of the opposition. And they believe that because the ANC is seen to speak for them - to express whom they are.

Lest this appear as a eulogy to the party in power, a similar dynamic was evident in the KwaZulu-Natal province, where, contrary to most poll predictions, voters turned out in great numbers to opt for the Inkatha Freedom Party, which is closely associated with traditional authorities in its home region. While some may have done this as an act of self-preservation, given the considerable power of traditional authority in the province's rural areas, many chose the IFP because it best expressed their identity, not because they saw it as a superior vehicle of "good governance". Nor are black rural traditionalists the only South African voters for whom identities are more important than public management - in differing and complex ways, just about all South African party politics, whether practised by white professionals in the suburbs or by black shack-dwellers, is about identities.

That neither most of the pollsters nor the pundits saw this was not so much a consequence of ignorance as of a myopia born of a deep ideological need to see South African voters as rationality maximising instrumental voters because political understanding among much of the country's elite is governed by an assumption that voters who choose on instrumental criteria are in some way superior to those who give greater priority to identities. Given the country's history, in which identities were manipulated for five decades in order to subjugate four-fifths of the populace, and the persistence of racial assumptions, which assume the average black voter to be a naive and primitive soul, this is understandable. Since the ideal type of the "Western" rational voter is a paradigm of the fully evolved democratic citizen, racism's opponents are reluctant to concede any ground to those who would argue that most South Africans have greater priorities than instrumental rationality. And yet the error lies with the ideal type: the "normal" democracy in which voters are motivated purely by technical rationality, is in reality abnormal since it describes, at best, a handful of democracies and certainly excludes several Northern states in which identity politics lurks just beneath the surface of what appears as pure "interest" politics: Italy, where voter allegiances were virtually cast in stone for five decades after World War Two, or Holland where religious identity has largely shaped political loyalties, are but two examples. For all its high-mindedness, it spawns assumptions, which can only lead away from a viable theory and practice of African democratisation.

But, while political culture remains an important variable, it seems likely that the compromise settlement was achieved at least partly because both the country's state and its economy seemed strong enough for both sides, despite the depredations of *apartheid*, to believe them worth preserving. Government's ability to meet material needs do not determine elites' and citizens' party loyalties, but they clearly play a significant role in influencing political calculations - and in discouraging potentially debilitating conflict.

A further feature of the transition was that organised political parties (primarily, but not exclusively the ANC and NP) with clear support bases faced each other across the table. Subsequent developments may show that the parties were not as organisationally strong as they then seemed - but this is relative. In much of the rest of Africa, parties - with the exception of some former liberation movements who have ruled for decades such as Tanzania's CCM and Kenya's KANU - are largely elite creations with little popular resonance. The effect in the South African case was to ensure that compromises reached by political leaders had a reasonable prospect of securing popular legitimacy, because party leaders had negotiated them. Interestingly, for those who yearn for Western-style interest parties in Africa, those in South Africa command significant voter identification precisely *because* they appeal to identities rather than interests.

Despite the important role played by parties and political leaders, another key feature of the South African negotiations was that they were not restricted to, nor did they entirely depend on, political elites. They were accompanied and probably underpinned by a parallel set of negotiations between interest groups: their expression was about a dozen national and hundreds of regional and local negotiating forums (Shubane and Shaw, 1993). The national forums all addressed socio-economic issues and their participants were, therefore, interest groups as well as parties. While they rarely achieved their stated purpose - to agree on post-apartheid socio-economic policy - they did assist in ensuring that both the culture and the practice of negotiated compromise were not restricted to political leaders. This obviously reminds us of the importance of civil society, however conceived, in democratic state formation and maintenance.

These structural factors notwithstanding, leadership played a key role in the settlement. Nelson Mandela and FW de Klerk may have simply been reading the writing on the wall, but there was no inevitability about the latter's ability to read it far earlier than he needed to: his counterpart across the Limpopo, former Rhodesian prime minister Ian Smith, never came close to this level of literacy. Nor was there any iron law of history, which forced Mandela to recognise the need for a settlement in the mid-1980s - or to devote much of his presidency to seeking a common sense of nationhood across the racial divides.

But the South African case is poor vindication for an attempt to scour the continent seeking similar visionaries. Important as their role was, neither Mandela nor de Klerk created a settlement *in vacuo*. Both chose to respond to propensities to compromise within their constituency - and both had at their disposal parties and constituencies, which they could steer towards it. Where African leaders lack the necessary political and institutional infrastructure, leadership is likely to be of little practical effect, however visionary it may be.

Some of these elements may explain the other unusual feature of the South African transition - that, five years on and two elections later, there has been no significant attempt by the new elite to curtail civil liberties. Nor, in contrast to some of Africa's new wave democracies, was there doubt that a competitive second election - whose result enjoyed legitimacy among all parties - would be held in 1999. Political culture, institutional continuity, civil society and leadership play crucial roles here.

Perils and Portends

There are, however, warning signs, which suggest that outcomes similar to those elsewhere on the continent are possibilities. The compromise achieved in 1993 is under some stress: racial division is more in evidence now than it was in the post-1994 period while the conflict surrounding the report of the Truth and Reconciliation Commission, convened to investigate human rights abuses both by the *apartheid* order and its opponents, has reminded us of the degree to which different understandings of the past remain. A key element in the ANC's response, therefore, was an angry rejection by its current leadership of the proposition that it could have been responsible for human rights abuses: those who fought against race domination, it insisted, could not be equated with those who sought to preserve it - even if the abuses of which they are accused were visited on *apartheid*'s victims, not its perpetrators. So, far from reconciling, the commission exercise largely confirmed the persistence of competing notions of justice whose present form is expressed in conflicts over distributional questions such as affirmative action in employment and admission to universities. Questioning the basis of the compromise became a preoccupation of President Thabo Mbeki who has repeatedly urged a new "national consensus" which, compared to that achieved in 1993, should be more explicitly shaped by the ANC's programme; the ANC has begun implementing a legislative and policy agenda which stresses majority interests in antagonism to those of the minority more clearly than at any time since 1994 (Friedman, 1998).

There are also signs of a desire by the ANC leadership to impose its stamp more firmly on both the movement - whose internal diversity is often the most palpable sign of civil society's influence - and the society. A close reading of the call for a "new consensus" suggests that it as much a reaction to criticism as to the concern to ensure that majority concerns are pursued more forcefully. The response to the Truth Commission report - in which Mandela advocated endorsement of its finding that the ANC committed human rights abuses during the "liberation" struggle, while much of the rest of its leadership sought to delay the report's publication - raises the possibility that the progress of the past five years was as much a consequence of Mandela's leadership as of the structural factors noted here.

It is worth stressing here that, for obvious reasons, difference is a more difficult problem in South Africa then in other sub-Saharan states: elsewhere, it was not used to buttress a system of minority power and privilege. Because it was used for precisely that purpose under *apartheid*, government attempts to eliminate those differences, which perpetuate inequity, are both inevitable and necessary. Nor is sensitivity to criticism necessarily a sign of intolerance among the elite: it stems often from the already-mentioned perception that many whites believe firmly that blacks are genetically unable to govern. This establishes a cycle in which white prejudice and black defensiveness feed off each other, making it difficult to clear sufficient space for a democratic pluralism. But it is easy in both theory and practice for justifiable irritation at bigotry to translate into discouragement of loyal dissent: understanding, even sympathy, for the roots of the problem do not minimise its potentially debilitating effects.

The state, while strong by continental standards, is weak by any others: witness the prevalence of crime or the failure of elected authorities to secure payment for public services - or, in many cases, taxes. Surveys suggest that public trust in government is generally low, with confidence concentrated disproportionately in the office and person of the former state president (Idasa, 1997). Pre-democratic authority structures (Chipkin and Thulare, 1997) and patterns of political behaviour (Gotz, 1997) remain influential - in some cases, as elsewhere on the continent, important areas of political and social life remain beyond the reach of the state.[5] Evidence of a democratic culture is ambiguous - almost half the respondents to a recent survey indicated that they would support a "strong", non-democratic, leader if democracy appeared not to be working (IDASA, 1996). While the finding that around half the citizenry would remain loyal to democracy even in that eventuality might be remarkable in any new democracy, there is enough support for an alternative to give would-be demagogues much with which to work. Nor is there any shortage of social issues which might fuel demagoguery, of which the low labour absorption capacity of the formal economy noted earlier, is but one example.

These threats to democracy and state-building are enhanced by the reality that the ANC, like all other successful African liberation movements, has remained intact - inhibiting the formation of parties expressing the differing values and interests within the liberation tradition (Shubane, 1997 - and faces no credible challengers. Given the society's racial divisions and the congruence between identities and party support, only a split in the governing party is likely to produce a challenger. But, while a break is regularly predicted as the ANC's two allies, the Congress of Trade SA Trade Unions and the SA Communist Party, contest its partial embrace of market-friendly economics, there is a strong likelihood that the purportedly fragile "broad church" will cohere for decades. Assured electoral victory vastly reduces the incentives for office holders to remain accountable to voters - and the prospect of a growing divide between state and society is enhanced by the reality that, ironically given its dominance, the ANC is weak organisationally, having lost up to two-thirds of its dues-paying membership since 1994. Since its dominance ensures that politics within the movement are at least as an important an indicator of democratic prospects than relations between it and the opposition, recent evidence of centralising tendencies inside the ANC are significant (Rapoo, 1998).

Centralisation is not simply a matter of concentrating more power in the upper echelons of the ANC. A stress on "delivery" - the dispensing of social goods and services to the citizenry - has served as rationale for the centralisation of government administrative decision-making and a consequent diminution of enthusiasm for the powers of sub-national government. This reflects on two of our themes. First, centralisation is seen as a formula for resolving technical difficulties which are held to be more pressing concerns than the maintenance of principles such as diversity of political representation through three levels of elected government. Citizens, we are told, have suffered material discrimination under *apartheid* and their chief concern now is to be delivered to rather than to enjoy the luxury of diverse representation. And yet what evidence we have, through a variety of public opinion surveys, suggest that "lack of delivery" is a far lesser concern to voters than a lack of trust in levels of government which are seen as remote and unaccountable. Again, citizens appear to value the intangibles far more than the elites prefer to believe. Second, while centralisation is justified on technocratic criteria, there are echoes of the integrative nation-building which has failed elsewhere on the continent, a particularly strong temptation in a society in which difference was exalted as an ideological rationale for minority hegemony.

Similarity Beneath the Surface

All these portents suggest that a South African reversion to the weak and authoritarian state to which the present wave of democratisation is an intended antidote is not impossible. But South Africa faces these threats not despite its differences with the rest of the continent, but because in some respects it is not different enough. Some of the reasons have already been suggested or implied: limited state capacity and the fact that the market economy remains beyond the reach of significant sectors of society. And civil society, while again far more significant than in any other African state, remains relatively shallow encompassing - with the partial exception of the trade union movement - only a relative elite.[6]

Mamdani's analysis helps illuminate some of the dynamics. In his view, South Africa's new democracy suffers from the same flaw as that of its counterparts elsewhere on the continent: it has dismantled one aspect of apartheid (or colonial government) - the racial national state - but not the other, "customary power" which was used as an instrument of indirect rule by colonial administrations. The result is an urban democracy - and civil society - constrained by the persistence of rural authoritarianism. (Mamdani, 1995: 29)

The diagnosis is flawed, for reasons mentioned earlier: it also overestimates the salience of the rural in South African politics and society and, therefore, the influence of power structures in the countryside. But, as a reminder of how much democratisation has left untouched, it is an important warning. Despite its achievements, the new South African polity is weakened by: the persistence, in some rural areas, the migrant hostels of the cities and peri-urban shack settlements, of non-democratic authority structures and patterns of behaviour beyond the reach of the democratic state (Chipkin and Thulare, 1997; Gotz, 1997); civil society's shallowness combined with an enthusiasm to incorporate parts of it into public decision-making despite its limited representativeness[7]; and the frequent absence of the implied "social contract" between state and society.

The reasons are "subjective" and "objective". On the first score, they are a consequence of a marked gap between the policy agenda of the new elite and that of its constituents confirmed in several empirical works by the Centre for Policy Studies. (Charney, 1995; Tomlinson, 1997) One symptom is a propensity for many citizens to be excluded from political participation by a stress - rhetoric to the contrary notwithstanding - on English as the language of public life, despite the fact that it is the first language of only a small fraction of the citizenry. To return to our first-mentioned theme, one cause is the elite's desire to model itself in the image of European or American "best practice" rather than in domestic reality. As in much of the rest of the continent, an elite tendency to measure success by the - perceived - standards of Washington and Paris tends to obstruct democratic and social progress. On the second, to the extent that severe income inequalities and low labour absorption mean that many South Africans remain beyond the reach of the market economy, they continue to lack both the means and incentives to political participation.

Balancing Tendencies

While the dangers are real, they - and the diagnosis from which they stem - are in all probability overstated. While the post-Mandela ANC leadership may prefer a more restricted democracy - perhaps one similar to that in Malaysia, where the form of multi-party democracy coexists with a centralised and often intolerant state, the market economy with a lengthy experiment in racial redistribution - there are significant countervailing factors.

The political culture noted above may ensure no overt challenge to democracy. The balance of forces between majority and minority, which ensures that the current demand for a new consensus is not an attempt to abrogate the 1993 compromise but to re-negotiate its terms[8], the diversity in the ANC alliance and the increasing absorption of the black majority - albeit at a slow pace - into the market economy as owners and managers may ensure that the costs of authoritarian ventures outweigh their benefits. While democratic participation remains available in substance only to part of society, and the withdrawal of large sections of the majority and minority from politics remains a real danger, it is a large enough part to create severe barriers to anti-democratic recidivism.

Whatever the outcome, the indicators of success or failure are likely to be the success of the post-1994 state-building endeavour and the fate of the market economy, which has done much to underpin the transition. South Africa's experience confirms the centrality of conflict resolution, state building and the development and broad extension of markets as the key requirements of African democratisation. Its uncertain future poses a challenge both to those who seek to promote democracy and to those who wish to understand the continent's prospects of achieving it: to embark on a new attempt to identify its African preconditions.

Conclusion: The Abyss and Beyond

Africa's search for democracy, it should be apparent by now, occurs in a context in which the stakes are significantly higher -and the issues to a degree different - than in most other parts of the globe. At issue is not whether citizens will enjoy sufficient expression to ensure them a degree of autonomy from state and market (Barber, 1998) - important as this question is in the North, it loses much of its relevance where neither state nor market are givens where, indeed, they often remain aspirations. Similarly, democracy's prospects in Africa will determine not whether citizens are to enjoy full expression in established states and - relatively - secure societies, but whether the continent's inhabitants will enjoy respite from decades of violence and its crushing effects on social and economic life.

As noted above, this ensures that the issues are far more basic and immediate than they are in the North: what is taken for granted in the latter, such as the preconditions for freedom from state initiated violence and the institutions necessary to pursue basic social and economic goals within a common community, are still to be won in much of Africa.

But, while issues such as the preconditions for ending armed conflicts, ensuring the basics of a functional state and generating market economies remain salient in Africa, these are not the only issues which will determine whether democracy does take root on the continent: normative questions such as the nature of democracy, the importance of difference and the value of self-expression remain essential to any intellectual activity or political practice capable of establishing and sustaining African democracy. A politics, which reduces citizens to economic actors or to beings concerned only with the satisfaction of basic needs is as inappropriate to a continent whose predicament is as stark as Africa's as it is elsewhere on the globe.

In his inaugural address, new South African President Thabo Mbeki, reflecting on centuries of colonial subjugation, followed by more than three decades of predation at the hand of new elites, described Africans as "the children of the abyss" and committed his government to working for a route away from this legacy. While democracy remains, in the view of this analysis, an essential element in any sustainable strategy to end these horrors, the past lies heavily upon the continent and many of the degradations of the abyss make a way out of it perilous and uncertain. The emergence of a new intelligentsia, which sees democracy as an essential ingredient of, rather than an alternative to, nation-building and reconstruction suggests that an African renewal, in which democracy will be a necessary ingredient, is inevitable. The constraints described here suggest that it may be longer in the making than those who aspire to a new Africa might wish. While many of the obstacles are structural, not all are. The debate on the good society in Africa must proceed in tandem with that on its structural preconditions.

References

Barber, Benjamin *A Place For Us: How to Make Society Civil and Democracy Strong, (Hill* and Wang, New York, 1998)

Bayart, Jean-Francois *L'etat en Afrique: la politique du ventre* (Paris, Fayard, 1989)

Bratton, Michael and Nicolas van de Walle : *Democratic Experiments in Africa: Regime Transitions in Comparative Perspective* (Cambridge, Cambridge University Press, 1997)

Downs, Anthony: *An Economic Theory of Democracy* (Harper and Row, New York, 1957)

Dumont, Rene: *False Start in Africa*, (London, Earthscan, 1988)

Etzioni, Amitai: *The New Golden Rule: Community and Morality in a Democratic Society (*Basic Books, New York, 1998)

Friedman, Steven (ed.): *The Long Journey: South Africa's Quest for a Negotiated Settlement* (Johannesburg, Ravan, 1993)

Friedman, Steven and Doreen Atkinson (eds.): *The Small Miracle: South Africa's Negotiated Settlement* (Johannesburg, Ravan, 1995)

Linz, Juan J and Alfred Stepan: *Problems of Democratic Transition and Consolidation: Southern Europe, South America and Post-Communist Europe* (Baltimore and London, Johns Hopkins, 1996)

Mamdani, Mahmood: *Citizen and Subject: contemporary Africa and the politics of late colonialism* (Kampala, Fountain 1995)

Migdal, Joel S *Strong Societies and Weak States: State-Society Relations and State Capabilities in the Third World* (Princeton, Princeton University Press, 1988)

Ottaway, Marina: *Africa's New Leaders: Democracy or State Reconstruction?* (Carnegie, Endowment for International Peace, Washington DC, 1999)

Rodrik, Dani: *The New Global Economy and Developing Countries* (Overseas Development Council, Washington DC, 1999)

Sisk, Timothy D: *Democratization in South Africa: The Elusive Social Contract* (Princeton, Princeton University Press, 1995)

Simone, T Abdou Maliqalim: *In Whose Image?: Political Islam and Urban Practices in Sudan* (Chicago, University of Chicago Press, 1994).

Tripp, Aili Mari: *Changing the Rules: the politics of liberalisation and the informal economy in Tanzania:* (Berkeley: University of California Press, 1997)

Articles from Books

Cruise O'Brien, Donal 'Does Democracy Require an Opposition Party?' in Hermann Giliomee and Charles Simkins (eds.): *The Awkward Embrace: One-Party Domination and Democracy*, (Harwood, Amsterdam, 1999).

Friedman, Steven: 'South Africa: Divided in a Special Way' in Larry Diamond, Seymour Martin Lipset and Juan Linz (eds.) *Politics in Developing Countries* (Boulder, Lynne Rienner, 1995)

Friedman, Steven and Louise Stack: 'The Magic Moment: The 1994 Election' in Friedman and Atkinson.

Chris Landsberg: 'Directing from the Stalls?: The International Community and the South African Negotiating Forum' in Friedman and Atkinson, 1995

Simone, Abdou Maliq: 'Urban Societies in Africa' in Richard Humphries and Maxine Reitzes (ed.) *Civil Society After Apartheid* (Johannesburg, Centre for Policy Studies/Friedrich Ebert Foundation, 1995)

Zartman, William: 'Prenegotiation: Phases and Functions' in Janice Gross Stein (ed.): *Getting to the Table: The Process of International Prenegotiation* (Baltimore, Johns Hopkins University Press, 1989)

Articles from Periodicals

Ake, Claude 'The Unique Case of African Democracy' *International Affairs* 69, 1993

Friedman, Steven: 'Bonaparte at the Barricades: The Colonisation of Civil Society', *Theoria* Special Edition, University of Natal, Durban, 1992;

Joseph, Richard 'Africa, 1990-1997: From *Abertura* to Closure': *Journal of Democracy* (Volume 9, Number 2, April 1998)

Rustow, Dankwart A: 'Transitions to Democracy: Toward a Dynamic Model' *Comparative Politics* 2 (3) 337-63, 1970

Schmitter, Philippe and Terry Karl, 'What Democracy Is ... And Is Not' *Journal of Democracy* 2, 1991

Simone, Abdou Maliq 'Between the lines: African civil societies and the Remaking of Urban Communities' *Africa Insight* 22 (3) 1992

Monographs

Bernstein, Ann, Peter Berger and Bobby Godsell: 'Business and Democracy: Cohabitation or Contradiction' in *Development and Democracy*, (Johannesburg, Centre for Development and Enterprise, No. 10, May 1996).

Charney, Craig: *Voices of a New Democracy: African Expectations in the New South Africa* (Johannesburg, Centre for Policy Studies, 1995);

Chipkin, Ivor with Paul Thulare: *The Limits of Governance: Prospects for Local Government after the Katorus War* (Johannesburg, Centre for Policy Studies, 1997)

Institute for Democracy in South Africa (IDASA) Public Opinion Service *Building a Democratic Culture in KwaZulu Natal: The Present Terrain* Cape Town, Idasa, POS Reports No. 9, June 1996

Institute for Democracy in South Africa (IDASA), *A Submission to The White Paper Secretariat by the Idasa Public Opinion Service*, December, 1997

Landsberg, Chris and Claude Kabemba, with Richard Cornwell *Partnership Real Africa: Swedish donor assistance, democratisation and economic growth in Africa* (Johannesburg, Centre for Policy Studies, 1997)

McGaffey, Janet: 'Domination and Resistance in Zaire: resisting the shadow state through the international trade of the second economy', paper delivered at the African Renewal Conference, Massachusetts Institute of Technology, March 1997

Rapoo, Thabo *A Twist in the Tail? The African National Congress and Provincial Premiers*, CPS Policy Brief, Johannesburg, Centre for Policy Studies, 1998

Shubane, Khehla and Mark Shaw: *Tomorrow's Foundations?: Forums as a Second Level of a Negotiated Transition in South Africa* Johannesburg, (Centre for Policy Studies, 1993)

Shubane Khehla: *Yesterday's Remedies: Political Parties, Liberation Politics and South African Democracy*, (Johannesburg, Centre for Policy Studies, 1997)

Tomlinson, Mary: *From Rejection to Resignation: Beneficiaries' Views of the Government's Housing Subsidy Scheme*, (Johannesburg, Centre for Policy Studies, 1997)

White, Caroline: Nkosana Dlodlo and Walter Segooa, *Democratic Societies? Voluntary Association and Democratic Culture in a South African Township*, (Johannesburg, Centre for Policy Studies, 1995)

Unpublished Papers

Friedman, Steven: *South Africa After 1999: Trends and Prospects* Johannesburg, (Centre for Policy Studies, Unpublished paper prepared for Swedish International Development Agency, January 1998)

Gotz, Graeme: *The Limits of Community: the Dynamics of Rural Water Provision*, (unpublished report for Rand Water, Johannesburg, Centre for Policy Studies, 1997)

EndNotes

[1] In principle, free electoral competition is permitted, but party formation is proscribed. Museveni's National Resistance Movement is, in theory, not a party but a movement expressing national aspirations.

[2] The date assembled in Bratton and van de Walle, *op. cit.*, indicate substantial differences between democratisation paths - see for example Table 4, p.120

[3] Opposition politicians and commentators have, for example, repeatedly expressed fears of a 'typical African one-party state'.

[4] The term is used by Linz and Stepan (1996:11) to denote the capacity to 'command, regulate and extract'.

[5] For an account of alternative, non-state, social and political organisation in Abidjan see Simone, 1992 and 1995.

[6] For a critique of the claims to representativeness of civil society organisations see Friedman, 1992. For the limited reach of associational life see White, Dlodlo and Segooa, 1995.

[7] Much of this is justified by the rhetoric of 'participatory democracy'. But, as Mamdani observes (1995: 299), many shack settlements 'began with an emphasis on participation and ended up with a shacklord'

[8] To name but one example, only hours after the ANC leadership had, at the movement's conference in Mafikeng, North West Province, in December 1997, attacked white lack of commitment to the new order, deputy president Mbeki announced an intention to tour white farming areas to persuade the farmers to endorse the new society.

13

The Commodification of Violence, Private Military Companies and African States

Anna Leander

Over the past decade a very instructive and interesting debate about the nature of the state in Africa has developed. Authors from a variety of perspectives have tried to capture the peculiarity of states whose borders were drawn largely by external powers and which have developed in the context of an intrusive international system. Jackson (1990) has described them as "quasi-states" resting on legally defined sovereignty and Clapham (1996) insists on the role of the international system in shaping them. In addition to this, there is a growing body of literature depicting the specific kind of politics, which characterises these states, and in particular the blurred distinctions between private and public authority. Thus, Bayart (1997b) has developed the idea of "occult power structures" which surround (and even dominate) the formal ones and Reno describes the development of a sui generis form of politics which he dubs "war-lord politics" (1998). Certainly much to the dismay of these scholars, their insights have been translated into politics through the popularisation of the ideas of "failed" states.

In this chapter, I want to focus on one recent development which affects many African states and which, I will argue, feeds into and cements, the particularity of states in the region, namely the rapid development and presence of Private Military Companies (PMCs). I will make the point that PMCs are increasingly present on the continent, that their presence is widely accepted, and that they are likely to remain part of the picture of how violence is regulated in Africa for the foreseeable future. I will then proceed to argue that this expansion of PMC activities has profound implications for states. It affects their role in the regulation of violence and hence one of the basic features of statehood. It does so both via its impact on the direct regulation of violence and via its effect on the foundations of state authority. So the bottom line is that the commodification of security tied to expansion of PMCs is bound to reinforce the particularity of many African states.

The Growth of Private Military Companies

The sale of security services is not a novelty on the African continent or anywhere else. On the contrary, many, f not most past conflicts have involved some degree and some form of it (Møller 2001). However, over the past decade important changes have occurred. There is more private security and private business companies are increasingly involved in its sale.

It is impossible to find authoritative and comprehensive information on the sale of private military and security services.[1] In Africa (and elsewhere) the issue is (and will remain) highly sensitive, largely occult and hence not reported and documented with any precision. This said, private security, in its various guises, holds an increasingly central place in the accounts of how violence is regulated in, and among most African countries. And according to most specialists, there has been a sharp increase in mercenary involvement in armed conflict during the 1990s. And this consensus is probably the most solid indicator of the growing importance of the phenomenon one can get. An indication of the magnitude is given by the compilations of available information on "mercenary activity" in Africa from the 1950s onwards. One such compilation shows 15 entries for the 40 years spanning 1950-1989 and 65 for the period 1990-98 (Musah and Fayemi 2000). Similarly, the recent Foreign and Commonwealth Office Greenpaper (2002: Annex A) shows 15 entries for the period 1950-1989 and 80 for the period 1990 onwards.

There is not only more private security; the sellers are increasingly international or transnational. The conventional image of private security services as being sold mainly by (local) gang leaders, mafias or warlords and by (foreign) individuals or mercenaries is obsolete. Of course, these sellers continue to exist and arguably play a growing role in contexts where the policing and judiciary systems have either broken down or were never established. But to this image one has to add an international business component: the PMCs.

In part, this business grows out of para-public defence industries and armies whose budgets are under pressure and who are being directed to become more commercial. The end of the cold war and regime changes in Russia and South Africa have led to a profound restructuring of the military in the direction of privatising and diminishing the role of the state. Moreover, there is a general trend to "commercialise" defence by making publicly owned and/or controlled entities compete for contracts on international markets (Edmonds 1998). At the same time, decreased state priority to military questions is visible in dwindling resources, status and paycheques allotted soldiers. The overall number of men in the armed forces has dropped from 28 to 21 million between 1985 and 1999 (IISS 2000). And those who stay often need to make arrangements to complement their income. The result is a combination of large numbers of qualified military personnel in search of alternative, complementary and/or more lucrative work, with the growing number of para-public commercialised firms in search of international contracts (Harding 1997; Harker 1998; Shearer 1998; Adams 1999; Isenberg 2000).

But it would be a mistake to deduce that the PMCs are merely a branch of the national armed forces of their country of origin. Many of them are not. Even when they are set up and staffed by former militaries they can operate as genuinely private companies. Their services are offered on international markets. Their size, scope and type vary. Some are very small, specialised and with a clear national anchoring. Others are large multinational businesses, traded on stock markets, with headquarters in tax havens, and with highly professional advertising and public relations departments.

The group of PMCs, which has attracted the greatest attention, is that where the firm is part of a large diversified corporate group; no doubt because of the many obvious parallels between the operations of these companies and the grand style colonial companies. The most frequently cited (but by no means only) examples are Executive Outcomes (closed in 1998) and Sandline. They are part of the Brach Heritage Oil and Gas group, which covers a wide range of mining, extractive, military support and logistics and financial activities. The business model - which Howe (2001) calls "the EO model" - consists of offering security, a stable source of tax revenue, and continuous foreign exchange inflows to governments in exchange for concessions. For example, to mine diamonds (in Sierra Leone) or extract oil (in Angola).

Accepting the Commodification of Violence

The most spectacular aspect of the PMC development is that the commodification of security entailed, is widely accepted. It is far more so, than at any other time during the past century. In sharp contrast with the situation that has prevailed since the mid 18th century when piracy, privateering and mercenaries were outlawed (Thomson 1994), states now (again) seem to accept a prominent role for private business interests in the regulation of violence. They use it themselves and allow or encourage others (NGOs, firms and international organisations) to do the same.

The overarching reason for this altered status of PMCs is that they have managed to constitute themselves as credible alternatives to the insufficient or inexistent public means of regulating violence. Indeed, in many African states the arguably always-vacillating public control over violence has further eroded over the past decade. A variety of reasons well described and discussed elsewhere[2], have conspired in this development. What matters here is that the incapacity of public authorities to impose their authority, with the help of public forces, on the regulation of violence has made private military companies stand out as useful and necessary. The bottom line is that the private companies do what the state should perhaps be doing but is neither willing nor capable of getting done.

The image of PMCs as a respectable alternative is grounded not least in the fact that they are extensively used by the public authorities themselves. An important part of the explanation for why this is so, is the financial squeeze on government budgets (and hence on spending for armed forces) created by the post-cold war withdrawal of the great powers from the region and the effects of conditionality and "financial globalisation". This squeeze has made the outsourcing of security and military operations a very attractive alternative for governments. They only have to pay for the intervention they ask for, whereas standing armies and/or police forces have to be paid independently of what they do. Payments in concession rights saves scarce foreign exchange and has the advantage of making sure that the extractive activities can continue; hence securing continued revenues. Finally, allowing PMCs to operate has the great advantage of shifting costs from the public to the private (or international) sector as private firms, international organisations and NGOs take on the costs of providing for their own security.

And indeed, outsiders are increasingly relying on private companies to compensate for the absence of effective state control over violence. They have to protect their installations and their personnel. They need protection from racketeering, abduction, and attacks. And in situations where the public armed forces and police are either unavailable, ineffective, or involved in the activities against which protection is needed, private solutions seem to be the credible only ones. Hence, even when (as is often the case) aid workers and firms resent the necessity to rely on PMCs, they are also painfully aware that the alternative is not to continue or engage in operation in conflict areas. And this is not an option. For firms declining to work with PMCs would mean an investment lost. For "humanitarians" it would imply that they could not work where they are needed. Consequently, both firms and humanitarians rely extensively on PMCs. DSL (Defence Systems Limited), lists among its humanitarian clients: the International Rescue Committee, CARE, Caritas, USAID, GOAL and World Vision. And in the UN system the UNHCR, UNICEF, UNDP, WFP amongst others declare to have used private security services (Spearin 2001).

Also outside governments have been increasingly positive to the idea of relying on PMCs. There are multiple and overlapping reasons for this. Firstly, it is related to the general trend to look for private solutions and privatise. Secondly it is that governments want to intervene in conflicts but do not want to see any body bags coming back as a result. Thirdly, it is that they wish to circumvent the political debate necessary to get support for international interventions. And lastly, economic interests are no doubt involved. As pointed out above, many companies are para-public and certainly pressure their governments to support them (as would most companies). Granting a great variety in the weight of these considerations, there has been an overall shift in the direction of increasing reliance on private companies (O'Brien 2000; Mandel 2001).

The widespread acceptance of PMCs is enshrined in the mounting efforts to make it possible for the UN to contract PMCs for peacekeeping and peace enforcing operations. For this to be possible would entail a revision of the existing conventions condemning the use of mercenaries[3]. To argue for such a change, advocates point to the PMC successes in particular the role of EO in Angola[4] and in Sierra Leone[5]. They contrast these with the abysmal failures of the international community to intervene and react in serious crisis situations, Rwanda in particular, where Kofi Annan complained that he could have saved thousands of lives with a very small number of troops. The advocates argue that it is the height of hypocrisy to rely on, accept and work with PMCs in all situations except when it comes to settling conflict. Instead of having Africans die by the thousands it would be enough to "write a check to end the war" (Brooks 2000b).

Although this view is far from unanimously shared, it is clear that we are in a rather novel situation (that is, comparing with the past century and a half). The bottom line is that PMCs are definitely part of the African security picture. Most actors who have security concerns in the region rely on them. The rather unsurprising outcome is that a wide range of governments, multilateral and private aid agencies, NGOs and private firms support the PMC lobbying. And it consequently seems that independently of whether or not this lobbying actually results in altered and clarified regulations of "mercenary activity", PMCs are bound to remain an important de facto part of the African security picture.

This raises a number of important and interesting questions, but the one I want to address here is how it affects state authority. And it seems an essential one. If reliance on PMCs has become so extensive and so accepted as a consequence of the difficulties states face in controlling violence, it is clearly important to ask how that capacity fares under the influence of PMCs activities. And I want to address this question by splitting it into two parts; looking first at what increased PMC presence entails for the direct capacity of states to control violence directly and then at how the more long-term foundations of state authority are influenced by an increased PMC presence.

PMCs and Direct State Control over Violence

Regarding the first issue of how PMCs affect state authority to control violence, I want to make the point that even if PMCs are mostly employed by governments to ensure precisely that authority, reliance on them creates difficulties of their own. Indeed, there are fundamental differences between the regulation of violence through a market where private business enterprises compete for selling their services and a regulation that is done through publicly controlled armed forces (police or military). This might sound rather self-evident. But it is not a point on which observers agree. Rather many of those advocating a more extensive role for PMCs claim that PMCs are merely tools that can be used by governments and hence have little or no influence on state authority. However, as this section shows, this is not the case. Relying on PMCs creates a set of difficulties for state regulation of violence. It does so by loosening state control over their own use of violence as well as more generally over who uses what violence how. But more profoundly it tends to loosen up the accountability (national and international) of states for the acts of violence carried out by their nationals.

First, the reliance on PMCs makes it increasingly hard for states to control that their decision-making authority can actually be translated into actual military operations. There is always the risk that the private firms will not fulfil their contracts, or not do so fully. And there are many examples (including recent ones) where this has happened, including to the most influential and powerful governments of the world. For example, Brown & Root reportedly failed to deliver or severely overcharged on 4 of its 7 obligations to the US Army.[6] There is also the risk that PMCs will shift sides in the middle of a conflict or simply run away when the situation becomes too unpleasant. In 1994 for instance, the Gurkha fled Sierra Leone after their commander had been killed (and reputedly cannibalised). And, finally, PMCs may turn against their employers and work for their overthrow by a ruler more sensitive to their own concerns. It seems that EO was active in the 1996 ousting of the president of Sierra Leone. In reality, Machiavelli's discussion of how to deal with the "whores of war" has regained its relevance.

Second, reliance on PMCs alters the capacity of states to decide *who* is entitled to use *what kind* of force. Indeed, by definition private firms are in the business to make a profit. For some firms this might require keeping a good reputation for selling only to respectable clients. The larger PMCs have repeatedly protested that their activities might contribute to fuelling conflicts and empowering non-state actors. They must care for their reputation. But this is not necessarily a concern shared by all. Some firms may see the market more as a one shot opportunity and be less concerned. And even if one grants that reputation is mostly important, there is no monitoring system in place to check firms. Moreover, the notion of respectable client is highly circumspect in internal war situations. Consequently, it is hardly surprising to find numerous allegations to the effect that firms sell services to non-state organisations including rebel groups, extractive firms, or outright organised crime involved e.g. in drug trading, human trafficking, or trade in illegally extracted diamonds (UN 2001).

Third, privatisation is affecting *the way that decision making authority* is exercised in the state and possibly more widely the structure of state institutions. The consequence of privatisation tends to be a de-politicisation of the use of violence. Privatisation moves the question of "what kind of force is being used where by what nationals" out of the public arena of debate. Private firms (unlike governments) do not need political approval. The de-politicisation is further accentuated by a lower level of concern with what firms on contract do or do not do. A contracting firm can reasonably be asked to take responsibility for its engagements (it did not have to accept them). By contrast public armed forces do not have the same possibility to refuse tasks placed upon them. Therefore, in countries intervening, the definition and debate about these tasks is far less important and central when it is done by PMCs. Similarly, in states buying private military services, the balance between political actors is shifted. The government does not have to find support among powerful groups (including the military itself) when it turns to the PMCs provided it could find the resources to pay the bill.

Finally, the development of PMCs leads to a situation where the *accountability* for violence is blurred (Zarate 1998; Cullen 2000). For one, governments are unclear on how to treat the individuals employed by PMCs as epitomised by the general confusion surrounding the status of mercenaries. They are denied the various protections granted to soldiers in the Geneva Convention, and therefore do not have prisoners of war status. But it is not at all clear what the alternative is. Are those foreigners to be treated as common criminals when they kill people as part the job they are contracted for? For two, there is increasing uncertainty about what the expansion of PMCs entails for accountability for violence in the international sphere. Armies are tied to states and can be held accountable through them. But what about companies? The answer since the mid 19th century has been that states accept responsibility for acts of violence by their nationals beyond their borders (Thomson 1994). Yet, because of the increasing privatisation, states can and do deny responsibility for violence and crimes of their nationals by pointing out that it is private. This return of a policy of "plausible denial" (by states of responsibility for violence) of course leaves wide open the dual questions of who is to be responsible instead and who is to enforce the consequence of that responsibility.

It is clear that the reliance on PMCs does affect the way that the state regulates violence. It affects its direct authority over it, it leads to the creation of a market that is outside state control, it tends to de-politicise the use of violence and it blurs the lines of accountability. Whether or not this entails a weakening of state authority to control violence is an open question. The answer depends on what authority the state had before as well as on how effective the contracted firm turned out to be. Indeed, there are many cases in Africa where (theoretically public) armed forces escape control and pursue private profits with a ruthlessness most PMCs would find it hard to equal, as illustrated by many of the so called resource wars (Cilliers 2000; Le Billon 2000) and complex emergencies (Duffield 1994). Moreover, many African states face insurgencies and private violence, which PMCs might help hinder rather than develop. And, finally, there is all reason not to grant unquestioning approval to the systems of accountability for the use of force in many African states. Many armed forces and governments are no more accountable than are PMCs.

Hence, it is impossible to make any generalisation on the relationship between PMCs and state authority. However, what the argument does underline is that it is a chimera to believe that relying on PMCs to regulate violence does not create difficulties of its own for the state control over violence. And these problems need to be addressed both when we think about state authority in Africa and when we consider whether or not we ought to join the bandwagon of those who now advocate an expanded role for PMCs.

PMCs and the Foundations of State Authority

I want to continue the above argument when discussing the impact of PMCs on the foundations of the states' authority in Africa. It is important to outline from the start that there is no underlying claim to the effect that these foundations are unproblematic or made problematic solely by PMC presence. On the contrary (again), the overarching justification for the increased reliance on PMCs is precisely that in most African countries, the foundations of state authority are just as problematic as the exercise of direct authority over the regulation of violence. However, this should make it seem even more urgent to think about what the implications of PMC presence are. It certainly should not serve as a pretext for neglecting these implications. And there are two ways in which PMCs create difficulties for the foundations of state authority: the first is through their role strengthening the private authority over the regulation of violence and the second is through their effect on the balance among state institutions.

The first point about the effect of PMCs on the foundations of state authority is that it tends *to consolidate the private control of violence*. It is indeed a particularity of "the business of private security" (Gambetta 1993) that it deals in a commodity that is not like all others. The market for it is by definition inscrutable. Insecurity is a potential risk and no objective testing of competing offers for how to ensure against it is possible (Gambetta 1994). Moreover, it is a market where the suppliers tend to create their demand (commonly racketing). And finally, it is a market that tends to distort competition also for other things (public contracts, markets, or social life). The overall result is that (as one might have expected?) the business of private protection tends to serve the private interests of that business, not the state. A closer look at the fate of state authority in Columbia and Sicily, both notorious for their businesses of private protection, might be instructive for those advocating founding state authority on private business.

PMCs are not the Mafia, but the basic thrust of the argument that the private business of protection is a peculiar one with a tendency to anchor and perpetuate private authority still holds. Also PMCs operate in markets that are inscrutable. It is a classical insight that the definition of security - and of what is required to ensure it - is not something objectively given. Rather it depends on perceptions of what is a threat and on the "securitisation" of issues and problems (Jervis 1976; Buzan, Wæver et al. 1998). It should, therefore, come as no surprise that PMCs put great effort into consulting, training, and equipping armies. This evokes the "Dr Strange-Love problem" of allowing the military to define threats and how to deal with them. Professional training and background tend to make them particularly prone to present and see the military aspects and needs and hence fuel demands for security. However, there is a specific twist to the Dr Strange-Love problem: It is not any military that is defining threats. It is a private one. Hence, threats posed by public forces and the superiority of private solutions are bound to be an integral part of the advising. This is something that seems to be amply confirmed by the considerable time and effort PMCs spend curing their image and reputation as well as explaining their superiority to public alternatives.

This leads straight onto the point that PMCs operate in a market where the supply tends to create demand. There is no foundation for, or reason to, accuse PMCs of racketing states as the mafia would a shopkeeper: at the point of the gun. The mechanisms are subtler. When PMCs sell protective capacity to one side, it increases the (perceived) insecurity of the other side. This will lead the other side to arm and hence we are in conventional arms race logic. And the result is that the price to pay for security increases steadily and there is an ever-increasing market for PMC services. Two things might amplify this. The first is that both sides in a conflict will try to rely on PMCs, usually different ones.[7] If one adds the tendencies of the PMCs to proliferate, offer services to different parties, and actually become actors in their own right it seems clear that in addition to paying a higher price for protection against one enemy, the number of enemies grows steadily as well. This is a crucial part of Reno's story about the transition to "war lord politics" (1998).

Lastly, the intensive debate about what the nature of the (denied and unacceptable) links between PMCs and various economic interests - and in particular around the so-called EO model (selling security against mining or extractive rights) - confirms is that there are tendencies for PMC activities to spill over into other sectors. However, it deserves underlining that according to most accounts[8], the link is not that PMCs enlarge their activities to include other sectors but the other way around. Firms operating in conflict areas create, ally with or hire PMCs. This might not matter fundamentally for the argument though. Because even if the link goes from the firms to the PMCs, the linking up of their interests is likely to create powerful structures which favour the reliance on private security.

That is the business of private protection, including when it is the business of PMCs, tends to perpetuate the private authority over the regulation of violence. It does so by contributing to a definition of the security needs which accords a key place to PMCs; by contributing to the creation of a supply led demand which perpetuates the need for PMCs; and finally by tying PMCs into other economic sectors which are likely to advocate and rely on PMCs.

The second point I want to make about the relationship between PMCs and the foundations of state authority is that PMCs influence *the balance between state institutions* in ways that are likely to have an eroding effect on the basis of state authority. They do so first, by "crowding out" state institutions. Indeed, the presence of PMCs relieves the state of the need to build institutions capable of providing security. Instead of investing into costly and politically dangerous armies and police forces, rulers can chose to rely on private companies. Relying on PMCs is all the more attractive since, as argued by Reno, "states do not necessarily prefer a state monopoly over legitimate violence" (Reno 1998: 72). Control over commerce (and not territory) is the name of the game, he argues, and that might go with various forms of control over violence. A state monopoly may be neither the most effective, nor the most appropriate means to that end. However, the flip-side of such "innovative political strategies" (Duffield 1998) is that rulers do not need to build the most basic institutions of statehood: the armed forces (police or military).

In addition to this, the presence of PMCs tends to skew the distribution of security. By making the control of violence something that is payable and decided upon according to economic criteria, PMCs tend to accentuate the divergence between those who command the control over resources and consequently can demand security and those who cannot. And I would like to stress that it is a matter of accentuating. One of the points often underlined in the literature of contemporary state building in Africa is that it is not because so often certain groups "opt out" that states split up and fall apart into regions. Rather more frequently, it is because states push people out. They "abandon people who could contribute little to a political alliance and would make demands on scarce political resources" (Reno 1998: 10). The gap between *l'Afrique utile* and *l'Afrique inutile* is widened (Bayart, Ellis et al. 1997a). Clearly, PMCs cannot be charged with creating the gap. However, the increased commodification of violence entailed by their presence certainly does not diminish it. On the contrary, it widens the gap and hence deepens the authority problems of states providing selective, rather Swiss cheese like, security coverage.

Ultimately, the presence of PMCs contributes to reduce the importance of legitimacy for states - something that is bound to weaken their authority decisively. Indeed, the role of legitimacy is already reduced in many countries. Power depends more on the approval of external authorities and access to international credits than it does on the "forging of mutual constraints between rulers and ruled" Tilly described as essential for the "civilianising of European states (1985)[9]. However, military companies push this trend further. The control over violence can be bought, the conditions is to command sufficient resources. Commanding adherence is of secondary importance. Moreover, the presence of private military personnel--in and of itself--is often seen as delegitimising the state and/or regime (Howe 2001). It is both a confirmation of the reduced import of legitimacy and something that further diminishes it.

To sum up, an increased PMC presence seems to cause trouble for the foundations of state authority in two ways: 1) by durably anchoring control over violence with the private sector; and 2) it tends to shifts the relative importance of (state) institutions in a way which undermines the long- term authority of the state. It does so by reducing the importance of constructing state controlled armed forces; by linking security and command over resources, which results in a Swiss cheese like security coverage, and by further diminishing the importance of legitimacy.

Conclusion

This chapter has argued that over the past decade we have witnessed an increased commodification of the regulation of violence on the African continent, which is epitomised by a growing and largely accepted presence of PMCs. The chapter went on to argue that the increased reliance on PMCs has profound implications for state authority. It alters both the direct control of states over the regulation of violence and the foundations of the authority by which they exercise this regulation. Throughout, the chapter has underlined that whether these implications entail a weakening of state authority or not, is something about which it is impossible to generalise. It depends on what kind of state and what PMC intervention is under discussion.

Hence the aim of this chapter has not been to vilify PMCs or their activities in Africa. Rather it has been to underline an obvious but often forgotten point: the privatisation of security impinges on public authority. This is no less the true where that public authority is highly problematic and contestable (such as in many post-colonial African states) than it is elsewhere. And it is important to keep this in mind and confront it, before jumping onto the bandwagon, following the enthusiasts advocating the reestablishment of order (and presumably public authority) on the basis of private intervention. "War is not polite recreation but the vilest thing in life, and we ought to understand that and not play at war" (Tolstoy). Therefore it is of essence to think about whom we grant authority to go to war and to control the means of war.

References

Adams, Thomas K. (1999): 'The New Mercenaries and the Privatisation of Conflict', *Parameters* 29, 2, pp. 103-116.

Bayart, Jean François, Stephen Ellis and Béatrice Hibou (1997a): 'De l'Etat kleptocrate à l'Etat malfaiteur?', in Jean François Bayart, Stephen Ellis and Béatrice Hibou, eds.: *La criminalisation de l'Etat en Afrique*, (Paris: Editions Complexe, pp. 17-54).

--- (1997b) *La criminalisation de l'Etat en Afrique*, (Paris: Editions Complexe).

Brooks, Doug (2000a): 'Messiahs or Mercenaries? The Future of International Private Military Services', *International Peacekeeping* 7, 4, pp. 129-144.

--- (2000b) 'Write a cheque, end a war: Using private military companies to end African conflicts', *Conflict Trends*, 1.

Buzan, Barry, Ole Wæver and Jaap de Wilde (1998) *Security. A New Framework for Analysis*, (Boulder, London: Lynne Rienner).

Cilliers, Jackie (2000) 'Resource Wars - A New Type of Insurgency', in Jackkie Cilliers and Christian Dietrich, eds.: *Angola's War Economy: The Role of Oil and Diamonds*, (Pretoria: Institute for Security Studies, pp. 1-15.)

Clapham, Christopher (1996) *Africa and the International System. The Politics of State Survival*, (Cambridge: Cambridge University Press).

Cullen, Patrick (2000) 'Keeping the New Dog of War on a Tight Leash: Assessing the Accountability for Private Military', *Conflict Trends*, June, pp. 36-39.

Duffield, Mark (1994) 'The Political Economy of Internal War: Asset Transfer, Complex Emergencies and International Aid', in Joanna

Macrae, Anthony Zwi and with Mark Duffield and Hugo Slim, eds, *War and Hunger. Rethinking International Responses to Complex Emergencies*, (London and New Jersey: Zed Books, pp. 50-69).

--- (1998) 'Post-modern Conflict: Warlords, Post-adjustment States and Private Protection', *Civil Wars* 1, 1, pp. 65-102.

--- (2001) *Global Governance and the New Wars. The Merging of Development and Security*, (London and New York: Zed Books).

Edmonds, Martin (1998) 'Defence Privatisation: From State Enterprise to Commercialism', *Cambridge Review of International Affairs* XIII, 1, pp. 114-129.

Foreign and Commonwealth Office (2002) *Private Military Companies: Options for Regulation*, (London, see the website below) http://www.fco.gov.uk/Files/kfile/mercenaries,0.pdf.

Gambetta, Diego (1993): *The Sicilian Mafia: The Business of Private Protection*, (Cambridge: Harvard University Press).

--- (1994) 'Godfather's Gossip', *Archives Européennes de Sociologie* XXXV, 2, pp. 199-223.

Harding, Jeremy (1997): 'The Mercenary Business: Executive Oucomes', *Review of African Political Economy*, 71, pp. 87-97.

Harker, John (1998): 'Mercenaries: Private Power, Public Insecurity?' *New Routes*, 4.

Howe, Herbert M. (2001): *Ambiguous Order: Military Forces in African States*, Boulder CO.: Lynne Rienner.

IISS (2000): *International Institute for Strategic Studies: The Military Balance 2000-2001*, London: Oxford University Press.

Isenberg, David (2000): 'Combat for Sale: The New, Post-Cold War Mercenaries', *USA Today*, March, pp. 12-16.

Jackson, Robert H. (1990): *Quasi-States: Sovereignty, International Relations and the Third World*, Cambridge: Cambridge University Press.

Jervis, Robert (1976): *Perception and Misperception in International Politics*, Princeton: Princeton University Press.

Le Billon, Philippe (2000) 'The Political Economy of Resource Wars', in Jackie Cilliers and Christian Dietrich, eds, *Angola's War Economy: The Role of Oil and Diamonds*, (Pretoria: Institute for Security Studies, pp. 21-43).

Leander, Anna (2002): 'Wars and the Un-Making of States: Taking Tilly Seriously in the Contemporary World', in Stefano Guzzini and Dietrich Jung, eds, *Copenhagen Peace Research: Conceptual Innovations and Contemporary Security Analysis.*

Mandel, Robert (2001) 'The Privatisation of Security', *Armed Forces and Society* 28, 1, pp. 129-151.

Musah, Abdel-Fatah and Kayode J. Fayemi, eds (2000): *Mercenaries: An African Security Dilemma*, (London: Pluto Press).

Møller, Bjørn (2001) 'Private Militære Virksomheder og Fredsoperationer i Afrika', *Militært Tidskrift* 130, 3, pp. 175-199.

O'Brien, Kevin (2000) 'Private Military Companies and African Security, 1990-8', in Abdel-Fatah Musah and Kayode J. Fayemi, eds, *Mercenaries: An African Security Dilemma*, (London: Pluto Press, pp. 43-75.)

Reno, William (1998): *Warlord Politics and African States* (Boulder, London: Lynne Rienner)

Shearer, David (1998): 'Outsourcing War', *Foreign Policy* Fall, pp. 68-81.

Singer, P. W. (2001/2): 'Corporate Warriors: The Rise of the Privatised Military Industry and Its Ramifications for International Security', *International Security* 26, 3, pp. 186-220.

Spearin, Christopher (2001): 'Private Security Companies and Humanitarians: A Corporate Solution to Securing Humanitarian Spaces?', *International Peacekeeping* 8, 1, pp. 20-43.

Thomson, Janice (1994): *Mercenaries, Pirates, and Sovereigns: State-building and Extraterritorial Violence in Early Modern Europe*, (Princeton: Princeton University Press).

Tilly, Charles (1985): 'War Making and State Making as Organized Crime', in Peter Evans, Dietrich Rueschemeyer and Theda Skocpol, eds, *Bringing the State Back In*, (Cambridge: Cambridge University Press, pp. 169-191).

UN (2001) Report by Enrique Bernales Ballesteros, *On the question of the use of mercenaries as a means of violating human rights and impeding the exercise of the right of peoples to self-determination, pursuant to Commission resolution 2000/3*, (New York: UN, E/CN.4/2001/19, available at http://www.unhchr.ch/Huridocda/Huridoca.nsf/0/b6e7abef3d39af97c12 56a140059c839/$FILE/G0110170.pdf.)

Zarate, Juan Carlos (1998): 'The Emergence of a New Dog of War: Private International Security Companies, International Law and the New World Disorder', *Stanford Journal of International Law* 34, 1, pp. 75-162.

EndNotes

1. In principle, private military services differ from private security services. However, practically the links between the two are close and there is a grey boarder zone where security and military services coincide (Brooks 2000a).
2. In particular: Clapham (1996); Reno (1998); and Duffield (2001).
3. The 1997 OAU Convention; and the 1989 UN Convention.
4. EO played a crucial role in bringing UNITA to the negotiating table, which eventually resulted in the 1994 Lusaka protocol.
5. The operations in Sierra Leone involved the reestablishment of order. But they went far beyond that: EO also organised the return of children and teachers who had been trapped, it organised the integration of hundreds of child-soldiers in rehabilitation programmes, and it supported the government against disgruntled RSMLF officers whose diamond trading was threatened by the government (Zarate 1998).
6. This and the two next examples stem from Singer (2001/2).
7. There are allegations of one firm working for both sides in a conflict such as that EO in Angola Reno (1998: 64).
8. I have personally never read a different account.
9. This point is discussed in more detail in Leander (2002 forthcoming).

14

Does the world owe Africa a living?

Desmond Davies

During the first half of 2003, citizens of the Democratic Republic of Congo and Liberia were under serious threat from rampaging assailants – armed with an assortment of clubs, machetes, handguns and mortars. As their terror increased, they appealed to Western governments to intervene in order to put a halt to the mayhem. In Liberia, ordinary people called for the US to come to their rescue.

This begs the question: why should the West intervene in an African conflict? Granted that those who are calling for foreign intervention are the helpless ones who are being terrorised by fighters who basically do not have any ideology to back their armed insurgency save that of gaining power. Why should Africans, in the first place, be killing each other in such high numbers in the 21st century? Answers have to be found to this because it really does not make sense to witness such senseless acts going on in Africa.

Rebels purport to be carrying out their campaigns in order to change society for the better. But how can they explain the unnecessary death and destruction that they cause? Once they have caused so much havoc during the conflict, what would be left for them to control? Take the case of the Revolutionary United Front of the late Foday Sankoh in Sierra Leone. When the rebels, who had invaded Freetown on January 6 1999, were being pushed back by Nigerian forces, after 12 days of occupation, they burnt half of the properties in the east end of the city, including churches, mosques and schools.

Eventually, when peace prevailed and Sankoh was given a position within the government, he complained bitterly that the government was taking its time to find suitable accommodation befitting his position. But the problem was that there was a housing crisis caused by the actions of the rebels.

It is the same situation that is being played out in areas of conflict in Africa. In the end those who are responsible for this destruction will turn to the outside world for assistance. It is not surprising, therefore, that there is a reluctance to help Africa. The onus thus lies on Africans to take action themselves to rectify the situation on their continent. The question Africans have to ask themselves first of all is why, after more than 40 years of independence, they are still searching for the right path towards African advancement? It would appear that after 40 years of independence, African leaders still do not seem to have a clue as to what is good for their countries.

But again, are we sure that African leaders do not know what is needed for Africa's development or are they just not interested in doing the right thing? I believe that African leaders are not interested in doing the right thing to lift their countries out of perpetual poverty and conflict. Every so often we hear of plans, initiatives and programmes to uplift African countries. But where have all these led the continent? Not very far on the road to development, it would seem. Even UN Secretary-General Kofi Annan was moved to bemoan the fact that these plans, initiatives and programmes for Africa have not achieved much. He said: "Over the decades, the United Nations system has been involved in so many development initiatives that even I cannot remember what the acronyms stand for. Unfortunately, few, if any, of them have been effective."

This is the problem we face in Africa. Why have the plans, programmes, and initiatives not delivered the goods? Is it because ordinary Africans and their leaders really do not have the interest of the continent at heart? To a certain extent, this might seem to be the case. For how can we explain the mindless behaviour of some Africans and their leaders when it comes to running their countries? Corruption is rife and political incompetence is the order of the day.

The greatest excuse for the failure of Africa to take off has been that of tribalism and ethnic divisions. These have caused much destruction to the continent's political, social and economic fabric. But why should tribalism and ethnic divisions be so rife in Africa? Is Africa the only continent with such problems? I don't think so. Indeed, according to statistics, only about 20 countries in the world - such as Japan and Portugal - are mono-ethnic. The rest are multi-ethnic. And I am not even talking about the recent immigration phenomenon. I am referring to nation-states that are made up of the same race but have their ethnic divides. But these nation-states, mainly in Europe, have managed in varying degrees, to overcome these problems and become successful. It could of course be argued that it has taken them a long time to achieve unity. But why should Africa be bogged down by deep-seated ethnic divisions, which are not taking the continent anywhere?

If, on the other hand, domination by one powerful ethnic group is to continue be the norm in Africa, why should this not be used in a positive manner? After all, this was what happened in South Africa during the days of apartheid when the Afrikaner tribe held sway. Its members who controlled the reins of power exploited all the other ethnic groups but ensured that the country was developed - at least for the minority tribe. Now, the new leaders in South Africa are benefiting from this.

South Africa, like many other African countries, has abundant natural resources. The Afrikaner tribe, while exploiting the other ethnic groups, used these natural resources to build their country. In the rest of Africa, the natural resources appear to be a curse to the countries that have them. That is the only explanation one can give for the way in which these countries have frittered away their wealth. Take Nigeria, for example. What did the northern military rulers do with the country's oil wealth? They stole the money and stashed it in foreign banks. Is this how Africa will move forward? In the cases of Sierra Leone, Angola and the Democratic Republic of Congo, the various factions stole the wealth and made Europeans richer.

The most important thing for Africa is that - ethnicity or not - Africans should owe their allegiance to the nation-state in which they live. After all, if the fortunes of the nation-state improve, those living within its boundaries would also prosper. But as long as we continue to destroy the nation-state in which we live - because this or that ethnic group is not in power, Africa will not move forward. Sadly, many Africans do not believe in their nation-states. They owe their allegiance to their ethnic groups - and this will continue to hold the continent back.

African leaders also do not inspire confidence in their people. They pay lip service to democracy, human rights and development. They are forever complaining about the unfairness of the global trade system that puts Africa at a disadvantage. But have they made any effort to change things themselves? No. African leaders have to take the lead in order to show the outside world that they mean business.

There are basic problems that have not been seriously addressed, as has been indicated in the United Nations Development Programme's (UNDP) Human Development Report (HDR) for 2003. It actually spells misery for African countries. The report, developed in 1990, publishes a Human Development Index (HDI) that measures achievements in terms of life expectancy, literacy and income. Thirty out of 34 countries at the bottom of the HDI – that is, the ones referred to as "low development" countries are in Africa. Some African countries though – such as Benin, Ghana, Mauritius, Rwanda, Senegal and Uganda – significantly improved their positions on the HDI. But, in the main, according to the report, the economically hard-pressed countries in Africa are facing an acute crisis in development.

According to the HDR, between 1990 and 2001, 21 countries went backwards – 14 of these in Africa. "Reversals in HDI are highly unusual as these indicators generally tend to edge up slowly over time," pointed out March Malloch Brown, UNDP Administrator. "The fact that over the course of the 1990s, 21 countries experienced a decline – in some cases a drastic drop – signifies an urgent call for action to address health and education as well as income levels in these countries."

The report pointed out that the rich countries ought to pay more attention to helping the less fortunate countries get out of the rut. But I think that these countries must also make better efforts to improve things with the resources available to them rather than wait until their fortunes change for the better. Jeffrey Sachs, Special Adviser to the UN Secretary-General on the Millennium Development Goals, made this point in the HDR. "Poor countries cannot afford to wait until they are wealthy before they invest in their people," he argues. "This is the wrong way. They need rural health clinics, schools, roads, safe drinking water and sanitation, so that economic growth can take root in the first place. Investment in meeting basic needs isn't just desirable in its own right for ending human suffering, but it is also a key part of an overall strategy for economic growth."

There is also the small matter of politics. Malloch Brown notes in the HDR. "Poverty can be a political problem. This report shows that there are many countries where income levels are high enough to end absolute poverty, but where pockets of deep poverty remain, often because of worrying patterns of discrimination in the provision of basic services."

Indeed, there is no point in African leaders urging foreign investors to pump their money into the continent if these basic necessities are not available to the mass of African people. An unskilled workforce is of no use to an investor. An unhealthy workforce is of no use to an investor either. Erratic electricity and water supplies will not entice foreign investors to Africa.

Regarding the above situation, I believe that African leaders tend to put the cart before the horse. If the basic needs of investors are not in place, how else can they explain the clamour for $64 billion to fund the New Partnership for Africa's Development (NEPAD)? Apart from South Africa, there is no country in sub-Saharan Africa, to my mind, that has the capacity to handle such a huge amount in investment money. Out of a continental GDP of $540 billion, South Africa's contribution is $120 billion. North African contributes $200 billion while the rest of the continent provides another $200 billion.

The problem with programmes such as NEPAD is that Africans place too much trust in Western countries, believing wrongly that they are genuinely out to help. The truth is that all they are interested in is to ensure that there is no crisis for capitalism. Western countries are always on the lookout for more consumers to buy the immense number of goods that roll off their industrial assembly lines. As Western domestic markets become saturated with competing brands, manufacturers have been driven to seek global economies of scale in the production and marketing of their goods.

But African countries can resist this expansion of Western corporations. If, as Ghana has complained, the French placed a 300 per cent tariff on chocolate from Ghana, why has Ghana not imposed a 1,000 per cent tariff on French cars? After all, do we need such luxury cars - and other luxury imports, for that matter - in Africa? If, as Africans are constantly being told, Africa is poor, why should they spend their hard-earned cash on Europeans goods?

I am not sure whether this will work anyway because the people who are supposed to protect their countries in Africa from unfair trade are the very ones who spend money on unnecessary foreign imports. Africans do not have their priorities right. What is the purpose of having an expensive car when there are no good roads to drive them? What is the purpose of having a satellite dish to watch foreign television programmes when there are constant power failures? What is the purpose of building an expensive house surrounded by slums?

So how can African countries improve rapidly to catch up with a world that is fast running away from the continent? I believe that the African Union will have to take the lead in changing things. Health, communications, agriculture, road, transport and energy – sectors that are providing immense challenges to Africa's development prospects, will have to be handled by the AU, acting as a supranational body.

Once the AU is allowed to act on behalf of all of Africa in the development process, I believe that the pressure on individual countries would be reduced and this would be good in the long run for Africa. Policies will be drawn up in the interest of the whole continent. It is now clearly obvious that African countries will not develop if they go it alone.

What is needed is the political will to support the AU. Member countries must ensure that their contributions are paid regularly. They should take the attitude that they took when dealing with the old OAU Liberation Committee, which was based in Dar es Salaam. Contributions to the Committee were never in arrears because, I think, African leaders believed in its aims and objectives: that of freeing the continent of colonialism and apartheid. This belief appears to be lacking among Africans and their leaders today.

As stated earlier, I believe that Africans and their leaders know what should be done to take their continent forward. But they are not interested in doing the right thing because it suits them to preside over a chaotic continent. So they are forever looking for excuses and passing the buck. Africans must begin to believe in themselves and in their continent if they are to move forward and become less dependent on the rest of the world to sort out their problems.

References

UNDP's, *Human Development Report*, 2003
Kofi Annan, Jeffrey Sachs and Malloch Brown were as quoted by the HDR, 2003.
West Africa magazine, various issues.

Part IV

Afro-Arab Relations: Co-operation or Conflict

15

Pan-Africanism and Pan-Arabism: Back to the Future?

Akram Hawas

While pressures on Africa have dramatically increased from many sides, the continent has also experienced the re-launching of the project of pan-Africanism. Globalisation has catapulted the continent on the world agenda. Africa is about to be re-discovered and there is a talk about re-colonisation. Against this threat, Pan-Africanism is re-emerging as an alternative to fragmentation and possible re-colonisation. Some African intellectuals have joined the optimists of some politicians seeking a renaissance in Africa.

Is the project of Pan-Africanism merely a reaction to the new challenges, or is it a more productive initiative that seeks to challenge the Western conception of "Afro-Pessimism"? The dreams of renaissance, however, sometimes go in the direction of a unity of sovereign states and other times even transcend the bitter reality of extreme fragility to prefigure a United States of Africa. Among the enthusiastic leaders is colonel Gaddafi of Libya, who seemingly expresses a desire to Africanise the Arab. This may indicate a prospect towards finding a new basis once more for strengthening Arab-African relations. One could call it, *neo*-Pan-Africanism, because Nasser of Egypt in his time pursued also Pan-Africanism but on different grounds. These grounds were obviously based on the political and intellectual foundations, which were available in the 1960s, and Nasser's interest in Africa aimed mainly to liberate the continent from direct Western colonisation.

Now Gaddafi is expected to think and act on the basis of the current political and economic demands and constraints. However, the demands of the current global evolution may present some positive opportunities in the form of theoretical openness, the risk is that the project of pan-Africanism can be reduced to a reaction against the bad and negative impacts of the globalisation process as it is conceived popularly in the Third world. For Gaddafi, the project can even be a sign of frustration with regard to the ability of Arab-nationalism to achieve any of its historic goals. Looking back at Gaddafi's own political history, he was in the time of Nasser a radical pan-Arabist. The question is whether Gaddafi has changed his ideological attitude from pan-Arabism to pan-Africanism. Are his current overtures to pan Africanism a new political mobilisation aimed at challenging the West and globalisation? Is Gaddafi pursuing a developing and flourishing Africa as other Africans may dream, or is he projecting a new world bloc in form of a globalisation *contra* globalisation? And a not less important question is whether Gaddafi will be able to mobilise the Arabs to pan-Africanism more than he achieved with regard to his failure to mobilise them to pan-Arabism.

This chapter tries to discuss the future Arab-African relations through a critical re-reading of some historical conjunctures. It considers the question of how to go beyond what is available, and seeks to explore a future that can be built firstly in the minds.

Issues in Africa-Arab Relations

Inspired by the theories of globalisation, its mechanisms, impacts and opportunities, the paper treats the Arab-African relations and future perspectives on the basis of a consideration of a few issues. The latter appear and are selected in no particular historic sequences. To start with, there is a speculation about what African leaders may have in mind in all their interactions with others. Next, the Arab-African relations are examined on the basis of a re-reading of the history, and experiences of modern times and the lessons learnt. The last part will examine possible Arab-African interaction. Finally, a conclusion sums up the discussion and opens up possibilities for further perspectives.

A dream beyond the dream

In 1991-92, I was in London doing my internship at Amnesty International. There I met a Sudanese colleague, Jameel. He told me two short stories, which I think are relevant to this discussion. A friend of Jameel was working in one of the Arab Gulf countries. Once he was going for a walk with some new immigrant Sudanese workers. A man passed, looked at them, shook his head and muttered something. Jameel's friend guffawed. The others could not guess: what did the man say? He said: "*Mal tayeh*". What does that mean? It means "wasted resources".

The other story was about an African professor who was travelling in a train outside London. There was a lady with her little daughter sitting. The little girl was staring at the professor. He tried to tease her and began to speak to her. The little girl jumped surprisingly: "Oh mum, it speaks".

To understand the Africans' dilemma, one may wonder: Who can be called *poor* in these two examples? The Arab man who still considers that it is a waste of resources to see an African taking a walk; the little English girl who cannot imagine a non-white human being; or the African who sometimes appears to confirm the stereotypes about himself. Is it always the task of the weak, in this case the African, who must prove the anti-thesis? Or can this African also demand that the others also should change their views and considerations? What can change these views? Both the Arabs and the Europeans had brought their beliefs to Africa. First the Arab brought Islam, and later the Europeans re-established and further spread Christianity.

Did that indicate a change in their views? Far from direct intervention by the colonial powers, the civil war in Nigeria was internally a conflict between the Muslims and Christians[1]. This social cleavage has since created a tradition of tension that flares up from time to time between these two groups of populations. The tensions usually open up opportunities for new intervention from outside. But would the former "masters" mind? Did the Arab and the European learn anything from the two great religions of Islam and Christendom?

In recent times a similar frontier has arisen. In the Sudan there have been clashes between the Northern Muslims and the Southern Christians. Among other negative consequences of this civil war is evidence of the re-emergence of slave trade. The Sudanese example represents also a line of division between Arab Africa and African Africa, with local cultural and religious distinctions, playing a big role in the unending conflict to date, despite numerous peace talks between the warring parties. Libya and Egypt had united and split up at different times. However these two countries have their own agendas. Libya was looking for influence in the Sudan, which historically was considered an area of Egyptian interest. Egypt on the other hand was looking for a way to cripple the Islamic sentiments of the Sudanese regime.

Some of the crucial questions here are: Can the Arabs transcend a reductionist Arab nationalism? Can the slaves of the past be the brothers of the future? Can the Arab learn more from Islam that pursued "once a Muslim, one is also a brother" policy that has operated since fourteen centuries ago? Can the African learn more from the *pre-slavery African empire and civilisation?* Can Africa re-articulate the world to manifest its humanity with an agency of freedom and unity? Is pan-Africanism an African resistance or an attempt to re-position Africa by some redefinition of globalisation?

Pan-Conceptualisation

The word "Pan" means "including all". This *all*, in order to be included, may share something that differentiates it from others. By this way we may have an African "peculiarity" and a different *other*. Are the Africans different? Can the Africans and Arabs be treated as one? Historically, neither the Africans nor the Arabs have shown any sign of oneness. Politically, economically, socially, culturally they have been fragmented. Is *neo* Pan-Africansim a striving to bring together the fragments within fragments? If it is the *colour,* then Africans do not share the same complexion. If it is geography, then a great number of Africans live outside the continent. The Arabs too do not have the same colour as those in North Africa have not the same colour as the peoples south of the great Sahara. Also, while Arabic is the dominant language in the North, the rest is divided between English, French, Spanish, Portuguese and numerous local language speakers. People fight each other not only on ethnic and religious affiliations, but also because they share modern political-ideological identities. The economy is still derived by and for the interest of non-Africans.

All in all, Africa is no longer what it once was. The continent has to be in the hands of Africans who are both inside and outside the continent. This fragility raises the question of whether a political approach can re-articulate all these: the Africans, the African Diasporas and non-Africans in one historic bloc? Are we talking about a pure political approach without any economic, social and cultural infrastructures? What should this approach be built on? The bitter reality, the vague future, or the history of slavery? Or can this project be based on the history of pre-slavery as some African scholars indicate? What can an excavation of the pre-slavery history benefit in this respect?

The *Other* of the *Others*

Recent anthropological studies tend to rest on an earlier hypothesis that Africa is the grand land of all human beings. If everyone is African in origin, one may so ask, who are the others in this connection? Is that, for example, history itself?

The Africans, as we know them now, or the peoples who stayed in the old continent, have gone through terrible experiences in the last few hundreds of years, namely slavery and colonialism. Ironically, the hijackers and the colonial powers were somehow the migrated grandchildren who came back to Africa, not to thank and reward but to kidnap and subjugate the grandparents and the grand land.

Who should be blamed, the despotic power and disrespect of the sons or the weakness and inability of the fathers; the limitless ambitions or the humble satisfaction; the inhumanity or the humanity; the aggression[2] or the submission? The problem that human beings face is sometimes the difficulty of determining who is the oppressor and who is the victim. Some human rights studies tend to see power and weakness as two faces of the same coin. So the coin bears origins of both the motivation of oppression and the nature of the vulnerability of the victim. Where to start then? We may recognise that we need equality, but can we put together the two cultures of aggression and submission? Or should we only dream of a historical moment when we can do what we actually cannot do? These questions may help us to *re-consider* Arab-African relations, not only with regard to the time of slavery when the Arabs' role is in question, but also in relation to the contemporary time, which is equally worthy to be re-studied.

From Arabisation to Africanisation

One of the main problems of seeking equality is that everyone thinks that by submitting the others into his own cultural context, equality can be achieved. But is that real equality? Such considerations have shaped the Arab's view towards the African in contemporary history. The revolutionary Nasser of Egypt considered his country's identity as partly African. In the so-called circles of belonging, Nasser saw African culture as the next source after the Arabic, and then followed by the Islamic. Nasser and other Arabic leaders supported many African countries in their struggles against direct colonialism. The campaign against the apartheid system in Rhodesia (Zimbabwe) and South Africa was at that time led from Cairo[3]. Nasser worked together with many African leaders - Nkrumah, Ahmed Sekou Toure and Lumumba to stand up against imperialism. But Nasser's main concern was Israel. He wanted African help against Isreali occupation of Palestine and Arab land. Nasser considered Arab nationalism as the core in combating imperialism as well as he considered Israel as the frontier between the imperialist powers and the imperialised peoples. In this way, one may say that he was trying to arabise the African concerns and attitudes.

Now Gaddafi seems to do the opposite. He tries to take the Arabs to Africa. There he seeks refuge and security. He tries to convince the Arab to discard Arab nationalism, of which he was one of its frontal voices, and join a new nationalism that can be called Arab-Africanism or even only Pan-Africanism (inclusive of Arabs in Africa and outside Africa). But what is the nature of this Africanism in Gaddafi's mind? Is it about the historic rights and justice of Islam as he makes sense of it, or is it about an ad-hoc alliance that serves to act as a countervailing power to the West? In all these options, the discourse of mass mobilisation cannot be reduced to Arabs but also to anyone who may show interest. Gaddafi sought earlier to mobilise the Indians in the USA, and among many other countries he once pursued unification with Malta[4], which is now on its way to being a EU member. Is Pan-Africanism thus a re-definition of the priorities of a revolutionary man, like Gaddafi himself, where he changes his political methods from creating international revolutions to creating blocs? The latter may be methods fitting best in the conditions of the current world situation.

Gaddafi's turn to Africa can also be understood on the basis of the efforts of his Arab ancestors. The Arabs had earlier Islamised a part of Africa in the name of their own civilising missions and were at loggerheads with the much more powerful civilising mission of Christendom that led to the direct colonisation of Africa. Gaddafi is trying to imitate this historical parallel of building a strong Africa to counter current western hegemony on the continent through globalisation and other modes of interventions. But ironically and in contrast to Islamic principles, the Arabs have been accused of having initiated the hijacking of Africans into the slavery industry, which flourished in the West[5]. There are still many in Africa who have not been persuaded that Gaddafi means also well to Africans and Africa.

History: A Re-Reading

There is no doubt that it was Islam which gave the Arab their first historical opportunity to play a greater role than their hitherto limited power and capabilities permitted. In the former time before the emergence of Islam, there were mutual interactions between Arabs and Africans. The Arabs established trade connections with the African East Coast and partly also with Mid- and North Africa. They migrated to those areas, initiated colonies and managed to Arabise a part of the populations there[6].

On the other hand, Christian Africans from the Abyssinian (Ethiopian) Dynasty managed in the pre-Islam periods to penetrate the Southern Arabic Peninsula, the original home of the Arabs. They established a kingdom in Yemen and sought to convert the pagan Arabs into Christianity. They achieved only a little in this connection and primarily failed to conquer Mecca, which was sacred since Abraham and his sons Ishmael and Isaac had built it. The Quran describes this episode as, God sent *Tairel-Ababil*[7] to protect Mecca from the invasion of the army of *Abrahal-Ashram* (Abueksium), the Abyssinian King of Yemen. Later when Islam emerged, it was ironically the King of Abyssinia, the faithful to Christendom, *Nejashi*, who saved the life of an interim group of Muslims who fled from the despotic pagan Arabs of Mecca. Since that time Africa has become an open land for the Arabs.

This African open-heart and warm bosom may have paved the way for the Islamisation of great parts in the East, North and Mid-Africa[8]. The Northern part even went further[9]. The people there changed also their languages and accepted Arabisation. As Islam proved to co-exist with African local cultures[10], a degree of hybridisation also took place. Many Africans had participated faithfully and actively in the Islamic concerns, especially the wars of conquest in Southern Europe and elsewhere. African intellectuals have also made remarkable contributions to Islamic schools and participated in the Islamisation of parts of Africa. All this has further increased the Arab-African interactions.

Nevertheless, different forms of interactions were not out of the mind horizon of some Arabs. The accusations of possible Arab involvement in initiating the slavery system have posed a real challenge to the Arabic commitments to the Islamic principles as well as the Arab-African hybridisation.[11] This opened the way for European intervention to colonise both the mind and the soil of Africa.

In modern times, Nasser and other North African Arab leaders showed great interest in the African Unity Charter as an enterprise to re-establish Arab-African relations. In other words, the African Charter was seen as an attempt to re-operationalise the Arab-African homogenisation process. Economically, a series of bilateral relations have been established, and many rich Arab countries like Iraq, the Gulf countries, Algeria and Libya, have given economic aid to African countries. Some of this aid aimed to create development and most of it was politically motivated. Politically, Arab-African relations made more progress. One important thing was that most of the Africans countries cut relations with Israel in the aftermath of the 1967 war with Arabs[12]. This was considered as a manifestation of Arab-African solidarity.

Both the dreams of African unity and of Arab-African solidarity have faced essential challenges internally and have also been extremely restrained by Western intervention militarily, economically as well as culturally. While colonialism and the migration of Europeans to the southern part of Africa had earlier restrained the Islamisation process, an intensive missionary work to re-christianise African populations, among them many Muslims, has weakened Arab-African interactions in modern times. Things changed more dramatically as Egypt signed peace agreement with the Jewish state in the late 1970s. Many African countries also re-established relationship with Israel in the 1980s. The Jewish state even managed to transform *Falasha* from Ethiopia.

All these setbacks, in as much as they emphasised the inability of the Africans to stand against infiltration from outside, have indicated also the failure of Arab nationalism to establish organic ties with African societies and political systems.

A New Attempt

In many ways Gaddafi´s attempt can be understood in the light of the failure of the Arab Nationalism to achieve any of its objectives, primarily how to hold the homogeneity of the Arab world. Arab Nationalism, after about fifty years of intensive efforts, has never really succeeded in its project of forging Arab unity. The main reason may be because it failed to establish an effective political system that can articulate the aspirations of the Arabs and protect their interests. It failed also to preserve the sovereignty of the Arab states. While Iraq invaded Kuwait (both countries are Arabic) in 1990, two other Arab countries, Libya (already in 1988) and the Sudan (1998) came under restrictive UN sanctions, because of accusations of international terrorism.

American raids against Libya, including direct attacks at Gaddafi and his family in 1986 when his daughter was killed, and later sanctions in 1988 destabilised Gaddafi's Arab's hopes. While most African countries did not seem to care, it was several African leaders who showed solidarity and good intentions to break the sanctions. Collectively and singularly they disregarded the UN sanctions throughout the 1990s. This *unrecorded* brave initiative by the African leaders made Gaddafi to re-think Arab-African relations. He started re-considering the importance of geography. In a television interview, Gaddafi emphasised that, talking about Arab Nationalism without having the ground, the geographical infrastructure, may indicate racism[13]. This new political tone got many Arab intellectuals to react but Gaddafi asserted that this attitude aims only to strengthen Arabism in this historical moment.

In fact, historically one may agree with Gaddafi because the Arabs have never been united and collected in one geographical territory, neither in the pre-Islam period nor under Islam or in the modern time. However, Gaddafi´s solution seems like a simplification of the Arab dilemma as he calls even the Asian part of the Arab world to join Africa. Gaddafi's *theory* is based on a fact that Africa has always existed as a specific geographical entity, and that Arab-African relations are historical, which the continental division (Africa-Asia) could not hamper.

On the other hand, the importance of geography has also been re-emphasised in the light of the emerging regionalisation in the world. Regionalisation is now considered as one of the instruments and organisations that can protect nations from the harsh realities of a globalising world economy. The Arab world had initiated the idea of a common Arabic market prior to the Europeans in the early 1950s. Nevertheless, they could never realise the project, not only because of external interventions but also because of internal Arab-Arab conflicts and fragility in terms of political, economic and social ties. This means, that regardless of numerous efforts, the official Arab circles have not been able to establish a united and sustainable purpose and/or bloc.

Africa now is in the focus of the Western powers and world economic giants who look for new markets and investment opportunities. This in itself has made many to re-think Africa's position and potentials. The idea of African renaissance and the emergence on the agenda of Arab-African solidarity can also be seen on the basis of such considerations. So, *neo*Pan-Africanism can in a way express success for Arab Nationalism and thus is to be based on future perspectives of an effective African bloc to compete with the other world blocs.

From Failure to Success

When the Europeans decided to colonise Africa, they considered the continent as "vacant", legally *les nullius* (a no-man's land) and their intervention was motivated by the "3Cs: Commerce, Christianity and Civilisation, a triple of Mammon, God and Social Progress".[14] This justification for the colonisation of Africa can in some way have impacts on the latter studies of the continent and future perspectives. In this respect, the so-called concept of "Afro-Pessimism" seems more political than a real analytical prognosis. It was launched by European scholars to give the sense of the failure of Africans to modernise their societies and change their social foundations into Western defined contexts. Equally important, this has been said to apply to the Arabs as well. In the eyes of the West, the Arabs, like the Africans, are still governed by traditional rules and social relations.

The political efforts in both the Arab world and Africa, on the one hand to create modernisation, and on the other hand to challenge Western domination, failed to achieve the objectives. The reasons were essentially because the Arab and African political regimes have blindly adopted Western models of modernisation and depended exclusively upon Western conceptions and comprehensions in the consideration of the social evolution of their societies. These so-called traditional societies, in contrast to Western societies, have over thousands of years kept and still keep deep cultural, religious and historical roots.

Now the question is, whether the idea of *neo*Pan-Africanism is again an imitation of the current globalising mechanisms that undoubtedly also have been defined and presented by the West. So, again to act according to the determinations given by the mechanisms of globalisation can risk inconvenience. Unless the Arabs and the Africans are willing to re-innovate their own methodologies politically, economically and with regard to social initiatives, not much success can be expected.

However, under the current globalisation, the best which some of the Arabs and Africans could ever achieve has been attempts to transform their regions into huge markets for the industrial countries' goods, and so their labours may fuel those industries, and their nature and history may entertain the rich tourists. Many Arab countries in both the Gulf region and in North Africa have already experienced a degree of transformation. Others appear set to follow suit.

This sort of transformation can be seen as a reaction to earlier initiatives. Attempts to establish an Arabic bloc have not been successful. The Arab League remained toothless during the Iraq invasion of 2003 by American and British old style classic imperialism. The same can be said about the Africans who formed the African Union but who cannot still agree on a united foreign policy. The invasion of Iraq saw different African countries behaving individually rather than collectively. Even at sub-regional levels, there is no manifest regional will. Individualised initiatives remain central to African conduct. This may ultimately hinder effective regional economic cooperation and further weaken Africa's position as an effective member of the global village"[15]

The transformation into huge markets bears risks of paralysing the Arabs' and Africans' ability to innovate and more crucially further demean the role of their cultural, ethnical and social fundamentals. This fear of bigness can hamper looking for alternatives whilst increasing the dependency on the West.

With regards to Arab-African relations, while this transformation reminds us of the commercialisation of the Arabic mentality that played a role in the slave trade, the question is whether it will pose further challenges to future relations?

In this respect, and as already pointed out, the Arabs had in the pre-Islam history established trade relations with the African east coast. This also may have helped bring Islam to Africa. But it seems that Islam failed to cripple the commercial mentality. Undoubtedly, their knowledge and trade expertise and the warm bosom of the Africans enabled the Arabs to kidnap and enslave the Africans. The pagan Arab society was full of African slaves who served the rich masters. When Islam came, essential changes took place in the societal relations including the relations with former slaves. Many of these slaves were released and others were allowed to re-define their relations, such as from slaves to servants. But nevertheless, the nature of the exploitative relations remained. The latter Arab participation in enslaving the Africans can be read within this context. It means that Islam could not create the condition of total equality in this manner, and it failed to remove the mentality of enslaving the Africans from the minds of many Arab tradesmen.

In modern times, and under the enthusiasm of anti-colonialism and anti-imperialism, Nasser and other Arab leaders sought to re-establish the Arab-African economic, political and social relations on more equal basis. Hence there was direct involvement by Arab leaders in the anti-apartheid campaigns. But the cooperation areas remained extremely limited and much driven by political imperatives.

Because any semblance of cooperation is driven by political imperatives, the project has usually failed to initiate any permanent common future. The master-slave system also failed because it reduced humans to goods.

The Arab and the African social systems remained ineffective and fragmented. Besides internal fragmentation along ethnic, religious, economic and political lines in each state, the Arab and the African attitudes are divided and largely depended upon external determinations. The Arabs had historically been divided on the basis of geography - between the easterners and westerners. The first is known for its emotional and cultural emphases, and the latter for its political rationality. The first produced Arab Nationalism, while the second produced tendencies towards integration into Mediterranean (common culture with Southern Europe). Egypt and probably Libya stand in the middle of this division. The Sudan represents an attitude emphasising the connection to African culture. Somalia, Djibouti and the Comoro Islands (the recent members in the Arab League) are significantly (with regard to language, colour and identity) more African Muslims than anything else.

Africa on its part is not less divided. In addition to the main fault lines such as between North Arab Africa, North of the Sahara or South of the Sahara, the continent has also been divided on the basis of experiences with colonialism. Colonialism created two traditions for cultural and identity associations. The Francophone established roots in Arab North and the west coast of Africa. The British Commonwealth has impacted on the South and partly the Eastern parts of the continent. Recently, Americanism has gained grounds in both the Arab world and Africa.

The unavoidable question is whether the enthusiasts of the *neo*Pan-Africanism can make efforts to redefine the attitudes and mobilise the masses on the basis of new methodologies and epistemologies that can avoid imitation and dependency by focusing on what the Arabs and the Africans themselves can innovate. This needs fundamental mind change and real commitment.

In fact, Gaddafi's Arab-African vision seems to merge the political and economic perspectives. Nevertheless, there is no clear sign of how history can play an innovative role. The question is, how much of this dream can change in the political and economic evolutions of both the Arab world and Africa. There is also the question of what each of the Arabs and Africans expect from this project of pan-Africanism.

Future Perspective

To make a personal evaluation is not my work. Similarly to reduce Arab-African relation to Gaddafi-Libya's politics is also a shortcoming, which I may have committed inadvertently in an effort to shed light on a complex combination. Gaddafi-Libya's central position in this discussion is related to his role as the only Arab leader who calls on incorporating Arab Nationalism into Africanism.

As said earlier, Arab-African connections go back to ancient history. In modern times, the mutual relations reached its peak in the 1950-60s under the boom of anti-colonialism, anti-imperialism and anti-apartheid. On the basis of these discourses the Arabs have also intervened in African affairs. One example is that many Arab countries supported the Eritrea Liberation Movement. This support came partly from a notion that considered Ethiopia as colonising Eritrea. The Arabs were also motivated by the revolutionary sentiments against traditionalism, which the regime of the Emperor Haile Selassie was representing. Later the revolutionary regime of Mengistu Haile Miriam was severely criticised for its communist and pro-Israeli politics. However a third and probably the most important reason for this support was that Eritrea was considered as a part of the Arab world. Ironically, once the Eritreans achieved their independence in the beginning of the 1990s, they neglected that Arabic illusion. This was yet another failure of Arab Nationalism.

Gaddafi´s Libya also gave another example of intervention in Africa affairs, namely in Chad. Chad has for a long time suffered from Libyan intervention both directly and indirectly. Libyan intervention in Chad came also under the motto of Arabic belonging as well as the struggle against imperialism. In other words, Libyan intervention occurred as an attempt to Arabise the country and revolutionise its politics[16]. The latter objective was one important pillar of Libya's foreign politics since Gaddafi's regime took over power in 1969.

The regime has undertaken a political discourse much greater than the country's real capacities. This extreme imbalance between the political objectives and the real capacities has created severe instability in Libya's relations both with the Arab world, neighbouring Africans and the rest of the world. Gaddafi has been known to many as a man who often changes his mind and regrets former decisions and political attitudes.

This raises the question of how to evaluate Gaddafi´s turn back to Africa. Africa's central position in Libya's new concerns can be interpreted or observed in different ways. One may in this respect note that in recent times the Libyan Satellite television has changed its logo: from Libya as brightening station within the Arab world, to Libya as the lighting green location in dark Africa. Another example is that over the last few years Gaddafi appeared as the imam to thousands of Muslims in African countries even though he is not known as an especially religious person. Recently, Gaddafi called on all Africans to move freely in the continent from Cape Town to Triploi.[17].

On the other hand, and far from these propagandist political discourses, what happens on the ground may disappointment the so-called Gaddafi's dream. In 2000, for example, there were severe clashes between Libyans and migrant African workers. Consequently a great number of African workers left or were directly or indirectly deported back to their countries.[18]

This unfair treatment of African labourers remind us of a similar deportation of Egyptian and Palestinian labourers earlier - something that questions Gaddafi´s practical commitment to Arab Nationalism. One may wonder whether the deportation of the Africans proves anything else.

Conclusion

Creating the future requires changing the mentality that pre-imagines the ideas and translates them into instruments for making the future. The first imagination is to do away with the lingering mental software for either enslaving or submission to domination that upsets the development of deep solidarity between Africans and Arabs. In history, there have been moments, which showed that either *wolf* or *sheep* was not the only choice. There is a need to recall the historical memory of national liberation in order to remove the false decolonisation of the Arab and the African. There is a need for a new mentality that innovates, instead of imitating all the time. That historical memory of national liberation must be recalled to serve the present and the future. This may indicate metaphysics, but what is wrong with a metaphysics of liberation?

Can dreams alone establish the future? Can the Arab-African bloc remain merely a dream? What kind of cooperation can these two groups of countries establish as a process towards full integration and bloc formation? And what could become of this dream if it is not realised? Such questions have to be taken into consideration in mapping out realistic strategies.

Undoubtedly, any cooperation between any two groups of countries outside the premises of the global forces is insecure. Attempts at establishing regionalisms in Africa have produced sub-regionalisms in the continent. These sub-regional groupings failed to establish mechanisms of innovations. In this context, bilateral economic relations have also experienced great retreat as the North-South polarisation has sharpened and South-South cooperation was changed by competition on who can achieve relations with the West on better conditions.

Two political episodes took place in recent years, both of which the Arab played a great role in connection with Africa. Gaddafi presented the project of transforming the Organization of African Unity to African Union, and the great explosions in Nairobi and Dar el Salam were linked to Arab terrorism. While the second may bring the Americans to the continent, the question is about the future perspective of the first initiative in re-articulating the Arab and African outlooks.

Nevertheless, so far, Gaddafi's efforts have only achieved a symbolic success, that is, the project of transforming the Organisation of African Unity into the African Union. The Arab and the Africans are still operating within the world determinants. And both groups of countries are among the weakest in the world both politically and economically.

Challenging globalisation on this weak basis will make them further vulnerable. Both the Arab world and Africa are under pressures as well as vulnerable to polarisations. Debts are dropped from the shoulder of some of the poorest countries of the world, among them African and Arab countries. Other countries receive economic aid. A sort of globalisation is also going on in form of privatisation, democratisation and openness.

How the project of *neo*Pan-African will deal with these challenges and changes is not clear. There is no doubt that both the Arab world and Africa are rich in raw materials and human resources, but they still need to re-consider how these resources can be re-transformed, that is, from the decisions that so far has attracted colonial powers, to something positive that helps self-building. Both the Arabs and the Africans need to find the way to self-perception and re-consideration of their own capacity and capability. The project of *neo*Pan-Africa is meant to create the spirit of this self-transformation.

References

Akano, Olasupo (2000), *Openness, Capital Accumulation and Economic Growth.* Eastern African Social Science Research Review, 16, pp. 25-47: 2
Ayogu, Mevin D. (2001): *Corporate Governance in Africa.* African Development Review, 13, pp. 308-330: 2
Breda Pavlic; Raul R. Uranga; Boris Cizelj (eds.) (1983): *The Challenges of South-South Cooperation* (Boulder, Col.: Westview Press)
Cavatorta, Francesco (2001): "Geopolitical Challenges to the Success of Democracy in North Africa", *Democratisation*, 8, pp. 175-194: 4
Clements, Poul (2001), "Challenges for African States", *Journal of Asian and African Studies*, 36, pp. 295-305:3
Lyons, Michal (2001), "The Changing Role of the State in Participatory Development", *Community Development Journal*, 36, pp. 273-288: 4
Padayachee, Vishnu (2001): *Changing Gear?* Transformation, 46, pp. 71-83
Saul, John S. (2001): "Cry for the Beloved Country" in *Review of African Political Economy*, 28, pp. 429-460: 89
Vetinde, Lifongo (1999): "Utopias, Transgressions", *Hybridity. Ufahamu*, 27, pp. 5-26:1/3

EndNotes

[1] See for example, Simon O. Ilesanmi, *Religious Pluralism and the Nigerian State*, Monographs in International Studies, African Series, 66, Athens OH: Ohio University Centre for International Studies, 1997

[2] Aggressivity can be described as the culture that justifies aggressive acts.

[3] Horas Kampel (trans. Helmi Sharawi), Tahaddi Nizamel-Apartheid menal-Qahera (Challenging Apartheid System from Cairo, in Peter Nyongo (ed), Min Tajarub el-Harakatel-Demoqratiyah fi Afriqiya wal Watanel-Aarbi (Experiences of Democratic Movements in African and the Arab World), , the Center for Arab Strudies, Cairo 1995 pp. 215-253

[4] Since he came to power in 1969, Gaddafi sought unification several times with Arab countries like Egypt, Syria, the Sudan, Tunisia and Morocco, as well as

with African countries like Chad and Mali.

[5]*New African*, November 1999, p.16, writes in the cover story on the basis of Duncan Clarke's book *Slaves and Slavery* that: 'Arab slavers were the first, and last, in modern times to ship millions of Africans out of the continent as slaves'.

[6] Oded, Arye (2000), *Islam and Politics in Kenya*, London, Lynne Rienner, pp. 1-3

[7]Quran describes: And send down (to prey) upon them birds in blocks. Casting against them stones of baked clay. So, He (God) rendered them like straw eaten up. Quran, 105, 3-5.

[8]See in this respect Neil McHugh, Holymen of the Blue Nile: The Making of an Arab Islamic Community in the Nilotic Sudan, 1500-1850, Evanson IL: Northwestern University Press, 1994

[9]See more in Elizabith Savage, A Gateway to Hell, A gate Way to Paradise: The North African Response to the Arab Conquest, Studies in Late Antiquity and Early Islam, vol. 7, Princeton: Darwin Press, 1997

[10] J. Spencer Trimingham, The Influence of Islam upon Africa, Second Edition 1980, London and New York, Longman, Librairie du Liban, First Impression 1968, pp. 44-45

[11] However, the Arab participation in the enslaving of Africans is disputable. Arab archives go in some way in the direction of underscoring. Kullu Shai' Wal-Dunia, an Egyptian Weekly, interviewed in 1934 an Arab tradesman who worked exclusively with slavery. The man was living in Egypt (no nationality is given) and he admitted that he has sold ten thousand women brought over from the Ethiopian-Sudanese border. He said: 'we were threatening the slaves of killing their families if they resisted'. Re-published in Majaletel-Ayam, No. 3, June-July 2001, Damascus.

[12] Bagenda, P. M.: "The Genesis of Africa's Response to the Middle East Conflict" in Haroub Othman (ed.) (1985): *The Palestine Question*. Harare: Tanzania-Palestine Solidarity Committee (publ.), pp. 48-9

[13] Interview in **Al-Jazeerah**, An Arabic TV broadcasts from Qatar, 17 November 1998 (my translation). The Economist also writes: 'Qaddafi Says Farewell, Arabia, and Sets His Sights on Africa', vol. 351, Issue 8116, April, 24, 1999, pp. 43-44

[14] Pakenham, Thomass (1991), The Scramble for Africa, London, Weidenfeld and Nicolson, pp. *xv-xvi*

[15] Akokpari, John K. (2001), *Globalisation and the Challenges for African States*. Nordic Journal of African Studies, 10, pp. 188-209 (201): 9

[16] Libya once sought unification with Chad. See former notes.

[17] Reviewed in Al-Hayat, February 4, 2002

[18]Quoting Libya's information secretary to have denied that racism or xenophobia was behind the disturbances, a correspondent of the London-based *New African* (November 200, p. 12), writes under the title: "Who's Spoiling Gaddafi's Dream?" that ' the Africans immigrants (about 2.5 millions) now inhabit their own zones within Libyan residential areas'. While Gaddafi blamed "foreign hostile hands", *New African* concludes that 'the violence...was clearly a setback to that dream'.

16

The Struggle for the Africa-Nation versus Arab Nationalism[1]

B.F. Bankie

 The struggle for the decolonisation of Africa and its Diaspora was largely inspired by a narrow concept of the Africa-nation. In the mid-twentieth century, African nationalism was more often than not seen as the struggle within the colonial entity for independence. Even there, once self-government was achieved, the objectives of the struggle were promptly abandoned – for example land distribution, the Freedom Charter, and so forth.

In the new millennium, the African national struggle does not seek to strengthen the neo-colonial states created at the Berlin Conference at the end of the 19th century. Today the African national struggle seeks the ending of the neo-colonial entity and its merging into a Pan-African entity called the Africa-nation, which links Africa, south of the Borderlands with its Diaspora. This is the challenge.

The concept of the Africa-nation predates the creation of the neo-colonial state. It was referred to by the founding fathers of the Pan-African movement, by people such as Marcus Garvey and Wilmot Blyden. Even in Southern Africa, the African National Congress (ANC) as originally conceived was not limited to South Africa but straddled all of Southern Africa, with branches in places such as Zambia.

- The struggle for Pan-African nationalism today encompasses the following issues:
- A definition of the Africa-nation which takes cognisance of the reality in the Borderlands, being that part of Africa running from Mauritania in the west through countries such as Mali, Niger, Chad and Sudan to the Red Sea in the east;

- The right to reparations not only for western slavery, but also for Arab slavery, and not only for African descendants, but for continental Africans;
- That there should be no "select" identity for Diasporans, that the infatuation with Egypt should end, but that all Diasporans have a right to the African citizenship;
- The right to repatriation is a right belonging to all Africans living in the Diaspora. There is nothing radical or unusual in this. All nations, be they Chinese, Arab, Indian or others, recognise that their nationals living in the Diaspora, have citizenship rights on their return home. The Africans in their Organisation of African Unity (OAU) denied states peopled in their majority by Africans (e.g. Haiti) the right to join the OAU. The OAU also denied Diasporans the right to work in its Secretariat.

Pan-Africanism or continentalism?

The crucial question today is what is to be done, given the Arab aggression against Africans dating back thousands of years, which pushed Africans down from the Mediterranean Coast southwards into the arid regions of the Sahel, so that today the point of conflict is no longer in North Africa, but in the South Sudan, Mauritania and the Borderlands in general, where slavery is still applied; and given the continuing ambition of Arab nationalism to push its control to the equatorial, lush and verdant parts of Africa? Bear in mind that North Africa appears to be hostile to the African Diaspora participating in any continental unity project. Also bear in mind that North Africa, specifically Egypt, has always opposed the issue of the Sudan being discussed within the OAU structure, stating that Sudan was an "internal matter" (that is, for discussion only within the Arab League). Afro-Arab relations need to be reviewed and overhauled in the light of history and the facts.

Walter Rodney's paper for the 6th Pan-African Congress in Dar-es-Salaam in 1974 analyses, amongst other things, the role of the African elite in general as the agents of the former colonial powers in the post-colonial states. It should not be a surprise that some of these elites in government are hostile to the Diaspora. At the United Nations World Conference Against Racism held in Durban, South Africa in 2001, both the Senegalese Head of State and that of Nigeria opposed reparations for slavery.

Rodney observed that the postcolonial state mirrors the interest of the political elites and not the democratic will of the African people. This represents a major contradiction in the pursuit of the unity among Africans and also a main source of incoherence in African international relations.

The key link of Africa should be with its Diaspora. If this link is not made structurally, Africa will remain weak. For Africans to develop, they need to interact in a continuous and structured basis with the African Diaspora in the West as well as the African Diaspora in Arabia and the East. The key link in the African unity project is therefore the linkage of Africa with its Diaspora.

Conclusion

The issues that the Borderlands raise date back thousands of years. That area provides a sharp and more holistic definition of the African nationality project than that hitherto offered by the black consciousness movements of the Americas and Southern Africa.

In the Sudan a minority group of Arabised black people, who do not consider themselves Africans, rule the country and participate in the oppression and enslavement of the majority African population. What is at stake here is not a matter of colour, but a question of culture. What the Borderlands teach us is that the African nationality question is primarily cultural, not racial. This has implications for the African unity movement in the new millennium. It means wiping the slate clean and returning to the drawing board.

With hindsight, the conclusion is that too much emphasis was placed on race, politics and economics at the expense of culture. For the youth, the need to create awareness around PanAfricanism, the Africa-nation and culture should be kept constantly in view and reviewed in schools, at the universities and within the learning process in general.

The Pan-African tradition comes to us with left and right philosophical options. Padmore taught us not to be dogmatic in dialectics. In a period of globalisation with the dominance of capital, we could enrich our choices with Marxist analysis when, for instance, we are faced with questions involving social stratification. Where monetarist matters need resolution such as stock market investments, we use the economic imperative.

Africa in general is in the early stages of anti-imperialist national democratic struggle. This struggle has begun on the military level. "National" refers to an increasing awareness amongst Africans of their common destiny as the only geo-political solution available in the face of the development challenge.

There is also an increased awareness that the post-colonial state by its nature tends to be undemocratic and autocratic, and that meaningful solutions come from bottom-up, rather than top-down approaches.

The late Mohamed Babu stated in the late 1990s that the basic problems of Africa require radical solutions. This holds also true for the problems in the Borderlands, which are hundreds of years in the making, and will not be resolved by peace pacts, which only provide respite before further conflict. Unless there is fundamental radical change in the thinking about the area, the relentless push southwards will not be reversed.

Conflict in Africa is increasingly generalised, most of it originating from non-African interference, including from the Arab. The G8 countries, assisted by the African elite seek to conserve the homogeneity of the neo-colonial state. From the national democratic phase, the duration of which remains unknown, should emerge a strengthened Pan-African nationalism, able to hold its own globally.

Whereas the African middle classes/bourgeoisie/elites lead the struggles for state independence, they thereafter privatised the state, which they exploited for their own narrow class as they stepped into the shoes of the departing colonialists.

Half a century later there are some relatively rich Africans. But the present African bourgeoisie has proven unpatriotic – it has ignored the Africa-nation. Whereas it has brought money back to Africa to support narrow ethnic faction fights, it has generally refused to advance African research and Pan-African endeavours.

References

The Conference on Arab-led Slavery of Africans, convened in Johannesburg on 22 February, 2003. For further information contact e-mail address wau@worldonline.co.za

Mortimo 'Bro Cummie' Planno – The Pan African Nationalist I Know", by B.F. Bankie, being a draft paper for publication.

"Towards the Sixth Pan African Congress" by Walter Rodney, appears in Resolutions and Selected Speeches from the Sixth PanAfrican Congress, published by the Tanzania Publishing House, Dar-es-Salaam, 1976

Pan-Africanism or Continentalism: The Coming Struggle for Africa, by George Padmore, published by Dobson Books Ltd, London, 1956

EndNote

[1] This paper is drawn in part from a draft work-in-progress, being a chapter contribution entitled "Mortimo 'Bro Cummie' Planno – The Pan African Nationalist I know" to a book dedicated to Ras Mortimo Planno, the Elder.

17

Africa and Arabia in the post-September 11 World Order

Mammo Muchie

"In a world still growing unequal our hope for orderly co-existence lies in global cooperation and an uncompromising multilateral approach to problems and challenges."
Nelson Mandela, the *Mirror*, UK, July 11,2003

"Because the Arab people are too weak to demand democracy, the US should intervene to liberate the Arab world from its tyrants."
Condoleezza Rice quoted in Al-Hayat, November 6, 2002

"If people want to say we're an imperial power, fine."
William Kristol, leader of the Neo-Conservative Policy think–tank: New Project for American Century, editor of the Weekly Standard, quoted in the *Washington Post*: US: A Mighty Empire August 17, 2003)

Military Unilateralism for a Unipolar Order

The post-September 11, 2001 and the May, 2003 US/UK invasion of Iraq have provided full expression of the US unilateralism that has been aspiring to guide and shape the emerging new world order with a singular imposition of the US government's will on the world since the collapse of the former USSR. Attacking others has been at the same time licensed and used as an excuse to export "made in the USA" brand of democracy and liberty. The idea of "a US empire of liberty" - an oxymoron- has come from fellows at the US Council of Foreign

Relations in order "to spread democracy" throughout the world. (*Washington Post*, August 17, 2003).

The principle of going to war in self-defence against aggression and the imminent threat of aggression, endorsed by the UN as part of international law is seen as no longer adequate. The unilateral approach dictates immediate action, on the part of US authorities, to sanction the killing of a potential enemy first, by a self-validated anticipation of a possible future attack from that enemy. Thus the new doctrine says, anticipate attack and prevent it by attacking first long before the potential to attack is fully developed, let alone the attack being carried out.

Future threat can also justify pre-emptive action. If the enemy is shadowy, invisible and unpredictable, the US Government reads this to mean there is a permanence and urgency to the threat. US military action has to be ready to be deployed to reduce this state of global permanent threat. The power of the threat is not that there could be any enemy in the planet that can deploy military action to the scale that the US can deploy. It lies in the fact that it is diffused and its targets are indiscriminate.

The doctrine of the national security state of mutually assured destruction (MAD) has changed into a new national security doctrine, namely the assured destruction of the enemy alone, with a vengeance going beyond seeking the redressing of injustice by looking for him anywhere in the globe, using a covert and overt deployment of US intelligence services and military power. The US has managed to proclaim to the world that it has the military capability and the resolve to remove the possibility of a threat before it becomes a real threat. Kill first in anticipation of a killer. Kill terrorists before they kill us said Paul Bremer, the US Viceroy of Iraq. Prevention is better than cure. Thus pre-empt using overwhelming force and prevent first rather than waiting to defend after an attack or an imminent danger of an attack occurs. Thus the hallmark of the new doctrine is expressed through the unlimited resort and uses of US preponderant force and the global projection and reach of this dominant US military might. If it has been conceived as prevention by a comprehensive deployment of economic, social, political, cultural and military engagement, it may be something else. The story is presented in terms of building massive military force to deal with any anticipated threat. It is conceptualised through a militaristic optic and wishes to justify this action morally and politically without the sanction of a moral underpinning emanating from the legality of the post World War II political settlement.

The danger is that the very act of such unilateralist military preemption leads to a never-ending use and reliance on the same military logic and military means to deal with real or imagined threats. As imagined threats are derived partly from real threats and partly from a metaphysical anxiety that a threat would occur, the US commitment to chase an invisible enemy until it is caught, makes the job endless in time, space and mental and psychological preoccupations. The US military-industrial complex has found an enemy that will never go away, will always exist and thus assuring what the US power structure sorely needed: a justification of why so much wasteful resources have to continue to be pumped or squandered to beef up the military after the "evil empire" has re-joined the fold and has become a normal run of the mill type of state. The US government also tries to build and amass e-weapons with enhanced command, control and communications capabilities which could fight in all weather conditions across land, sea, space, desert or storm. This is as much driven by power as by the psychology to beat down fear through technological mastery. This reliance on spending more and more to build modern weaponry creates huge imbalance between spending less and less for bread or more and more for guns. Resources will be hugely distorted in favour of the gun when in actual fact genuine freedom from threat requires giving high priority to spending more for bread and less for producing and using the barrel of the gun.

This new national security doctrine appears to be a response to terrorist attacks against US targets since 9/11. But it is broader than a response to terrorism or the atrocities from 9/11. It is how a sole superpower, unchallenged, and without any credible competitor or challenger, wishes to rule (kratos) by imposing unipolar political and economic power structures across the globe to control the various parts of a vastly discontented empire. Military threats alone do not require US military intervention. According to the neo-conservatives, US military power is necessary to spread American political ideas of "democracy and freedom" and to reorganise far-flung countries in the image and values of America. Interventions have been variously justified for humanitarian reasons (for example, Balkans), to liberate people and remove the threat of weapons of mass destruction (for example, Iraq), to warn others not to provide haven for terrorists (for example, Afghanistan). More interventions are likely to come. Under threat are areas in the Arab world and Africa where the US seeks to set up military bases and seeks to assure the flow of resources such as Arabian and African oil. Africa and Arabia are particularly vulnerable to regime change because they have resources the USA seeks. At the moment Washington has sent veiled or even open threats to countries like Iran, Syria, Zimbabwe, Cuba, North Korea and others that may be unlucky to have active terrorist cells and activities in their countries. Tomorrow it could be any number of other countries that the USA deems strategic to its purposes and that are not towing the line according to the understanding (or misunderstanding) of the US incumbent Republican Administration and its neo-conservative die-hard ideologues.

This militarisation of politics to give fuller play of the unipolar ambition of the US and its chief European ally - Britain, and the willingness of these two allies to justify intervention in sovereign states using sanctimonious and moral arguments, provide to the post-Cold War unilateralism, an unusually sharp distinction in international relations. US unilateralism has pronounced the end of the Westphalian sovereignty of states, having provided notice that any state not towing the preferred line by Washington can be attacked massively and with rapid reaction forces or any other means. The current US administration wishes to impose a unilateralist social arrangement to rule over international relations for generations, even a century. The neo-conservatives wish the 21st century to become a US century. They seem to have an intellectual and political project called: the Project for a New American Century!

The fatal weakness of this US activist unilateralism is that it is built on an exaggeration of the so-called contemporary adversary: global terrorism. To be sure, terrorist attacks have occurred and will probably occur in the future. A terrorist or the network uses hit-and-run tactics and shadowy structures. However offensive terrorist actions are, no terrorist network should be made to occupy the position of the former USSR in opposition to US power. That is simply to gratuitously bestow such networks power that they do not possess. The fact that an individual or state is attacked by the USA ironically bestows power and myth to that individual and state. This has happened both to the Islamic cleric Osama bin Laden and the secular Saddam Hussein. Were the USA to choose a less excited approach and were to prefer to

315

understate rather than overstate the danger from terrorists or states it does not see eye to eye with, there is no doubt such figures would not have had the disproportional importance they have been accorded way beyond any power they really possess.

The new national security doctrine is also built on an exaggeration of the global terrorist threat from states like Saddam's Iraq. Even if these threats were real, it is not wise to assume that those who are opposed to the US's strategies of fighting the terrorists are necessarily supporting the terrorists. This is politics of blackmail. It is not a politics of providing enlightened leadership to expunge terrorism root and branch. It is more emboldened on form rather than substance.

Ironically the Cold War political software and cognitive frame for polarising the world disposition of political forces seems not to have changed at all. During the Cold War, countries that were not with the US were treated as if they were strong allies of the former USSR. Gamal Abdel Nasser was attacked for wishing to pursue an Arab national agenda which was neither pro-USSR nor pro-USA. Similarly Kwame Nkrumah got overthrown for trying to pursue an African national agenda. The US ruling circles will fight any attempt by any state or political figure of any repute who tries to be out of reach and control in assisting them to implement their exclusive agenda, such as, for example, the war on Iraq. Such a narrowing of perspective is too self-serving and does not do justice to the aspirations of some 80 per cent of the world population, who are primarily interested in their work and their families.

"Unilateralisation, unipolarisation and militarisation" are the new national security doctrine just as "privatisation, stabilisation and liberalisation" have, for the past twenty years, been the core of the so-called Washington consensus for the political economy of distressed underdeveloped countries. Together they mirror how the new Republican US Administration wishes to establish a new global economic and security order. Sun Tsu taught the world, as a law of war, that when the enemy advances, the forces opposed should retreat if they cannot take on the advancing forces. Likewise when the enemy retreats, the opposing forces should advance. The new US national security doctrine seems to say pursue permanently the enemy anywhere and at any time. Find him and kill him. This policy seems therefore to elevate war into a tool for creating a global security order. In reality this will create a global security disorder. Goliath is seeking to kill David. The latter has dated weapons and some native cunning at his disposal, whilst the former has the latest high-tech armoury. But David can evade, inflict damage and hide like fish in a sea of people who find US overreaction unpalatable though they find also David's terror tactics reprehensible. Where the development and use of human and social technology rather than military technology may be more effective, the US opts for the logic of an eye for an eye. This spreads rather than diminishes terrorism. The world will continue to experience spasmodic and unpredictable earthquake-like terror attacks with some interval of time. Military deployment for such an invisible enemy can disorganise the terrorist network, but it will not eliminate terrorism. To eradicate the scourge of terrorism for good, the causes that give rise to it have to be faced fair and square with courage and not anger or vengeance. It is justice not violent retribution that can attenuate terrorist attacks.

Many commentators have seen in the new national security doctrine the creation of international anarchy, the collapse of international legality, the end of the UN and the breakdown of the normative, legal and moral authority of the advocates of permanent war. The world has been made to be ontologically more insecure than at any time in world history with the new political dispensation roaring from Washington DC. And this is taking place with singular and unbending ferocity without any diplomatic decorum and subtlety. The neo-conservatives tell it like it is.

Military unilateralism to perpetuate the unjust system

Military unilateralism is a luxury in a world ripped with poverty and inequalities. Arabs and Africans are struggling to emerge out of their historical humiliation. Their hope lies in changing the unjust system - not being forced to live under it by military threat from the sole superpower and its faithful ally. The new national security doctrine of externally and militarily forced "regime change", unilaterally arm-twisting specific states in Africa and Arabia to pursue US military-corporate interests and seeking to expand US control over strategic resources such as oil, offers no deal except to continue the age-old imperialist divide and rule of Arabia and Africa. This US posture can only threaten to perpetuate their subjugation and oppression rather than allowing them to break out of their state of historical humiliation.

Iraq has now become the prime example and victim of the new permanent war to continue the unjust world order.

If the Gulf War in 1991 was more about a demonstration of power by the USA in establishing a new world order, the American invasion of Iraq in 2003 is even more so - as one of its overriding objectives is to show how "awesome" the technology of war has become over the last ten years. Iraq, as a weak Arabian state, was chosen as a scapegoat. Its unprovoked attack on a false pretext was an entirely deliberate, strategic and pre-planned affair hatched by those around the current Pentagon chief and the vice-president since 1996. With the force of a bayonet, they installed an occupying force at the heart of the Middle East, which would likely recognise Israel and thus further divide the Arab states.

Iraq was not attacked because of 9/11. What the events of 9/11 did was add fuel to the already pre-planned mission to attack Iraq. In 2003 the "war" on Iraq was forced on the world and a pretext had to be manufactured to justify it. There were series of contradictory claims and lies by those who were looking to justify their indefensible desire to bomb a weak third world state in Arabia. There is merit to the argument that this was not a war in the sense of two opposing armies facing each other and vying for total victory. There was only Mike Tyson in the boxing ring equipped with the training, boxing skills, fans and media to egg him along to do his thing. The opponent had no training, had none of the weapons or skills to match the champion. There was only one side that showed its armada: its army, air force, navy and the embedded journalists that did much to inform, misinform or mislead a captured public. There was no army from the side of Iraq, no air force, no navy and even journalists except for the Iraqi information minister who curiously and astonishingly played the role of the army, the government, the minister and journalist - all rolled into one. This was more about an American exhibition and projection of power. It was not merely a violent engagement for controlling resources - as it is becoming clearer with the passing of every day under the American occupation; it was more sinister than that. It has been borne as unprovoked violence to show who is to be in the driving seat, controlling the history and shaping the futures of the weak, oppressed and vulnerable hitherto colonised peoples and nations.

Iraq has been a demonstration case and a marketing advert for the rest of the one-time colonised Afro-Asian and Latin American world.

The message is loud and clear from Washington DC and London. If the ex-colonised peoples will not do what the Washington-London axis want them to do, they run the risk that the might of the US military will rain its B-52 bombs, cruise missiles, oxygen-depleting weapons, cluster bombs, daisy bombs, microwave bombs, bunker-busters and uranium-depleting weapons on their largely undefended populations. Iraq is the guinea pig - the showcase for others to learn the lesson and change their conduct if they had aspirations to do things differently from those assigned by the chief cop of the western empire. The empire is ready to do the Iraq on anyone, and is prepared to carry out pre-emptive strike ferociously. The agency to determine the future of the weak and the powerless is in the hands of the most powerful.

The battle for Iraq resonates beyond the control of Iraq. It has become a battle to own the terms and means of shaping the destiny of the weak by deliberate terror and the revival of a more modern edition of Victorian style imperial-colonialism. In the 18th century, we had the metaphor that the sun never sets in the British Empire. Incredulous as it may be, we are witnessing right before our eyes in the 21st century the resurrection of the empire - this time in the form that the sun also never sets in the American empire. Unlike the previous empire, the latest empire aspires for a total control of everything: physical space, water, oil, land, the galaxy, politics, the body, mind, soul and spirit spanning all creatures, peoples, nations and religions. The right to be different is perceived as a threat. Nations are safe when they are similar to the US image and value of Government.

This new American muscular foreign policy to impose American-style political ideas on others has resurrected old imperialism. The ideologues are open about it. They think describing the USA as an empire is "fine".

The extension of dominion through conquest throws history twenty steps backward and no step forward. History is forced at gunpoint to move back to shape the future of the weak. The weak nations are seen as always wrong. The winner is always right. The UN could not bring itself to condemn an imperial violation of international legality when two lethally armed nations descended on a helpless and already highly vulnerable country. Weak nations cannot rely on the good offices of the UN to rescue them when the empire decides to strike. This enjoins all weak nations to take up the new imperial challenge. They can no longer take for granted what little independence they may possess will be safe under their own fragmented custodies. It can be snatched by the whims of the uncrowned emperors of our time.

If history is rolled back two hundred years to re-invoke the logic of empire by the oppressor nations, weak nations should also roll back history fifty years to revive the spirit of the national liberation movement. They need to unite and create strong nations. They should create a strong and free Africa, and a strong and free Arab nation. They should also forge Afro-Arab and Afro-Asian alliances from the grassroots to the state level. This should be one of the most urgent challenges of our time as it could be the bulwark against future imperial aggressions. Without unified nations and common defence, Arabia and Africa will always remain playthings in the hands of the modern-day emperors of America.

The global disposition of forces in the 18th century was between the empire and those who tried to be free from it, and the rivalries amongst them. After World War II, there were four main contradictions that characterised the world disposition of political and economic forces. There was first, the systemic contradiction between socialism and capitalism, followed by the colonies trying to be independent and of the imperial powers trying to accommodate or fight that aspiration. There was a residual rivalry between the French, the British and other allied nations grouped under American hegemony to resist the Soviet ambition during the cold war. There were also social, workers and citizens movements for rights, visibility, peace, equality and safe environment - all protesting the injustices they confronted as a community, group and interest stakeholders. Today, the systemic contradiction has dropped out. The national liberation movement lacks focus. The aspiration to express different voices by some European countries has infuriated the current US rulers, prompting them to threaten punishment of a core European nation. The social and workers movements have been active in forging solidarity against the inequities and injustices of the go-go globalisation driven by the major corporations. There is now an attempt by those who wish to extend the tenure of US imperial power to reduce the contradiction to one: that between the unalloyed and untrammelled domination of the US Empire over the rest. That is the mission of the Project for the New American Century. The imposition of US power on the future destiny and history of the world appears to be what the latest military show against Iraq is all about. The US does not wish to earn respect. The current rulers prefer to be feared and to impose themselves on other nations. This is an extraordinary moment in history. "No legal issue arises when the US responds to challenge to its position, prestige or authority." This was said in the 1950s. It is now the US Government official doctrine to strike anywhere and at any individual or regime, should the US rulers perceive threat to their interests. It has become the age of preventive/pre-emptive war and violently externally executed "regime change" by the powerful. Might is right is back on the international political scoreboards. This is the new rule of the game by which all aspiring to be out of line will be dealt with.

It is the prerogative of emperors to divine their rule by allusion to transcendental mysteries. The neo-conservatives believe the US is not simply a country but it is also a "cause." To defend this nation, which is a cause in itself, means that it is beyond temporal jurisprudence. It is spiritual. The temporal rules, norms and laws are there to be broken to defend the idea of the "US as a cause". The US empire is thus above the law and above justice. Its stewards have freed themselves to arrogate democracy when they violate it, freedom when they flaunt it. It has been stated that the need for justice makes democracy desirable whilst the prevention of injustice makes it necessary. With the current US Empire, the logic is twisted; the emperor and his courtiers invoke democracy loudly to spread injustice, and freedom to deny a true self-expression of freedom for the cause of preserving the USA as a cause. George Orwell is here to stay. Anyone who dares to think differently and question the idea of the USA as a cause is cast as anti-American. Any divergence from the thought patterns established by the powerful will be condemned. The idea of freedom to think differently from established power does not make sense to the imperial ideologues from the US.

The imperial demonstration of violence against Iraq was distinguished not only by the spectacular exhibition of warfare, but also by the most unscrupulous organisation and dissemination of deceit and hypocrisy: false words, disarming euphemisms, false witnesses, planting false news, double-standards, and repeated lies victimised not simply the truth but everyone. It is as if everyone was being stabbed in the front and the back by lies. Such fraudulent deceitful behaviour was not an isolated incident. It was deliberate. It was part of the grand demonstration as it was part of the imperial prerogative to hoodwink at will. The US Government and British Government claimed that Iraq had weapons of mass destruction capable of creating a global threat. As it is becoming clear by the day, there were no weapons of mass destruction to be found under the possession of Iraq. The secular Ba'athist regime had no proven links with the clerically controlled al-Queda network. Lies, lies and damned lies. This is the only phrase that can truly describe the behaviour of the war-mongers who seem to have not anticipated or planned for the chaos that would ensue after the removal of the Ba'athist regime.

The occupying American and British forces have not yet stabilised the situation. They have not even assured electricity and water supplies. Almost every day Iraqis seem to be killed in retaliation by the occupiers for the random action taken by Iraqis to kill the occupation soldiers. The US and British regimes went and violently overthrew the Ba'athist regime against the expressed will of their own citizens who came out in unprecedented global demonstrations. Today, they have not fully pacified the Iraqis because wherever there is imperialism, there will be national liberation struggle sooner or later.

There is a big myth that the violent engagements made against Iraq by the imperial super power of the 21st century are to promote democracy and freedom. Nothing can be further from the truth. If the overriding objective were to shape the destiny of weak nations, then they would not be helping themselves to their resources. Imperial greed abhors democracy and freedom as nature abhors a vacuum. In Iraq, US soldiers did the infamy of protecting the oil ministry whilst looking on curiously at the most savage looting of human civilisation at the Museum of Baghdad. To date the US has refused to allow the UN to oversee the transition, neither has it allowed Iraqis to control the transition from Baathist rule to any new form of Government the Iraqis may want to establish. The US is directing the process and the Viceroy boasts that the US will "impose its will on Iraq" by its occupations. The name of the game is this: Install a weak regime that can only willingly authorise Iraq's national wealth to be plundered by the new imperial masters of the universe - and drone it with the description of democracy and freedom, and congratulate yourself for "liberating" the Iraqi people - that is the antithesis of democracy and freedom, not their expression and realisation. US Governments have done and will continue to do everything to install the group most amenable to fulfil their desire. That is what is emerging in Iraq, as indeed it happened in Chile and other places. Democracy and freedom are earned and are home-grown affairs, never gifts to be droned by the local population through external imposition or cruise missiles. The home based democracy and freedom may be rough, but it is real, not imposed, not imported, not distorted, not slick and without a need of any foreign stamp and imprint. The social movement for national liberation can create freedom and democracy and shape the future by using the native resources for nurturing them.

The Short and Long term Consequences of the Iraq war for Africa and Arabia

Both Africa and the Middle East are resource-rich regions. They contain the world's 18 per cent and 22 per cent of oil, making them regions that will not be left alone by the US, Europe and Japan. At the same time, they have the largest number of population in the world crushed by grinding poverty, disease and ill-being. The resources of Africa and Arabia have not been used to help develop the people of the region. They have been used to help internal elites and external robbers in the form of big transnational corporations. The war in Iraq underscores this unjust social relation in the two mineral resource and agricultural regions of the world.

The US needs more from these regions than they want from her. Even if these regions can say we do not want you, the US and the West will not leave them alone. The US has a large shopping list that cannot be easily satisfied. It requires forward military bases. It sees the regions as hotbeds of international terrorism and subject to its constant surveillance. The US Administration has used divide and rule tactics ignoring largely African and Arab efforts through the African Union and the Arab League to bring cohesion and solidarity amongst the regions. For example, Bush who postponed his January 2003 trip to Africa because of the then imminence of the Iraq war was unwilling to change his schedule in July when he made a five-day five states stint (safari) across Africa. That trip coincided with the meeting of the second African Union meeting. It was potentially disruptive of that meeting where African leaders were pulled off to meet him, when they should be concentrating and giving their undivided attention to construct enduring solidarity. He did more to divide the African leaders by cajoling some to sign bilaterally for the citizens of the USA to be exempted from extradition if called by the International Criminal

Court (ICC). Botswana, a country that has ratified the ICC has thrown its weight in support of America. (*New African*, August/September, 2003, p.26). Gambia had earlier done so. This encourages division amongst African countries. The US also selected certain countries for a Bush visit and others to be invited to see him in the capital city of the chosen leader. This will no doubt encourage division and unhealthy competition. The US selects certain countries to install military bases and proffer assistance. This too exacerbates inter-African rivalry.

Similar problems exist in the Arab world where certain countries are supported for providing facilities, bases and ready assistance to the USA. The Arab countries are divided and the Arab League is made ineffective.

The attack on Iraq signals that Washington will go to any length to protect its military bases and access to resources, specially African and Middle Eastern oil. The US is ready to sharpen the division amongst the countries and will not see kindly to the unity, cohesion and solidarity amongst African countries or Arab countries, let alone inter-African and Arab cooperation. The new doctrine of the US poses a grave threat to the construction of a new cooperative solidarity amongst Africans and Arabs and between each other.

The long-term interest of the two regions lies in Arab unity and African unity and the cooperation between the united entities of the Arab and African nations. This is the only way they can resist the age-old game of divide and rule directed at them. Though colonialism left formally, its divide and rule relics and antics have not been removed.

The existing global system and the current much-trumpeted globalisation have not reduced poverty in the two regions. The current military activism to forcibly change regimes will entrench the unjust world order further. The struggle to create solidarity amongst Africans and Arabs must be premised on the doctrine of mobilising their own resources to eradicate poverty, preventing the unequal relations between the rich world and themselves and to meet the Millennium Development Goals and other targets collectively.

The unjust system the USA is striving to protect with overwhelming military might has these flaws with respect to the interest of the poor world.

Unfair terms of trade inflict heavy burdens on the regions. For example, both regions suffer, like all developing regions, from the unfair and unequal global trade arrangements. As the President of the

World Bank admitted: "For too long we have viewed as normal a world where less than 20 per cent of the population in the rich countries dominate the world's wealth and resources and takes 80 per cent of its income." (James Wolfsholn, UN Meeting on Financing Development, Monterrey, March 25, 2002).

The July 21 International *Herald Tribune* put the global injustice that characterises the world thus: "By rigging the global trade game against farmers in developing nations, Europe, the United States and Japan are essentially kicking the development ladder out from under some of the world's most desperate people. This is morally depraved. America's actions are harvesting poverty around the world." The famous paradox is this: Nearly one billion people live on $1.00 a day whilst European cows net an average of $2.00 a day. Farms in Europe, America and Japan were subsidised with $320 billion in 2002 whilst the aid for the same year was $50billion. Mr Bush has signed $180 billion subsidy to US farmers whilst trying to steal the show in Monterrey, Mexico for increasing US assistance by $5 billion.

"The United States and its wealthy allies will not eradicate poverty - or defeat terrorism - by conspiring to deprive the world's poor farmers of even the most modest opportunities."(*Herald Tribune*, July 21)

The world economy has to be reformed to increase the voice of Africa and Arabia. But the military unilateralism of the US wants to impose more of the same system by extending its tenure, as it exists today. It is happy with a world economy evolving into a huge casino run by a global military industrial complex led by the USA. It wishes to continue offering limited assistance while imposing logic of aid that leads to debt: give a little with one hand and expect to reap windfall debts with the other hand. That neither helps to eradicate poverty nor terrorism.

The global institutions that are surrogates to US and Western interests (the rich world, in fact) that govern the world economy (the IMF, World Bank, WTO) are not responsive to the needs of Africa and Arabia. US activist unilateralism renders the external environment less conducive to reform than if the world was disposed to accommodating diverse voices by allowing their expression. Terrorism has been ruptured from the poverty from which it feeds itself. Whilst military unilateralism wishes to attack the former, it has no stomach to deal with the causes of terrorism. It wishes to perpetuate the unjust order by military domination, high tech armoury and fear generated through threats of death rather than sustaining life by war against poverty.

All the goals to reduce poverty require, as a necessary condition, the reform of the unjust system. The UN Millennium goals that were set, and the African countries that expected an international environment to fulfil the targets, remain largely pipedreams. Despite pledges of $10 billion in the Millennium Challenge Account and $15 billion for fighting HIV/AIDS by the US, the millennium goals will not be met. The verdict has been pronounced by recent studies by the World Bank and the UN's Human Development report, 2003. The key issue is that for the millennium goals to be fulfilled, the international political and economic architecture has to be reformed. That is a minimum requirement. But the way the current USA and UK regimes are defining international politics and economics is to perpetuate the existing order. What they call the new world order is in reality the old order. A number of approaches have been expressed to create a new world order.

The first is the dominant approach: to continue the existing unjust order by offering huge amounts of rhetoric such as the speech by Tony Blair that Africa is the scar on the conscience of the world, implying that if the world does not act, the losers will get angrier. This approach offers some charity, but often far lower than the resources they siphon out of the poor by heavy trade barriers and subsidies to their farmers. The basic approach is comprehensive control of the poor by building overwhelming military technology, armed and police forces and prisons. The correlate of this externally aggressive posture is matched by heavy intrusion in restricting civil liberties in the domestic setting of the rich world, including the use of arbitrary detention and threats to imprison and use the death penalty.

The second approach comes from movements that call for reforming the international political, economic and financial order. This has been expressed in the form of New International Economic Order in the 1970s and the reform of the Bretton Woods Institutions to arrive at what a Nobel Prize winner in Economics called "the Post-Washington Consensus", where "liberalisation, privatisation and stabilisation" were imposed as a blanket measure without any let-up on the entire poor world.

The third approach is from the World Social Forum where social solidarity is emphasised more than the market.

A fourth approach is to revive the Bandug spirit and bring back African-Arab cooperation and more broadly Afro-Asian national solidarity. It is in part like the second approach but the reforms are framed within a national liberation project explicitly against imperialism. There is a need to counter the imperial challenge with the resurrection of the national liberation movement, which will bring back the national project of the 1960s to counter the imperial project that harks back to the dream of Victorian empire to define and appropriate selfishly the 21st century. The Iraq war was a classic implementation of imperialism. It is pure colonial occupation.

The uncompleted nations (or aborted nations) of Africa and Arabia have to be born. A determined struggle has to be waged to resist the resurrection of old imperialism in the 21st century by building a comprehensive national project. Pan-Africanism and Pan-Arabism have to be revived. This is the only way the humiliation from imperial spectacular attacks will stop. I am suggesting a solid unified movement, not the self-defeating and self-killing strategies adopted by the "focoist" or terrorist groups today. Such tactics as human bombs, random killing of civilians and other isolated terrorist attacks disorganise more those who wish to resist injustice than hurt the perpetrators of injustice. It is the absence of strong national and social movements and the lack and fragmentation of ideology that has created the space for terrorism to proliferate as a phenomenon. Lack of secular ideology opens the space for all sorts of mystical and clerical ideas to take centre stage. Clericalism and terrorism feed the need of the military-industrial complex to construct the world as a dangerous place in order to justify huge expenditure to manufacture more and more the technology of death. Both are fundamentalists and jealous in fighting for what they perceived to be their interests. Both are intolerant. What they share is more than their differences. It is that simple. Perversely they become strange bedfellows in destruction and disorganising movements with roots in class, social, national, rights and interest foundations. Look how easy it was for the empire to nudge MPs in Britain and America to sign a bill authorising the use of billions of taxpayers' during the assault against Iraq. To exterminate or incinerate life, there are always huge sums that can be raised instantly. To save, educate and create life, there is always a reluctance to spend.

I propose that the post-Iraq world should send a compelling message: that people want justice, countries want freedom and particularly, that nations that have been aborted as a result of internal and external factors should be given the space to give birth to themselves, first and foremost as the Arab nation and the African nation. President Mubarak of Egypt lamented when asked about what Egypt could do during the Iraqi episode: "I tell the Arab world: it is not possible every time there is a crisis to ask where is Egypt?" Where is the agreement for joint Arab defence?" (*Al-Haram*, April 16). True, Egypt alone cannot do much. But Egypt has the historical opportunity of facilitating the most impregnable defence of Arabia and Africa. Egypt is in Africa. Egypt is also in the Arab world. Under Gamal Abdel Nasser it stimulated both African national liberation and Arab national ambitions. Nasser made the connection as follows: "We cannot, under any condition, even if we wanted to, in any way stand aloof from the terrible and terrifying battle now raging in the heart of the continent between five million whites and 200 million Africans ... the people of Africa will continue to look at us – the guardians of the continent's northern gate – as the ones who constitute the connecting link between the continent and the outer world."(Nasser, *Philosophy of the Revolution*, 1952)

That project, long abandoned, needs to be resuscitated.

References

Nelson Mandela, July 11 the *Mirror*, UK, 2003
Al-Ahram, April 16 (quoted in *Al-Haram* English weekly), 2003
The Herald Tribune (July 21, 2003)
Al-Hayat, November 6, 2002
James Wolfsholn, UN Meeting on Financing Development, Monterrey, March 25, 2002
Washington Post, August 17, 2003
Nasser, A.G: *The Philosophy of the Revolution*, Cairo, 1952

Part V

Africa-Nation, Pan-Africanism and the African Renaissance: Alternative Guideposts

18

Wither Africa? –Reflections on alternative guideposts

Jacques Hersh

The theme of whether Pan-African integration is an idea whose time has come should be seen in the context of two interrelated processes. One is the internal evolution on the socio-economic and political levels of the various countries and societies of the African continent. The second is related to the question of whether Africa is being marginalized or incorporated in the globalisation process, which is supposedly taking place at the planetary level. Seen in this perspective, the task for concerned Africans and friends of Africa is to determine whether Pan-Africanism or institutionalised regionalisation should be conceived as conducive to greater and better integration within the globalisation process or be understood as a defensive strategy.

This question is appropriate at a time when the notion of "Afro-pessimism", deploring marginalisation, seems to have been replaced by the discourse of "Afro-optimism" implying an increasing participation in the world economy. However, a sober analysis might lead to a more sceptical position. The first conceptualisation sees Africa as belonging to the Fourth World in contrast to the newly industrialised and competitive Third World of East Asia and Latin America (Amin 1996: 200). The second projection is based on the apparent growth of African economies in the 1990s and the implementation of the Structural Adjustment Programmes (SAPs) of the Bretton Woods institutions.

What the proponents of the two theses have in common is that they both seemingly accredit the situations to the role of the state. For Afro-pessimists, the states and bureaucracies, with their important role in modern societies have stipulated, because of internal shortcomings and on the basis of the recommendations emanating from the SAPs, reduced the scope of policies and strategies which in the past translated into a relatively positive degree of social equity and development. Afro-optimists, in contrast, see the states and bureaucracies as having accepted a certain degree of democratisation and on the advice of the International Financial Institutions retrenched from controlling market and productive forces. According to this line of thinking the strategy of unleashing the market released economic growth.

In the optimistic framework whatever improvements, coming on the heels of the defeat of the apartheid system in South Africa, are cited as evidence of a kind of African Renaissance marking what is projected to be a second independence. The optimism of African leaders such as Adebayo Adedeji (former Executive Secretary of the UN Economic Commission for Africa) calling for a more self-reliant development strategy or South Africa's President Thabo Mbeki's vision of an African Renaissance has been "hijacked" by opinion-makers and academics in the West.

For example, the "Bretton Woods sisters" (the World Bank and the International Monetary Fund), have declared in unison that "Africa is on the move" (Braütigam 1998: 204); a few years ago, *The Economist* (June 14, 1997) had a cover story on "Emerging Africa"; also UNCTAD (UN Conference on Trade and Development) highlighted not too long ago Africa's new role as a promising emerging market. (*Le Monde*, July 13, 1999). In the realm of international politics, an African, that is a black African, has for the first time been appointed General Secretary of the United Nations. Another landmark were the visits to Africa by Bill Clinton - a continent largely ignored by American presidents. This apparent lacuna is paradoxical given the fact that a large minority of Americans have their roots in Africa. Even in the realm of sports, the national football team of Cameroon won the gold medal at the Olympics in Sidney. The euphoria around this evolution has created a new interest in Africa. As the editor of *Le Monde Diplomatique* put it:

"We see that investors, international institutions, research centres and universities show a new interest for Africa." (Ramonet 2000: 7)

Clouding this rosy picture of the African condition is, aside from the ethnic violence within countries, the emergence of a new phenomenon: political-military conflicts pitting armies and countries against each other, in what has been called "Africa's scramble for Africa". (Weinstein 2000:11-20) These evolutions – the renewed Western interest and the spectre of a continent at war with itself, have given rise to voices calling for the re-colonisation of the continent in order to protect the human rights of the African populations. In other words, a return to a variant of the ideological notion of "the White Man's burden"!

This notwithstanding, the recent emergence of inter-state wars on the continent is a development which needs to be taken seriously, given the disparities in power among the states in sub-Saharan Africa. Fundamentally, the dilemma revolves around the issue of whether the map of Africa should be redrawn on the basis of ethnic compositions of the different entities. In this respect, it should be recalled that in the past the Organisation of African States always affirmed the legitimacy of the notion of national sovereignty established by the Westphalian system in Europe and which formed a cornerstone of the United Nations Charter.

The acceptance of the legacy of the colonial borders drawn during the European scramble for Africa, provided the post-independence regimes with the opportunity for consolidating their political positions, and gave rise to the development path of nationalist populism. This is not the time or place to go into a discussion of the concept of populism, but in the African context of the time it might have been appropriate to consider it as an ideological response, and resistance of rural traditionalist peasant society to the spreading of capitalist relations (Saul 1973: 152-179). An attempt was made to resolve the dichotomy between nationalism – as a developmental project - and populism - as a discourse based on an undifferentiated appeal to the people or masses, by appealing to traditional loyalties while simultaneously carrying out a national modernisation project to appease the different social sectors in the society. The tensions of the specific conditions of post-independence, under these conditions, were related to the need for self-affirmation by drawing on pre-colonial cultural antecedents. There was also awareness that the past would be superseded in a new developmental project that drew from the Western example and therefore risked undermining the claims to autonomy. As the African scholar, Abiola Irele, points out:

For despite frequent use of the rhetoric of archaism, it was always clear to African Nationalists that the African past to which they appealed was, in the final analysis, irretrievably lost. To be meaningful, nationalism requires a prospective rather than a retrospective vision. (Irele 1992: 299)

The developmentalism put into effect by the new elites did generally show positive results in the first periods of independence. However, the specific political projects, by appealing simultaneously to traditional and national identities contributed in weakening the thrust of "Pan-Africanism". This notion had been launched by Kwame Nkumah and supported by a number of African leaders in the post-independence period with the purpose of surmounting the heritage of colonialism and strengthening the emergence of Africa.

While some internal forces were thus pushing in the direction of strengthening national identity at the expense of African unity, Western powers did their bit to scupper the Pan-African project. In fact, they had earlier on violated the Congolese independence. By intervening overtly (Belgium) and covertly (US and Britain), with the tacit approval of the United Nations, in the overthrow and murder of Patrice Lumumba (Gibbs 2000:359-382), the Western powers in effect eliminated the possibility of the emergence of a force that could have decisively strengthened the evolution of Africa towards a more continent-centred political and economic development. Because of its central location and wealth, the Congo could have been a key player in strengthening Pan-Africanism. In fact, the demise of the democratically elected Lumumba was one of the darkest chapters of Western great power involvement in African affairs in modern times, and the consequences of that are still felt in the present conflict in Central Africa. Other Pan-African leaders were likewise targeted and removed from power through overt or covert Western great power manoeuvres on the international market for primary good (for a vivid analysis of this kind of operation with regard to the demise of Kwame Nkrumah, see Fitch and Oppenheimer, 1966).

In contrast to the intra-African conflicts, which the continent is presently experiencing, during the Cold War period, although some African states did act as surrogates for the superpowers and South

Africa, this was more the exception than the rule. By and large African states did not invade one another (Weinstein 2000:15). Now the chicken is coming home to roost, and the present chaos in the Congo can, to no small extent, be ascribed to the imposition by the West of the corrupt Mobutu regime in 1960. Most of the intervening states have been motivated by the extraction of rents obtained through control of the Congo's mineral and other resources. In other words, what we are seeing is African state formations not acting in a pre-modern fashion, as some analysts claim, but very much in accordance with an economic rationality reminiscent of the colonial metropoles. This is not to detract from the fact that involvement by some neighbouring countries in the Congo war are dictated by considerations of personal gains on the part of leading politicians in these countries. The extent of the involvement of Western actors in these events is less direct than in the overthrow of Lumumba. Nevertheless, the United Nations has recently issued a report documenting the degree to which the Congo war serves the economic interests of some of the West's staunchest allies, and an array of foreign businesses. Commenting on the report, the New York *Times* in its editorial wrote that "Africans have exploited Congo's natural resources in league with reputable foreign companies and financial institutions (reproduced in the International *Herald Tribune*, May 31, 2001).

At this juncture, the future evolution evolutionary paths for the African continent   may be conceptualised in the following **possible scenarios**: 1) a continuation of positive economic growth leading to economic integrations and regionalisms; 2) a continuation of the "African scramble for Africa", perhaps leading to selective Western interventions and re-colonisation; 3) a return to the vision of Pan-Africanism involving an alternative societal project.

Concerning the **first scenario**, it is not impossible that the continent will experience continued economic growth and that industrialisation will ensue. This would signify greater integration into the world economy, which itself is undergoing transformations. The old contrast conceptualised by the dependency theory equating industrialisation with the core countries of the world system and non-industrial regions with peripheries is in need of revision. What we may be seeing is the emergence of an international division of labour, which permits the spread of industrialisation while at the same time intensifying the polarisation of the world. The new centre-periphery dichotomy might very well be spearheaded by the five monopolies located in the core with influence all over the world. These are the monopolies of science and technology, financial flows of global capital and large-scale enterprises, control over (not necessarily) ownership of the resources of the planet; control of communications and the media which besides the financial gains, also allows for the spreading of a specific cultural and political message and discourse; and finally the monopoly of advanced armaments and weapon systems.

It is within this context of the West's (including Japan's) domination of the commanding heights of the world economy that a number of countries of East and Southeast Asia, South Asia and Latin America have been moving and developing the capacity of being competitive in the global market (see various recent writings by Samir Amin). But as far as Africa is concerned, the continent appears to have been lagging behind in this evolution. However, in light of the renewed Western interest for Africa, the possibility of a similar process might not be inconceivable. Until now however, although labour is cheap, the inferior productivity and the acutely weak infrastructure make most of Africa still less competitive than many Asian countries with higher wages. This is reflected in the worldwide flow of foreign direct investment. According to Deborah Bräutigam:

... in comparative perspective, the new interest in Africa is still quite marginal. Foreign direct investment in Africa, while growing, accounts for only a little more than 2 per cent of FDI going to developing countries. Columbia and the Czech Republic each received more FDI in 1995 than all of sub-Sahara combined. (Bräutigam 1998: 205)

Due to the fact that many of the African nation-states would have difficulties surviving as viable economic entities we may see the emergence of larger units of economic collaboration. Such a trend would not be contrary to the evolution of the regionalisation of the world economy, which can also be observed in the core countries with the formation of the European Union and NAFTA. The director of the Africa studies programme at the Council on Foreign Relations in the United States proposes that a reasonable approach to "unbundling " Africa is to start thinking of five distinct sub-regions. As far as the African policy of the United States is concerned such a regional integration should imply recognising five countries as the target for American involvement: South Africa and Congo in Southern and Central Africa, Nigeria in West Africa, Kenya in East Africa, and Algeria in North Africa (Booker 1998:200-l).

The second scenario, based on a continuation of the observed malfunctioning of African societies leading to chaos and violence implies a political evolution, which is difficult for the rest of the world to comprehend. Since the 1990s, politics in this part of the world has been marked by breakdowns of order, and in some cases the vanishing of the central authority of the state. The analysis of this evolution has seen different approaches being used: some analysts invoke globalisation and the implementation of structural adjustment programmes, others put the emphasis on the crisis of the patrimonial state, while others still introduce social and cultural factors as key parameters of the explanation.

There can be little doubt that the process of state collapse in Africa under the impact of internal dynamics has given rise to a degeneration of the social order and an increase in outbreaks of violence. The main socio-political features occurring with this evolution have been the decline or disappearance of state functions and offices; abusive use of the surviving institutions, that is the army and police; central authority becoming fragmented or disappearing, thereby opening the way for chaotic and anarchic conditions; the conflictual coexistence of state and society on the basis of either mutual avoidance or violence and resource extraction. This influences the economy in a negative manner through the contraction of state economic activity and decline of the upkeep of infrastructure, law and security, etc. In most cases, much of the formal economy is replaced by informal sector activities, a process which is seen by some as an advantage to the former resource extraction activities of the state. However, together with the implementation of the SAPs (structural adjustment programmes) these societies are facing deterioration in the social, health and education sectors of a large magnitude. (For a more detailed analysis of the internal violence and state collapse in Africa, see Allen 1999: 367-384.)

The theoretical analysis of internal wars and violence tends to have evolved from the rather primitive way of considering them to be irrational. There is still a tendency to explain violence and internal war by treating all cases of the phenomenon as being in principle similar and thus leading to a uniform prototype explanation. There are however differences in the kinds of conflicts with regard to their origin, character and outcome. As pointed out by a French Africanist, the ethnic conflicts are at times only names hiding real political tensions between social groups as well as manipulations by the former colonial power (Engelhard 1998:31). However, regardless of their origin, it is a fact in most cases that the impact of the violence has been on the civilian populations.

From the perspective of international law, the African continent has been experiencing inter-state conflicts on the basis of the self-proclaimed right of intervention by the intervening parts in contravention to the Charter of the OAU, now defunct. The centrepiece in this development is of course the disintegration of the Congo. The course towards African inter-state wars cannot be separated from the greater interest the United States and the former European colonial powers still have in the continent. On the one hand, because of the disintegration of states in certain parts of Africa and due to the disparities of wealth and resources between countries, there has been a tendency toward the creation of new African geopolitical arrangements based on spatial groupings around key countries (Mbembe 2000: 13-15).

As touched upon previously, American strategists are already planning on the basis of a certain regionalisation of the African continent around five countries on which the United States ought to concentrate its attention. At a time of globalisation under the leadership of the United States, Africa is increasingly considered to be an untapped area of opportunity offering US capital profitable investment outlets. This is taking place at a time when a former colonial power like France, some forty years after the wave of independence of its former colonies, is in the process of re-arranging its relations with its former African dependencies and looking towards the entire continent as an arena of competition with the United States (Leymarie 2000:76-78). The stakes might not at first glance appear to be high. But appearances can be deceptive. Although Africa is still considered to be a high-risk investment area by international rating agencies, estimates are that while foreign investors in developing countries normally earn returns of some 16 to 18 per cent, profits on African investments average from 24 to 30 per cent (Bräutigam 1998:205). Besides this interest for investment placements, the US Assistant Secretary of State for African affairs told a conference on Africa of the advantages of the enormous market of some 700 million people, of the immense unexploited resources, and of the possibilities for the creation of American jobs (Stern: 1998).

It is in the context of the socio-economic and political chaos and conflicts facing many African countries that the interests for economic intercourse with the continent on the part of Western powers should be analysed. It is with this backdrop in mind that the talk of "recolonisation" should be scrutinised. Such a process need not involve direct Western political-military involvement if African intermediaries or private Western mercenaries can be counted on to keep order while economic ties are intensified in what could evolve into a kind of blurred institutionalised neocolonialism.

While the scenario of regression and re-colonisation builds on the conceptualisation of Africa as an example of failed development, there is another take on the evolution of African societies whose line of argumentation ought to be an object of further research. The approach is related to the question of modernisation and how Africa has fared in this process. In contrast to conventional thinking which sees Africa as a failure, the French Africanists Patrick Chabal and Jean-Pascal Daloz suggest that the African experience has to be seen in the context of the possibility that there might be different types of modernity. While Western modernisation has been successful in combining science and technology with bureaucratic and managerial efficiency, Africa in contrast seems to have evolved a form of modernity, which provides for the ability to use the tools of Westernisation (technology and science) and to remain stubbornly "traditional" on the social and cultural levels (Chabal 2000:9). According to this way of thinking, Africa should not be seen as moving backward or engaged in a notional return to age-old ways but as following its own specific form of modernisation. As the two authors put it: "It is in fact, quite possible that this part of the world is heading in a distinct, decidedly non-Western, direction: modernity without development." (Chabal and Daloz 1999: 125)

The specificity of African modernity as contrasted with Western modernisation at a time of globalisation (that is, the spread of capitalist logic and relations both at the societal and inter-societal levels) demands some forms of organisation enabling the nations of the continent to either integrate or protect themselves. This is where the discussion of the **third scenario** comes in. In the post-colonial era, the political elites of the newly born nation-states were concerned with modernisation projects either through nationalism, Pan-Africanism or state capitalism. Developmentalism under these conditions was based on co-opting and harnessing traditionalism to the modernisation of society in the shape of external models.

The call for African socialism, which the Pan-Africanist current promoted in its rhetoric never materialised. As argued above, internal conditions of post-colonial society demanded that traditions be taken into consideration in the political strategies of implementing economic development. The Cold War accentuated divisions between countries and even the defunct Organisation of African Unity promoted a variant of the European state system instead of a project of continental dimension. We have seen how the Western powers, in fear of socialism which the discourse of Pan-African solidarity promoted, intervened in the Congo to make sure that the resources of this rich country would remain within the Western sphere of interest.

In order to resurrect Pan-Africanism from the past, it is of importance that efforts be made by Africans to surmount the legacy of the state system and base continental modernity on the two logics discussed by Chabal and Daloz (1999). In this regard, two types of project confront Africans. One is based on regional economic integration in terms of common markets. This is in the interest of the global bourgeoisie and local compradors whose interests lie in the intensification of capital accumulation through a specific modernisation process. This will not reduce inequalities between societies and harmonise economic levels between them. On the other hand, in order to fulfil its calling, the Pan-African vision would have to face the issues of the contradictions within the particular societies as well as the external challenges facing the continent. Although Pan-Africanism has a mobilising content, it has to take into account ways to confront the menaces which globalisation carries with it before acquiring the status of ideological hegemony. In the view of Samir Amin, the doctrine has to retreat from culturalism and by bringing politics back, devise an alternative societal order which avoids the pitfalls of the modernisation model proposed by the conventional development paradigm. This could have a more universal value at a time when globalisation is revealing itself as a detrimental project for the majority of humankind.

"... certainly Africa needs Pan Africanism but I don't think the cultural rhetoric on Pan Africanism will do the job. It has to be supportive of meeting the real challenge: actually existing capitalism, not European culture but actually existing capitalism. That is the challenge; we need to discuss it in terms of programmes but not exclusively in terms of culture. There are African cultures, in Europe, there are European cultures; we should look at moving from our cultures towards universal culture, the universal dimension of the future we want for all humankind. (Amin 1998: 482)

It is often forgotten in the discussion that Africa has been subjected to three centuries of violent integration into European capitalism and colonialism. The process took various forms: slave trade, disorganisation of political and economic structures, colonisation and imposition of neocolonial states and military regimes, etc. This experience ought to be sufficient to foster a felt-need for viable alternatives for Africa. The implication ought surely to be that another development path should be implemented. In this respect the need to return to the hopes and aspirations of the African national liberation struggle could be appropriate. Accordingly, we could do much worse than quote Franz Fanon, who in the immediate post-independence period warned against following the European model:

We can do anything today on the condition of not imitating Europe, on the condition of not being obsessed by the desire of catching-up to Europe. (Fanon 1966: 239-40)

Pan-Africanism is sandwiched between Afro-optimism and Afro-pessimism. It is optimistic because it embodies hope, possibility and African aspirations realised through the unity of Africans in Africa and the world outside Africa. It betrays pessimism because fragmented states may not be able to realise fully the complete liberation of their people. Pan-Africanism resists the continued fragmentation of the continent, and instils hope in the unity of the continent. Understanding the dilemma of Africa is of course a necessary first step, but not sufficient in itself. As Antonio Gramsci wrote at the time, concrete analysis is not an end in itself but depends on how it can lead to "practical activity". In this relation, the project of Pan-Africanism might be conducive to surmounting the tension between the "pessimism of the intellect" and the "optimism of the will". As formulated by a student of Gramsci, "what is possible is also related to what is desired"(Sassoon 1999). Africans can think of their unity and make it.

References:

Allen, Chris (1999) "Warfare, Endemic Violence & State Collapse in Africa" in *Review of African Political Economy*, no. 81.

Amin, Samir (1998) "The First Babu Memorial Lecture" in *Review of African Political Economy*, no. 77.

Booker, Salih (1998) "Thinking Regionally About Africa" in *Current History*, May.

Bräutigam, Deborah (1998) "Economic Take-off in Africa" in *Current History*, May

Chabal, Patrick (2000) "Africa: Modernity Without Development" in *ISIM Newsletter* (International Institute for the Study of Islam in the World), no. 5, June.

Chabal, Patrick and Daloz, Jean-Pascal (1999) *Africa Works: Disorder as Political Instrument*, Oxford: (James Currey and Bloomington Ind.: Indiana University Press).

Engelhard, Philippe (1998) *L'Afrique – Miroir du Monde?*, Paris: Arlea

Fanar, Frantz (1966) *Les damnés de la terre*, Paris: Francois Maspero.

Fitch, Bob and Openheimer, Mary(1966): Ghana: End of an illusion, *Monthly Review,*Vol.18, no.3 (July-August)

Gibbs, David N (2000) "The United Nations, international peacekeeping and the question of 'impartiality': revisiting the Congo operation of 1960" in *The Journal of Modern African Studies*, 38, 3.

Irele, Abiola (1992) "The Crisis of Legitimacy in Africa – A Time for Change and Despair" in *Dissent*.

Leymarie, Philippe (2000) "Washington á la Conquete d'espaces vierges" in *Maniere de voir*, no. 51, May-June.

Mbembe, Achille (2000) "Vers une nouvelle géopolitique africaine" in *Maniere de voir*, no 51, May-June.

Ramonet, Ignacio (2000) "Un Continent d'avenir" in *Maniere de voir*, no. 51, May-June.

Sassoon, Anne Showstack (1999) "The space for politics: globalisation, hegemony, and passive resistance" in Johannes Dragsbaek Schmidt and Jacques Hersh (eds.) *Globalisation and Social Change*, (London and New York: Routledge).

Saul, John S. (1973) "On African Socialism" in Giovanni Arrighi and John S. Saul *Essays on the Political Economy of Africa*, (New York/London: Monthly Review).

Stern, Alexandra (1998) *Africa International*, January.
Weinstein, Jeremy M. (2000) "Africa's Scramble for Africa – Lessons of a Continental War" in *Foreign Policy*, Summer.

19

NEPAD: It simply won't work

Guy Arnold

The beginning of the new century has witnessed the transformation of the OAU into the African Union, the launch of a New Partnership for Africa's Development (NEPAD) and the South African insistence that the time has come for an African renaissance. At the same time Africa faces the new neo-colonialism represented by the World Bank, the IMF, the World Trade Organisation - the international financial institutions - that, whatever their ostensible purpose, have been turned into instruments of Western manipulation and control. The question of how Africa can shake off dependence upon the outside world is quite separate from engagement with that world. Despite the fanfare about NEPAD and the visit to Africa in July 2003 by US President George Bush, the West at most is only marginally interested in Africa as Africa, as opposed to what it can extract from it, and if African leaders pause to think about this, they should be relieved rather than upset. If past history, both colonial and post-colonial, is any guide, neither European nor American interest has done the continent any favours. NEPAD, the launch of the African Union and an African renaissance are closely intertwined as part of the same exercise: how to rid Africa of the weight of external pressures that force it to develop as the West requires it instead of in its own fashion.

The African problems that engage external attention have been well rehearsed: poverty, lack of development, aid, dependence, debt, corruption, civil wars, lack of democracy, failed states. It is a depressing list. The question is how best to tackle these problems? Awareness of their debilitating impact upon Africa's potential for growth has been behind these new continental initiatives. Let us begin with the new African Union. There will be no point in transforming the OAU into a new African Union unless the core issue of enabling Africa to speak with one voice is tackled. The newly independent nations of Africa rejected moves towards real union in the immediate post-independence era, for understandable reasons, and instead opted for a weak OAU. However, the need for African unity has never been more urgent than today, as the process of world globalisation is pushed ever harder by a dominant West. It should in fact be at the top of the continental agenda. Fifty-four weak states will be permanently subservient to western interests and pressures unless they learn to act as one in relation to the United States and the European Union. Even the strong work together rather than separately. The donor nations, for example, invoke IMF or World Bank conditionalities when they wish to evade one-to-one decisions and the EU bargains as a collective with individual African countries. Given the power disparities between the West and Africa, it becomes essential that the AU should speak for the whole continent, most especially at the present time when the United States is seeking new bases in Africa. The aims of the African Union, as set out in its new charter - unity, harmonisation of policies, economic integration - are impeccably correct, but are they also meaningless? Africa has made many attempts to achieve regional economic integration and ECOWAS and SADC are at present the best examples of this, but what the continent needs is a single economic voice.

The second task for the AU, one that is only too apparent at the present time, is the need for it to take control of peacekeeping in Africa. In troubled Sierra Leone, Africa appears only too ready to allow the former imperial power, Britain, to do the peacekeeping. When Côte d'Ivoire went up in flames, the African Union's first chairman, President Thabo Mbeki of South Africa, had a unique opportunity to involve the AU in a peacekeeping exercise; instead he gave his blessing to a Paris initiative under the arch neo-colonialist, President Jacques Chirac. Africa does not lack soldiers and it is time some of these were placed permanently at the disposal of the AU for peacekeeping operations anywhere on the continent. African independence owed much to United Nations pressures in the 1950s and 1960s and the integrity of the UN is of the greatest importance to its weakest members, yet when the United States and Britain arrogantly bypassed the UN to invade Iraq without a UN mandate to do so, Africa was noticeably mute in its response to this deliberate downsizing of the world body, giving rise to the suspicion that it was desperate not to offend the two western powers because it was relying upon their generosity to make NEPAD work.

And what has the AU been prepared to say, let alone do, about events in the Democratic Republic of the Congo? It has said and done nothing about the predatory activities of the Congo's neighbours, especially Uganda and Rwanda whose raping of the country's resources is straight international piracy. And it has been equally quiet about ethnic violence in the Ituri region of northeast Congo between Lendu and Hemu that threatens to spark off full-scale genocide; Africa appears content to allow a French-led UN intervention deal with the problem. Article Four - Principles - of the Constitution Act of the African Union lays down:

(h) The right of the Union to intervene in a Member State pursuant to a decision of the Assembly in respect of grave circumstances, namely war crimes, genocide and crimes against humanity.

There is no ambiguity about this principle; as yet there has been no sign that the AU or any member state is prepared to invoke it. Yet, until Africa is seen to be ready to deal with such crimes on the continent, despite the ingrained habit of non-interference in the internal affairs of member states, there can be little hope of an African renaissance that has any meaning.

The NEPAD concept arose out of the October 2001 meeting at Abuja, Nigeria, when African leaders reviewed the dangers of terrorism. They also discussed the New Africa Initiative (NAI) that had been formulated in July 2000 at the final OAU summit in Lusaka. They agreed to rename NAI as NEPAD and establish its headquarters in Pretoria. They envisaged three African commitments: clear accountability and open government; an end to gross human rights abuses; and an end to African wars and the imposition of African peacekeeping. In return, the West would provide more aid for infrastructure, development and education as well as increased investment and the lifting of existing trade barriers. This represented a neat equation, and though the initiative should not be decried, it was depressingly similar to past occasions when, in return for promises of good governance, Africa asks for more aid. It is surely a humiliation, to put it no higher, that 40 years after independence, Africa is collectively promising to behave well in return for more aid. Libya's Colonel Gaddafi put his finger on the blatant neo-colonialism of the NEPAD concept when he said: "We are not children who need to be taught. They (the colonial powers) made us slaves, they called us inferior but we have regained our African name and culture." Thus, it has to be asked, will NEPAD do anything other than tie Africa more closely to the West just when it should be breaking free? The only NEPAD initiative that would make ground-breaking sense would be one that brought an end to US and EU subsidies to their farming sectors so that they opened their markets to African agricultural products in the way President Bush asks Africa to open its markets to the more advanced western economies.

NEPAD presupposes a new relationship between Africa and the North, especially Britain, France, the EU and the United States. This requires us, first, to look at the old relationship. Forty years ago, the leaders of the newly independent Africa nonetheless recognised that the West was determined to continue controlling the economies of Africa and this has not changed. Poverty, and the manipulation of the poor by the rich, is central to the world's current problems. Almost all international gatherings over the last ten to fifteen years have revealed a hardening of attitudes between North and South, with both sides finding confrontation easier than consensus. Moreover, no matter how many initiatives have been launched, for example over debt relief, the rich get richer and the poor poorer, and though we have the knowledge as well as the resources to bridge all the gaps that exist, the rich do not have the will to do anything of the sort. Those who have wealth and power do not want to equip the poor to rival them.

Demonstrations against the annual meetings of the G8, the World Bank and IMF, the WTO or the Davos meetings are symbolic of the yawning divides that separate North and South. Far from altering anything, these demonstrations simply emphasise the fact that the world is divided into two camps: smug power facing desperate poverty. Finding solutions to an unequal relationship always founders on two realities: the first, that the weak have very few weapons to hand with which to tackle the strong; and the second, that the strong are always determined, by whatever means, to maintain their advantages. Thus, when we consider NEPAD we must ask: what does the EU want of Africa and what does the United States want? Aid has been the West's principal means of manipulating African economies since independence and the attitudes that divide the rich donors from their African recipients were formed during the 1960s and have changed little since that time.

It is historically instructive that the donors only recognised the value of aid after African countries had become independent; prior to independence, colonies were largely supposed to pay for themselves. As a broad generalisation, aid became a weapon of economic management for donors while for recipient rulers it relieved them of responsibilities to their people that could not have been avoided if there had been no aid. The result of decades of aid has been to create aid dependency on the one hand, and mountains of debt on the other that between them deprive African countries of any freedom of economic choice. Further, it is pertinent to ask just what aid has achieved over the last forty years of the 20th century and why so many African countries, despite aid, are either no better off or even worse off than they were at independence. It is naive to imagine that a NEPAD funded by the West will do anything other than tie Africa more closely into an economic system it cannot control.

At the G8 summit of July 2002 in Canada, a deputation of African leaders, including South Africa's Thabo Mbeki and Nigeria's Olusegun Obasanjo were invited to attend and present the case for NEPAD. They obtained a firm promise of an additional $1bn of aid for Africa ($22bn was promised Russia, the former superpower). Now, whatever NEPAD is about, it should not require African leaders acting as supplicants, like Oliver Twist, asking for more. Britain's prime minister, Tony Blair, is reportedly a firm supporter of NEPAD, which is an African-led initiative but just what do statements of support for the initiative mean? Will NEPAD simply legitimise the present North-South relationship under a new name and attract marginally more aid for Africa? Or, does it amount to something more valuable? At the March 2002 UN Monterrey summit in Mexico - the International Conference on Financing for Development with the grand title, Confronting the Challenge of Financing Development, A Global Response – which discussed eradicating African poverty and elaborated on the Millennium Development Goals, targets were set for universal education and a two-thirds reduction of child deaths by 2015. President Bush spoke of a "compact for development", in which US aid would only go to countries that rooted out corruption, restructured their economies and opened their markets. Then reluctantly, under intense

EU pressure (since the Europeans did not wish to bear the greater part of the aid "burden"), Bush agreed a small increase in US aid from $10bn to $15bn by 2006 (a rise from 0.1 per cent to 0.15 per cent of GDP as opposed to the EU average of 0.33 per cent which was to rise to 0.39 per cent, both far below the UN target of 0.7 per cent.) The inclusion of rooting out corruption in President Bush's "compact for development" must have appeared unbelievably arrogant to anyone from Africa or elsewhere in the South at a time when the Enron scandal, the largest corporate corruption case in history, was unfolding. Almost as soon as NEPAD was born, British MPs were suggesting that Britain ought not to support it, unless first, President Mbeki of South Africa had exerted pressure upon Zimbabwe's President Mugabe to change his ways; this was to revert to classic aid tactics: behave politically as we (the donors) tell you and aid might be forthcoming. In other words, nothing had changed.

An aspect of the New World Order, first proclaimed by George Bush senior, is the democratisation and greater accountability of countries in the South. Now accountability and open government is accepted as part of NEPAD though exactly what is expected is difficult to analyse. In order for it to work, democracy must be an indigenous growth. It cannot be imposed from without. The people of a country have to want it and fight for it themselves, as has been happening over much of Africa in recent years. Similarly, accountability is not to be imposed from outside. Western governments make much of the need for accountability though their own actions are often not accounted for at all. Recently and uniquely, the Zambian parliament voted unanimously to lift ex-President Federick Chiluba's immunity against prosecution for corruption although such actions are still something of a rarity in Africa.

Even so, it is in stark contrast to the action of the Italian parliament, which in July 2003 passed legislation to exempt Prime Minister Silvio Berlusconi from prosecution on massive corruption charges. Once more, we are treated to the spectacle of double standards. What the West insists Africa must do is contemptuously disregarded in Europe. This raises another question about this most uneven of relationships. Should aid donors that claim to believe in democracy only deliver aid to countries that practice democracy (as the West understands it) or should they continue, as they do, to deliver it to tyrannies and so help keep the tyrants in power. And this leads, naturally, to another question: what to do about the decision-makers of major institutions that are responsible for so much that takes place in Africa. These comprise the United Nations, the World Bank, the IMF, and the G8 itself. The United Nations may try to speak on behalf of the poor and least developed, yet all-important decisions are subject to scrutiny by the Security Council where the five permanent members have the veto, which enables them to override the wishes of the majority as they frequently do. The World Bank and the IMF are even less democratic in terms of either transparency or democracy where the weighted voting power of the major donors always enables the West to control policy. At the present time Britain, France, Germany, Japan, Canada, Russia, Saudi Arabia and the United States control 46 per cent of the World Bank and 48 per cent of IMF's voting rights. The US always appoints the head of the World Bank, Europe, of the IMF. These institutions above all, since so much of their work concerns the developing world, should themselves be made fully transparent and democratic, with one country one vote, no matter the size of their monetary contributions. The democratic structure of the WTO has been subverted by the rich nations who make key decisions in conclave before open sessions take place. Given such practices in the developed world, why should African countries be expected dutifully to accept western prescriptions about accountability?

NEPAD raises awkward questions about western trading practices. For example, would the President of the United States – any president risk losing votes by insisting upon a reduction of US living standards that would follow if certain measures to achieve a more equitable world trading system were adopted. The most obvious of these would be an end to subsidies to American farmers so as to allow African agricultural products a chance to penetrate the huge American market while also bringing an end to subsidised US cotton undermining African cotton production. Similar considerations apply to the EU with its iniquitous CAP support system for its farming sector. Another cause of concern is the constant western pressures upon African countries to privatise state assets. Such privatisation in a poor country where few of its citizens are able to purchase shares merely ensures that western companies can move in to buy up the assets whose control may then pass out of the continent. The strong argue for free trade (though in the matter of agriculture they ignore their own precepts) while the poor need protection. Dependence upon commodities remains the key to African exports and nine major commodities account for 76 per cent of the continent's agricultural exports. Almost all initiatives emanating from the North require Africa to open its markets to outside competition while ignoring the fact that the North, where it has political groups to protect, does not do the same thing.

The next issue to consider is whether globalisation and NEPAD are compatible. A growing proportion of people worldwide, especially in the developing world, oppose globalisation yet seem unable to prevent its spread despite all their protests. If NEPAD is to mean anything it must be about altering the balance between rich and poor. But globalisation - the rapid spread of corporate power - hardly seems the instrument to alter this balance except in one direction only, towards the rich.

There have been too many uncritical African responses to globalisation as though the process is inevitable when, in fact, it is nothing of the kind. There appears to be something of a consensus in Africa: if you cannot beat it, join it. It is an attitude that turns the state into a conduit for capital rather than an instrument for controlling it so as to ensure that it is used to bring about greater social equity. The West, greatly assisted by the international financial institutions, appears to have been only too successful in selling the "inevitability" of globalisation to those countries least able to cope with it.

What, then, will constitute an African renaissance? Nelson Mandela first used the term in 1997 and Thabo Mbeki has sponsored the idea ever since. First, any real change for the better in Africa's situation can only be effected from within; if the renaissance relies upon assistance from outside the continent it will be a non-starter. Africa must put Africa to rights; outsiders, whatever their proclaimed objectives, always have their own agendas and these, naturally, favour their particular interests.

Moreover, it is inherently unlikely that any renaissance can take place as long as African economies remain in the grip of aid donors and the international financial institutions. Too many African leaders look outside the continent for solutions to their problems instead of relying upon self-transformation. They do so for two main reasons of which one is excusable, the other not.

Most preside over such small weak economies that they have only limited room in which to manoeuvre; many, however, are more concerned about keeping themselves in power at almost any cost rather than pursue genuine development. The cost, as a rule, is accepting western capitalist pressures and adopting policies approved by the donors.

The prospects for an African renaissance at the present time are not encouraging for a continent that has a higher proportion of civil wars and failed states than any other region in the world. The best hope for an African renaissance lies with Nigeria and South Africa, the continent's two regional great powers, creating a working axis between them. Thabo Mbeki is president of the most developed and potentially richest country in Africa and he has done much to bring both the AU and NEPAD into existence. South Africa should be the continent's economic powerhouse: it is self-sufficient in food, has the best industrial-commercial infrastructure in Africa (the Johannesburg Stock Exchange is ranked tenth in world terms) and is a storehouse of mineral wealth. It also has substantial military capacity that should be used for peacekeeping and is one of the very few African countries strong enough to pursue a relatively independent foreign policy. Nigeria possesses oil, has Africa's largest market and a highly developed entrepreneurial capacity. It has also, through ECOMOG, deployed its military forces on a number of peacekeeping operations. Neither country is in receipt of aid, except on the margins, and both are major exporters. If these two states work together to spearhead an African renaissance there is a real possibility that it could take off.

The problems are daunting and Africa has fallen into a habit of dependence that must be broken. When the two old colonial powers, Britain and France, suddenly show a renewed interest in Africa, as they have done over the last few years, the continent should be wary. Both Tony Blair's interest in NEPAD and Jacques Chirac's sudden rescue operation in Côte d'Ivoire reek of neo-colonialism. And when a hard rightwing US Republican President decides to visit Africa, the continent should analyse his every move and promise, with courtesy of course, but also with suspicion. Already the Democratic Republic of Congo, Djibouti, Egypt, Gabon, Gambia, Ghana, Madagascar, Mauritania, Rwanda, Seychelles, Sierra Leone, Togo and Tunisia have allowed themselves to be bullied by Washington into agreeing to accept the iniquitous US demand that in the case of US citizens committing crimes in their countries they bypass trial by the ICC and send them back to the United States.

International relations are all about power: who has it and who does not. Africa has little power, a fact that attracts the major powers like vultures to a carcass to be exploited. How best, then, can Africa deploy what power and influence it has to ensure that it develops in its own way? NEPAD funded by the West is not the answer.

References

"Africa and the World" in West *Africa* magazine (Issue 4357, 23 Dec.-12 Jan.2003)
"Iraq and Western Disunuty" in *West Africa* magazine (Issue No. 4364, 24 Feb. - 2 March 2003)
"What does Mbeki stand for?" in *West Africa* magazine (Issue No. 4366 10-16 March 2003)
"After the Iraq War a New World Order" in *West Africa* magazine (Issue No. 4368 24-30 March 2003)
The quote comes from: Constitutive Act of the African Union (AU), published by the *Department of Foreign Affairs*, Republic of South Africa

20

NEPAD: Can it succeed without reforming the global economic System?

Mammo Muchie

"The emancipation of Africa is the emancipation of man."

K.F. Nkrumah, Consciencism: Philosophy and Ideology for Decolonisation: Panaf, London, p.78

"The hand that receives is always under the one that gives""
African Proverb

Not economic exploitation, as often assumed, but the disintegration of the cultural environment of the victim is the cause of the degradation. The economic process may, naturally, supply the vehicle of the destruction, and almost invariably economic inferiority will make the weaker yield, but the immediate cause of his undoing is not for that reason economic; it lies in the lethal injury to the institutions in which his social existence is embodied. The result is loss of self-respect and standards, whether the unit is a people or a class, whether the process springs from so-called 'culture conflict' or from a change in the position of a class within the confines of a society.

> Karl Polyani, The Great Transformation "Class Interest and Social Change" Ch.13, 1944

Introduction

Like many contradictory processes, the demise of colonialism brought mixed blessings to Africa. It led to the formation of multiple states while fragmenting the ex-colonial entities from their much wider territorial and trade extent into many mini and micro states. Except for a few, African states can hardly sustain a credible national development strategy without major inputs from outside. Fragmentation has one overriding consequence: it left the existing states vulnerable to outside help. If they could not access outside assistance, they came to believe that they might not undergo profound transformation. Unfortunately, outside help has not been given (or perhaps may not likely be given) on a scale to bring fundamental change in Africa. Instead it created an unhealthy competition for limited donor funds, loans and grants amongst African states. Nearly every African state has suffered from a constraint akin to something like a prisoner's dilemma for this external assistance. As the foreign assistance in the form of ODA and foreign direct investment declined after the cold war[1], the foreign policy of the heavily indebted states of Africa has become largely an unimaginative posturing to solicit foreign aid. The African states reel under the power of aid.

While donor involvement functioning within a nationally framed and specified strategy can be made probably productive, the current pattern leaves a lot to be desired. What states win in terms of cash and funds comes with a heavy price by sacrificing social capital that is needed to overcome the fragmentation of Africans. One of the ways of advancing African integration is to reduce such destructive competition with cooperation and trust. Independent industrial, technology and innovation strategies cannot be carried out without inviting the donors to drive the process. Most of the fragmented African states lack independent agency to carry out policies to transform their economic structure.

It is from this failure that the need for African integration has been proposed as a possible alternative. Even the re-grouping of African states into regional blocs has not diminished, but has rather intensified regional rivalry for external assistance. The prisoner's dilemma will not go away with the mere institution of a regional concept. It matters how regional arrangements are conceptualised, framed and activated. How stakeholders articulate their interests, aspirations and influences in shaping any regional economic reconfigurations has also a major influence on how a regional concept is articulated.

The rationale for African integration should emerge from the desire to activate and mobilise Africa's agency for undertaking and managing effectively the development process (understood as comprehensive structural transformation). Development must be anchored in the principle to remove ill-being and promote and habituate well-being development and human security. There is a need to identify how to counter the degradation of people, nature and knowledge by ventilating arrangements, structures, actors, activities and practices for their subtractive and additive qualities to human well-being development. The subtractive or additive outcome to human well-being should be the main criterion used in assessing any regionalisation process. Thus African integration can make sense if it is designed to respond to the needs and aspirations of ordinary people.

One of the main reasons for embarking on African integration is thus to expand the opportunities and identify the problems in orienting development from being elite driven to one being driven by the people. It is part of the strategy to help undo the current mismanagement of Africa's development. There is no merit in hankering for a wider African trade and economic regime, if the majority of ordinary people (the workers and farmers) are made to lose in the process. The emancipatory underpinning to the regional integration project must not be lost. By the ordinary people I mean the productive social classes such as the workers, farmers, innovators and producers. I do not mean external donors, foreign business interests and local ruling elites with aspirations to connect with external interests and create their own materially comfortable world with callous indifference and moral abandon in the midst of massive poverty in their own societies.

One of the reasons for arguing for regional integration is to undertake an internal mobilisation of resources and finance through a combination of trade creation, diversification and diversion to connect the regions. Africans need resources that can be harnessed from regional integration. The latter will assist or deter the revitalisation of development in Africa depending on whether the people and the localities enjoy much latitude by employing something like the subsidiarity principle. That is to say within the regional framework self-action by different communities and actors can be expressed with freedom and self-determination

NEPAD and the Problem of Deepening and Broadening African Integration

Africa has experienced a number of regional integration traditions. As a regional integration project, which tradition does NEPAD wish to build upon? This is an important issue for the elaboration of the concept, strategy and policy of African structural transformation through integration.

There are two main types of integration and five approaches to African integration. The two are voluntary and involuntary integration. An example of deliberative and cooperative schemes that have been formed and undone is the East African Community. The states drove and broke the regional cooperation and are trying to re-make it. Market driven regional cooperation tends to be cross-border, mostly informal trade corridor linkages. The approaches to African integration have come from:

-The Pan-African movement (whose source is the US and Caribbean-UK Diaspora)
-The colonial enlarged estates (UK, France, etc.)
-The post-colonial state driven continental unity aspiration (for example, OAU, AU, NEPAD)
-Actual sub-regional groupings based on the policies and laws of the existing states (for example, ECOWAS, COMESA, SADAC, etc.)
-Cross-border flows through refugees, pollution, wars and other disaster induced migrations (as a result of conflict, violence, social and nature degradation.)

There is a need to evaluate the merit of the different models of integration. The movements, states, trade and trans-African migrations via war and refugees are creating novel re-arrangements of economic transaction and may create the new trans-state-national African citizen. New hybrid identities are being formed that may dissolve petty loyalties and narrow regional and ethnic ties. It is not true that Africans think through tribal and clan association, units and entities. Tanzania provides a very good example of the fallacy of such casual and superficial observation. The most enduring legacy of Nyerere's era in Tanzania is the de-ethnicisation of that society. That augurs well to suggest that provided there is an enlightened political project, which is pursued with integrity and sincerity, an African national citizen can be made.

NEPAD and African Integration

It will be useful to relate NEPAD to the different types of integration described above. NEPAD is a state driven process. It came as an initiative of the leaders of South Africa, Nigeria, Algeria and Senegal. It shares in the optimism of the millennium to wish for a better African future. African leaders converted the Organisation of African Unity into the African Union (AU) in 2000, claiming that the OAU had accomplished its mission by ending colonialism and apartheid. A year later the New Partnership for African Development (NEPAD) came on the scene. But there seems to be contradictions in the approaches taken by the two initiatives. In the course of time however these contradictions were ironed out. The AU and NEPAD seem to come closer together than drive apart, as it was feared.

The European Union appears to serve as a model for the new AU, whose Constitution suggests that it wants to fight poverty and establish a regime of human rights and government by law, citizen participation and accountability. There are plans for a single currency, a common African market and even a peace, security and cooperation council.

While the AU aspires to "pull fragmented sovereignties together" by building political unity and solidarity among African states and peoples, NEPAD aspires to capture and to define the continent's developmental agenda. It thus gives priority to the economic, technological and business strategy for the transformation of African economic structures. NEPAD is thus the latest proposal amongst a series of earlier plans such as the Lagos Plan of Action having a go at trying to dent the problem of structural transformation of African economies. The NEPAD document describes Africa's unacceptable marginalised position in today's world economy and puts forward a programme of action. The document recognises that the private sector and the partnership of the private and public sectors in forging the African public economic sphere forms one of the key strategies for transforming the structure of African economies. In addition, while NEPAD does not ignore the importance of mobilising domestic finance, it expects the bulk of the finance to come from the outside. This formula of stressing the role of the private sector and donor funding to define the African development agenda has been questioned. Some analysts suggest that NEPAD represents a "class project". Some say that South Africa and Nigeria are using NEPAD to express their hegemonic aspirations in Africa (private communication from the Research Director, Nordic Africa Institute).

Although NEPAD is not mentioned in the AU constitutive Act, it was clearly stated at the Durban founding meeting of the AU that NEPAD is the economic programme of the AU, and not a rival to it. It appears that NEPAD has been endorsed by the "trade union" of African heads of states. The charge that it has been smuggled by a few elite leaders has now been overcome by its endorsement by the assembly of heads of states. In terms of African integration, the AU is like an imagined African national community while NEPAD becomes the economic arm in deepening and widening the integration process. The problem is whether the two processes can reinforce each other or create further obstacles to the prospect of African integration. This issue cannot be settled in the abstract.

NEPAD[1] as a Development Agenda and its Problems

Forty years has gone since an externally imposed development model, based on grants, loans, scanty foreign investment and unequal trade relations involving the extraction of African agricultural and mineral rights for foreign exchange to buy foreign manufactures replaced the direct colonial system. There is now recognition, that far from this externally orientated development model denting growing poverty and inequality, it has produced debt (including debt servicing) in Africa and has foreclosed Africa's right to independent development.[2]

How can Africa earn its right to develop and structurally transform? What future; what destiny for Africa: a free future or an externally manipulated future? That is the "to be or not to be" question - the so-called "Hamletian dilemma". When one looks at Africa through the mirror of its history, one finds it is not Africa that has failed, but the external development model and the way it has been imposed on African politics, economics, society, governance and culture by others.

It is their project of development, their specific remedies and strategies that have been unjust. Should Africa rectify or justify the unjust system and its ideas that have failed it or not? Given the current convergence or confluence of information technology and financial services that have together formed speculative or casino capital on a global scale, it is important to ask whether Africa can ever make it to the promised land by playing dice in the fast globalising casino-type of world economy?

I shall start by according the benefit of doubt to African leadership. Let us assume their intention is good and let us give NEPAD a generous read. The authors of NEPAD think that Africa can pursue a self-reliant strategy while integrating in the globalised world economy. To put the point across in the leaders' own language:

> "The New Partnership for African Development is a pledge by African leaders, based on a common vision and a firm and shared conviction, that they have a pressing duty to eradicate poverty and to place their countries, both individually and collectively, on a path of sustainable growth and development, and at the same time to participate actively in the world economy and body politic. The Programme is anchored on the determination of Africans to extricate themselves and the continent from the malaise of development and exclusion in a globalising world." (NEPAD Document, 2001:1)

No one can fault the sincerity with which the leaders made their pledge to "eradicate poverty", and/or defined NEPAD to occupy the centre stage of Africa's "sustainable development" agenda. The problem lies at the same time in their assignment to NEPAD to provide the framework for Africa's participation and inclusion in the world economy. Given the bad record of Africa's participation and inclusion in the world economy since the time of slavery, what is new in "NEPAD" that will make a difference? Can the leaders' expressed commitment to "eradicate poverty" and embark on "sustainable development" be attained while participating in a world economy whose *modus vivendi* has not changed, in the main, in relation to Africa since the fifteenth century?

One can also understand that autarchy for Africa is not an option. Engagement with the world economy is unavoidable. However, it is the terms of that engagement that has been fudged by the leaders' eagerness to pledge to the people of Africa to deliver on poverty eradication, while assuring the transnational actors that NEPAD is far from being a subversive pledge. The deontological commitment by the leaders to "eradicate poverty" suggests that NEPAD aspires to carry out an emancipatory project. However, the willingness to play by the rules of the game within the world economy subjects the emancipatory ambition to the vicissitudes and impersonal interplay of economic forces shaping the world economy. It depends how much African social actors play the game and succeed. Is there no alternative to this uncertain custody of poverty eradication to the logic and working out of the games played by impersonal forces of the world economy? Does the world economy that operates with the logic of the law of value - where there has to be losers and gainers - tie or free African efforts to eradicate poverty rapidly? What is there to offset Africa from being a loser once more? How can it join the gainers in this game? We are dealing with an economic system that builds wealth through widening inequalities and poverty. And Africa becomes included or participates in the world economy without any affirmative action or equal opportunity provision to compete with well-established players. Where does Africa's support come from? How would the desire for a new partnership with the "international community" help precisely? What is the "international community" anyway? There is a world order under the unipolar management (or mismanagement) of the Anglo-Saxon Empire led by the USA. How does this world order treat Africa? As a partner or a region to be dealt with, and to keep open its source of raw materials and market provision at dirt-low prices, dictated and driven by the buyer power in the global value chain?

To quote Karl Marx may not be in fashion now, but what he said about capitalist production and the institutions for enforcing its expansion is relevant:

"Capitalist production, by collecting the population in great centres, and causing an ever-increasing preponderance of population, destroys at the same time the health of the town labourer and the intellectual life of the rural labourer...Moreover, all progress in capitalist agriculture is a progress in the art, not only of robbing the labourer, but of robbing the soil; all progress in increasing the fertility of the soil for a given time, is a progress towards ruining the lasting sources of the fertility. The more a country starts its development on the foundation of modern industry, like the United States for example, the more rapid is this process of destruction. Capitalist production, therefore, develops technology, and the combining of various processes into a social whole, only by sapping the original sources of all wealth - the soil and the labourer." [2]

The importance of this debate is this: capital's economic expansion (the thing it can still do best) is said to be purchased by a dialectical co-relate of the expansion of massive social waste and destruction, radical inequalities and poverty (the thing it is not good at correcting in space and time). Capital embodies in its mode of existence and dynamics social waste and economic expansion. It is so ontologically insecure that it needs to control the social fallout from the rigours of accumulation by employing more and more prisons, more and more military organisation, employing more and more controlling personnel and technology against the possible crimes of the losers and their supporters.[3] The international institutions for capital expansion and social regulation on a planetary scale such as the IMF, World Bank and WTO are implicated in this dialectic of capital's economic growth and social waste. Their spokespersons bemoan through various international fora that the social inequities that keep growing as capitalist production expands is not inherent to the logic of capitalist production, and keep proposing anti-poverty and anti-environmental degrading measures without touching the foundations of capital's systemic logic. This has prompted angry retorts by activists:

The IMF and the World Bank, far from bringing economic stability and reducing poverty, are destroying the environment and impoverishing people. Their calls for dialogue are just a public relations ploy and the announced reforms are cosmetic. The Bretton Woods institutions should be abolished and all the Third World debt cancelled. Moreover, the entire political and economic system of global capitalism needs to be overhauled. This is to be achieved by a global movement of solidarity opposed to the neoliberal model imposed by multinational companies, the rich countries, and their minions at the World Bank and the IMF.[4]

Can Africa eradicate poverty without some reform of the capitalist world economy? Is it an illusion to desire poverty eradication while wishing fully to participate in the system that is known to increase poverty and inequalities especially in the most vulnerable territories of Africa, Latin America and Asia? This is an important issue that NEPAD has not fully addressed. The terms of engagement with the capitalist global economy are too important to leave out. It is important to specify with what agency and options one engages and how Africans engage with such a system. Seeking partners is fine, but are we talking of partners to reform the system or simply to sympathise and increase the aid budget? NEPAD should have clearly stated, like the proposal of the NIEO in the 1970s, that what Africa requires are partners that will struggle to reform a system that has become synonymous with injustice itself in relation to the poor people of the world including workers and farmers.

Perhaps the leaders of Africa may have made an appraisal of the world economy different from what is now conventional wisdom. Is there a window of opportunity in the post-cold war US dominated empire to include Africa on better terms than, say, what Africa had during the Cold War? Is today's unipolar moment/conjuncture favourable to Africa's inclusion and participation in the world economy on beneficial terms? Is that what the leaders have premised NEPAD upon?

The current debate on globalisation has taken a variety of forms. At the core is whether there is fundamentally a new logic to the capitalist system different from that suggested by K. Marx (see quote above!) capable of self-generating economic advance by preventing regression into social decay and destruction, including in certain circumstances war. Is globalisation the latest version of "imperialism" in the classic way those socialist-radical thinkers such as Kautsky, Hilferding, Lenin–Stalin, Luxembourg, Trotsky, Bukharin and Mao Tse Tung and non-socialists such as Schumpeter and Hobson have described? Or is globalisation an extra-capitalist phenomenon inaugurating a different political economy to capitalist development by resolving the bifurcation of simultaneous economic progress and social regress with new bridges and new spaces? Has globalisation modified the workings of capital sufficiently to imagine and realise economic gains without sacrificing social and environmental security? Or, is globalisation an expression of the facilitation owing to digital, molecular and advanced material technology and telecommunications, of the fast movement of capital in bewildering and proliferating varieties? Has the unstable features of capital been attenuated by the creation of global capital and global markets? Is the capital logic still there with its uneven territorial concentration of wealth and poverty? Is the capital logic giving way to a new integrated and even development of the system? Following Max Weber's the Spirit of Capitalism, is there a NEW SPIRIT OF CAPITALISM characterised by even development territorially and socially?

I ask these questions because if Capitalism can expand economic activity while at the same time expanding social inequality, need Africa integrate into this economic structure without demanding changes in the first place? Does NEPAD have a neutralising safety net to provide a beneficial integration of Africa into the world economy?

If on the other hand the capitalist logic bifurcates economic expansion with social waste, NEPAD may be spreading an illusion to pledge poverty eradication within a system known to exacerbate poverty and inequality by its systemic creation of winners and losers territorially and socially.

If the type of neo-liberal capitalism that dominated the last twenty years is anything to go by, according to the World Bank, some 80 per cent of world income is known to be concentrated where 20 per cent of the world population lives. The same 20 per cent of the world population occupies 80 per cent of the world environmental space. That does not augur well for NEPAD's expressed desire to eradicate poverty while playing by the rules of the capitalist game or spirit. Territorial and social inequalities are still inherent features within present day world economy. Unfortunately, much as one wishes to see it, Africa may not see the number of its poor people grow less. On the contrary the number of the poor may likely grow unless there are robust social policies to make sure the number of poor people is reduced. A pro-poor social policy implies that one cannot let one's hands be tied behind one's back by integrating lock, stock and barrel into the capitalist global economy. Africa needs to evolve a selective intervention strategy where it retains the initiative for social policy-making by pursuing strategies of defence and offence to eradicate poverty and to embark on sustainable development.

However African leaders wish to play it, the larger context of the state of the dynamics of the capitalist system cannot be ignored to pursue any development strategy nations wish to follow to eradicate poverty. If they wish to develop policies to eradicate poverty, they may come up against the interests of powerful debtors who will insist that Africans produce minerals and primary commodities to pay and service debt. They will be coerced to abandon industrial, economic, technology, innovation and social policy. If they refuse, they will be denied budget subsidies and other funds. If they go it alone, one by one, without a common strategy of defence or offence to deal with structural inequities in the world economy, they will be victimised one by one. It is this catch-22 situation that they must avoid by pooling their sovereignties together to plan the eradication of poverty across Africa.

The most interesting lesson for Africa about the Lagos Plan of Action is not whether its implementation would have been smooth sailing. It would not. They would have been problems had it been taken up and implemented. But it was shunted aside due to the fact that African states were too fragmented to deal with the challenges from the Bretton Woods Institutions. The other important consideration was the fact that the structural adjustment policy adoption virtually every African government in the 1980s was rewarded with loans whilst the Lagos Plan of Action was largely looking for self-finance, Africa's development and long–term structural transformation.

NEPAD faces the same challenges as the Lagos Plan of Action: can it overcome internal fragmentation by promoting an African shared national project; and can it overcome the temptation to surrender policy independence for cash?

To give credit to African leaders, they call for a "new partnership" with the industrialised world. Does it mean a call for systemic reform or is it a desire to prevent their conditionalities from subverting any policy independence the leaders wish to pursue?
This is how they put it in their own words:

"[NEPAD] is a call for a new relationship of partnership between Africa and the international community, especially the highly industrialised countries to overcome the development chasm that has widened over centuries of unequal relations." (NEPAD, 2002: 2)

But what does it mean to say "a new partnership" with the industrialised world? Does it mean a call to reform the global economy? Does it mean to rescue policy independence and initiative in the face of expected demands from powerful external actors like the international financial institutions? How much are those who benefit from the world economy (and who have helped themselves to Africa's rich minerals and agricultural commodities) willing to negotiate a new deal for Africa? This confusion is very important to clarify.

If "new partnership" means that Africa can re-negotiate the rules of the game of the world economic system, then there is something "new" to, and in NEPAD. If it means inserting Africa in the unequal world economic division of labour, it would mean back to the old scoreboards. Africa's hands will be tied and carrying out any meaningful anti-poverty eradication measures would become a long haul.

Who drives NEPAD? Here African leaders clearly state that they are in the hot seat and only desire for the rest of the world to "complement" and not lead in setting Africa's development agenda. In their words:

> "We will determine our own destiny and call on the rest of the world to complement our efforts. There are already signs of progress and hope. Democratic regimes that are committee to the protection of human rights, people-centred development and market-orientated economies are on the increase. African peoples have begun to demonstrate their refusal to accept poor economic and political leadership." (NEPAD Document, 2002:2)

I take the statement by the leaders that "We will determine our destiny" to mean a striving to reveal African independent agency in international relations, foreign policy and diplomacy. There is at once a desire to form an African will, to make African perspective to guide Africa's interest in international relations and a willingness to deal with problems by mobilising Africa's combined energy. The making or claiming of the 21st century as Africa's century means nothing else other than inscribing at the centre of Africa's interest, aspiration and perspective in the emerging world arrangement or international social contract.

If putting Africa at the centre is the new benchmark, this can be certainly taken as a positive aspect of the leaders' intention. Putting together market-orientated economies with people-centred development appears to show another confusion. In a document like NEPAD such conceptual confusion should have been clarified before release to the public.

While Africa's leaders' understanding of the political economy of the global economic system is contentious, on the whole NEPAD resonates a positive tone echoing very much the upbeat talk of the African renaissance. The development plan and agenda is supposed to have been owned by Africans, which means that African leaders will take responsibility for the failure and success of NEPAD. The leaders seek a new partnership that may or may not mean a diplomatically couched demand for reforming the existing structure of global power. The leaders pledge to democratise society and respect human rights and this is meant to be monitored through a peer-review mechanism. Poverty eradication is an essential foundation to protect human rights. They also pledge to ensure macro-economic stability, accountability and transparency of both leaders and institutions and the institutional and policy support to market relations. They pledge to pursue regional integration at both the regions and the level of the continent. They seemed to take Pan-African integration more as a step-by-step, incremental, geographical, economic and political integration from the sub-regions to the continent. The danger of sub-regional incremental evolution in relation to the option of a big-bang burst into continental integration remains real. In addition, they have not addressed the issue of the historic African Diaspora and the recent Diaspora that migrated after the creation of the largely authoritarian post-colonial system of African Government.

The leaders have put forth four initiatives to address the programmatic implementation of the NEPAD concept: a) the Peace and Security Initiative, b) Democracy and Governance Initiative, c) Economic and Corporate Governance Initiative and d) the Sub-regional Approaches to Development. It remains how effective these initiatives will be and whether they will be consistent and lead to overall synergy and social innovation.

4. Evaluating criticisms of NEPAD: selecting the seeds that will grow from those that will not.

There are broadly two types of critical commentaries. The first is the ideologically-driven critique[5], which sees NEPAD as a class project[6], while the second is related to those who wish to identify positive and negative features in the NEPAD document. [7]

Criticisms of NEPAD as a neo-liberal document are too sweeping and simplistic. There is confusion in the document, but it does not merit an outright dismissal as a neo-liberal document. Critics that dismiss NEPAD outright have been primarily driven by ideological impulse. It is difficult to make contribution to the debate if the critique is so pitched at an immanent level. It is difficult to engage African leaders with such criticisms.

Some question the sincerity of the leaders that propose NEPAD. Betrayal and sell-out has been attributed to the leaders. There was also a peroration suggesting that NEPAD may have been influenced by the G8.

The main reason why so many criticisms were levelled against NEPAD is the confusion in the document that I pointed out above. It opens the floodgate for all sorts of criticisms. Had the people of Africa owned NEPAD (rather than African leaders), there would have been an opportunity to raise all these issues. That opportunity was not available and the document claims to define and own Africa's development agenda for the 21st century. Hence the interest and the sharp criticisms that ensued.[8]

Some of the scholarly criticisms have come from within civil society by pointing out the contradictions, especially in the NEPAD document. Critics take to task the authors of NEPAD for calling for self-reliance while relying on external finance and support. It accuses the "new international partnership" initiative of ignoring past and existing efforts by Africans to resolve Africa's crises and move forward, describing NEPAD as "a top-down programme driven by African elites and drawn up with the corporate forces and institutional instruments of globalisation, rather than being based on African peoples' experiences, knowledge and demands".

They even question who will benefit from NEPAD: they claim that the main beneficiaries of the new approach to African economic development would be largely foreign businesses and those local actors working with them. There are those who claim African development should lift the underdogs – what Fanon called in his book "the

Wretched of the Earth". They say that efforts to date to give prominence and voice to Africa's ordinary people have made little real difference. If we are to develop a strategy for African development where local, regional, national and continental combinations can take place, the starting point for evolving a shared purpose and action emanates from a commitment to change the prevailing ill-being state of the population into a well-being state for the large majority of ordinary people.

Thabo Mbeki appears to have heard or read some of the criticisms on NEPAD. His response which appeared as a South African Foreign Ministry release was picked up by the Harare based SEATIN and the *New African* magazine of October 2002. Mbeki took a broad swipe at all the critics declaring:

> "It is important that we study both the NEPAD and Africa Action Plan closely, to understand and act on the possibilities they open up for African development, eschewing easy, routine, uninformed and cynical conclusions and the lazy and expensive option of disengagement."(Thabo Mbeki, Building Africa's Capacity Through NEPAD, reprinted in *New African* October 2002, p.66)

Mbeki has picked up the main weakness in much of the criticism of NEPAD. He mentioned 120 specific actions that the G8 action plan and the EU have committed themselves without specifying some of them. He advises against a counter-productive campaign against "Governments and institutions" of the North, while keeping the right and the duty "to protest against an unjust world order." The need to engage "our development partners in the true NEPAD partnership" must balance" the necessary exercise" to keep the right to protest against the unjust system open.

Mbeki said that NEPAD tries to break the unwholesome relationship between hapless African aid-seekers and benevolent Donors. Mbeki challenged criticisms directed at the shortfall of aid that would flow to Africa from the June G8 meeting in Canada as broadly uninteresting because it reflects the "demeaning view of Africans."

Mbeki mentions that resource mobilisation will ensue from "our own partnership" and affirms Africa's rejection (and the Donor's endorsement of such rejection) of Donor aid to fill Africa's "begging bowl". He mentioned specific areas where the G8 have promised in their action plan (to be reviewed in 2003 to assess implementation):

-Capacity building for peace support operations at regional and continental levels
- Generating larger inflows of foreign direct investment.
-Support to increase agricultural production and productivity.
-Help in building infrastructure project proposals.
-Opening their markets to African products.
-Increase funding to relieve debt.
-Support in securing affordable drugs and medicine and in building a health infrastructure.
-Clean water, sanitation and management of water resources.

Mbeki positively appraises the G8 Africa Action Plan issued from their June 2002 meeting in Canada.

Thabo Mbeki wishes Africa not to extend its begging bowl in the form of grants and suggests that the G8 will generate foreign direct investment and allow Africans to raise funds from the private capital market. There is of course nothing new in this relationship. The problem is that their promise may or may not be honoured. Most likely it will not. Whilst there is much to appreciate to reject the demeaning view of Africans as beggars, there is still that old relationship in the way the G8 will relate to Africa if they continue to donate and Africans also expect them to donate to them.

If the EU and US do not over-subsidise their farmers, African agriculture would have increased its productivity and Africa can potentially build the capacity to feeding Europe. But at the WTO, the EU and the US always support their protectionist farmers while preaching and forcing trade liberalisation on the weaker developing countries of Africa, Asia and Latin America. The expectation that the EU and US will support African farmers can be misguided. These powers seem to say: do as we tell you, but not as we do! Even if the subsidies and tariffs were to be lifted, other non-tariff barriers have to be surmounted. A concrete example is how cheese from camel milk from Mauritania was blocked from the German market. The German consumer loved the cheese and continued to purchase despite high tariff barriers, which reached about 70%. When customer preference beat the authorities, they brought in methods of production, quality, standard, health and safety barriers to block the cheese from being exported to Germany.

What this example shows is that there will be a lot of tariff and non-tariff barriers that will be imposed on the African farmer or agro-manufacturer. Thabo Mbeki may be too optimistic about the possibilities regarding G8 promises. Talking is one thing, delivering is another.

Whilst Thabo Mbke's rejoinder is very interesting, much of the concerns about NEPAD and the relationship with G8, private capital market, opening the markets of the North for African products, support for building Africa's physical, intellectual, social and financial infrastructure depend in "reforming the unjust and inequitable system." The latter is not available yet, making the broad positive possibilities from NEPAD to come to fruition uncertain. There must be a practical way of changing the unjust world order to make the G8 and others recognise Africa's interest and aspirations.

Crystallise an African National Project to Anchor Development through Self-reliance

It is important to crystallise a new African synergy beyond the current de-colonised fragments. The Western world that feels it has much to lose and its local allies have often castigated the Pan-African vision as a daydream. But after 40 years of political independence, the case for constituting a Pan-African national project is more compelling now than in the 1960s when it was unfurled by the first generation of progressive African leadership. There is a clear need to forge an African nation going beyond the existing fragile, ineffective and fragmented state system. All nations are imagined communities. The Italian nation and the German nations that emerged as a consequence of national unification were also imagined Communities. Africa's unity has been aborted by the historical compromise of the national liberation movement in both accommodating and retaining colonial interests at independence. The abandonment of Pan-African directions meant that the ex-colonial powers retained colonial-like presence in partnership or alliance with the local ruling elites. They instituted a loan-grant and debt regime to rule Africa indirectly.

While unity has been an easy rhetoric on the lips of Africa's post-colonial leadership, it has been, nevertheless, elusive and difficult to forge for the last forty years. Unity is a rich concept in Africa as it is the necessary foundation for Africa's free future. It is thus more than a territorial agglomeration of the existing states. African unity is first and foremost the development of an African national consciousness to transform, build, guide and finally realise an African national project by thinking beyond the existing state frontiers. It represents above all the African conquest of a unity of purpose and unity of action to confront the many challenges Africans face in today's fragile and chaotic world. Unity will be the way for Africa to reclaim fairness in dealing with others in an unequal world. Such unity can be said to be made when Africans evolve a collective identity and platform and a common conception for collective action in relation to four major matters:

A shared conceptual framework on how to bring an integrated and comprehensive structural transformation of Africa.

A common and united conception and approach in dealing a system with which continues to have a logic and modus operandi that is massively unjust and unfair to Africa.

A compelling moral clarity, intellectual confidence and political commitment to assist ordinary Africans to be the main beneficiaries of Africa's wealth, resources and environment.

A united approach to bring to bear a co-ordinate political, executive, legislative, judicial and scientific authority to prevent nature degradation.

Together the above will assist Africa to define and set its own agenda and deal with hostile environments while learning to respond to the friendly in the world. At the moment Africa is neither fully free nor fully self-reliant. It needs to reveal and build a collective independent agency to put African transformation and perspective at the centre of international relations.

Unity at a Pan-African level is preferred to unity at any other level because unity, on any other basis, will not bring to birth emancipated or free Africa. I can enumerate a number of other levels at which unity could be constructed: the family, the clan, the ethnic group, the community, the church, the trade union, social movements, political parties, the nationality, the institution that can serve as the organising principle to bring the fullness or richness of ethnic group, the existing artificial states or the current neo-liberal inspired creations such as the growing and conflicting or competing number of NGOs, civil society, the private sector (businesses), new regions and so on. While these institutions, identities and hybrids are important and may be necessary; none of them could bring about a broader conception of Africa's role and place in the wider and larger scheme of things. The reason is simple: they are too dispersed, discrete and it is difficult to transform their specific interests and aspirations into a general interest. Each of these social units or arrangements leave the door open for division and for others who do not mean well for Africa to get in and sow discord and distrust. We must wake up to the fact that Africa's long history from ancient Egypt to the present day provides a clarion call and a compelling case for its unity. It is easier to unite on the basis of an African identity than on any other. It is all-inclusive and does not exclude on the basis of territorial, religious, regional, ethnic, linguistic and other criteria. Since 1963 there has been official rhetorical lip service to Pan-African unity. What is absent is not the rhetoric for this need of Africa's unity. There is an inflation of rhetoric inversely proportional to the deflation in action. All the governments of the defunct OAU have signed to some notion of Pan-African ideal. But a large number of states have been named and shamed by *New Africa* magazine for not having paid their dues. They thus pay lip service to the organisation. Most now have ratified the AU. But judging by the way they treated the OAU, the future of the AU is uncertain. AU may be, as one analyst quipped - OAU without the "O".

What is disturbing is that there is massive hypocrisy by the leaders: talking Pan-African and acting anti-Pan-African and, at the same time, excluding those with committed interest to realise the political and economic unification of the continent. There is a great need for a moral and intellectual resolution and clarity to make free or emancipated Africa. Africa as a civic nation based on the emancipated citizen must be forged. Free Africa needs a new kind of being - a citizen of the African world with a globalised African soul free from petty allegiances and labels, possessing a revitalised sense of a civic-African self and personality as a premier identity. We have Africa. It is high time we made the Africans.

Notes

NEPAD's priority areas are agriculture, the private business sector, infrastructure and regional integration.

The figure of US$64 billion for the year 2002 was flaunted at the G8 meeting in Canada, an expectation that seems unrealistic in view of the G8's greater interest in good governance than in dishing out the cash.

For example, the Lagos Plan of Action (1980), the Abuja Treaty (1991), the African Alternative Framework to Structural Adjustment Programs (AAF-SAAP, 1989), the African Charter for Popular Participation and Development (Arusha Charter, 1990) and the Cairo Agenda (1994).

References

"NEPAD: A False or True Start to Transform Africa": (Special Lecture, 38 Anniversary of African Liberation Day, May 25, 2002, Aalborg, Denmark).

5. M. Muchie, " NEPAD and The African Public Sphere", *Journal of West Asia and Africa* (translated into Chinese), No.4. June-July, 2002.

M. Muchie, Feature Article: "2 +2 = 5 or 2 +2= 3: A Question for African Civil Society" in, *Alliance*, Vol.7, no.4 December 2002.

M. Muchie, in World Bank *'s World Encyclopaedia*, The Organisation of African Unity, July-August, 2002.

M. Muchie, World Bank's *World Encyclopaedia*, The African Union, July-August, 2002.

M. Muchie, contributions into various electronic debating forums: Mathiba*, Centre for Civil Society, University of Natal, Durban South Africa, and Debate at the Wits*. University, South Africa.

M. Muchie, "NEPAD and African Integration", (EADI 10th International Conference, Ljublijana, Slovenia, September 19- 21, 2002)

M. Muchie, "NEPAD and African Development, *Dir Working Paper, No. 104*, (Aalborg, Denmark, July-August, 2002)

M. Muchie, "Towards a Theory for Re-Framing Pan-Africanism: an Idea Whose Time Has Come": *DIR Working Paper*: No. 83, 2000, Aalborg: Denmark

M. Muchie, "Pan-Africanism and National Liberation", Translated in Chinese by the Chinese Academy of Social Science, *Journal of West Asia and Africa*, March-April, 2001

M. Muchie, Pan-Africanism: An Idea whose Time Has Come, *Politikon,* 2000

K.Liskova African: One of the leaders of the movement against economic globalisation: *Global Civil Society*, 2001.

K. Marx, *Capital* Vol. 1, FLPH, Moscow, 1959.

Peter Anyang'Nyong, Asghedech Ghimaths(z)ion & Davinder Lamba (eds.), *NEPAD a New Path?* (English Press Ltd, 2002)

17. Stefano Ponte, "Aid Policy & Practice", *CDR Issue Paper*, January, 2002.

18. P. Bond, 2002: *Fanon's Warning: A civil Society Reader on the New Partnership for Africa's Development*: (Trenton, NJ: Africa World Press)

19 J. O. Adesina: "NEPAD and the Challenge of Africa's Development: Towards a Political Economy of A Discourse", (CODESRIA 10th Conference, unpublished paper).

20. T. Mbeki: "Building Africa's Capacity Through NEPAD", *New African*, No.411, October, 2002.

21. Fidel Castro, Speech on 1, June 2002, Havana, Cuba.

22. Yash Tandon, Director's Comment and Feature articles, Various Issues of the SEATIN Bulletin, Harare, Zimbabwe.

23. Karl Polyani, The Great Transformation "Class Interest and Social Change" 1944

K.F. Nkrumah, *Consciencism: Philosophy and Ideology for Decolonisation*: (Panaf,London),

Endnotes

1   See my own comments: M. Muchie, "NEPAD: A False or True Start to Transform Africa?" (*Special Lecture, 38 Anniversary of African Liberation Day*, May 25, 2002, Aalborg, Denmark: M. Muchie, "Public Sphere", *Journal of West Asia and Africa* (translated into Chinese),, No.4, June-July, 2002;, M. Muchie, Feature Article: "2 +2 = 5 or 2 +2= 3: A Question for African Civil Society" in, *Alliance*, Vol.7, no.4, December,2002, and M. Muchie, in World Bank 's *World Encyclopaedia*, The Organisation of African Unity,July-August,2002, M. Muchie, World Bank's: *World Encyclopaedia*, The African Union, July-August,2002 , M. Muchie, "NEPAD and African Integration", *EADI* 19th

Conference, Lublijana, Slovenia, September 19-21, M. Muchie, "NEPAD and African Development", *DIR Working Paper*, no.104, July-August,2002, including contributions into various electronic debating forums: Mathiba, Centre for Civil Society, Durban and Debates at the Wits.

[2] The important issue is how free are Africans to set their own development agenda. Does their dependence on aid distort their policy making power as it did in the 1980s and 1990s.

[3] K. Marx, *Capital* Vol. 1, FLPH, Moscow, 1959 PP. 506-507
[4] In the USA, –Americans of college age bracket are more in prison than in universities and it has been suggested most of them are innocent.
[5] K.Liskova African: One of the leaders of the movement against economic globalisation: *Global Civil Society*, 2001

[6] P. Bond, 2002, **Fanon's Warning**: A civil Society Reader on the New Partnership for Africa's Development: Trenton, NJ: Africa World Press
[7] J. O. Adesina, NEPAD and the Challenge of Africa's Development: Towards a Political Economy of A Discourse, CODESRIA 10th Conference, unpublished paper, p.1; Adesina claims that the petty bourgeois leaders of Africa have bourgeois aspirations. Far from committing class suicide a la Amilcar Cabral, they are working to enrich themselves to escape their petty-bourgeois status into a bourgeois status. Thus NEPAD is a class project in this embourgeoisment of the African ruling classes.
[8] See Yash Tandon and the SEATIN Bulletin, where recognition of the positive content has been recognised along with the negative features of the NEPAD document.
[9] The Third World Network (Accra), CODESRIA (Dakar), African Civil Society Declaration on NEPAD, South Africa, and the Heinrich Boll Foundation financed a conference in Nairobi from which criticisms were labelled against NEPAD from every angle. Adebayo Adedeji defended the Lagos Plan of Action and showed how NEPAD has not been informed by its lessons. Dani Nabudre criticized NEPAD from a historical presentation of Pan-Africanism. Thandika Mkandawire criticised the economic governance and resource mobilisation. Others critiqued the democracy and governance aspect, the environment, gender, regional integration and partnerships. Since the conference the Foundation has published "the voices and critiques of the Forum on NEPAD" in a book edited by Peter Anyang'Nyong, Asghedech Ghimaths(z)ion & Davinder Lamba, NEPAD a New Path? English Press Ltd, 2002

Part VI:

General Conclusions

21

General Conclusions

Mammo Muchie

It has been said that if one wants to hide a leaf, one should put it in a forest. Similarly if Africans want to liberate themselves for good, they have to undertake a root-cutting project from the hegemonic power that has cast in stone for over five hundred years their historical and contemporary status of oppression. They can stay as a leaf outside the forest and face the music of oppression and continue to do themselves in or join the dense tropical forest that can hide and protect them inside a liberated Africa-nation founded on a radical Pan-African historical imagination.

In editing *The Making of the Africa-Nation* and linking dialectically the projects of Africa-nation, Pan-Africanism and African Renaissance, we wish to drive home that Africa needs to evolve its own power of definition, discourse, ideology, narrative, myth and metaphysics to deal with, and overcome the imperialist-colonial domination that militates against its chances of becoming free, empowered and attaining a comprehensive agency. Pan-Africanism, African Renaissance and Africa-nation are Africa's counter-hegemonic projects for instantiating and inscribing Africans' will not to remain isolated leaves but to become part of a dense network that the tropical forest symbolises. Pan-Africanism has to be resurrected as the logo embedding free and united Africa. We think the broad thrust of the arguments made in this book is a ringing call to bring back African nationalism through the Pan-African and the African-Renaissance movements to become the grand narratives that will define this new counter-hegemonic projects.

Over five hundred years has passed since the system of slavery scattered Africans to the New World. A hundred years has passed since the Pan-African movement began. Nearly sixty years has passed, when in 1945 in Manchester, England, Africans from the Diaspora and the continent met and united to defy the colonial system by declaring solemnly that they will use armed resistance if the colonial powers stood against the African national liberation movement. Forty years has passed since many of the existing states in Africa acquired formal political independence.

Africa has been passing through reversals, compromises, forgiveness and forgetfulness during its long walk (still unfinished!) to national liberation. It could not run as the methods chosen to claim its national identity disallowed speed and making the right turns to reach the goal. After receiving the crown of formal political independence, Africa surrendered the economic jewels to the internal structures left by the departing colonial powers to perpetuate Africa's servitude. The colonial powers fought tooth and nail African nationalism and its key nationalist proponents. The pact between the new syndicate/local African elite and the former colonial powers created a discourse of economic development that misdirected Africans from establishing Pan-Africanism as the ideology of African liberation. Africa entered a period of sabotage and technicist and economistic tinkering, abandoning largely Pan-Africanism. Decolonisation therefore became false decolonisation. Africa was forced to lose its way. The elite decided to mask its loss of direction under the banner of Pan-Africanism. The latter got watered down to the point that the external enemies of Africa and their local collaborators triumphantly proclaimed (through such policies as the IMF/World Bank-supported structural adjustment programmes of the 1980s and 1990s), the end of Pan-Africanism as an emancipatory project.

To be sure, all is not gloom and doom. There is much to build upon that is positive in Africa, made by Africans, and for Africans over the last half-century. It is true that Africans have distinguished themselves in every walk of life and broken through every glass ceiling previously defined for them by their oppressors.

Though Africans have achieved much, every bit of their success was fought hard for, and nothing was given to them on a silver platter. Despite this, Africa is still on the road to freedom - with some running, others walking and still others not knowing whether to walk or take it easy. Africa's ordeal of struggle is therefore not over. It has actually become a very complicated process. Having suffered many abortions due largely to externally induced miscarriages and sometimes also due to self inflicted activities, free or emancipated Africa is yet to be born. African nationalism has to create and liberate the Africa-nation. The debate to revive Africa's national rebirth is all the more urgent with the revolutions in science and technology imparting a turbo-generating logic to the world economy while Africa still remains tethered to the bottom of the league in all indices of socio-economic development.

Africa needs to build its own national house and protect itself from the current globalisation discourse, ideology and policies, which will not produce wealth and prosperity for the continent but rather poverty and ill-being. If the task is to accelerate the industrial and technological growth of the continent, and economically empower every African, then joining the existing global rat race (even if it were possible) will not deliver the goods. For Africa to benefit from the current global system, it has to first create its national house and then challenge the inequities and the marginalizing competitive thrusts inherent in the system.

Various contributions in this book suggest forcefully that the emancipatory projects for Africa will be alive and current for a long time. Those who think otherwise by declaring and celebrating the death of the emancipatory projects for Africa are therefore bound to be disappointed. The idea of the African and the Africa-nation to anchor the African renaissance and provide the historic Pan-African imagination's current and future relevance have been proposed in order to mobilise the latent native energy in the continent and the Diaspora to challenge outside interference. The African national project gives primacy to the concept of centring rather than continuing to peripheralise African perspectives and voices in international relations. It assists in providing the historical imagination and ideational resources to capture the power of Africa to define its problems and solutions and challenge the often-uninvited outsiders who use their money and other temptations to misdirect Africa's striving to reveal its agency. The disempowering external domination can be challenged only with an African national project.

Pan-Africanism provides the logo for the re-launching of the counter-hegemonic emancipatory project. The state of fragmentation and the systemic arrangement that has trapped Africa to the addictions of loans, grants and debt have liquidated Africa's striving to manifest a unified voice. Freedom for Africa lies in forging a unification-nation. Divide and rule has to be replaced by unite and be truly sovereign.

The project of completely decolonising Africa requires continuous debate and exploring new avenues. The contributors have asked the difficult questions and have proffered suggestions on how to move forward in order to complete the African liberation project. The debate must continue.

Notes on the Contributors

Abdulai, David N.

David N. Abdulai holds a Ph.D in International Economics and Technology Analysis and Management from the Graduate School of International Studies, University of Denver. His Masters degree is in International Development from the School of International Service, American University, and his Bachelors degree in Political Science and Journalism from Howard University in Washington, D.C. He is currently the CEO of Nolaygewerks Initiatives in Kuala Lumpur, and had previously worked at the Bank for International Settlements in Switzerland as a Senior Officer.

Ankomah, Baffour

Baffour Ankomah, 46, editor of *New African* magazine, has been a journalist for 23 years. From 1983-1986, he was editor of *The Pioneer*, the oldest existing newspaper in Ghana, his home country. He moved to the UK in August 1987 to escape a second arrest by Ghana's then military government headed by Flt-Lt Jerry Rawlings. He had earlier been arrested in February 1985 and tortured by the same government. He spent 50 days in hospital and at home nursing his injuries.

In June 1988, he joined the London-based *New African* magazine (which he had been writing for while doing further studies in Journalism in Paris in 1985-86). He started at *New African* as assistant editor, then became deputy editor in 1994, and editor in June 1999.

He has written and spoken extensively in the UK and abroad on "Africa in the Western media". In 2002, the Ugandan-based AFRICA ALMANAC website (www.africaalmanac.com) founded by Timothy Kalyegira named him at No. 53 (ahead of Kofi Annan, the UN Secretary General, No.54) as one of the "Top 100 Africans of 2001, in order of ranking" and among the "700 Best-Known Africans, All Time". The citation that came with the honour simply said: "Baffour Ankomah (Ghana), editor, *New African* magazine. This London-based magazine is doing more than most publications to feature some important themes and currents of contemporary Africa, notably newsmakers, and highlighting the fact that Africa is not all aflame and collapsing."

Arnold, Guy
Guy Arnold has been visiting and writing about Africa since the 1960s. His books include *Kenyatta and the Politics of Kenya, Aid in Africa, Wars in the Third World Since 1945, The End of the Third World* and *The New South Africa*. He is a regular contributor to *West Africa* magazine.

Bankie, B.F.
Born 1 January 1946 in England, of Ghanaian and Gambian parentage, Bankie Forster Bankie is a lawyer by profession. His research interest is international relations, with emphasis on Africa and Asia. B.F. Bankie has worked in a number of West and Southern African countries and is currently serving in an administrative capacity at the Centre for Advanced Studies for African Society (CASAS) in Cape Town. He is a member of the General Council of the Sudan Commission for Human Rights (SCHR).

Bercu, Silvia
Sylvia Bercu, Medical MRCPsych, is a Consultant Forensic Psychiatrist in London, UK, with interest in development issues. She has been developing health, education and infrastructure projects in Kenya and Ghana since 1999 through the Humanist Movement and RelayNET, a registered Charity. Dr Bercu has participated in many international seminars and conferences including The Academics for a World Without War conference, at Berkeley University, San Francisco (1996), where she presented a paper on "The Psychological Consequences of War".

Chimutengwende, Chen
Honourable Chen Chimutengwende was born on 28 August, 1943 in Zimbabwe and is a highly respected Pan-Africanist writer and activist. He is the President of New Africa International Network (NAIN) and has been a Member of Zimbabwe's Parliament since 1985. He was a Government Minister for ten years, from 1990 to the year 2000. He has been a Senior Lecturer in Mass Communications and International Affairs at the International Press Institute, City University, London (1979-1982); Executive Director of the Europe-Third World Research Centre in London (1969-1974) and Director of the School of Journalism at the University of Nairobi, Kenya.

He holds a Masters Degree in Peace Studies from Bradford University, UK (1976), and enrolled in the same University for his PhD degree. His uncompleted Ph.D. dissertation was on "Mass Media and the State in the Socio-economic Development Process". He has published extensively on mass communications, politics and international relations. He wrote this article in July 2003. His e-mail address is: chenchim@yahoo.com or nain@unitednewafrica.com

Davies, Desmond

Desmond Davies has been Editor of the London-based weekly magazine, *West Africa,* since 2001. He has been a journalist for 30 years, 25 of which he has spent in London writing on African affairs for a variety of magazines. He holds an MA in Mass Communications from the University of Leicester in the UK.

Friedman, Steven

Steven Friedman is Senior Research Fellow at the Centre for Policy Studies, an independent policy research institute, in Johannesburg, South Africa. He is the author of Building Tomorrow Today, a study of the South African trade union movement, and editor of two books on South Africa's transition - *The Long Journey* and *The Small Miracle*. He has also published widely on democratisation and related topics.

Hawas, Akram

Akram Hawas obtained his PhD in the sociology of development and international relations from Aalborg University in 1999. He has participated in various international conferences and has been hosted as guest researcher in many research centres in Europe and the Middle East. He has written and published on issues of development, globalisation, world evolution, and on Middle East and Arab relations. He is currently a researcher at the Centre for Oriental Studies, Copenhagen University.

Hersh, Jacques

Professor Jacques Hersh, Dr.Sc.Soc, is the director of the Research Centre on Development and International Relations at Aalborg University, Denmark. He was educated variously in Paris, New York, Vienna and Copenhagen University. He has visited and lectured at various institutions in the world. Professor Jacques has published profusely on development strategies and international politics, in different languages. His special research interest is on the injustices and inequities of the global capitalist system and strategies for creating a community of resistance to such a system.

Jamison, Andrew

Andrew Jamison is professor of technology and society at the Department of Development and Planning, Aalborg University, Denmark and guest professor in environmental science at Malmö University, Sweden. His books include *The Making of Green Knowledge: Environmental Politics and Cultural Transformation* (Cambridge 2001); *Seeds of the Sixties* (California 1994) and *Music and Social Movements* (Cambridge 1998). He is co-author (with Ron Eyerman) of *Social Movements: A Cognitive Approach* (Polity 1991).

Kebede, Messay

Messay Kebede is Associate Professor of Philosophy at the University of Dayton, Ohio. He obtained his PhD from the University of Grenoble in France. He has previously taught philosophy at Addis Ababa University (Ethiopia). He is the author of two books, *Meaning and Development* (Rodopi 1994) and *Survival and Modernisation* (Red Sea Press 1999). He has also published numerous articles. The most recent include: "The Rehabilitation of Violence and the Violence of Rehabilitation: Fanon and Colonialism (*Journal of Black Studies* 2001) and "Directing Ethnicity toward Modernity" (*Social Theory and Practice* 2001).

Leander, Anna

Anna Leander, (PhD), is a researcher at the Institute of International Studies (Copenhagen University, Denmark) and Assistant professor of political science (on leave) at the Central European University (Budapest, Hungary). She is also external lecturer at the University of Copenhagen and at the University of Malmö. Her current research interest is in International Political Economy, with special focus on the regulation of the use of force. Her publication list and on going research projects is available at www.copri.dk.

Li, Xing

Xing Li is a lecturer and researcher at Aalborg University, Denmark. He holds a PhD in Development Studies and International Relations. In recent years he has published a number of articles, book chapters and essays on both general and specific questions on global politics, international relations and development issues with empirical focuses on China and East Asia, and other topics relating to debates on Marxism and Chinese socialism.

Muchie, Mammo

Mammo Muchie was born in Ethiopia and educated until matriculation in Gonder. He did his undergraduate studies at Columbia University, New York City and obtained his MPhil and DPhil degrees from Sussex University at the IDS and SPRU respectively. He also studied Measurement Science in Petrograd, Russia. Professor Muchie has taught and researched at various universities in the USA and Europe including Cambridge University and the Middlesex University (UK); the University of Aalborg (Denmark) and Limburg University, Maastricht University and Amsterdam University (The Netherlands). He was made honorary professor at the Jianxing University in China.

He is currently on secondment from the Middlesex University Business School to the University of Natal, Durban, South Africa, where is he is director of the research programme on Civil Society and African Integration. He has been editor of many academic journals, and is also on the editorial board of some, including *Social Epistemology, Transformation and Tinabantu*. He has published profusely in scholarly journals and is also co-editor of *The Making of African Innovation Systems and Competence* (forthcoming, Aalborg University Press).

Nehusi, Kimani S.K.

Kimani S. K. Nehusi is an *Afrikan* (He insists on the African being spelt with a 'k' rather than 'c') who was born in Queenstown Village on the Essequibo Coast of Guyana, in South America. He entered into formal political activity at age twelve and served in a number of offices in community groups in his village before leaving to attend Teachers College. He continued to combine activism with academic pursuits while earning the BA and MA degrees from the University of Guyana, PhD from the University College, London and Diploma in Egyptology from the University of London. He has taught at primary and secondary schools, the University of Guyana and the University of London, and given special lectures at a number of universities and institutes in Africa, North America, the Caribbean and Europe. Dr Nehusi has been Director of the Africa Studies Centre at the University of East London and is currently a lecturer in the School of Education and Community Studies at the same university. Previous works include A *Book of African Names* (1982), *Ah Come Back Home: Perspectives on the Trinidad and Tobago Carnival 2000* (co-edited with Ian Smart) and "From Medew Netjer to Ebonics" in Clinton Crawford (ed.) *Ebonics and Language Education* (2001).

Prah, K.K.
Professor Kwesi Kwaa Prah is retired Professor of Sociology at the University of the Western Cape. He is currently Director of the Centre for Advanced Studies of African Society (CASAS) at Cape Town, South Africa. Educated in Ghana, he took university degrees in the Netherlands and has held research and teaching posts in Sociology and Anthropology in various universities across Africa as well as in Germany, the Netherlands, England and China. Prah has written many books including *Beyond the Colour Line* (1998), *African Languages for the Mass Education of Africans (1995)* and Capitein. He also published *A Critical Study of an 18th Century African* (1992), *The Bantustan Brain Gain* (1989), *and Mother Tongue for Scientific and Technological Development in Africa (2000)*

westernisation, 25, 93

Ordering this Book

*Wholesale inquiries for this book should be directed to any of the following:

Wholesale inquiries in the UK and Europe should be directed to one of the following:

Bertram, The Book Wholesaler:
+44 1603216 666: email: orders@bertrams.com

Gardners Books Ltd
+44 1323 521777: email: custcare@gardners.com

In the USA, wholesale inquiries should be directed to one of the following:
Ingram Book Company (ordering)
+1 800 937 8000 website: www.ingrambookgroup.com

Baker & Taylor (General and sales information)
+1-800-775-3700 Email: btinfo@btol.com

*Online Retail Distribution: www.amazon.co.uk, www.amazon.com

*Shop Retail: Ask any good bookshop or contact our office:
http//:www.adonis-abbey.com
Phone: (44) 020 7793 8893

The ebook version of this print is also available in PDF format.
Please contact: sales@adonis-abbey.com

Other Books by Adonis & Abbey include:

Broken Dreams (fiction/Town Crier Series 1)
By Jideofor Adibe

Wooden Gongs and Drumbeats: African Folktales, Proverbs and Idioms (fiction/Town Crier Series 2)
By Dahi Chris Onuchukwu

Nigeria and the Politics of Unreason (politics/political economy/history)
By Victor E. Dike

The Challenge of Authenticity: African Culture and Faith Commitment (religion/philosophy/theology)
By Jacob Hevi

www.ingramcontent.com/pod-product-compliance
Lightning Source LLC
Chambersburg PA
CBHW020331270326
41926CB00007B/141